D0032727

National Audubon Society
Field Guide to
North American Wildflowers

A Chanticleer Press Edition

# National Audubon Society Field Guide to North American Wildflowers

Western Region

Richard Spellenberg,
Professor of Biology,
New Mexico State University

Visual Key by
Susan Rayfield and Carol Nehring

Alfred A. Knopf, New York

This is a Borzoi Book
Published by Alfred A. Knopf, Inc.

Copyright © 1979, 1995 by Chanticleer
Press, Inc. All rights reserved under
International and Pan-American
Copyright Conventions. Published in the
United States by Alfred A. Knopf, Inc.,
New York, and simultaneously in Canada
by Random House of Canada Limited,
Toronto. Distributed by Random House,
Inc., New York.

Prepared and produced by
Chanticleer Press, Inc., New York.

Color reproductions by C. Angerer &
Goeschl, Vienna, Austria.
Type set in Garamond by Dix Type Inc.,
Syracuse, New York.
Printed and bound in Japan.

Published July 26, 1979
Fifteenth printing, August 1995

Library of Congress Catalog Card
Number 78-20383
ISBN 0-394-50431-3

# CONTENTS

# NATIONAL AUDUBON SOCIETY

*The mission of the* NATIONAL AUDUBON SOCIETY *is to conserve and restore natural ecosystems, focusing on birds and other wildlife for the benefit of humanity and the earth's biological diversity.*

In the vanguard of the environmental movement, AUDUBON has 560,000 members, regional and state offices, and an extensive chapter network in the United States and Latin America, plus a staff of scientists, lobbyists, lawyers, policy analysts, and educators. Through our sanctuary system we manage 150,000 acres of critical habitat.

Our award-winning *Audubon* magazine, sent to all members, carries outstanding articles and color photography on wildlife and nature, and the environment. We also publish *Audubon Activist,* the newsjournal; *Audubon Field Notes,* a journal reporting seasonal bird sightings; and *Audubon Adventures,* a bimonthly children's newsletter reaching 600,000 students.

Our *World of Audubon* television specials air on TBS. NATIONAL AUDUBON SOCIETY sponsors books and electronic programs on nature, plus eco-trips to exotic places like Antarctica, Africa, Australia, South America, and the South Pacific.

For membership information:

NATIONAL AUDUBON SOCIETY
Membership Department
700 Broadway, New York, NY 10003
(212) 979-3000

# THE AUTHOR

Richard Spellenberg is a Professor of
Biology at New Mexico State
University. He has collected and
studied plants in all the western states
and has specialized in desert plants of
the Southwest and Mexico. From 1968
to 1972 he was associated with the
New York Botanical Garden, aiding in
the production of *Wildflowers of the
United States, Vol. 5. The Pacific
Northwest* (1970), and *Vol. 6. The
Central Mountains and Plains* (1973) by
H. W. Rickett. He has published a
number of scientific papers and is a
specialist on the threatened and
endangered plant species of New
Mexico.

# ACKNOWLEDGMENTS

A book such as this is a synthesis from numerous sources, and for the help received from many people I am deeply appreciative. Six are especially important. My wife Marie typed the entire manuscript more than once and did much preliminary editing. My friend David Sutherland provided many valuable comments and corrections. William Niering and Nancy Olmstead, while deeply involved in preparing the companion guide on eastern wildflowers, helped solve many problems of organization and arrangement. Finally, I am grateful to two fine teachers, Dennis Anderson and C. Leo Hitchcock, whose enthusiasm encouraged my own interest and studies in the western flora.

The staff at Chanticleer Press has been a tremendous help and a pleasure to work with. I would like to thank the publisher Paul Steiner and Gudrun Buettner for their creative support and guidance. Also to be thanked in this regard are Milton Rugoff, Susan Rayfield, Richard Christopher, Helga Lose, and Carol Nehring. In addition, I only wish I could thank each of the photographers whose lovely work makes this book a pleasure to view.

Richard Spellenberg

# INTRODUCTION

It is not easy to define a wildflower; what one person considers a wildflower may be a weed to another. All we may safely say is that they are wild plants with flowers and that they may be found almost anywhere, from cracks in city sidewalks to vast empty deserts, pristine forests, or mountain meadows. This guide is directed toward the reader whose interest in wildflowers has just been awakened, as well as toward the nature devotee who knows many of the common or showy western wildflowers but desires to learn more. Because space in a book is necessarily limited, only a portion of the thousands of western wildflowers can be discussed or illustrated. Our plan, therefore, is to cover most of the flowers that attract attention because they are showy or because of their unusual nature, to represent with at least one example most genera of western wildflowers, and to represent the kind of variation found among species of some of the huge western genera such as Lupines, Beardtongues, and Evening Primroses.

Geographic Scope: In many guides covering the eastern and western United States, the dividing line between the two regions has been arbitrarily set at the 100th meridian. For topographical and other reasons, we

BERING
SEA

BEAUFORT
SEA

GULF
OF
ALASKA

C          A

PACIFIC OCEAN

U

S          T

0          500          1000 Miles

have chosen what we believe to be a more natural boundary (see map), which more or less parallels this demarcation line as it runs along the eastern base of the Rocky Mountains, then shifts southeast as it goes across Texas to the Big Bend region. This line marks a pronounced change in the kinds of native plants, with few species extending very far beyond on either side. The guide covers the entire region from this line westward to the Pacific Coast, and from Alaska to the Mexican border.

Major Western Habitats:   The wide range of habitats in the western United States accounts for the great number and diversity of native plants. Near the Pacific coast moist conditions prevail, with warmer temperatures in the south, cooler in the north, creating a general division between plant species. In the mountains, there are dense coniferous forests, most with few wildflowers, some with meadows that bloom with a profusion of colorful species. The high Pacific mountains, some with cold, wind-swept tundra on their ridges, receive most of the rainfall from the west. As a result, there is a wide area of arid grasslands and deserts to the east of the Sierra Nevada and Cascade ranges. A cold desert lies at lower elevations with many gray shrubs, especially sagebrush. The hot southern Mojave, Sonoran and Chihuahuan deserts have mostly an olive-green shrub, creosotebush, and a completely different set of plants from those in the cold desert. Ponds, streams and coastal salt marshes provide habitats for many kinds of aquatic plants. Species growing along the coast and in low, interior desert pools must be tolerant of salty soils.

Photographs:   Although many flower books are illustrated with drawings or paintings, we have chosen to use color photographs because they show flowers as seen in nature, rather than as interpreted by an artist. In using the work of America's leading wildflower photographers, we believe we are adding an exciting new dimension to what generally appears in guides as drawings. A good photograph captures the natural color of a wildflower in its natural setting, making identification that much easier. Finally there is the beauty itself of pictures taken by outstanding photographers: this guide is meant to be a delight to look at as well as use.

In selecting our photographs, we have tended to emphasize the flowers themselves, but leaves and other identifying features are also shown in many instances. Where useful, a number of line drawings are included among the text descriptions.

Captions:  The caption under each photograph gives the common name of the flower and height data for the plant. It also gives one of the following flower dimensions: the average flower width ($w.$) or flower length ($l.$); approximate cluster length ($cl.$) or approximate cluster width ($cw.$). [For further details, see note preceding the color plates.] This information is especially helpful where flowers are shown larger or smaller than life-size. Plant height is not given for plants classified as aquatics, vines, or creepers. The term "creeper" is used here not in the botanical sense of a prostrate plant rooting at the nodes but, more loosely, to describe any trailing or sprawling plant. The caption ends with the page number of the species description.

Arrangement by Color:  Since most inexperienced wildflower enthusiasts notice flower color first of all, we have grouped the flowers by color, though we realize that this, like any identification technique has its limitations. The color groups are in the following order:

Green
White (includes Cream)
Yellow
Orange
Brown
Red
Pink (includes Lavender)
Blue (includes Purple)

Where a flower has more than one prominent color, it may be included in two different color sections. Where a plant has a conspicuously colored or unusual fruit, the fruit may also be shown.

Flower Subgroups: Within the larger color groups, such as Yellow, we have further organized the flowers having a somewhat similar structure or form. To accomplish this, we have devised six basic subgroups: Simple-shaped flowers; Daisy- and Dandelion-like Flowers; Odd-shaped Flowers; Elongated Clusters; Rounded Clusters; Vines, Shrubs, and Trees. These subgroups will be discussed in more detail later in this Introduction.

Flower Types: When one looks directly into the face of a flower, its overall symmetry is evident. If its petals radiate in wheel-like fashion, it is termed radially symmetrical or regular (a). If it is divisible into two equal halves only along one line through the center, it is bilaterally symmetrical or irregular (b). For accurate identification, a plant's type of symmetry must be observed. Since radial symmetry is the basic form, we mention symmetry only when it is bilateral.

a

b

Flower Parts: Most flowers consist of four series of parts. The outside series, often green, is the calyx; its individual parts are the sepals. Inside this is the corolla, composed of petals and usually showy. The calyx and the corolla together are called the perianth. In some plants sepals and petals may look alike; in others, petals may be missing and only green sepal-like structures are present. In a very few plants there are no petals, but the sepals are petal-like, which is understandably confusing to the beginner. Sepals may be joined to one another and form a dish, bell, or tube; petals may also be joined in such shapes. In our description of a flower with separate petals, the number of petals is given; in a flower with joined petals, the number of lobes on the corolla is given.

Just inside the petals, and often attached to the corolla in plants with joined petals, are the stamens. Each stamen consists of a relatively slender stalk, the filament, and a pollen bearing body, the anther. The pollen inside the anther produces the sperm that fertilizes the egg.

In the very center of the flower are one or more pistils. The pistil has a swollen basal portion, the ovary, containing ovules that will grow into seeds. Above the ovary is a stout or slender, sometimes branched style, topped by the stigma. Pollination occurs when either wind, an insect or a small animal carries the pollen to the stigma.

Flower Forms: Flowers may be borne singly at the end of the stem or singly all along the stem in the leaf axils (the angle between the stem and the leaf stalk). More frequently, flowers are arranged in a cluster and are set apart from the rest of the plant. Technical names for flower clusters have been avoided in our text wherever possible; but some are very helpful in identification, and their technical names must be used. This is true of the Carrot Family (Apiaceae), where the flower cluster has a number

# Parts of a Flower

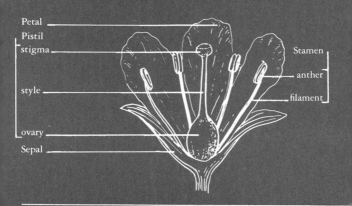

Petal

Pistil
  stigma

  style

  ovary

Sepal

Stamen

anther

filament

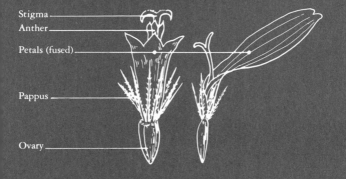

**Disk Flower**    **Ray Flower**

Stigma

Anther

Petals (fused)

Pappus

Ovary

# Composite Flower

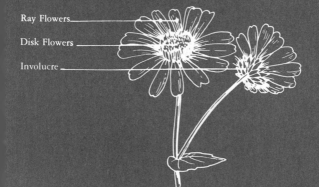

Ray Flowers

Disk Flowers

Involucre

## Arum

Spathe

Spadix

## Pea Flower

Banner

Wing

Keel

## Iris

Standard (petal)

Petal-like Style

Crest

Fall (sepal)

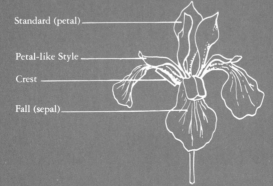

# Cluster Types

Umbel

Corymb

Cyme

Panicle

Raceme

Spike

of branches all attached at one point, a form called an umbel. It is also the case in the Sunflower Family (Asteraceae). Here a cluster of tiny flowers, some forming the button-like center, others forming the rays, are collectively called the head, which resembles a single radially symmetrical flower. (Such commonly used botanical terms are explained in the Glossary and appear in labeled drawings.) Reduced leaves in the flower or inflorescence are called bracts.

Leaves: Leaves can be an important aid to identifying a wildflower. Each leaf has two parts, a stalk (petiole) and a blade. In this guide we use two of the many technical terms to describe the outline of the blade: lanceolate (shaped like the tip of a lance), and ovate (egg-shaped, but with a pointed tip). In addition, leaves may be simple with smooth, toothed, or deeply lobed margins, or they may be compound. Compound leaves are composed of many little leaves (leaflets), either arranged along a central stalk (pinnately compound), or attached at the end of a stalk, spreading like fingers on a hand (palmately compound).

There are several common arrangements of leaves on plants. In the usual arrangement, called "alternate," each leaf is attached at a different level on the stem. If two leaves are attached at one level but on opposite sides, they are said to be "opposite." If three or more are attached in a ring, at one level, the leaves are described as "whorled." Leaves that appear at ground level are called "basal;" if there are many, they form a basal rosette. In the text we mention leaf arrangement only if it is not the usual, alternate one.

Classification and Names: The common name of a plant is often used only by people in one area. A geographically widespread plant may

# Leaf Types

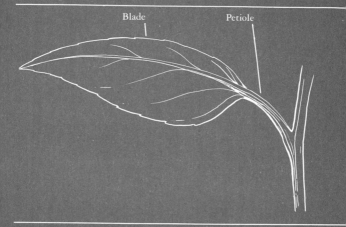

Blade      Petiole

Entire      Toothed      Lobed

Linear      Lanceolate      Ovate

# Leaf Arrangements

Opposite

Basal

Alternate

Whorled

Clasping

Perfoliate

Palmate

Once Pinnate

Twice Pinnate

have several common names, while plants that have more restricted distributions may have none at all. In the mid-18th century, the great Swedish botanist Carolus Linnaeus developed the scientific nomenclature in use today. The names are structured in Latin, and many have Greek roots. The first part of the scientific name is the genus (pl., genera); it is always capitalized and is usually assigned to a number of species with many characteristics in common. The second part is the specific name, usually lowercase, which often tells something about that particular species, such as its flower color, size, where it grows, or who its name honors. The two parts together form the species name, which is used uniformly around the world. Just as species may be grouped in genera according to characteristics they have in common, so genera may be grouped in larger aggregations called families.

Text
Descriptions:
The text contains descriptions of each species shown in the color plates. The species descriptions are arranged alphabetically by scientific name within genera, and the genera within families. This arrangement tends to put closely related species nearby, thus allowing for easy comparison of similar species.

*Description:*
Each species entry begins with a statement about the main visible features of the plant, so that the guide user can quickly decide whether he is on the right track. Detailed information then follows about flowers, leaves, fruit, and height. As an additional aid, prominent features of the plant are italicized.

*Flowering:*
Each entry covers the blooming period, which may vary considerably depending on climatic conditions. In one locality, the plant may flower only for a short period of the total span given in the

text, which is the span for the entire geographic range. Also, plants of a species that occur in southern locations tend to bloom earlier than those in more northerly sites; plants of a species that are found at low elevations tend to bloom earlier than those at higher levels.

*Habitat:* Knowing the general environment where a plant occurs is often very helpful in its identification, for most plants grow only in certain situations. Under "Habitat" we also mention commonly associated trees or shrubs; the reader should become familiar with these in order to fully understand some habitat descriptions. They are: pine, fir, spruce, and hemlock; piñon (a bushy pine); juniper (also called "cedar" in parts of the West); creosotebush; and sagebrush.

*Range:* The listing of geographic range begins as far as practical in the northwest part of a plant's range and proceeds from north to south, then west to east.

*Comments:* These notes give additional information about the plant, such as the origin of its names, its uses and various other legend and lore.

Endangered Many native wildflowers have been
Species: seriously depleted because of land development, lumbering, farming, and intensive grazing. By 1973 the impact of man on his environment had become so severe that Congress passed the Endangered Species Act giving some protection to plants faced with extinction. State laws, which vary widely, offer additional protection for many species and are often strictly enforced. Therefore, the reader is advised to check the laws of his state carefully before removing any plant. However, in the wide open spaces of the West, plant laws are often difficult —if not impossible—to enforce. Conscience is the best guide if we are to save our rarest wildflowers from extinction.

| | |
|---|---|
| How to Find the Flower: | First determine which of the major color groups the flower belongs in. To make it easy to locate each color group, and the shapes within the larger color groups, a thumb tab showing the color and shape is provided. Flowers are complicated structures and not every flower, of course, will fit precisely into any one grouping. Therefore if you fail to find your flower in one likely subgroup, try another subgroup in the same color category. Then turn to that color section and see if the flower matches the photograph. The Orange and Brown color sections have only a few species and so are not further subdivided. The larger color sections, White, Yellow, Pink, and Blue, are further divided according to flower or plant shape, into 6 subgroups as follows: |
| *Simple-shaped Flowers:* | The individual flowers tend to stand out separately; most flowers are radially symmetrical, usually with 4 or 5 petals (occasionally 3 or 6). |
| *Daisy- and Dandelion-like Flowers:* | Flower head with a button-like center and many radiating, strap-like petals (actually ray flowers) or flowers with many rays and no button-like center. |
| *Odd-shaped Flowers:* | Flowers or plants with an unusual overall appearance (generally bilaterally symmetrical), often difficult to classify in terms of shape. |
| *Elongated Clusters:* | Elongated masses of flowers either tightly or somewhat loosely arranged along the stalk; individual flowers may be symmetrical or asymmetrical. |
| *Rounded Clusters:* | Rounded masses of flowers either tightly or somewhat loosely arranged on a stalk; individual flowers may be symmetrical or asymmetrical. |
| *Vines, Shrubs and Trees:* | Climbers, and woody plants with one or many stems. |

If the photograph and the flower seem to match, read the caption beneath the picture and refer to the text description to confirm your identification.

An inexpensive hand lens is useful in studying the flower, and will also expand your appreciation of the minute perfection and beauty of the individual flower parts.

## HOW TO USE THIS GUIDE

Example 1    You have found a plant with bright
*Red Flower*    red, tubular, radially symmetrical
  *in Woods*    flowers.
    1.  Turn to the color plates labeled *Red
      Flowers,* and look for a flower with the
      form described. You will note several
      flowers of this type, all grouped
      together, but only one will seem
      exactly right: Firecracker Flower. The
      caption under the photograph gives
      information about the plant height and
      the size of the flower, as well as the
      page number of the text description.
    2.  You check the text description and find
      that your plant matches only
      Firecracker Flower and that it is a
      woodland plant.

Example 2    You have found a plant in open
*Blue-violet*    grassland with blue-violet flowers in a
*Flower in*    rounded cluster atop a long leafless
*Grassland*    stalk, with a few grass-like leaves at the
      base.
    1.  Turn to the color plates labeled *Blue
      Rounded Clusters.* You think your plant
      resembles the Forktooth Ookow.
    2.  Turning to the descriptions in the text,
      you find it does resemble Forktooth
      Ookow, but you note that your flower
      has round rather than forked teeth.
      From reading the Comments, at the
      end of the text description, you find
      that your plant is a kindred species,
      Roundtooth Ookow.

Example 3
*Green Fruit*
*along Roadside*

You have found a round, green fruit with green spiny projections growing on a leafy weed along a roadside.

1. Turn to the section labeled *Green Fruit*. Among the 4 photographs in this section only one resembles your specimen: the Buffalo Bur.

2. Upon reading the species description, you find that another plant, the Melonleaf Nightshade, also grows in the same habitat. Since the flowers on your specimen are blue-violet, not yellow, you correctly identify your specimen as the Melonleaf Nightshade.

# Part I
## Color Plates

## Key to the Color Plates

The color plates on the following pა
are divided into eight color groups:

Green
White (includes Cream)
Yellow
Orange
Brown
Red
Pink (includes Lavender)
Blue (includes Purple)

Within the larger color groups—
White, Yellow, Pink, and Blue—the
flowers are further divided by shape and
form into six subgroups:

Simple-shaped Flowers
Daisy- and Dandelion-like Flowers
Odd-shaped Flowers
Elongated Clusters
Rounded Clusters
Vines, Shrubs and Trees

Thumb Tabs  Each subgroup is indicated by a colored
symbol on a thumb tab at the left edge
of each double-page of plates. The
smaller color groups—Green, Orange,
Brown, and Red—are represented by
the General Flower Thumb Tab, with
the Green and Red color groups having
an additional thumb tab for fruit.

## Subgroup

### Simple-shaped Flowers

The individual flowers tend to stand out separately; most flowers are radially symmetrical, usually with 4–5 petals (occasionally 3 or 6).

### Daisy- and Dandelion-like Flowers

Flower head with a button-like center and many radiating, strap-like petals (actually ray flowers), or with many ray flowers and no button-like center.

### Odd-shaped Flowers

Flowers or plants with an unusual overall appearance (generally bilaterally symmetrical); often difficult to classify in terms of shape.

### Elongated Clusters

Elongated masses of flowers either tightly or somewhat loosely arranged along the stalk; individual flowers may be symmetrical or asymmetrical.

### Rounded Clusters

Rounded masses of flowers either tightly or somewhat loosely arranged on a stalk; individual flowers may be symmetrical or asymmetrical.

## Examples

Poppy

Violet

Trillium

Daisy

Desert Dandelion

Dandelion

Iris

Clover

Fairybell

Goldenrod

Larkspur

Purple Loosestrife

Milkweed

Wild Carrot

Field Mint

| Subgroup | |
|---|---|
| **Vines, Shrubs and Trees**<br>Climbers, and woody plants with one or many stems. | |
| **Fruit**<br>The dried or fleshy reproductive parts of a flower. | |
| **General Flower Thumb Tab**<br>Used for the Green, Orange, Brown, and Red color groups. Whenever possible, the flowers and fruit within these groups are arranged according to similar shapes. | |

## Examples

Morning Glory

Rhododendron

Palo Verde

Bittersweet Berries

Spiny Berry

Devil's Claw Pod

# How to Read the Captions under the Plates

Example:
454   Western Sea Purslane, $1-2'$, $w.$ ½", $p.$ $319$
1—   2————————— 3— 4— 5——

---

*w.* (*width*)          refers to average *width* of the flower. In
                        Sunflowers or Clovers it is the width of
                        the entire flower head.

---

*l.* (*length*)         refers to average *length* of the flower.
                        Given for some tubular and pendant
                        flowers as well as some extremely
                        recurved flowers where the length of the
                        flower in profile is its most noticeable
                        dimension. In Sunflowers and Clovers it
                        is the length of the entire flower head.

---

*cw.* (*cluster*        refers to range of *cluster width*. Given
*width*)                for broad clusters, usually umbels,
                        compound umbels, corymbs and cymes.

---

*cl.* (*cluster*        refers to range of *cluster length*. Given
*length*)               for elongated clusters, usually spikes,
                        racemes and panicles.

1 Plate number.
2 Common name of plant.
3 Height of typical mature plant. Usually a ran
given; if only one figure is shown, it refers to
maximum height.
4 Dimensions of the flower (see chart below).
5 Page number of species description.

Sunflower

Lily

Bunchberry
(bracts conspicuous)

Coneflower

Orchid (lip)

Fairybell

Buckwheat

Wild Carrot

Fairy Duster

Smartweed

Corn Lily

White Sweet Clover

1   Dingy Chamaesaracha, *creeper, w. ½", p. 784*

2   Green Passion Flower, *vine, w. ¾", p. 659*

3   Globe Berry, *vine, w. ½", p. 473*

4  Monument Plant, 4–7', *w.* 1¼", *p. 523*

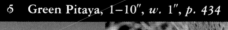

5  Green Pitaya, 1–10", *w.* 1", *p. 434*

6  Teddybear Cholla, 3–9', *w.* 1¼", *p. 437*

7 Early Coral Root, 3–12", *l.* ¼", *p.* 637

8 One-sided Wintergreen, 2–8", *l.* ¼", *p.* 699

9 Five-point Bishop's Cap, 4–16"; *w.* ¼", *p.* 739

10  California Pitcher Plant, 3', *l.* 2½", *p.* 733

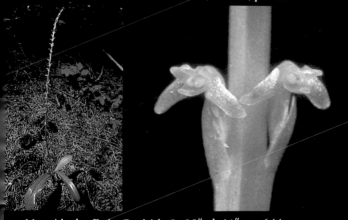

11  Alaska Rein Orchid, 8–32", *l.* ⅛", *p.* 644

12  Broad-leaved Twayblade, 2–14", *l.* ¼", *p.* 645

13   Devil's Claw, *creeper, l.* 5″, *p.* 612

14   Buffalo Bur, 16–32″, *w.* 1″, *p.* 790

15 Flatpod, 1–5″, *w.* ½″, *p. 419*

16 Bladderpod, 2–8′, *l.* 2″, *p. 447*

17 ...ted Saxifrage, 2–6″, w. ⅜″, p. 741

18 Meadow Chickweed, 2–20″, w. 1″, p. 452

19 Douglas' Meadow Foam, 4–16″, w. ¾″, p. 599

20 Wood Nymph, 2–6″, *w.* ¾″, *p. 696*

2   Broad-leaved Montia, 4–16″, *l.* ½″, *p. 683*

D warf Hesperochiron, 1–2″, *w.* 1″, *p. 534*

23  Rattlesnake Weed, *creeper, w. ⅛", p. 484*

24  Fringed Grass of Parnassus, *6–20", w. 1", p. 740*

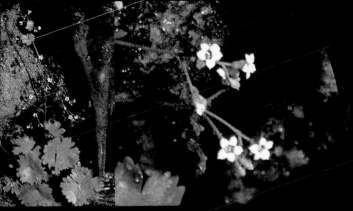

26 Coast Boykinia, 6–24″, *w.* ¼″, *p.* 736

27 Roundleaved Sundew, 10″, *w.* ⅜″, *p.* 477

29  Northern Fairy Candelabra, 1–10″, *w.* ⅛″, *p. 688*

30  Alpine Collomia, *creeper, w.* ¾″, *p. 662*

31  Nuttall's Linanthastrum, 1′, *w.* ½″, *p. 668*

32  Velvety Nerisyrenia, 8–24″, *w.* ¾″, *p.* 423

33  Bladder Campion, 3′, *w.* ½″, *p.* 456

34  White Campion, 1½–4½′, *w.* ¾″, *p.* 453

35 Miner's Lettuce, 1–14″, *w.* ³⁄₁₆″, *p.* 684

36 Bunchberry, 2–8″, *w.* 4″, *p.* 466

37 Canada Violet, 4–16″, *w.* 1″, *p.* 798

38    Beautiful Sandwort, 2–12″, *w.* ½″, *p. 451*

39    Fendler's Sandwort, 4–12″, *w.* ½″, *p. 451*

40    Queen's Cup, 2½–6″, *w.* 1¼″, *p. 575*

41    Apache Plume, *7′, w. 1¼″, p. 721*

42    Dwarf Bramble, *creeper, w. ½″, p. 730*

43    Richardson's Geranium, *8–32″, w. 1″, p. 528*

44 Water Buttercup, *aquatic, w.* ½″, *p.* 714

45 Beach Strawberry, *creeper, w.* ¾″, *p.* 722

46 White Mountain Avens, *creeper, u* . 1″, *p.* 720

47 **Elegant Cat's Ears**, 2–8″, *w.* 1″, *p.* 570

48 **Sego Lily**, 6–18″, *w.* 1½″, *p.* 572

49 Western Wake Robin, 4–16″, *w.* 2″, *p.* 591

50   Alpine Lily, 2–6″, *w.* ¾″, *p.* 586

51   Sweet-scented Heliotrope, 4–16″, *w.* ¾″, *p.* 406

52   Southwestern Thorn Apple, 5′, *l.* 6″, *p.* 7

53  Sand Lily, 8″, *w*. 1¼″, *p*. 584

54  Desert Lily, 1–6′, *l*. 2½″, *p*. 583

55   Avalanche Lily, 6–10″, w. 2½″, p. 580

56   Cascade Lily, 2–7′, w. 3½″, p. 586

57 Globeflower, 4–20″, *w*. 1¼″, *p*. 716

58 Western Pasque Flower, 8–24″, *w*. 1¼″, *p*. 701

59  Marsh Marigold, 1–8″, *w.* 1″, *p. 708*

60  Fragrant Water Lily, *aquatic, w.* 5″, *p. 622*

61    Birdcage Evening Primrose, *creeper, w. 2½″, p. 631*

62    Great Desert Poppy, *8–20″, w. 2½″, p. 652*

63  Matilija Poppy, 3–8′, *w.* 6″, *p.* 657

64  Prickly Poppy, 4′, *w.* 3″, *p.* 653

65  Blackfoot Daisy, 6–20″, w. 1″, p. 379

66  English Daisy, 2–8″, w. 1″, p. 349

67 Mojave Desert Star, 1–2″, *w.* ¾″, *p.* 380

68 Oxeye Daisy, 8–32″, *w.* 3″, *p.* 354

69 Spreading Fleabane, 4–28″, w. 1″, p. 360

70 Engelmann Aster, 1½–5′, w. 2″, p. 345

71   Desert Anemone, 4–16″, *w.* 1¼″, *p.* 703

72   Yerba Mansa, 1′, *cl.* 1–2″, *p.* 735

73  Stemless Daisy, 1–2″, w. 1½″, p. 391

74  White-rayed Mule's Ears, 6–32″, w. 4″, p. 395

75   Tobacco Weed, 12–28″, *w.* 1½″, *p. 347*

76   Desert Chicory, 6–20″, *w.* 1¼″, *p. 384*

77 Str[...]flower, 2–6″, *w.* 1½″, *p. 457*

78 Common Ice Plant, *creeper, w.* 1″, *p. 318*

79 **Wavy-leaved Soap Plant**, 2–10′, *w*. 1¼″, *p. 574*

80 **Coville's Columbine**, 8–14″, *w*. 1½″, *p. 707*

81    Wartberry Fairybell, 1–2′, *l.* ½″, *p. 578*

82    Southwestern Ringstem, 4′, *l.* 1½″, *p. 618*

83   Angel Trumpets, *creeper*, *l.* 5″, *p. 616*

84   Sweet Four O'Clock, 1½–5′, *l.* 5″, *p. 619*

85   Mountain Lady's Slipper, 8–28″, *l.* 1″, *p. 639*

86   California Lady's Slipper, 1–4′, *l.* ¾″, *p. 638*

87  White Globe Lily, 1–2′, *l.* 1″, *p. 568*

88  Northwestern Shooting Star, 6–16″, *l.* 1″, *p. 689*

89   White Clover, *creeper, w.* ½″, *p. 513*

90   Sour Clover, 4–32″, *w.* 1½″, *p. 512*

91 Phantom Orchid, 9–20", *l.* ¾", *p. 640*

92 Indian Pi

93 White Prairie Clover, 1–2′, *l.* 2½″, *p. 509*

94 English Plantain, 6–24″, *l.* 2″, *p. 660*

95 Desert Tobacco, 1–3′, *l.* ¾″, *p.* 786

96 Cotton Grass, 8–40″, *w.* 2½″, *p.* 475

97 Enchanter's Nightshade, 4–20″, *w.* ⅛″, *p. 625*

98 Round-leaved Rein Orchid, 8–24″, *l.* ⅝″, *p. 643*

99 False Mitrewort, 8–16″, *w.* ¼″, *p. 747*

100 Hooded Ladies' Tresses, 4–24″, *cl.* 2–5″, *p. 646*

101 Bog Rein Orchid, 6–52″, *cl.* 4–8″, *p. 642*

102 Coastal Rein Orchid, 8–16″, *cl.* 1½–4″, *p. 642*

103　Northern Inside-out Flower, 6–20″, *l.* ½″, *p.* 399

104　Merten's Saxifrage, 4–16″, *w.* ¼″, *p.* 742

105 One-sided Wintergreen, 2–8″, *l.* ¼″, *p.* 699

106 Fringe Cups, 32″, *w.* ½″, *p.* 746

107   Vanilla Leaf, 10–20″, *cl.* 1–2″, *p. 397*

108   Baneberry, 1–3′, *cl.* 2–4″, *p. 701*

109 False Lily of the Valley, 6–14″, *cl.* 1–2″, *p.* 587

110 False Solomon's Seal, 1–3′, *cl.* 1–8″, *p.* 589

111 **Partridge Foot**, 2–6″, *cl.* 1–2″, *p. 725*

112 **Poker Heuchera**, 6–36″, *cl.* 1–4″, *p. 737*

113 Sticky Tofieldia, 4–20″, *cl.* ½–1″, *p. 591*

114 Western Bistort, 8–28″, *cl.* 1–2″, *p. 678*

115    California Corn Lily, 4–8′, *cl.* 8–20″, *p.* 594

116    Bear Grass, 5′, *cl.* 4–24″, *p.* 595

117  Goatsbeard, 3–7′, *cl.* 4–16″, *p. 720*

118  Case's Fitweed, 2–7′, *cl.* 2–5″, *p. 519*

119    **White Sweet Clover,** 2–10′, *cl.* 1½–5″, *p. 506*

120    **White Milkwort,** 8–14″, *cl.* ¾–3″, *p. 673*

121  Sickletop Lousewort, 6–20″, *l.* ½″, *p.* 767

123 White Snapdragon, 4½', *l.* ½", *p.* 748

124 White Loco, 3–16", *l.* ¾", *p.* 507

125 White Checkermallow, 1½–3′, *w.* 1″, *p.* 608

126 Plains Larkspur, 5′, *w.* 1″, *p.* 713

127  Arrowhead, *aquatic, w. 1″, p. 322*

128  Grass-leaved Sagittaria, *aquatic, w. ½″, p. 321*

129  Elegant Camas, 6–28″, *w.* ¾″, *p. 597*

130  Lonely Lily, 6–12″, *w.* 1″, *p. 579*

131  Lance-leaved Draba, 2–10″, *cw.* ¾–1″, *p. 415*

132  Watercress, *creeper, cw.* 1–1½″, *p. 422*

133  Heartleaved Bittercress, 4–32″, *cw.* 1–2″, *p. 412*

134 Spectacle Pod, 2', *cw.* 1½–2½", *p. 414*

135 Western Peppergrass, 16", *cw.* 1–1½", *p. 420*

136 Western Smelowskia, 2–8" *cw.* 1–1½" *p. 425*

137 Ballhead Gilia, 8–12″, *cw.* ¾–1″, *p.* 665

138 Alpine Saxifrage, 1–3″, *cw.* ½–1″, *p.* 744

139 Western Saxifrage, 2–12″, *cw.* ¾–2″, *p.* 742

140 Leatherleaf Saxifrage, 2–10″, *cw.* ¾–1″, *p. 738*

141 Diamond-leaf Saxifrage, 2–12″, *cw.* ¾–1½″, *p. 744*

142 Bedstraw, 8–32″, *cw.* 1–3″, *p. 732*

143   Yerba Buena, *creeper, cw. ¾–1¼", p. 559*

144   Nuttall's Pussytoes, *6", cw. 1–2", p. 344*

145   Pearly Everlasting, *8–36", cw. 2–5", p. 343*

146 Beach Silvertop, 2½″, *cw.* 3–4″, *p. 329*

147 Ranger's Button, 1½–7′, *cw.* 2½–4″, *p. 330*

148 Northern Buckwheat, 4–20″, *cw.* 1–4″, *p. 674*

149   Estevé's Pincushion, 4–10″, *cw.* ¾–1¼″, *p. 353*

150   White Hyacinth, 10–28″, *cw.* 1½–4″, *p. 593*

151   Snowball, 4–20″, *cw.* 1–3″, *p. 614*

152　Popcorn Flower, 6–20″, *w.* ¼″, *p. 410*

153　Quail Plant, *creeper, w.* ¼″, *p. 407*

154　Bouncing Bet, 1–3′, *w.* 1″, *p. 454*

155 Buck Bean, *aquatic, w. ½", p. 613*

156 Wild Candytuft, 1¼–16", *cw. ¾–1¼", p. 428*

157 Shepherd's Purse, 6–16″, *cw.* 1–1½″, *p. 412*

158 Water Plantain, *aquatic, w.* ½″, *p. 320*

159   Hoary Cress, 8–20″, *cw.* 1–1½″, *p. 413*

160   Downy-fruited Vervain, 4–24″, *cw.* 2–5″, *p. 792*

161   Rocky Mountain Rockmat, 3", *cw.* ³/₄ [illegible] 25

162   Yerba de Selva, *creeper, cw.* ¹/₂–1" *p.* 532

163    White Milkweed, 3–10′, *cw.* 1½–2½″, *p. 336*

164    Poison Milkweed, 4′, *cw.* ¾–1¼″, *p. 338*

165   Fendler's Waterleaf, 8–32″, *w.* ⅜″, *p.* 535

166   Clammyweed, 4–32″, *cw.* 1½–2½″, *p.* 447

167  Water Hemlock, 1½–7′, *cw.* 3–5″, *p.* 326

168  Cow Parsnip, 10′, *cw.* 5–12″, *p.* 329

169  Wild Carrot, 1–4', *cw.* 3–6", *p. 327*

170  Yarrow, 12–40", *cw.* 2–5", *p. 341*

171    Western Serviceberry, 4–30', *w.* 1½", *p.* 719

172    White Virgin's Bower, *vine, w.* ¾", *p.* 710

173    Bindweed, 1–3', *w.* 1", *p.* 463

174 White Heather, 2–12″, *l.* ¼″, *p.* 479

175 Deer Brush, 3–13′, *cl.* 3–6″, *p.* 718

176 California Buckeye, 40′, *cl.* 4–8″, *p.* 530

177   Trapper's Tea, 2–7′, *w.* ½″, *p.* 481

178   Mockorange, 4–10′, *w.* 1″, *p.* 531

179　White Rhododendron, 3–7′, *w. ¾″, p. 482*

180　Pacific Dogwood, 6–65′, *w. 4″, p. 467*

181    Night-blooming Cereus, *1–3′, w. 2½″, p. 431*

182    Climbing Milkweed, *vine, cw. 2–4″, p. 339*

183 Saguaro, 50′, *w.* 3″, *p. 430*

184 Our Lord's Candle, 4–11′, *cl.* 3–9′, *p. 597*

185   Sotol, 6–17′, *cl.* 5–8′, *p.* 576

186   **Parry's Nolina**, 10′, *cl.* 18–30″, *p.* 587

187   Mojave Yucca, 4–15′, *cl.* 2–3′, *p.* 596

188   Blue Yucca, 5′, *cl.* 1–3′, *p.* 595

189    Redwood Violet, *creeper,* w. ½", p. 802

190    Stream Violet, 2–12", w. ⅝", p. 799

191    Douglas' Violet, 2–6", w. ⅝", p. 798

192    **Yellow Wood Violet**, *4–14″, w. ¾″, p. 800*

193    **Goosefoot Violet**, *2–6″, w. ⅝″, p. 801*

194    **Twinleaf**, *4–16″, w. ½″, p. 491*

195   Beach Primrose, *creeper, w. ¾", p. 631*

196   Douglas' Meadow Foam, *4–16", w. ¾", p. 99*

197   Common Silverweed, *creeper, w. ¾", p. 726*

198    Large-leaved Geum, 3', *w.* ½", *p. 722*

199    Sagebrush Buttercup, 2–8", *w.* 1", *p. 715*

200    Subalpine Buttercup, 2–10", *w.* 1", *p. 714*

201    Common Purslane, *creeper, w.* ¼″, *p. 684*

202    Tinker's Penny, *creeper, w.* ¼″, *p. 542*

203    Desert Rock Nettle, *1–2′, w.* 1½″, *p. 602*

204    Rough Menodora, *14"*, *w. ¾"*, *p. 624*

205    Goat's Head, *creeper, w. ⅜"*, *p. 805*

206    Tansy-leaved Evening Primrose, *4"*, *w. 1"*, *p. 633*

207   Whispering Bells, 6–20″, *l.* ½″, *p.* 533

208   Cream Cup, 4–12″, *w.* ¾″, *p.* 657

209   Fringed Gromwell, 2–12″, *l.* 1″, *p.* 407

210  Buffalo Bur, 16–32", *w.* 1", *p.* 790

211  Klamath Weed, 1–3', *w.* 1", *p.* 543

212  Blazing Star, 1–3', *w.* 4", *p.* 603

213   Rain Lily, 9″, *l.* 1″, *p.* 324

214   Desert Rosemallow, 4′, *w.* 1½″, *p.* 605

215   Sticky Cinquefoil, 20″, *w.* ⅝″, *p.* 727

216 Comb Draba, ½–4″, *cw.* ¾–1¼″, *p. 416*

217 Fendler's Bladderpod, 1–16″, *w.* ½″, *p. 421*

218 Desert Gold, 2–4″, *w.* ⅜″, *p. 669*

219   Hooker's Evening Primrose, *2–3′*, *w. 2½″*, *p. 632*

220   Yellow Willow Herb, *8–28″*, *w. 1¼″*, *p. 628*

221   Rock Rose, *8–12″*, *w. 1″*, *p. 458*

222  Indian Pond Lily, *aquatic, w. 3", p. 623*

223  Alpine Poppy, 2–6", w. 1¼", p. 656

224  White-bracted Stick-leaf, 6–12", l. 1¼", p. 603

225   Desert Mariposa Tulip, 4–20″, *w.* 1½″, *p.* 570

226   Yellow Mariposa Tulip, 8–24″, *w.* 1¼″, *p.* 571

227   Mexican Gold Poppy, 16″, *w.* 1¼″, *p.* 655

228 Ghost Flower, 4–20″, *l.* 1¼″, *p. 763*

229 Chihuahua Flax, 4–20″, *w.* ¾″, *p. 601*

230 Flower-of-an-Hour, 1–2′, *w.* 1½″, *p. 606*

231    Fragile Pricklypear, 8–10″, *w.* 1¾″, *p. 438*

232    Plains Pricklypear, 3–6″, *w.* 2½″, *p. 440*

233 Rainbow Cactus, 4–12″, *w*. 2½″, *p. 432*

234 Barrel Cactus, 3–10′, *w*. 2″, *p. 434*

235　Chinchweed, 2–8″, *w.* ½″, *p. 381*

236　Yellow Spiny Daisy, 6–14″, *w.* 1″, *p. 369*

237　Sunray, 6–18″, *w.* 3½″, *p. 360*

238 Stemless Golden Weed, ½–6″, *w*. 1½″, *p.* 368

239 Arrowleaf Groundsel, 1–5′, *w*. 1¼″, *p.* 387

240 Orange Sneezeweed, 2–4′, *w*. 2½″, *p.* 369

241 Woolly Daisy, ½–4″, *w.* ¼″, *p.* 364

242 Threadleaf Groundsel, 1–3′, *w.* 1¼″, *p.* 387

243 Five-needle Fetid Marigold, 4–8″, *w.* ¼″, *p.* 358

244   Little Golden Zinnia, 3–9″, *w.* 1¼″, *p.* 396

245   Paperflower, 4–20″, *w.* ¾″, *p.* 383

246   Brittlebush, 3–5′, *w.* 2½″, *p.* 359

247　Common Sunflower, 2–13′, *w.* 4″, *p.* 370

248　Heartleaf Arnica, 4–24″, *w.* 2½″, *p.* 345

249 Mule's Ears, 12–32″, *w.* 4″, *p.* 395

250 Arrowleaf Balsam Root, 8–32″, *w.* 4½″, *p.* 348

251　Cowpen Daisy, 4–60″, *w.* 1¾″, *p.* 394

252　Golden Yarrow, 4–24″, *w.* 2″, *p.* 363

253 Rosin Weed, 1–4″, *w.* 1″, *p. 352*

254 Desert Sunflower, 1–3′, *w.* 2″, *p. 365*

255  Stemless Hymenoxys, 3–12″, *w.* 1½″, *p.* 372

256  Old Man of the Mountain, 1–12″, *w.* 3½″, *p.* 373

257 Desert Dandelion, 6–14″, *w*. 1¼″, *p*. 379

258 Snakehead, 4–20″, *w*. 1¼″, *p*. 378

259   Curlycup Gumweed, 1–3′, *w.* 1½″, *p.* 366

260   Desert Marigold, 12–20″, *w.* 1½″, *p.* 347

261   Golden Aster, 8–20″, w. 1″, p. 354

262   Common Madia, 1–4′, w. 1½″, p. 377

263   Goldfields, 4–10″, *w.* ¾″, *p. 373*

264   Cutleaved Coneflower, 2–7′, *w.* 4½″, *p. 385*

265 Mexican Hat, 1–4′, *l.* 2″, *p.* 385

266 Greeneyes, 1–4′, *w.* 1½″, *p.* 350

267    Common Dandelion, 2–20″, *w.* 1″, *p. 390*

268    Pale Agoseris, 4–28″, *w.* 1″, *p. 342*

269 Yellow Salsify, 16–32″, w. 1¾″, p. 392

270 Alpine Gold, 6–14″, w. 2½″, p. 371

271  Silvery Luina, 6–16″, *cw.* 1–2″, *p. 375*

272  Hawk's Beard, 8–28″, *w.* ¾″, *p. 358*

273 Silvercrown Luina, 1–3′, *w.* ⅝″, *p.* 351

274 Yellow Head, 2–8″, *w.* ½″, *p.* 393

275   Desert Trumpet, 8–40″, *cw.* ¼–½″, *p. 675*

276   Yellow Skunk Cabbage, 12–20″, *cl.* 4–8″, *p. 333*

277 Turtleback, 2–5″, *w.* ¼″, *p.* 383

278 Powdery Dudleya, 4–14″, *w.* ⅜″, *p.* 469

279 Yellow Globe Lily, 8–20″, *l. 1″, p. 569*

280 Yellow Fawn Lily, 6–12″, *l. 2″, p. 579*

281 Ground Iris, 6–8″, *w*. 3″, *p*. 545

282 Yellow Bell, 4–12″, *l*. ¾″, *p*. 582

283  Common Bladderwort, *aquatic, l.* ¾″, *p.* 564

284  Deer Weed, 1–3′, *cw.* ¾–1¼″, *p.* 500

285  Snub Pea, 2–3′, *l.* ½″, *p.* 498

286　Seep-spring Monkeyflower, 3', *l.* 1", *p.* 761

287　Dwarf Lousewort, 4", *l.* ¾", *p.* 768

288　Devil's Claw, 1', *l.* 1¼", *p.* 612

289　Golden Columbine, 1–4′, *l.* 2½″, *p.* 704

290　Green-flowered Macromeria, 3′, *l.* 1½″, *p.* 409

291　Wright's Birdbeak, 2′, *l.* 1″, *p.* 755

292 Wright's Deer Vetch, 8–16″, *l.* ½″, *p.* 501

293 Hill Lotus, *creeper, l.* ¼″, *p.* 499

294 Tufted Loosestrife, 8–32″, *cw.* ¾–1¼″, *p.* 692

295  Fringed Loosestrife, 1–4′, *w.* ¾″, *p. 691*

296  Bog Loosestrife, 8–32″, *w.* ⅝″, *p. 692*

297    Moth Mullein, 1–5′, *w.* 1″, *p. 781*

298    Woolly Mullein, 2–7′, *w.* ⅞″, *p. 781*

299   Tree Lupine, 2–9', *cl.* 4–12", *p. 501*

300   Yellow Pea, 2–4', *cl.* 4–8", *p. 511*

301    Butter and Eggs, 1–3′, *l.* 1¼″, *p. 758*

302    Butter Lupine, 12–32″, *cl.* 2–8″, *p. 503*

303    Yellow Rattle, 6–32″, *l.* ½″, *p.* 779

304    Yellow Parentucellia, 4–28″, *cl.* 2–4″, *p.* 765

305    Towering Lousewort, 3', *cl. 3–8", p. 766*

306    Yellow Owl's Clover, 4–16", *cl. 2–5", p. 764*

307   Desert Plume, 1½–5′, *cl.* 4–24″, *p. 426*

308   Meadow Goldenrod, 1–5′, *cl.* 4–18″, *p. 388*

309 Narrow Goldenrod, 2–32″, *cl.* 2–8″, *p. 389*

310 Sulfur Paintbrush, 6–20″, *cl.* 2–6″, *p. 752*

311   Golden Ear-drops, 1½–5′, *l.* ½″, *p. 520*

312   Yellow Cryptantha, 3–10″, *w.* ⅜″, *p. 403*

313   Nodding Groundsel, 1–3′, *w.* ½″, *p.* 386

314   Hog Potato, 4–12″, *w.* ¾″, *p.* 496

315    Arizona Jewel Flower, 1–2′, *l.* ½″, *p.* 427

316    Mountain Jewel Flower, 8–40″, *l.* ½″, *p.* 427

317   Golden Smoke, 4–24″, *l.* ¾″, *p. 518*

318   Canada Milkvetch, 12–32″, *cl.* 1–3″, *p. 488*

319    Golden Stars, 6–24″, *w.* ¾″, *p.* 567

320    Pretty Face, 4–18″, *w.* ¾″, *p.* 593

321    Yellow Bee Plant, 1½–5′, *cw.* 1–2″, *p.* 445

322 Golden Alexanders, 8–24″, *cw.* 1–2½″, *p. 331*

323 Sweet Fennel, 3–7′, *cw.* 2–7″, *p. 328*

325 Alpine Wallflower, 2–8″, *w.* ⅝″, *p. 418*

326 Plains Wallflower, 6–14″, *w.* ¾″, *p. 416*

327 Menzies' Wallflower, 1–8″, *w.* ⅝″, *p. 418*

328   Double Bladderpod, *creeper, w.* ½", *p. 424*

329   Desert Primrose, 1–30", *w.* ¾", *p. 630*

330   Yellow Sand Verbena, *creeper, cw.* 1–2", *p. 615*

331   Wayside Gromwell, 8–24″, *cw.* 1–1½″, *p. 408*

332   Hedge Mustard, 1–3′, *cw.* ½–1″, *p. 424*

333   Charlock, 1–3′, *cw.* 1–2″, *p. 411*

334 Gordon's Ivesia, 8″, *cw.* ½–¾″, *p.* 724

335 Sierra Sedum, 1–7″, *cw.* ½–1″, *p.* 469

336 Sulphur Flower, 4–12″, *cw.* 2–3″, *p.* 676

337  Bird's Foot Trefoil, *creeper, l. ½", p. 498*

338  Large-flowered Brickelbush, *1–3', l. ½", p. 350*

339   Northern Dune Tansy, 8–24″, *w.* ½″, *p. 389*

340   Yellow Peppergrass, *creeper, cw.* ½–1″, *p. 419*

341    Tree Tobacco, 26′, *l.* 1¾″, *p.* 786

342    Yellow Twining Snapdragon, *vine, l.* ½″, *p.* 749

343    Trixis, 1–3′, *l.* ¾″, *p.* 393

344 Buffalo Gourd, *creeper, w. 2½", p. 473*

345 Melon Loco, *creeper, w. 1½", p. 472*

346 Tree Poppy, *4–20', w. 1½", p. 653*

347   Giant Coreopsis, 1–10′, *w.* 3″, *p.* 357

348   Creeping Oregon Grape, 4–8″, *w.* ¹₂″, *p.* 398

349   Snakeweed, 6–36″, *cw.* 1–2″, *p.* 367

350   Bladderpod, 2–8′, *w.* 1″, *p. 447*

351   Shrubby Cinquefoil, 6–36″, *w.* 1″, *p. 727*

352   Rabbit Brush, 7′, *cw.* 1–2½″, *p. 355*

353   Blue Palo Verde, 33′, *w.* ¾″, *p. 492*

354   Scotch Broom, 10′, *l.* ¾″, *p. 493*

355    Lechuguilla, 7–10′, *cl.* 1–5′, *p. 323*

356    Parry's Century Plant, 10–16′, *cl.* 3–6″, *p. 324*

357   Orange Bush Monkeyflower, 2–4′, *l.* 1½″, *p.* 760

358   Flannel Bush, 5–30′, *w.* 2″, *p.* 791

359   Tiger Lily, 2–4′, *w.* 2½″, *p. 584*

360   Desert Poppy, *creeper, w.* 2″, *p. 804*

361   California Poppy, 8–24″, *w.* 1½″, *p.* 654

362   Desert Mariposa Tulip, 4–20″, *w.* 1½″, *p.* 570

363 Fire Poppy, 12–24″, *w*. 1″, *p. 655*

364 Orange Agoseris, 4–24″, *w*. 1″, *p. 342*

365 Coulter's Globemallow, 8–60″, *w.* ⅞″, *p. 611*

366 Scarlet Globemallow, 20″, *w.* 1″, *p. 610*

367 Western Wallflower, 6–36″, *w.* ¾″, *p. 417*

368 Amber Lily, 3′, *w.* 1″, *p. 566*

369   Scarlet Pimpernel, *creeper, w. ¼", p. 687*

370   Flame Flower, 6–14", w. 1", p. 685

371   Butterfly Weed, 3', *cw. 2–3", p. 339*

372 Fiddleneck, 1–3′, *w.* ⅛″, *p. 402*

373 Pericome, 2–5′, *w.* ½″, *p. 382*

374 Winged Dock, 6–20″, *cl.* 2–8″, *p. 678*

375  Western Peony, 8–24", *w.* 1¼", *p. 651*

376  Clustered Lady's Slipper, 2–8", *l.* ½", *p. 639*

377 Fetid Adder's Tongue, 8″, *w*. 1″, *p*. 588

378 Mission Bells, 1–4′, *l*. 1″, *p*. 580

379 Rosy Twisted-stalk, 6–16″, *l.* ⅜″, *p.* 590

380 Stenanthium, 4–20″, *l.* ½″, *p.* 589

381 Vase Flower, 8–24″, *l.* 1″, *p. 709*

382 Mountain Jewel Flower, 8–40″, *l.* ½″, *p. 427*

383   Long-tailed Wild Ginger, *creeper, w.* 3½' *p. 334*

384   Meadow Rue, 1–3', *w.* ⅜", *p. 715*

385    Roseroot, 1¼–12″, *cw.* 1–2″, *p. 470*

386    California Ground Cone, 4–10″, *cl.* 4–10″, *p. 647*

387    Spotted Coral Root, 8–32″, *w.* ¾″, *p. 636*

388    Texas Purple Spike, 12″, *w.* 1⅛″, *p. 644*

389    Stream Orchid, 1–3′, *w.* 1¼″, *p. 641*

390  Striped Coral Root, 6–20″, *w.* 1″, *p.* 637

391  Desert Candle, 1–2′, *l.* ½″, *p.* 414

392  Pinedrops, 1–3′, *l.* ¼″, *p.* 697

393   Indian Pink, 6–16″, *w.* 1¼″, *p.* 455

394   Indian Blanket, 1–2′, *w.* 2″, *p.* 365

**395 Scarlet Fritillary** 1–3′, *l.* 1″, *p. 582*

**396 Red Cinquefoil** 1–2½′, *w.* 1″, *p. 728*

397 Scarlet Creeper, *vine, l. 1″, p. 464*

398 Desert Globemallow, *20–40″, w. 1″, p. 609*

399 Rocky Mountain Lily, 12–28″, w. 2½″, p. 585

400 Crimson Columbine, 6–36″, w. 2″, p. 706

401   Crimson Woolly Pod, 4–8″, *l.* 1½″, *p.* 488

402   Canyon Dudleya, 4–8″, *l.* ½″, *p.* 468

403   Candystick, 4–12″, *cl.* 3–9″, *p. 695*

404   Snow Plant, 8–24″, *cl.* 7–20″, *p. 699*

405 California Fuchsia, 1–3', *l.* 2", *p.* 634

406 Red Shrubby Penstemon, 12–20', *l.* 1¼", *p.* 769

407 Chuparosa, 5', *l.* 1¼", *p.* 315

408     Crimson Sage, 20″, *l.* 1½″, *p. 557*

409     Scarlet Bugler, 1–4′, *l.* 1¼″, *p. 769*

410     Red Monardella, 4–20″, *l.* 1½″, *p. 553*

411   Texas Betony, 3′, *l.* ⅞″, *p.* 561

412   Firecracker Flower, 1–3′, *l.* 1¼″, *p.* 577

413  Skyrocket, 6–84″, *l.* 1″, *p.* 664

414  Golden-beard Penstemon, 3′, *l.* 1¼″, *p.* 768

415   Cushion Buckwheat, 1–12″, *cw.* ¾–1¼″, *p. 675*

416   Bighead Clover, 4–12″, *w.* 1½″, *p. 512*

417 Desert Paintbrush, 4–16″, *cl.* 2–8″, *p.* 750

418 Giant RABI A A A S A B B T1

419    Cardinal Flower, 1–3′, *l.* 1¼″, *p. 443*

420    Coral Bells, 10–20″, *l.* ⅜″, *p. 737*

421    Showy Thistle, 2–4′, *l. 2″, p. 356*

422    Red Clintonia, 10–20″, *cw. 1–2″, p. 574*

423   Claret Cup Cactus, 2–12″, *w.* 1¾″, *p.* 433

424   Scarlet Bouvardia, 3′ *l.* 1″ *p.* 731

425 Western Coral Bean, 15', *l.* 3", *p.* 495

426 Ocotillo, 30', *l.* ¾", *p.* 517

427    Baneberry, 1–3′, *w.* ⅜″, *p. 701*

428    Kinnikinnick, *creeper, w.* ⅜″, *p. 478*

429   Desert Christmas Cactus, 3', *l.* ½", *p.* 439

430   Freckled Milkvetch, 4–16", *l.* ⅝", *p.* 490

431   Moss Pink, 1–2½″, *w.* ½″, *p. 455*

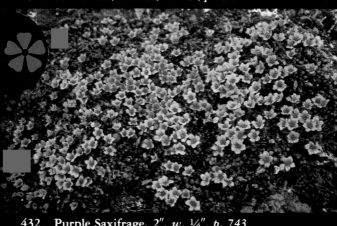

432   Purple Saxifrage, 2″, *w.* ¼″, *p. 743*

433   Smooth Douglasia, *creeper, w.* ⅜″, *p. 691*

434　Alpine Collomia, *creeper, w. ¾", p. 662*

435　Dwarf Purple Monkeyflower, 4", *l. ¾", p. 762*

436　Shaggy Tuft, 2½", *w. ⅝", p. 316*

437    Mustang Linanthus, 4–24″, *w.* ¾″, *p.* 669

438    Prickly Phlox, 1–3′, *w.* 1″, *p.* 667

439    Desert Four O'Clock, 18″, *w.* 1″, *p.* 620

440  Violet Suksdorfia, 4–8″, *l.* ⅜″, *p.* 745

441  Honesty, 20–40″, *w.* ¾″, *p.* 421

442  Bridge's Gilia, 2–14″, *l.* ½″, *p.* 663

443    Redwood Sorrel, 2–7″, *w.* ⅝″, *p.* 650

444    Spring Beauty, 2–10″, *w.* ½″, *p.* 681

445    Little Pipsissewa, 2–6″, *w.* ½″, *p.* 695

446 Mountain Four O'Clock, 3′, *w.* ½″, *p. 621*

447 Mountain Wood Sorrel, 1–10″, *w.* ⅝″, *p. 649*

448 False Baby Stars, 2–12″, *w.* ⅝″, *p. 668*

449   Western Starflower, 4–10″, w. ½″, p. 694

450   Grass Pink, 8–24″, w. ½″, p. 453

451   Centaury, 5–24″, w. ½″, p. 522

452 Filaree, *creeper*, *w.* ½″, *p.* 527

453 Fagonia, 8–24″, *w.* ½″, *p.* 803

454 Western Sea Purslane, 1–2′, *w.* ⅙″, *p.* 319

455   Pigmy Talinum, 1–3″, *w.* ¾″, *p. 686*

456   Sticky Geranium, 1–3′, *w.* 1″, *p. 529*

457   Red Maids, 2–16″, *w.* ½″, *p. 680*

458    Trailing Four O'Clock, *creeper, w.* ¾″, *p.* 617

459    Stringflower, 2–6″, *w.* 1½″, *p.* 457

460    Rock Fringe *creeper, w.* 1″, *p.* 629

461  Sagebrush Mariposa Tulip, 8–20″, *w.* 2″, *p.* 572

462  Corn Cockle, 1–3′, *w.* 1″, *p.* 450

463　Pale Face, 1–3′, *w.* 1¼″, *p.* 606

464　Grass Widow, 4–12″, *w.* 1½″, *p.* 547

465    Desert Five Spot, 4–24″, *w.* 1″, *p.* 607

466    Farewell to Spring, 6–36″, *w.* 1¼″, *p.* 626

467　Bush Morning Glory, *4′, w. 2¼″, p. 464*

468　Beach Morning Glory, *creeper, w. 2″, p. 462*

469    Peyote, 1–3″, *w.* ¾″, *p. 435*

470    Fishhook Cactus, 6″, *w.* ⅞″, *p. 436*

471    Cushion Cactus, 1½–6″, *w.* 1½″, *p. 431*

472  Simpson's Hedgehog Cactus, 2–8″, *w.* 1¼″, *p. 441*

473  Beavertail Cactus, 6–12″, *w.* 2½″, *p. 436*

474  Tree Cholla, 3–7′, *w.* 2½″, *p. 439*

475   Leafy Aster, 8–20″, *w.* 1½″, *p. 346*

476   Mojave Aster, 1–2½′, *w.* 2″, *p. 377*

477 Seaside Daisy, 4–16″, *w. 2″, p. 361*

478 Showy Palafoxia, 1–2′, *w. 1¼″, p. 381*

479     Philadelphia Fleabane, 8–28″, *w.* ¾″, *p. 362*

480     Showy Daisy, 1–3′, *w.* 1¾″, *p. 363*

481   Sticky Aster, 1–3′, *w.* 1½″, *p.* 375

482   Sea Fig, *creeper, w.* 2″, *p.* 317

483    Steer's Head, 1–4″, *l.* ½″, *p. 521*

484    Calypso, 8″, *l.* 1¼″, *p. 636*

485    Lovely Clarkia, 1′, *w.* 1¾″, *p. 627*

486 Salt-marsh Club-flower, 8–16", *l.* ¾", *p. 754*

487 Common Henbit, 3–6", *l.* ⅝", *p. 551*

488 Desert Calico, 1–2", *w.* ½", *p. 666*

489   Bent Milkvetch, *creeper, w. 1″, p. 489*

490   Crescent Milkvetch, 2–10″, *w.* ⅞″, *p. 487*

491   Feather Peabush, 1–3′, *w.* ½″, *p. 494*

492 Mountain Pride, 6–12″, *w.* 1″, *p.* 774

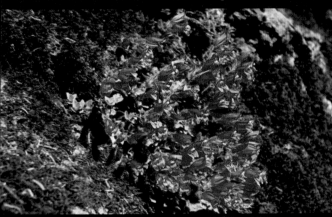

493 Cliff Penstemon, *creeper, l.* 1¼″, *p.* 776

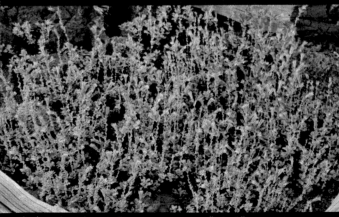

494 Davidson's Penstemon, 2–6″, *l.* 1″, *p.* 771

495 New Mexico Vervain, 3', *cw.* ¾–1¼", *p. 795*

496 Purple Prairie Clover, 1–3', *l.* 2", *p. 510*

497 Coyote Thistle, 20–40", *l.* 1", *p. 328*

498 Cow Clover, 4–32″, *w.* 1″, *p. 514*

499 Red Clover, 1–3′, *w.* 1¼″, *p. 513*

500 Musk Thistle, 1–9′, *w.* 2½″, *p. 352*

501    Prairie Smoke, 16″, *l.* ½″, *p.* 723

502    Adobe Lily, 1–18″, *l.* 1¼″, *p.* 581

503   Alpine Shooting Star, 4–12″, *l.* ⅞″, *p. 688*

504   Few-flowered Shooting Star, 4–24″, *l.* ⅞″, *p. 690*

505   Western Bleeding Heart, 8–18″, l. ¾″, p. 520

506   American Vetch, 2–4′, l. ¾″, p. 515

507　Twinflower, *creeper, l.* ½″, *p.* 449

508　Vase Flower, 8–24″, *l.* 1″, *p.* 709

509    Checkermallow, 1–3′, *w.* 1¼″, *p.* 609

510    Mountain Globemallow, 3–7′, *w.* 1½″, *p.* 607

511 Foxglove, 2–7', *l. 2", p. 756*

512 Western Sweetvetch, 16–32" *cl. 2–5", p. 496*

513　Harlequin Lupine, 4–18″, *cl.* ½–1½″, *p. 505*

514　Stinging Lupine, 8–40″, *cl.* 4–10″, *p. 503*

515　Showy Loco, 4–16″, *cl.* 2–5″, *p. 508*

516　Purple Loco, 4–16″, *cl.* 2–7″, *p. 507*

517　Lemmon's Sage, 1–3′, *l.* 1¼″, *p.* 558

518　Great Hedge Nettle, 2–5′, *l.* ¾″, *p.* 561

519  Bird Vetch, 4–7', *cl.* 2–5", *p. 515*

520  Telesonix, 2–8" *cl.* 1–4" *p. 746*

521   Purple Chinese Houses, 1–2′, *l.* ¾″, *p.* 753

523 **Balloon Flower,** 2–7', *l.* 1¼", *p.* 775

524 **Parry's Penstemon,** 4', *l.* ¾", *p.* 776

525    Great Plains Paintbrush, 4–12″, cl. 1–5   p. 751

526    Common Owl's Clover, 4–16″, cl. 2–5″, p. 764

527 Water Smartweed, *aquatic*, cl. ½–1½", p. 677

528 Bog Wintergreen, 6–16", w. ½", p. 698

529  Nettleleaf Horsemint, 1–5′, *cl.* 1¼–6″, *p. 550*

530  Rocky Mountain Bee Plant, ½–5′, *cl.* 2–8″, *p. 446*

531 **Elegant Clarkia,** 6–36″, *w.* 1¼″, *p. 627*

532 **Scarlet Gaura,** 6–24″, *w.* ½″, *p. 629*

533   Dotted Gayfeather, 6–32″, *cl.* 3–16″, *p.* 374

534   Elephant Heads, 28″, *cl.* 3–14″, *p.* 766

535  Purple Loosestrife, 2–7′, *cl.* 1–3′, *p. 604*

536  Fireweed, 2–7′, *cl.* 1–2′, *p. 628*

537   Spreading Dogbane, 8–20″, *l.* ¼″, *p. 332*

538   Long-leaved Phlox, 4–16″, *w.* 1″, *p. 671*

539   Western Pink Vervain, 8–16″, *w.* ⅜″, *p. 794*

540   Purple Mat, *creeper, w. ⅜″, p. 536*

541   Dagger Pod, *2–8″, w. ½″, p. 423*

542   Desert Sand Verbena, *creeper, cw. 2–3″, p. 616*

543   Sierra Primrose, *creeper, w. ¾″, p. 693*

544   Parry's Primrose, *3–16″, w. 1″, p. 693*

545   Fremont's Monkeyflower, *1–8″, w. ⅞″, p. 760*

546    Threadleaf Phacelia, *4–20″, w. ½″, p. 540*

547    Siskiyou Lewisia, *4–12″, w. 1⅛″, p. 682*

548    Bitterroot, *½–2″, w. 1¾″, p. 682*

549    Showy Milkweed, 1–4′, *cw.* 2–5″, *p.* 337

550    Nodding Onion, 4–20″, *cw.* 1½–3″, *p.* 566

551    Hooker's Onion, 4–12″, *cw.* 1–2″, *p.* 565

552 Umbrella Plant, 2–6′, *cw.* 2–7″, *p. 741*

553 California Thrift, 2–16″, *cw.* ¾–1″, *p. 661*

554 Pussy Paws, *creeper, cw.* 1½–2¼″, *p. 681*

555    Red Four O'Clock, 1–3′, *l.* ⅝″, *p.* 619

556    Silky Beach Pea, 8–24″, *l.* ¾″, *p.* 497

557    Field Milkvetch, 2–12″, *cl.* 1–1½″, *p.* 486

558    Kinnikinnick, *creeper, l.* ¼″, *p. 478*

559    Pink Mountain Heather, 4–16″, *l.* ¼″, *p. 482*

560    Alpine Laurel, 4–20″, *w.* ½″, *p. 480*

561   Red Clintonia, 10–20″, *cw*. 1–2″, *p.* 574

562   Lowbush Penstemon, 6–16″, *l.* 1½″, 773

563 Thistle Sage, 4–20″, *l.* ⅞″, *p.* 554

564 Lewis' Monkeyflower, 1–3′, *l.* 1½″, *p.* 762

565     **Range Ratany,** 6–24″, *w.* ¾″, *p. 549*

566     **Shrubby Coldenia,** 4–20″, *cw.* ¾–1¼″, *p. 403*

567     **Fairy Duster,** 8–20″, *w.* 2″, *p. 490*

568  Western Redbud, 6–17′, *l.* ½″, *p. 492*

569  Chaparral Pea, 7′, *l.* ¾″, *p. 510*

570  Autumn Sage, 3′, *l.* 1⅛″, *p. 557*

571   Nootka Rose, 2–13′, *w.* 2½″, *p.* 729

572   Western Azalea, 4–17′, *w.* 2″, *p.* 483

573   Morning Glory, *vine, w.* 2″, *p.* 465

574  Salal, 4–48", *l.* ⅜", *p. 480*

575  Desert Willow, 4–30', *l.* 1¼", *p. 400*

576  Texas Silver

577     Tufted Phlox, 2–6″, *w.* ⅝″, *p. 670*

578     Alpine Forget-me-not, 4″, *w.* ¼″, *p. 405*

579     Baby Blue Eyes, 4–12″, *w.* 1″, *p. 536*

580    Pale Trumpets, *2′, l. 1¼″, p. 665*

581    Purple Groundcherry, *creeper, w. ¾″, p. 787*

582    Arizona Blue-eyes, *1′, w. ⅝″, p. 463*

583   Blue-eyed Grass, 4–20″, *w.* 1″, *p.* 547

584   White Horsenettle, 3′, *w.* 1″, *p.* 789

585   Common Butterwort, 2–6″, *w.* ⅝″, *p.* 563

586     Western Pansy Violet, 2–5″, *w.* ⅝″, *p. 797*

587     Larkspur Violet, 3–8″, *w.* ⅝″, *p. 800*

588     Blue Violet, 4″, *w.* ⅝″, *p. 796*

589  Wild Blue Flax, 6–32″, *w.* 1″, *p.* 600

590  Blue Gilia, 10″, *w.* ¾″, *p.* 663

591  Pasque Flower, 14″, *w.* 1¾″, *p.* 703

592 Felwort, 2–20″, *w.* ¾″, *p.* 526

593 Blue Anemone, 4–12″, *w.* 1¼″, *p.* 702

595   Tahoka Daisy, 4–16″, *w. 2″, p. 376*

596   Sticky Aster, 1–3′, *w. 1½″, p. 375*

597   Salsify, 20–48", w. 2½", p. 392

598   Chicory, 1–6', w. 2", p. 356

599  Maiden Blue-eyed Mary, 2–16″, *w.* ¼″, *p.* 754

600  Small-bracted Dayflower, *creeper, w.* 1″, *p. 460*

601  Western Dayflower, 20″, *w.* ¾″, *p. 459*

602  Naked Broomrape, 1¼–4″, *l.* 1″, *p. 648*

603  Northern Gentian, 2–16″, *w.* ⅝″, *p. 524*

604  Limestone Columbine, 2–5″, *w.* 1¾″, *p. 706*

605   Blue Columbine, 3', *w.* 2½", *p.* 705

606   Rocky Mountain Iris, 8–20", *w.* 3½", *p.* 545

607 Tough-leaved Iris, 16″, *w.* 3½″, *p.* 546

608 Douglas' Iris, 6–32″, *w.* 3½″, *p.* 544

609 Explorer's Gentian, 2–12", *l.* 1¼", *p. 525*

610 Fringed Gentian, 4–16", *l.* 1½", *p. 525*

611  **Bluebell**, 4–40″, *l.* ¾″, *p. 442*

612  **Prairie Gentian**, 10–28″, *l.* 1½″, *p. 523*

613 Spike Broomrape, 4–20″, *cl.* 4–18″, *p. 648*

614 Dwarf Waterleaf, 4–16″, *cw.* 1–1½″, *p. 534*

615 Teasel, 1½–7′, *cw.* 1¼–2″, *p.* 476

616 Coyote Mint, 6–14″, *cw.* 1–1½″, *p.* 553

617 Bladder Sage, 2–3′, *l.* ¾″, *p. 554*

618 Creeping Charlie, *creeper, l.* ¾″, *p. 551*

619 Austin's Skullcap, 4–12″, *l.* 1¼″, *p.* 559

620 Marsh Skullcap, 4–32″, *l.* ⅝″, *p.* 560

621 Blue Toadflax, 28″, *l.* ½″, *p.* 757

622 Jones' Penstemon, 2–8″, *l.* ⅝″, *p.* 772

623 Narrowleaf Penstemon, 6–16″, *l.* ¾″, *p.* 774

624  Rydberg's Penstemon, 8–24″, l. ⅝″, p. 777

625  Platte River Penstemon, 8–40″, l. 1″, p. 770

626  Cascade Penstemon, 8–28″, l. ⅞″, p. 777

627 American Brookline, 4–40″, *w.* ⅜″, *p.* 782

628 Cusick's Speedwell, 2–8″, *w.* ½″, *p.* 783

629    Venus' Looking Glass, 6–24″, *w.* ⅝″, *p.* 444

630    Common Camas, 12–20″, *w.* 2″, *p.* 573

631   Southwestern Blue Lobelia, 8–28″, *l.* ¾″, *p. 443*

632   Parry's Larkspur, 1–3′, *w.* 1″, *p. 711*

633 Poison Delphinium, 2–6′, *w.* 1¼″, *p. 712*

634 Nuttall's Larkspur, 4–16″, *w.* 1″, *p. 711*

635   Western Monkshood, 1–7′, *l.* 1″, *p. 700*

636   Miniature Lupine, 4–16″, *cl.* ½–3″, *p. 502*

637 Coulter's Lupine, 8–16″, *cl.* 3–8″, *p. 505*

638 Blue-pod Lupine, 2–5′, *cl.* 6–24″, *p. 504*

639    Alpine Besseya, *6″, cl. 2–5″, p. 749*

)    Vinegar Weed, *2–5′, l. ½″, p. 562*

64 Mountain Kittentails, 4–24″, *cl.* 2–8″, *p.* 780

642 Purple Fringe, 16″, *cl.* 3–10″, *p.* 540

643   Many-flowered Stickseed, 1–3′, *w.* ¼″, *p.* 405

644   Hound's Tongue, 12–32″, *w.* ½″, *p.* 404

645   Sky Pilot, 4–16″, *w.* ⅝″, *p.* 672

646    Pine Spiderwort, 8–20", *w.* ⅝", *p.* 460

647    Snow Queen, 6", *cw.* 1–2", *p.* 780

648    Mountain Bluebell, 6–60", *l.* ⅝", *p.* 409

649   S...loped Phacelia, 6–30″, *w.* ¼″, *p.* 539

650   Wild Heliotrope, 8–32″, *w.* ¼″, *p.* 538

651   Silverleaf Phacelia, 8–20″, *cw.* 1–3″, *p.* 538

652 Desert Bell, 8–30″, *l.* 1″, *p.* 537

653 Field Mint, 8–32″, *cw.* ¾–1¼″, *p.* 552

654 Chia, 4–20″, *cw.* 1¼–2″, *p.* 555

655　Forktooth Ookow, 1–3′, *cw.* 1¼–2″, *p.* 576

656　Douglas' Triteleia, 8–28″, *w.* ¾″, *p.* 592

657 Elegant Brodiaea, 4–16″, *l.* 1¼″, *p. 568*

658 Western Polemonium, 1–3′, *w.* ⅝″, *p. 671*

659   Net-cup Snapdragon Vine, *vine, l.* 1", *p.* 759

660   Little Snapdragon Vine, *vine, l.* ⅞", *p.* 758

661 Bittersweet, *vine, w.* ⅝″, *p. 788*

662 Columbia Virgin's Bower, *vine, l.* 1½″, *p. 708*

663   Death Valley Sage, 1½–4′; *cw.*•¾–1½″, *p. 556*

664   Gray-ball Sage, 8–32″, *l.* ½″, *p. 556*

665  Deer Brush, 3–13′, *cl*. 3–6″, *p. 718*

666  Smoke Tree, 4–26′, *l*. ½″, *p. 494*

# Part II
## Family and Species Descriptions

The numbers preceding the species descriptions in the following pages correspond to the plate numbers in the color section.

## ACANTHUS FAMILY
(Acanthaceae)

Herbs or shrubs with seeds borne on characteristic hooked projections.
Flowers: often bilaterally symmetrical, with showy bracts. Corolla with 4–5 united petals, usually with 2-lobed upper lip and 3-lobed lower lip; sepals 4–5, stamens 2 or 4. All these parts attached at base of the ovary.
Leaves: simple, opposite, smoothly margined, with pale streaks or small bumps.
Fruit: 2-celled capsule.
About 250 genera and 2,600 species are native to temperate and tropical regions throughout the world. Many are cultivated as ornamentals.

407 Chuparosa
(*Beloperone californica*)
Acanthus Family (Acanthaceae)

Description: Numerous *tubular dull-red flowers* bloom on this *mostly leafless, densely branched, grayish-green shrub.*
Flowers: corolla 1–1½" (2.5–3.8 cm) long, deeply cleft into a 2-lobed upper lip and a 3-lobed lower lip.
Leaves: about ½" (1.3 cm) long, opposite, ovate, finely hairy, deciduous.
Height: to 5' (1.5 m), nearly as wide.
Flowering: February–June.
Habitat: Along desert watercourses, mostly below 2,500' (750 m) elevation.
Range: Southeastern California, southern Arizona, and northwestern Mexico.
Comments: Only one of the 60 species in this New World genus extends north into the United States. The common name is Spanish for "hummingbird;" these birds frequently visit the nectar-rich plants, pollinating flower after flower as they feed. Linnets and sparrows bite off the flowers and eat the nectar-filled bases. Sometimes known locally as

"Honeysuckle," Chuparosa is said to
have been eaten by Papago Indians.

---

436 **Shaggy Tuft**
(*Stendandrium barbatum*)
Acanthus Family (Acanthaceae)

Description: A dwarf, *tufted, grayish plant* with *short
spikes of pink-rose bilateral flowers* nestled
among the leaves.
Flowers: corolla about ⅝" (1.5 cm)
wide, its 5 lobes flaring from a narrow
tube, the 2 upper lobes slightly darker
than the lower 3.
Leaves: to 1½" (3.8 cm) long, opposite,
narrowly lanceolate, broader above
middle, densely shaggy with gray hairs.
Height: to 2½" (6.3 cm).

Flowering: March–June.

Habitat: Open limestone flats and rocky or clay
banks.

Range: Southern New Mexico and western
Texas; south to northern Mexico.

Comments: One of the first wildflowers to bloom in
the normally dry spring of western
Texas, its bright pink-rose flowers are
conspicuous against the gray limestone.

## ICE PLANT FAMILY
(Aizoaceae)

Usually fleshy herbs with showy flowers and simple leaves.

Flowers: radially symmetrical, commonly solitary or in small open clusters; sepals 5–8, often brightly colored and like petals; technically no petals but in many species the outer stamens are sterile, brightly colored, and resemble numerous narrow petals; stamens many. All these parts may either be attached at base or top of ovary.

Leaves: either opposite or alternate.

Fruit: capsule with 2–5 or more chambers.

There are about 130 genera and 2,500 species, most of which occur in South Africa. In the United States members of this family are most common in the West, especially near the warm coast. Several genera are cultivated as ground covers and dune stabilizers, and a few as succulent novelties.

---

### 482 Sea Fig
(*Mesembryanthemum chilense*)
Ice Plant Family (Aizoaceae)

Description: A mat-forming plant with *trailing, rooting stems,* bearing large *deep reddish-lavender flowers* nestled among the *erect, narrow, succulent leaves.*
Flowers: 1½–2½″ (3.8–6.3 cm) wide; sepals of different lengths, the larger like leaves; petals numerous, very narrow.
Leaves: 1½–3″ (3.8–7.5 cm) long, mostly opposite, straight, 3-sided.
Fruit: green, fleshy, plump, flat at top, with 8–10 chambers.
Height: creeper, with trailing stems up to 3′ (90 cm) long and flowering branches to 5″ (12.5 cm) high.

Flowering: April–September.

Habitat: Coastal sands and bluffs.
Range: From southern Oregon to Mexico.
Comments: The tongue-tangling genus name means "blooming at midday;" flowers only open in full sun. A similar species, Hottentot Fig (*M. edule*), introduced from South Africa, is used to stabilize dunes. It has 3-sided curved leaves with fine teeth on the lower angle, and yellow petals which become pinkish. The fruit is edible. Other cultivated species have "escaped" in parts of California. They have flat or nearly cylindrical leaves.

## 78  Common Ice Plant
(*Mesembryanthemum crystallinum*)
Ice Plant Family (Aizoaceae)

Description: A succulent plant with branched, reclining stems, covered with tiny *glistening beads; white or reddish flowers* in the upper axils.
Flowers: 1″ (2.5 cm) wide, with *many narrow petals* ¼–⅜″ (6–9 mm) long, and many stamens.
Leaves: ¾–4″ (2–10 cm) long, wavy, ovate or spatula-shaped.
Height: creeper, about 3″ (7.5 cm) high, with stems 8–24″ (20–60 cm) long.
Flowering: March–October.
Habitat: On sandy flats and slopes in open areas near the coast; also in deserts.
Range: Southern half of California to Baja California.
Comments: Found also in southern Europe and Africa, this plant was probably introduced to North America from the Old World. The beads on the stems are actually swollen with water; they are easily crushed, exude their contents, and give the plant a moist feel. The species name refers to the crystalline look of the water cells.

### 454 Western Sea Purslane
(*Sesuvium verrucosum*)
Ice Plant Family (Aizoaceae)

Description: A succulent grayish-green plant with branched prostrate or ascending stems and *star-like pink flowers*.
Flowers: about ½" (1 cm) wide, in upper leaf axils; *sepals 5*, green on outside, pink on inside, joined to form a bell-shaped base; on the back of each pointed tip is a small green horn. *No petals*. Many stamens.
Leaves: ½–1½" (1–3.8 cm) long, opposite, narrow or lanceolate, broadest above middle.
Height: 1–2' (30–60 cm).
Flowering: April–November.
Habitat: In open low spots in salty or alkaline soil.
Range: Southern half of California across the Southwest to Missouri; north into southern Utah, Colorado, and Kansas; south into Mexico.
Comments: The only species in the West. Others grow to the east or south, most in salty soil, some near the coast (thus the common name).

## WATER PLANTAIN FAMILY
(Alismataceae)

Aquatic or marsh herbs with long-stalked, simple basal leaves and a leafless stalk that bears whorls of small flowers in a much-branched cluster or raceme.
Flowers: radially symmetrical; sepals 3, green; petals 3, delicate, white or pinkish; stamens 6 to many; pistils 6 to many, separate.
Leaves: prominently veined, with bases sheathing stem.
Fruit: hard, 1-seeded.
The family includes about 13 genera and 90 species, widely distributed in shallow freshwater or muddy habitats in warm and temperate climates.

---

### 158 Water Plantain
(*Alisma plantago-aquatica*)
Water Plantain Family (Alismataceae)

Description: A tall *spindly plant* with basal leaves and a flower stalk with umbel-like clusters of *small white or pale pink flowers* near the ends of whorled branches.
Flowers: ¼–½", (6–13 mm) wide; sepals 3; petals 3; stamens several; 10–25 pistils in a circle.
Leaves: those above water: ovate blades 1–6" (2.5–15 cm) long on long stalks; those underwater: often narrow and grass-like.
Fruit: several in each flower, small, seed-like, arranged in a ring.
Height: aquatic, the flower cluster 3–4' (90–120 cm) above water.

Flowering: June–August.
Habitat: In shallow water, in marshy places, or on muddy shores.
Range: Throughout most of North America.
Comments: The submerged fleshy portion of several species of *Alisma* was dried and eaten by Indians. A second species, Narrow-leaved Water Plantain (*A. gramineum*),

with grass-like leaves and smaller pink petals, occurs across southern Canada and the northern United States.

### 25 Fringed Water Plantain
(*Machaerocarpus californicus*)
Water Plantain Family (Alismataceae)

Description: Several basal leaves and one or a few flower stalks with *white or pink fringed flowers* often in clusters on whorled branches.
Flowers: sepals 3; petals 3, broad, about ¾" (2 cm) wide, with *small, sharp, uneven teeth across ends.*
Leaves: ovate blades 1–3" (2.5–7.5 cm) long on long stalks.
Fruit: several in each flower, needle-pointed, arranged like wheel spokes.
Height: aquatic, the flower cluster 8–18" (20–45 cm) above water.
Flowering: April–August.
Habitat: Shallow water or mud in open areas.
Range: Northern half of California and adjacent regions of Oregon and Nevada to southwestern Idaho.
Comments: The genus name, from the Greek, refers to the fruit (*karpos*), which resembles a tiny dagger (*machaira*). There is only one species.

### 128 Grass-leaved Sagittaria
(*Sagittaria graminea*)
Water Plantain Family (Alismataceae)

Description: *Long grass-like leaves* emerge from water and surround shorter spindly flower stalks with *white flowers blooming on whorled branches.*
Flowers: about ½" (1.3 cm) wide; petals 3, broad; sepals 3, broad; upper flowers usually only with stamens; lower flowers usually only with pistils borne on hair-like, ascending, individual stalks.

Leaves: blades to 8" (20 cm) long and
1" (2.5 cm) wide, on long stalks, or
blades absent.
Fruit: many, seed-like, in a head about
½" (1.3 cm) wide.
Height: aquatic, the flower cluster
about 2' (60 cm) above water.

Flowering: April–November, occasionally
throughout the year.

Habitat: Mud or shallow water of ditches,
marshes, streams or ponds.

Range: Throughout eastern North America;
west on the Great Plains and to south-
central Texas.

Comments: Grass-leaved Sagittaria has consistently
narrow leaves. It barely enters the
eastern edge of this book's range.

---

**127   Arrowhead; Tule Potato; Wapato**
(*Sagittaria latifolia*)
Water Plantain Family (Alismataceae)

Description: *Arrow-shaped basal leaves* surround a
taller stalk with *small white flowers* at
ends of short, whorled branches. Sap
milky.
Flowers: ¾–1½" (2–3.8 cm) wide;
sepals 3, spreading out or bent back;
petals 3, 20 or more stamens in some
flowers; in others *many pistils form a
sphere.*
Leaves: with conspicuous veins; a long
petiole attached in "V" at base of blade.
Height: aquatic, the flower clusters to
3' (90 cm) above water.

Flowering: July–September.

Habitat: Ditches, ponds, and swampy areas.

Range: Most of United States; to South
America.

Comments: In mud, rhizomes produce starchy
tubers, once an important source of
food for American Indians. Wapato is
one of its Indian names; early settlers
called it Duck Potato. The genus name
comes from *sagitta,* Latin for "arrow,"
referring to the shape of the leaves of
some species.

## AMARYLLIS FAMILY
(Amaryllidaceae)

Herbs or (rarely) woody plants,
growing from bulbs or underground
stems, with narrow basal leaves and a
long, leafless flowering stalk.
Flowers: radially symmetrical; sepals 3
and petals 3, colored alike and united
below into a tube, sometimes with
additional parts in the center forming a
crown; stamens 6. All these parts
attached above the ovary.
Leaves: grass-like or blades rigid,
sharply pointed, and with teeth along
edges.
Fruit: capsule or berry.
Members of this family are mostly
native of tropical and warm regions.
About 86 genera and 1,300 species
exist; among them, Daffodils, Jonquils,
and Amaryllis are highly prized
ornamentals.

---

### 355 Lechuguilla
(*Agave lecheguilla*)
Amaryllis Family (Amaryllidaceae)

Description: A *tall, narrow cluster of flowers* grows
from a basal rosette of *erect, rigid,
sharply pointed leaves.*
Flowers: ¾–1½″ (2–3.8 cm) long,
grouped in small clusters along the
main stalk; 6 narrow, spreading, yellow
to red or purplish petal-like segments.
Leaves: 12–20″ (30–50 cm) long,
about 1″ (2.5 cm) wide, straight or
slightly curved.
Height: 7–10′ (2.1–3 m).
Flowering: May–July.
Habitat: Rocky limestone slopes.
Range: Southern New Mexico and western
Texas to Mexico.
Comments: This formidable plant was a dangerous
obstacle in early Southwestern
exploration. The sharp leaves pierced
horses' legs and a rider who fell might

lie impaled. Today, leaves of small plants puncture tires of off-road vehicles. Indians obtained fiber from the leaves.

### 356  Parry's Century Plant
(*Agave parryi*)
Amaryllis Family (Amaryllidaceae)

Description: A stout, tall flower stalk, like a huge candelabrum, grows from the center of a *compact rosette of thick, rigid, broadly lanceolate grayish-green leaves.*
Flowers: buds reddish, but *open flowers yellow* facing upward in clusters near the ends of branches, each flower with 6 petal-like parts about ¾" (2 cm) long and 6 stamens attached near upper edge of flower tube.
Leaves: 12–18" (30–45 cm) long, concave on upper side, each bearing a dangerously sharp terminal spine and a few smaller spines along the edges.
Height: 10–14' (3–4.2 m).
Flowering: June–August.
Habitat: Dry rocky slopes.
Range: From central Arizona to western Texas; also northern Mexico.
Comments: Century Plants require many years to flower, but not a century. They provided southwestern Indians with food, beverages, fiber, soap, medicine, and lances. Today the liquors mescal, pulque, and tequila are made from the juice of the Mexican species.

### 213  Rain Lily
(*Zephyranthes longifolia*)
Amaryllis Family (Amaryllidaceae)

Description: *Resembling a Daffodil,* but much smaller and more delicate, the single yellow, funnel-shaped flower is held erect on a slender stem.
Flowers: ¾–1" (2–2.5 cm) long, the 6

petal-like parts, yellow inside, copper-tinged outside, join above ovary.

Leaves: to 9" (22.5 cm) long, few, basal, very narrow, often not present at flowering.

Fruit: nearly spherical 3-chambered capsule about ¾" (2 cm) wide, filled with flat, black, D-shaped seeds.

Height: to 9" (22.5 cm).

Flowering: April–July.

Habitat: Sandy deserts and grasslands.

Range: Southern Arizona to western Texas and northern Mexico.

Comments: *Zephyranthes* means "flower of the west wind." Flowers of this species appear very soon after substantial rains; hence its common name.

## CARROT OR PARSLEY FAMILY
### (Apiaceae or Umbelliferae)

Usually aromatic herbs with hollow
stems and fern-like leaves. Small
flowers in umbels, further grouped into
a compound umbel.
Flowers: radially symmetrical, with
those near edge of the compound umbel
sometimes bilaterally symmetrical;
sepals 5 small; petals 5; stamens 5. All
these parts attached at top of the ovary.
Leaves: alternate, pinnately compound.
Fruit: splits into 2 halves, each 1-
seeded.
About 300 genera and 3,000 species,
mostly in the Northern Hemisphere.
Nearly a quarter of genera are native to
the United States, with several large
genera in the West. The family is
important for such foods as carrots,
parsnips, and celery and such spices and
seasonings as coriander, caraway, anise,
parsley, and dill. Some native species
are very poisonous.

---

167 **Water Hemlock**
(*Cicuta douglasii*)
Carrot Family (Apiaceae)

Description: A tall plant with flat-topped *umbels of
tiny white flowers* at the top of a stout,
hollow, leafy stem.
Flowers: in compound umbels up to 5″
(12.5 cm) wide; petals 5.
Leaves: 5–14″ (12.5–35 cm) long,
pinnately divided, those near leaf base
again pinnately divided into lanceolate
leaflets 1¼–4″ (3.1–10 cm) long, with
sharp teeth on margins.
Fruit: small, flat, round, with corky
roundish ridges.
Height: 1½–7′ (45–210 cm).
Flowering: June–September.
Habitat: Marshes, edges of streams and ditches,
and wet low places.
Range: Pacific Coast; east to the Rocky

Mountain region from New Mexico to Alberta; also in northern Mexico.

Comments: The swollen bases of the stems and usually the thick roots have horizontal chambers inside, a feature which helps identify this deadly poisonous species. Its toxin rapidly affects the nervous system, causing severe convulsions and usually death. Another tall member of this family, with white flowers, fern-like leaves, and purple-spotted stems, is Poison Hemlock (*Conium maculatum*). Judging from the symptoms, it was an extract of this hemlock that poisoned Socrates. Children also have been fatally poisoned by blowing whistles made from its hollow stems.

## 169 Wild Carrot; Queen Anne's Lace
(*Daucus carota*)
Carrot Family (Apiaceae)

Description: A few large, flat-topped *umbels with tiny white flowers* top hairy, sometimes nearly smooth, *lacy-leafed stem.*
Flowers: umbels about 6" (15 cm) wide; the central flower commonly purple or pink (sometimes all flowers pink). Branches of older umbels curl inward, resembling bird's nests.
Leaves: lacy blades 2–6" (5–15 cm) long, repeatedly pinnately divided into narrow segments.
Fruit: oval, with minute barbed prickles along every other rib.
Height: 1–4' (30–120 cm).
Flowering: May–September.
Habitat: Roadsides, fields, and old lots.
Range: Most of North America.
Comments: Ancestor of the cultivated carrot. The flowering heads served 18th-century English courtiers as "living lace," hence the common name.

### 497 Coyote Thistle
(*Eryngium leavenworthii*)
Carrot Family (Apiaceae)

Description: A stiff, *prickly, purplish plant* with narrow, leafy, forked stems topped by *spiny, egg-shaped, lavender or reddish flower heads.*
Flowers: heads to 1½" (3.8 cm) long; flowers tiny, with 5 purplish petals.
Leaves: to 2½" (6 cm) long with prickly edges.
Height: 20–40" (60–100 cm).
Flowering: July–September.
Habitat: Plains and prairies.
Range: Much of Texas; north to Kansas.
Comments: The prickly nature of this plant is unusual for the Carrot Family, but the individual flowers are typical. Though this one barely enters the range of this book, it represents the several species of *Eryngium* that grow in the West, all with flowers in prickly heads. In the West, "coyote" often means "false," for one of the Mexican meanings of the word is a "shyster," a "foxy" or "tricky" person.

### 323 Sweet Fennel
(*Foeniculum vulgare*)
Carrot Family (Apiaceae)

Description: A tall plant with *feathery leaves,* and on the upper branches *tiny yellow flowers in compound umbels.*
Flowers: umbels 2–7" (5–17.5 cm) wide; each flower with 5 petals, no sepals.
Leaves: to 12–16" (30–40 cm) long, triangular, pinnately divided several times into hair-like segments.
Fruit: ³⁄₁₆" (4.5 mm) long, cylindrical, bluntly tapered at ends, ribbed.
Height: 3–7' (90–210 cm).
Flowering: May–September.
Habitat: Roadsides, old lots, and fields.
Range: Most frequent west of the Sierra Nevada

and Cascade Mountains.

Comments: All parts are edible and have a mild
anise or licorice flavor. Sweet Fennel is
used in French, Italian, and other
cuisines. Young shoots are eaten,
cooked or raw as a vegetable, leaves are
used in salads and for seasoning, seeds
are used as a flavoring in cooking and in
candy and liqueurs. It is sometimes
called Wild Anise, although true Anise
is of the genus *Pimpinella*.

---

146 **Beach Silvertop**
(*Glehnia leiocarpa*)
Carrot Family (Apiaceae)

Description: This low, spreading plant has rosettes
of *pinnate leaves that lie on the sand,* and
from the center, on short stems, are
small, tight, round umbels with
numerous tiny *white flowers.*
Flowers: umbels 3–4″ (7.5–10 cm)
wide, with a few stout woolly branches;
conspicuous bracts beneath flower
clusters.
Leaves: 1–6″ (2.5–15 cm) long, fleshy,
hairy on underside, divided 3 times
into *3-lobed leaflets.*
Fruit: ¼–½″ (6–13 mm) long with
corky wings on edges and both faces.
Height: 2½″ (6.3 cm).
Flowering: May–July.
Habitat: Beach sands and dunes.
Range: Along the Pacific Coast from Alaska to
northern California.
Comments: *Glehnia* probably honors P. von Glehn,
19th-century curator at the St.
Petersburg Botanic Garden.

---

168 **Cow Parsnip**
(*Heracleum lanatum*)
Carrot Family (Apiaceae)

Description: A tall, leafy, stout plant topped by
large *umbels of tiny white flowers.*

Flowers: umbel to 12″ (30 cm) wide, often in groups; each flower with 5 petals, those at margin of umbel larger, about ¼″ (6 mm) long, cleft in middle.
Leaves: 6–16″ (15–40 cm) long, round, divided into 3 lobes or parts, edges coarsely toothed.
Fruit: flat, oval, broader above middle, the broad sides with 4 dark lines extending halfway down, alternating with 3 fine ribs.
Height: to 10′ (3 m).

Flowering: February–September.
Habitat: Moist, partially shaded places, up to 9,000′ (2,700 m) elevation.
Range: Most of North America from southern California to Georgia northward.
Comments: This is the largest species of the Carrot Family in North America. The genus is named for Hercules, who is reputed to have used it for medicine. Early in each year, Indians peeled and ate the young sweet, aromatic leaf and flower stalks. However, before eating any wild plants of the Carrot Family one should be sure of their identity, for some are deadly. This species, although edible, can cause dermatitis.

## 147 Ranger's Button; Swamp White Head
(*Sphenosciadium capitellatum*)
Carrot Family (Apiaceae)

Description: A stout, tall plant with numerous tiny white *flowers in compact, separate white "buttons"* at the ends of hairy branches.
Flowers: umbel up to 4″ (10 cm) wide; each flower with 5 petals, no calyx.
Leaves: 4–16″ (10–40 cm) long, broad, pinnately divided, lower segments again divided, the lanceolate leaflets 1–3″ (2.5–7.5 cm) long, their *edges with a few teeth above middle.*
Height: 1½–7′ (45–210 cm).

Flowering: July–August.
Habitat: Wet meadows, swamps, and stream

banks, from foothills to moderate elevations.

Range: From eastern Oregon and central Idaho to the mountains of southern California.

Comments: The name comes from the Greek *sphen* ("wedge") and *skias* ("umbrella"), probably referring to the shape of the flower cluster.

### 322 Golden Alexanders
(*Zizia aptera*)
Carrot Family (Apiaceae)

Description: Several leafy stems in a cluster have bright yellow flowers in a *compound umbel*.
Flowers: umbel to 2½" (6.3 cm) wide; each flower with 5 petals and 5 sepals.
Leaves: basal leaves 1–4" (2.5–10 cm) long, with long petioles, the ovate blades indented at base, edges with teeth; *upper leaves pinnately divided into 3 segments* with several narrow lobes, edges with teeth.
Fruit: elliptic, slightly flat, with low ribs.
Height: 8–24" (20–60 cm).

Flowering: May–July.

Habitat: Moist meadows or open woods, stream banks and low ground.

Range: From eastern Washington, northwestern Oregon, and northeastern Nevada to Colorado; north to Canada; much of eastern United States.

Comments: The genus is named for the German botanist Johann Ziz, who lived around the turn of the 19th century.

## DOGBANE FAMILY (Apocynaceae)

Herbs or shrubs (trees in tropical regions) with solitary or clustered flowers and milky juice.
Flowers: radially symmetrical; calyx with 5 united sepals; corolla with 5 united petals; corolla lobes often twisted in the bud; stamens 5. All these parts attached at base of ovary.
Leaves: simple; opposite, whorled, or alternate.
Fruit: 2 pods, often attached at tip by the style.
There are about 200 genera and 2,000 species, most abundant in the tropics and subtropics. Among them, Oleander and Periwinkle are popular ornamentals; other species produce valuable fruits; many are poisonous.

---

### 537 Spreading Dogbane
(*Apocynum androsaemifolium*)
Dogbane Family (Apocynaceae)

Description: A branched, bushy plant with drooping pairs of leaves, and *small, pink, bell-shaped flowers* in short open clusters at ends of stems or in axils. *Milky sap.*
Flowers: corolla ¼–⅜" (6–9 mm) long, with 5 outward-curved tips on rim.
Leaves: 1–2½" (2.5–6.3 cm) long, ovate.
Fruit: 2 *slender pods*, 5–7" (12.5–17.5 cm) long, each containing many seeds with long silky hairs.
Height: 8–20" (20–50 cm).
Flowering: June–September.
Habitat: Dry soil, mostly in coniferous forests at low or medium elevations.
Range: Throughout.
Comments: The popular name Dogbane is derived from the Greek word *apocynum*, meaning "noxious to dogs." Distasteful and poisonous, it is avoided by animals. Indians used fiber from the stems to make cords, nets, and cloth.

## ARUM FAMILY (Araceae)

Erect, prostrate, or climbing herbs with numerous small flowers crowded on a fleshy spike (spadix), surrounded by an often showy bract (spathe).
Flowers: bisexual or unisexual; sepals and petals absent or represented by 4–6 segments; stamens usually 4–6. All these parts attached at base of ovary.
Leaves: simple or compound, often on long stalks.
Fruit: berry.
More than 115 genera and about 2,000 species are found in shady, damp or wet places, most numerous and varied in the tropics. Many such as the Calla Lily, Philodendron, Dieffenbachia (or Dumbcane) are grown as ornamentals.

---

276 **Yellow Skunk Cabbage**
(*Lysichitum americanum*)
Arum Family (Araceae)

Description: A spike of minute flowers surrounded by a large, conspicuous *yellow or cream bract* open on one side; grows on a stout stalk in a cluster of giant, *erect, leaves.*
Flowers: bract to 8″ (20 cm) long, often appearing before leaves are fully developed; tiny flowers inconspicuous.
Leaves: 1–5′ (30–150 cm) long, the stalks usually much shorter than the oval blades.
Height: 12–20″ (30–50 cm).
Flowering: April–July, often as the snow melts.
Habitat: Swampy soil.
Range: From Alaska to near the coast in central California, east to Montana.
Comments: The common name refers to the skunk-like odor of the sap and the fetid odor of the flowers, which draws flies as pollinators. The peppery sap was once used as a treatment for ringworm. The short, fleshy underground stem is eaten by animals. Baked, it supplemented the winter diets of Indians.

## BIRTHWORT FAMILY
(Aristolochiaceae)

Herbs or woody vines with commonly heart-shaped leaves and medium to large, bizarre, often carrion-scented flowers.
Flowers: bilaterally or radially symmetrical; calyx 3-lobed or bent with united red, purple, or brown sepals; no petals; stamens usually 6 or more; all these parts attached to top of the ovary.
Leaves: alternate, basal, or stalked. The edges commonly smooth.
Fruit: capsule with 4–6 chambers.
This is a small family of about 6 genera and 400 species, widely distributed in tropical and temperate regions. Some are aromatic; a few are cultivated.

### 383 Long-tailed Wild Ginger
(*Asarum caudatum*)
Birthwort Family (Aristolochiaceae)

Description: A bizarre *brown-purplish to yellowish or greenish flower* is hidden by *heart-shaped leaves* growing in pairs from trailing, rooting stems that form dense patches.
Flowers: 1½–5″ (3.8–12.5 cm) wide; 1 in each leaf axil, with 3 petal-like lobes ¾–3″ (2–7.5 cm) long, tapering out from the bowl-like base to slender tips; stamens 12, tipped with scale-like appendages shorter than pollen sacs.
Leaves: ¾–4″ (2–10 cm) long.
Height: creeper, with leaf stalks 6″ (15 cm) high.
Flowering: April–July.
Habitat: Moist shaded woods below 5,000′ (1,500 m) elevation.
Range: From British Columbia and western Montana to northeastern Oregon; south on the western side of the Cascade Mountains and the Sierra Nevada to near the coast of central California.
Comments: The aromatic stems and roots were used by early settlers as a substitute for the

tropical ginger. There are 2 other
western species: Hartweg's Wild
Ginger (*A. hartwegii*), found in
southern Oregon, northern California,
and southward along the Sierra Nevada,
usually has mottled leaves, and
appendages on anthers longer than the
pollen sacs; and Lemmon's Wild
Ginger (*A. lemmonii*), from the Sierra
Nevada, with calyx lobes ½" (1.3 cm)
long or less.

## MILKWEED FAMILY
(Asclepiadaceae)

Herbs, shrubs, or vines, usually with thick milky juice, opposite or whorled leaves, flowers in umbel-like clusters (cymes), and tufted seeds in pods.
Flowers: radially symmetrical in flat or round clusters; sepals 5; corolla of 5 united petals with reflexed lobes; a 5-lobed crown between corolla and stamens; stamens 5. All parts attached at base of the 2 ovaries.
Leaves: simple, mostly opposite or in whorls.
Fruit: 2 pods often joined at tips by style, filled with many silky-haired seeds.
There are about 250 genera and 2,000 species, widely distributed but most abundant in tropical and subtropical regions. The unusual structure of the flower regulates pollination. Sacs of pollen snag on insects' legs, are pulled from the stamens, and then must be precisely inserted in slits behind the crown. If inserted backwards, pollen grains germinate in the wrong direction and are wasted. This may explain why so few pods occur on most plants. Insects too small to pull free die trapped on the flower.

---

### 163 White Milkweed
*(Asclepias albicans)*
Milkweed Family (Asclepiadaceae)

Description: Tall, *leafless, waxy-white stems* have woolly umbels of whitish star-like flowers on branches near the top. Sap milky.
Flowers: umbels about 2″ (5 cm) wide, with flowers about ½″ (1.3 cm) wide; sepals 5, small greenish; petals 5, *greenish-white* tinged brown or pink, bent back; 5 *round yellowish hoods* with short horns curved toward center of flower.

Leaves: ½–¾" (1.3–2 cm) long, hair-like, 3 at each node, dropping soon after development.
Fruit: Pods smooth, plump, about 4" (10 cm) long, containing many seeds with silky hairs.
Height: 3–10' (90–300 cm)

Flowering: March–May.
Habitat: Dry rocky places in desert.
Range: Southeastern California and southwestern Arizona to northwestern Mexico.
Comments: Asklepios was the Greek god of medicine, and some species of this genus have had medicinal uses. A similar species, Rush Milkweed (*A. subulata*), grows in the same region in desert washes and on sandy flats; it is distinguished by its narrow erect hoods about as long as the petals.

### 549 Showy Milkweed
(*Asclepias speciosa*)
Milkweed Family (Asclepiadaceae)

Description: A *grayish, velvety plant* with erect leafy stems and with *umbels of star-like pinkish flowers* in upper axils and at top. Sap milky.
Flowers: about ¾" (2 cm) wide; sepals 5, reddish; *petals 5, pink or reddish purple*, about ½" (1.3 cm) long, bent back; *5 pink erect hoods* in center with incurved horns.
Leaves: 4–8" (10–20 cm) long, opposite, broadly lanceolate or ovate with conspicuous veins from midrib to edge.
Fruit: pod 2–4" (5–10 cm) long, plump, covered with velvet and *small soft spines*.
Height: 1–4' (90–120 cm).

Flowering: May–August.
Habitat: Dry gravelly slopes, sandy areas, along watercourses, in brush and open forests.
Range: British Columbia to California, east of the Cascade Mountains; eastward to

central United States.

Comments:   There are recipes for preparing this species as a vegetable, but the plants should be positively identified as some of the Milkweeds are highly poisonous, and eating them can result in death.

164   **Poison Milkweed; Horsetail Milkweed**
(*Asclepias subverticillata*)
Milkweed Family (Asclepiadaceae)

Description:   *White star-like flowers in round umbels; 3–5 very narrow leaves in whorls* at nodes form feathery clumps or patches. Sap milky.
Flowers: umbels ¾–1¼" (2–3.1 cm) wide; each flower, almost ½" (1.3 cm) wide, has 5 tiny sepals, 5 petals, bent back, and 5 roundish hoods with long horns arched toward center.
Leaves: ¾–5" (2–12.5 cm) long, with dwarf branches and very small leaves in axils.
Fruit: broad, smooth pod 2–4" (5–10 cm) long, contains many seeds with long silky hairs.
Height: to 4' (1.2 m).
Flowering:   May–September.
Habitat:   Sandy or rocky plains and desert flats and slopes, common along roadsides.
Range:   Central Arizona, much of Utah, and western Colorado; east to Kansas; south to Mexico.
Comments:   This unpalatable species is very poisonous to livestock, which ordinarily avoid it. When better forage is unavailable, the animals may eat it, but with fatal results.

371 **Butterfly Weed; Orange Milkweed;
Chiggerflower**
(*Asclepias tuberosa*)
Milkweed Family (Asclepiadaceae)

Description: *Star-like orange, yellow, or red flowers*
bloom in umbels in the upper axils and
at the tops of leafy, hairy, clustered
stems.
Flowers: umbels to 3″ (7.5 cm) wide;
flowers about ½″ (1.3 cm) wide, with 5
small sepals, *5 petals, bent back,* and *5
erect hoods shaped like sugar scoops,* the
slender horns arched toward the center.
Leaves: 1¼–4½″ (3.1–11.3 cm) long,
almost opposite on stem, narrowly or
broadly lanceolate, base on some
indented, underside hairy.
Fruit: narrow, tapered pod 3–6″ (7.5–
15 cm) long, containing many seeds
with silky hairs.
Height: to 3′ (90 cm).
Flowering: April–September.
Habitat: Prairies and canyons, in brush or open
woods, generally dry places.
Range: From southern Utah east to Ohio; south
into Mexico.
Comments: Contrary to one of its common names,
this Milkweed has no milky sap. The
thick tuberous root was once used as a
cure for pleurisy.

182 **Climbing Milkweed**
(*Sarcostemma cynanchoides*)
Milkweed Family (Asclepiadaceae)

Description: A *smooth vine* with milky sap and *pale
white star-like flowers* in umbels, the *long
twining stems* often clambering over tops
of bushes.
Flowers: umbels up to 4″ (10 cm) wide;
each flower about ½″ (1.3 cm) wide,
with 5 sepals, 5 spreading white,
purplish, or pink pointed petals, and *5
white spherical hoods* near the center.
Leaves: to 2½″ (6.3 cm) long, opposite,
blades narrow, lanceolate, or narrowly

triangular with one or more glands on the midrib near the base.

Fruit: pods to 3″ (7.5 cm) long, plump, downy, containing many seeds with silky hairs.

Height: vine, stems to 10′ (3 m) long.

Flowering: April–August.

Habitat: In sandy or rocky soils, mostly in deserts, but also on dry plains and in brush near the coast.

Range: From southern California to southern Utah, Oklahoma, and Texas; south into Mexico.

Comments: *Sarcostemma,* coming from the Greek words *sarx* ("flesh") and *stemma* ("crown"), refers to the fleshy inner portion of the corona. There are several similar species in the Southwest, all hairy or downy.

## SUNFLOWER OR DAISY FAMILY
(Asteraceae or Compositae)

Herbs, sometimes shrubs or vines,
rarely trees. Flowers small, but
organized into larger heads resembling
a single, radially symmetrical flower
cupped by a ring of green bracts.
Flower-like heads composed of tiny,
radially symmetrical central flowers,
which form the disk, and larger flowers
around the edge, the rays, which are
strap-shaped and resemble petals;
however, all flowers in one head may be
disk flowers or rays.
Flowers: calyx absent, or modified into
hairs, bristles, scales, or a crown, which
often persists atop the fruits; corolla
with 5 united petals; and stamens 5; all
these parts attached to top of the ovary.
Leaves: simple or compound, alternate
or opposite.
Fruit: 1-seeded, with hard shell, seed-
like.
In this large, worldwide family there
are about 920 genera and 19,000
species. Cosmos, Sunflower, Zinnia,
Dahlia, and many others are grown as
ornamentals; Lettuce, Sunflowers, and
Artichokes provide food. Safflower oil is
obtained from this family. Ragweed
pollen causes hay fever.

---

170 **Yarrow; Milfoil**
(*Achillea millefolium*)
Sunflower Family (Asteraceae)

Description: An aromatic plant with *feathery, fern-
like leaves* on a tough fibrous stem, and
a flattish cluster of *small, white flower
heads* at the top.
Flowers: each head with 3–5 roundish
white (sometimes pinkish) rays ⅛" (3
mm) long and 10–30 disk flowers.
Leaves: to 1½" (3.8 cm) wide, blades
repeatedly pinnately divided into fine
segments.

Height: 12–40″ (30–100 cm).
Flowering: March–October.
Habitat: Open areas from lowlands to mountain highlands.
Range: Most of temperate North America.
Comments: Among this species' several common names Milfoil and Plumajillo ("little feather") refer to the divided leaves and Sneezeweed and Nosebleed may derive from the irritating odor. Spanish Californians once steeped leaves in water to treat cuts and bruises and to stop bleeding.

364 **Orange Agoseris**
(*Agoseris aurantiaca*)
Sunflower Family (Asteraceae)

Description: From a basal cluster of leaves grow several leafless stalks with milky sap, topped by *coppery-orange flower heads*.
Flowers: head about 1″ (2.5 cm) wide; *flowers all of ray type,* those in center of head very short.
Leaves: 2–14″ (5–35 cm) long, narrow, broadest above middle, often with a few large teeth.
Fruit: seed-like, with a stalk at tip about as long as the body, topped by fine silvery bristles.
Height: 4–24″ (10–60 cm).
Flowering: June–August.
Habitat: Meadows and grassy openings in coniferous forests in the mountains.
Range: Western Canada to California and New Mexico.
Comments: This plant is easily recognized. It is the only orange-flowered *Agoseris*.

268 **Pale Agoseris**
(*Agoseris glauca*)
Sunflower Family (Asteraceae)

Description: Several leafless stalks, each with a *yellow flower head* at the top, grow from a basal cluster of leaves. Sap milky.

Flowers: head ½–1¼" (1.3–3.1 cm) wide; *flowers all of ray type,* those in middle very short.

Leaves: 2–14" (5–35 cm) long, very narrow to broadly lanceolate, broader above middle, without teeth, with a few teeth, or sometimes deeply pinnately divided.

Fruit: seed-like, with fine ridges at tip and fine white hairs on tip of the stalk.

Height: 4–28" (10–70 cm).

Flowering: May–September.

Habitat: Open areas in coniferous forests and in sagebrush.

Range: Western Canada; south through the California mountains; east across the West to New Mexico, South Dakota, and Minnesota.

Comments: Several other yellow-flowered species of *Agoseris,* all called False Dandelion or Mountain Dandelion, are distinguished from this one by technical features of the fruit. The true Dandelion (*Taraxacum*) is also similar, but has minute pegs all over the top of fruit and usually has bracts curved back beneath the involucre.

145 **Pearly Everlasting**
(*Anaphalis margaritacea*)
Sunflower Family (Asteraceae)

Description: Several evenly leafy woolly stems in a small patch are topped by a crowded, roundish cluster of flower heads with *pearly-white bracts,* sometimes with a dark spot at base of each outer bract.

Flowers: heads about ¼" (6 mm) long; flowers minute, on some plants with stamens only, on others only with pistils.

Leaves: to 5" (12.5 cm) long, narrowly lanceolate, underside densely hairy, top less so or even smooth and dark green.

Height: 8–36" (20–90 cm).

Flowering: June–September.

Habitat: Commonly in forest openings but also along roadsides and in fields, from lowlands to high in the mountains.

Range: Most of North America; south to New Mexico, southern California, Arizona, Kansas, and eastern United States.

Comments: The dried stalks with their pearly-white heads are attractive in floral arrangements.

144 **Nuttall's Pussytoes**
(*Antennaria parvifolia*)
Sunflower Family (Asteraceae)

Description: From a small, *grayish basal rosette* rises an erect, sparsely-leaved flower stalk with *clusters of small, rayless, whitish flower heads.*
Flowers: heads nearly ½" (1.3 cm) long, the translucent, scale-like bracts barely darkened at the base.
Leaves: ½–¾" (1.3–2 cm) long, equally hairy on both sides, those in rosettes lanceolate but obviously broader near the top, those on the flower stalk much narrower.
Fruit: seed-like, with 5 white bristles at top.
Height: to 6" (15 cm).

Flowering: July–September.

Habitat: Openings in dry forests and on plains.

Range: From western Canada to eastern Washington and through the Rocky Mountains and the western Plains to Arizona and New Mexico.

Comments: Some plants in this species produce seed in the usual manner, by fertilization of eggs in the ovary; others do not require fertilization. The tightly clustered basal leaves and the near absence of dark bases on the bracts of the flower heads help distinguish Nuttall's Pussytoes from other members of this large genus.

## 248 Heartleaf Arnica
(*Arnica cordifolia*)
Sunflower Family (Asteraceae)

Description: Stems with *2—4 pairs of heart-shaped leaves* are topped by 1–3 broad yellow heads. Plants in patches.
Flowers: heads 2–3½" (5–8.8 cm) wide; with 10–15 rays each and many tiny disk flowers; bracts of head have long spreading hairs.
Leaves: those on separate, short shoots largest, 1½–5" (3.8–12.5 cm) long, with long petioles attached at notch; those on flowering stem with short or no petioles.
Fruit: seed-like, with a tuft of white or pale tan hairs at top.
Height: 4–24" (10–60 cm) tall.
Flowering: April–June, occasionally to September.
Habitat: In lightly shaded woods.
Range: From Alaska to southern California; east to the Rocky Mountains from Canada to New Mexico; also in northern Michigan.
Comments: In alpine areas or in open places along roads, the leaves may be narrower and without the notch at the base of the blade. All western species have paired leaves on the stems, but only this one has heart-shaped leaves.

## 70 Engelmann Aster
(*Aster engelmannii*)
Sunflower Family (Asteraceae)

Description: Stems leafy in the middle, but not below, and branched near top, and at ends of branches, *flower heads with a few white or pinkish rays.*
Flowers: heads with a yellow disk about 1½–2½" (3.8–6.3 cm) wide; surrounded by about 13 rays; bracts with a strong, raised midvein, pale and stiff at base.
Leaves: 2–4" (5–10 cm) long, lanceolate, without stalks, not hairy or

only lightly hairy, hairs densest on
lower side.
Fruit: seed-like, hairy, with a few fine
bristles at top.
Height: 1½–5′ (45–150 cm).
Flowering: June–September.
Habitat: Open places and openings in woods.
Range: Western Canada south to Washington,
northeastern Nevada, and northern
Colorado.
Comments: This is one of a number of tall Asters;
the stems straight, erect, few in a
bunch, branched only near the top. Its
heads, with a few often slightly curled
rays, have a ragged appearance.

### 475 Leafy Aster
(*Aster foliaceus*)
Sunflower Family (Asteraceae)

Description: Leafy stems with ascending branches,
terminated by several flower heads, each
with *many narrow lavender or purple rays*.
Flowers: heads 1–2″ (2.5–5 cm) wide;
rays surround a *yellow disk*. Bracts
around head overlapping; often
additional *outer, rather leafy, large bracts*.
Leaves: 5–8″ (12.5–20 cm) long, basal
ones lanceolate, gradually narrowing to
stalk-like base, those at midstem with
bases partly surrounding and clasping
stem.
Fruit: seed-like, smooth or sparsely
hairy on surface, topped by a tuft of
fine hairs.
Height: 8–20″ (20–50 cm).
Flowering: July–September.
Habitat: Moist places in woods, on road banks,
and in mountain meadows.
Range: Alaska to central California, Arizona,
and New Mexico.
Comments: Asters, "star" in Greek, have flower
heads which resemble those of
Fleabanes (*Erigeron*), another large and
complex western genus. The bracts of
*Aster,* however, usually vary in length,
overlapping like shingles on a roof.

Many Asters are tall and leafy; few
*Erigeron* are.

---

75  **Tobacco Weed; Parachute Plant**
    (*Atrichoseris platyphylla*)
    Sunflower Family (Asteraceae)

Description: A smooth, gray-green plant with a *flat
            rosette* of basal leaves, tall spindly stem,
            openly branched in the upper half, and
            *white or pale pink flower heads* at the ends
            of branches.
            Flowers: heads 1–2″ (2.5–5 cm) wide;
            *flowers all of ray type,* those in center of
            head smaller.
            Leaves: 1¼–4″ (3.1–10 cm) long,
            ovate, often purple-spotted, edges with
            uneven, tiny, spine-tipped teeth.
            Fruit: seed-like, shaped like a 5-sided
            club, without hairs.
            Height: 12–28″ (30–70 cm).
Flowering: February–May.
  Habitat: Sandy washes in deserts.
    Range: Southeastern California to southwestern
            Utah and northwestern Arizona.
Comments: The scientific name means the "flat-
            leaved" (*platyphylla*) "chicory plant
            without hairs" (*Atrichoseris*), referring to
            the absence of hairs on the fruit.

---

260  **Desert Marigold**
     (*Baileya multiradiata*)
     Sunflower Family (Asteraceae)

Description: A *grayish, woolly plant,* branched and
            leafy mostly in the lower half, with
            *brilliant yellow flowers* in heads, one
            borne at the end of each of many nearly
            leafless flower stalks.
            Flowers: heads 1½–2″ (3.8–5 cm)
            wide, with 25–50 oblong rays that
            after seed-set become papery and
            remain on head. No scales among the
            disk flowers.
            Leaves: broadly ovate, blades 1½–3″

(3.8–8 cm) long, pinnately divided into broad lobes, which are again divided or have roundish teeth.
Fruit: seed-like, pale tan or chalky white, lacking bristles or scales at top.
Height: 12–20″ (30–50 cm).

Flowering: April–October.

Habitat: Sandy or gravelly places in deserts, common along roadsides.

Range: Southeastern California to southern Utah and western Texas; south to northern Mexico.

Comments: Dense patches often form solid strips of yellow along miles of desert roadsides. In gardens a single plant grows into a perfect hemisphere of yellow, blooming throughout the hot summer and into fall. The name Marigold, given to several species of Asteraceae with sunny yellow or orange flowers, comes from "Mary's Gold," in honor of the Virgin.

## 250 Arrowleaf Balsam Root
(*Balsamorhiza sagittata*)
Sunflower Family (Asteraceae)

Description: An almost leafless stalk with 1 large *bright yellow flower head* at tip grows from a *basal cluster of large silvery-gray leaves* covered with felt-like hairs.
Flowers: heads 4–5″ (10–12.5 cm) wide, with densely woolly bracts, 8–25 rays, each 1–1½″ (2.5–3.8 cm) long, and many disk flowers, each enfolded by a parchment-like scale.
Leaves: blades to 1′ (30 cm) long, on petioles about the same length.
Fruit: seed-like, no hairs or scales at tip.
Height: 8–32″ (20–80 cm).

Flowering: May–July.

Habitat: Open hillsides and flats in grasslands, sagebrush, or open pine forest.

Range: From British Columbia south through the Sierra Nevada of California; east to western Montana, western South Dakota, and Colorado.

Comments: Indians prepared medicine from the roots. The very similar Deltoid Balsam Root (*B. deltoidea*), found in open places in California, western Oregon, and Washington, is only sparsely hairy, is much greener, and drops its rays soon after flowering. Several species of *Balsamorhiza* have pinnately divided leaves.

## 66 English Daisy
(*Bellis perennis*)
Sunflower Family (Asteraceae)

Description: Short, slender, leafless stalks, each bearing one flower head with *many narrow white or pinkish rays* and yellow disk flowers, grow from a basal rosette of leaves.
Flowers: heads about 1″ (2.5 cm) wide, with bracts the same length.
Leaves: to 1½″ (3.8 cm) long, the blade elliptic or round and with small teeth on edges, tapered at base to a broad petiole as long or longer.
Fruit: seed-like, no hairs or scales at tip.
Height: 2–8″ (5–20 cm).
Flowering: March–September.
Habitat: Lawns, fields, and roadsides.
Range: Introduced from Europe and found scattered throughout the United States; in the West most frequent from California to Washington.
Comments: It may be with this plant that the word "daisy" originated. It means "day's eye" and comes from Anglo-Saxon *daeges ege*. English Daisy folds up its rays at night and opens them again at dawn—the "eye of the day." This pretty flower is a common weed in lawns, especially in the cool moist region near the coast. A "double" form is planted as an ornamental.

### 266  Greeneyes; Chocolate Flower
(*Berlandiera lyrata*)
Sunflower Family (Asteraceae)

Description:   A leafy plant, often with many short
branches at its base and longer, leaning
ones that end in leafless stalks topped
by flower heads with *yellow rays and a
maroon disk.*
Flowers: heads about 1½″ (3.8 cm)
wide, with broadly ovate, nearly flat
bracts, 5–12 (usually 8) broad rays,
each ½″ (1.3 cm) long, their undersides
yellowish maroon or with maroon
veins, and a scale enfolding each disk
flower. Bracts of involucre, fruit of ray
flower, 2 nearby bracts and disk flowers
all shed together when mature.
Leaves: 2–6″ (5–15 cm) long, velvety,
either with scalloped edges or pinnately
divided into scalloped-edged segments,
*end segment largest.*
Fruit: seed-like, no scales or hairs at
tip.
Height: 1–4′ (30–120 cm).

Flowering:   April–October.

Habitat:   Grassy areas on limestone, common
along roadsides.

Range:   From southern Kansas and southeastern
Colorado to southeastern Arizona; south
to Mexico.

Comments:   The genus name honors Jean-Louis
Berlandier, a French-Swiss physician
who collected plants in northern
Mexico and Texas in the early 1800's.
A chocolate odor may be detected when
rays are plucked from the head.

### 338  Large-flowered Brickelbush
(*Brickellia grandiflora*)
Sunflower Family (Asteraceae)

Description:   Clusters of *creamy yellow rayless flower
heads* hang from short branches at tips
of leafless stalks borne in upper axils of
leafy stems.
Flowers: heads ⅜–½″ (9–13 mm)

long, the outer bracts ovate, with long
slender tips, and the inner bracts long
and narrow, all straw-colored and
striped with green.
Leaves: ¾–5″ (2–12.5 cm) long,
triangular blades, angles near the base
rounded, edges scalloped.
Fruit: slender and seed-like, with 10
ribs and fine hairs at tip.
Height: 1–3′ (30–90 cm).

Flowering: July–October.

Habitat: On banks and cliffs, in canyons, low to
moderate elevations, mostly in forests.

Range: Eastern Washington south to Baja
California; east to western Texas,
Arkansas, Missouri, and Nebraska.

Comments: This large and complex genus consists
mostly of shrubs. Some were used
medicinally by Indians.

---

### 273 Silvercrown Luina
(*Cacaliopsis nardosmia*)
Sunflower Family (Asteraceae)

Description: *Golden-yellow rayless flower heads* bloom
in a narrow cluster at the top of a stout
stem growing from a cluster of basal
leaves.
Flowers: heads ½–¾″ (1.3–2 cm) long,
the *bracts all about the same length, lined
up side by side* and barely overlapping.
Leaves: long stalks and *nearly round,
palmately cleft,* coarsely toothed blades
to 8″ (20 cm) long.
Fruit: seed-like, slender, with
numerous fine bristles at top.
Height: 1–3′ (30–90 cm).

Flowering: May–July.

Habitat: Meadows and open woods in the
mountains.

Range: Washington south along the Cascade
Mountains to northern California; then
south in the North Coast Range to
north of the San Francisco Bay region.

Comments: The only species in the genus.
Sometimes included in the genus
*Luina.*

### 253 Rosin Weed
(*Calycadenia truncata*)
Sunflower Family (Asteraceae)

Description: A slender, odorous plant with *yellow flower heads* in a narrow cluster, and very *narrow leaves,* the upper ones tipped with a broad *dish-shaped gland.*
Flowers: heads about 1″ (2.5 cm) wide, with *3–8 broad rays,* each about ¼–½″ (6–13 mm) long, with *3 teeth at end,* the central tooth narrowest.
Leaves: ¾–3½″ (2–8.8 cm) long.
Fruit: seed-like; those from disk flowers are slender, sparsely hairy, and topped by several short scales; those from ray flowers are short, squat, wrinkled, and without hairs or scales.
Height: 1–4″ (30–120 cm).
Flowering: June–October.
Habitat: Dry, sunny, sparsely grassy slopes.
Range: Southern Oregon to central California.
Comments: The genus name comes from the Greek *kalyx* ("cup") and *adenos* ("gland"), referring to the peculiar glands which distinguish all but one species of this primarily California genus. Rays on some species are white, changing to rose as they age.

### 500 Musk Thistle; Bristle Thistle; Nodding Thistle
(*Carduus nutans*)
Sunflower Family (Asteraceae)

Description: Tall and leafy, *prickly on the edges of the leaves and on thin ribs along the stem,* with large, handsome, *deep reddish-lavender rayless flower heads* at top.
Flowers: heads 1½–3″ (3.8–7.5 cm) wide, with prickly bracts, lower ones bent back.
Leaves: to 16″ (40 cm) long, stalkless, pinnately lobed, the lobes jagged.
Fruit: seed-like, with fine, long white bristles at top.
Height: 1–9′ (30–270 cm).

Flowering: June–October.
Habitat: Roadsides, pastures, and rangeland.
Range: Native to Europe and western Asia but now occurring throughout much of the United States, especially in the Rocky Mountain region.
Comments: Preferring disturbed ground, this unwelcome immigrant has become increasingly frequent in grazed areas. The more common Thistles, *Cirsium* species, are very similar but have tiny hairs along the bristles at the top of the fruit, giving the bristles a feathery appearance.

## 149 Esteve's Pincushion
(*Chaenactis stevioides*)
Sunflower Family (Asteraceae)

Description: A small, openly branched plant with heads of *white disk flowers,* those around the edge larger and somewhat ray-like.
Flowers: heads about 1″ (2.5 cm) wide, sometimes tinged with pink.
Leaves: ½–1½″ (1.3–3.8 cm) long, *lightly woolly, pinnately divided,* segments again pinnately divided into short narrow lobes.
Fruit: seed-like, club-shaped, hairy, with 4 lanceolate scales at top.
Height: 4–10″ (10–25 cm).
Flowering: March–June.
Habitat: Rocky or sandy deserts.
Range: Southeastern Oregon and southern Idaho to western Wyoming and Colorado; south to New Mexico and northwestern Mexico.
Comments: Other common names sometimes used are "False Yarrow" and "Broad-leaved Chaenactis." There are several species with white flowers.

### 68 Oxeye Daisy
(*Chrysanthemum leucanthemum*)
Sunflower Family (Asteraceae)

Description: A *dark green leafy plant* with several
stems in a cluster; at the top are nearly
leafless branches, each bearing a flower
head with *many white rays* and a yellow
disk. *Bracts of head each have a narrow
brown line near margin.*
Flowers: heads about 3″ (7.5 cm) wide,
including rays ½–¾″ (1.3–2 cm) long.
Leaves: lower ones 1½–6″ (3.8–15 cm)
long, broadly lanceolate, with long
petioles; upper ones smaller and lacking
petioles; margins of all leaves lobed or
cleft and also scalloped.
Fruit: seed-like, no scales or hairs at
tip.
Height: 8–32″ (20–80 cm).
Flowering: May–October.
Habitat: In fields, pastures, and along roadsides.
Range: Introduced from Europe and naturalized
throughout much of North America;
more common in northern half of
United States.
Comments: The genus name means "golden
flower." The Chrysanthemum sold by
florists, *C. morifolium* , derives from
eastern Asian sources, but the precise
history of its many variations in size
and "doubling" of head is unknown.
Shasta Daisy (*C. maximum*), commonly
cultivated, also grows wild west of the
Cascade Mountains. It resembles Oxeye
Daisy but generally has rays ¾–1¼″
(2–3.1 cm) long.

### 261 Golden Aster
(*Chrysopsis villosa*)
Sunflower Family (Asteraceae)

Description: A round plant with erect or spreading
leafy stems, with *yellow flower-heads in
branched clusters*. Stem covered with
rough, grayish hairs.
Flowers: heads about 1″ (2.5 cm) wide,

with yellow rays around yellow disk.
Leaves: lanceolate, those at midstem
½–1¼" (1.3–3.1 cm) long.
Fruit: seed-like; dingy white bristles in
two lengths at top, the outer shorter.
Height: 8–20" (20–50 cm).

Flowering: May–October.

Habitat: Open plains, rocky slopes, cliffs, from
low elevations into coniferous forests.

Range: From Canada to southern California;
east to Texas, Nebraska, and
Wisconsin; south into Mexico.

Comments: This species and its close relatives,
distinguished by their hairiness, are so
common in the West that they are
difficult to overlook. They are
everywhere in dry places, often in very
showy displays.

## 352 Rabbit Brush
(*Chrysothamnus nauseosus*)
Sunflower Family (Asteraceae)

Description: A shrub with *erect, slender, flexible
branches* covered with dense, felt-like,
matted hairs (often overlooked until one
scrapes the surface lightly), very narrow
leaves, and *small yellow heads* in dense
clusters at ends of stems.
Flowers: heads ¼–½" (6–13 mm)
high, slender, *without rays, bracts
oriented in 5 vertical rows,* outer bracts
short.
Leaves: ¾–3" (2–7.5 cm) long.
Fruit: seed-like, with fine hairs at tip.
Height: up to 7' (210 cm).

Flowering: August–October.

Habitat: Dry open places with sagebrush, or
grassland or open woodland.

Range: From western Canada to California,
Texas, and northern Mexico.

Comments: Rabbit Brush is a common and variable
species in a genus found only in western
North America. Some races are light
green, others have silvery hairs. Navajo
Indians obtained a yellow dye from the
flower heads.

### 598 Chicory
(*Cichorium intybus*)
Sunflower Family (Asteraceae)

Description: Wiry, branched stems, with few leaves
on upper part, have heads of *pale blue
ray flowers* that bloom along the main
branches. Sap milky.
Flowers: heads nearly 2″ (5 cm) wide,
each ray with 5 small teeth across blunt
end.
Leaves: those near base lanceolate, 3–
10″ (7.5–25 cm) long, pinnately
toothed or lobed, edged with small
sharp teeth; upper leaves smaller.
Fruit: seed-like, with tiny scales at tip.
Height: 1–6′ (30–180 cm).

Flowering: March–October.

Habitat: Roadsides, fields, and city lots.

Range: Introduced from Eurasia and now found
throughout most of United States; more
common in regions with ample rain.

Comments: Chicory is grown for its roots; ground
and roasted, they are added to or
substituted for coffee. Young leaves
may be used in salads or as a vegetable.
Endive (*C. endivia*), a close relative, is
cultivated as a salad plant.

### 421 Showy Thistle
(*Cirsium pastoris*)
Sunflower Family (Asteraceae)

Description: A *white, woolly, prickly plant* with
*crimson flower heads* at the ends of the
few upper branches terminating the
main stem.
Flowers: heads 1½–2½″ (3.8–6.3 cm)
long, with bracts the same length,
tipped with spines; bright red disk
flowers extend about 1″ (2.5 cm)
beyond the bracts.
Leaves: 4–12″ (10–30 cm) long,
narrow, pinnately lobed, edges prickly
and continuing down the stem as
narrow wings.
Fruit: seed-like, with long white hairs

at tip, each hair with many smaller
hairs along its length.
Height: 2–4′ (60–120 cm).

Flowering: June–September.

Habitat: Dry open slopes in brushy or grassy
areas, or in open woods.

Range: Northern California, southern Oregon,
and western Nevada.

Comments: With its blaze of red flowers
accentuated by white foliage, this is
perhaps the handsomest Thistle among
a group considered to be obnoxious
weeds. *Cirsium* comes from the Greek
*kirsos,* "a swollen vein," for which
Thistles (*kirsion*) were a reputed
remedy. Two similar California species,
neither quite so white and woolly, and
with nearly spherical heads, are
Coulter's Thistle (*C. coulteri*) and
Cobweb Thistle (*C. occidentale*).

## 347 Giant Coreopsis
(*Coreopsis gigantea*)
Sunflower Family (Asteraceae)

Description: Resembles a small tree, with a soft,
woody stem that branches near the top,
where *feathery leaves* grow and *large
yellow flower heads* bloom in clusters at
the ends of long leafless stalks.
Flowers: heads up to 3″ (7.5 cm) wide,
with bracts in 2 series, outer lanceolate
and shorter, inner ones broader; rays 2-
tone yellow, more deeply colored at the
base.
Leaves: up to 1′ (30 cm) long, broadly
ovate, repeatedly pinnately divided into
fine, fleshy, very narrow lobes. Stems
about 4″ (10 cm) thick.
Height: 1–10′ (30–300 cm).

Flowering: March–May.

Habitat: Coastal dunes and bluffs.

Range: Los Angeles County to San Luis Obispo
County, California.

Comments: Another species, Sea Dahlia (*C.
maritima*), stout but not woody, with
heads borne singly on stalks, grows in

coastal San Diego County. It is not a true Dahlia, a popular ornamental developed from wildflowers (species of *Dahlia*) found in the mountains of Mexico.

---

### 272  Hawk's Beard
(*Crepis acuminata*)
Sunflower Family (Asteraceae)

Description: Many *narrow heads of yellow ray flowers* form a loose, flattish or round-topped cluster on top of a branched, *leafy stem*. Sap milky.
Flowers: heads about ½–1″ (1.3–2.5 cm) wide, with inner bracts ⅜–⅝″ (9–15 mm) long, at least twice the length of outer bracts, and 5–10 flowers.
Leaves: 4–16″ (10–40 cm) long, lightly and softly downy, pinnately lobed, edges often with teeth.
Fruit: seed-like, with slender white hairs at tip.
Height: 8–28″ (20–70 cm).
Flowering: May–August.
Habitat: Open dry places in sagebrush and coniferous forests.
Range: Eastern Washington to eastern California; east to northern New Mexico, Colorado, and central Montana.
Comments: *Crepis* is Greek for "sandal," the reason for its application to this genus apparently lost in history.

---

### 243  Five-needle Fetid Marigold
(*Dyssodia pentachaeta*)
Sunflower Family (Asteraceae)

Description: A low, tufted, dark green *prickly plant* with a small, deep yellow flower head on each of several leafless stalks above the foliage.
Flowers: heads ¼–½″ (6–13 mm) wide, surrounded by bracts, upper parts

of which are dotted with conspicuous glands; 8–13 rays, each ⅛–¼″ (3–6 mm) long, surround a few disk flowers.
Leaves: about ½″ (1.3 cm) long, opposite, *pinnately divided into a few needle-like lobes.*
Fruit: seed-like, slender, with pointed scales at top.
Height: 4–8″ (10–20 cm).

Flowering: April–October.
Habitat: Open desert and arid, rocky plains.
Range: Southern Utah to Arizona, New Mexico, Texas, and Mexico.
Comments: This common low plant frequently grows near creosote bush and Snakeweed or among piñon and juniper. Its close relative, Prickly Fetid Marigold (*D. acerosa*), is more woody and prickly, with heads that sit among undivided leaves.

### 246 Brittlebush; Incienso
(*Encelia farinosa*)
Sunflower Family (Asteraceae)

Description: A round, *silvery-gray, leafy bush* with *bright yellow flower heads* that bloom in loosely branched clusters on branched stalks well above the foliage.
Flowers: heads 2–3″ (5–7.5 cm) wide, with 8–18 yellow rays, each ¼–⅝″ (6–15 mm) long, surround a yellow disk (or brown disk in southern part of range) with scales that enfold the flowers.
Leaves: 1¼–4″ (3.1–10 cm) long, ovate, hairy, with petioles.
Fruit: seed-like, without hairs or scales at top.
Height: 3–5′ (90–150 cm).

Flowering: March–June.
Habitat: Dry slopes and washes in the desert.
Range: Southeastern California across southern Nevada to southwestern Utah and western Arizona, and northwestern Mexico.
Comments: In full flower, Brittlebush seems a solid

hemisphere of brilliant yellow. The stems exude a fragrant resin that was chewed by Indians and used as incense in the churches of Baja California. A similar species, California Encelia (*E. californica*), which grows near the coast in southern California, has only one head on each stalk.

237 **Sunray**
(*Enceliopsis nudicaulis*)
Sunflower Family (Asteraceae)

Description: One or several *leafless stalks,* each with a *broad yellow flower head* at the top, grow from a *basal cluster of gray-green leaves.*
Flowers: heads 3–4″ (7.5–10 cm) wide, with about 20 rays and a broad central disk, each of the small disk flowers enfolded in a stiff bract.
Leaves: ovate blades ½–2½″ (1.3–6.3 cm) long, tapered to flat, long stalks.
Fruit: seed-like, flat, with hairs on sides nearly hiding 2 stiff bristles at top.
Height: 6–18″ (15–45 cm).
Flowering: May–August.
Habitat: Among desert brush.
Range: Central Idaho to Nevada, Utah, and northern Arizona.
Comments: Its beauty—golden heads held high above a tuft of gray foliage—makes it a worthwhile ornamental in dry regions.

69 **Spreading Fleabane**
(*Erigeron divergens*)
Sunflower Family (Asteraceae)

Description: A well-branched plant covered with *short, grayish hairs,* those on stems standing straight out; at the tip of each of the many branches blooms a flower head with *many narrow white, pink, or lavender rays* surrounding a *yellow disk.*
Flowers: heads about 1″ (2.5 cm) wide,

with very narrow *bracts, mostly lined up
side by side,* and not overlapping like
shingles; rays each ¼–½″ (6–10 mm)
long.

Leaves: largest in tufts at base, ½–1″
(1.3–2.5 cm) long, the lanceolate blade
evenly tapered to the stalk-like base;
those on stem numerous, but slightly
smaller.

Fruit: seed-like, with numerous fragile,
fine bristles at top.

Height: 4–28″ (10–70 cm).

Flowering: April–September.

Habitat: Open sandy areas in deserts, plains,
valleys, and foothills.

Range: Southern British Columbia to
California; east to western Texas,
Colorado, and Montana; also Mexico.

Comments: This is one of a large number of similar
species. Most usually can be recognized
as *Erigeron* by their low form, many
white, pink, or lavender rays, and
bracts around the head all of about the
same length.

---

**477 Seaside Daisy**
(*Erigeron glaucous*)
Sunflower Family (Asteraceae)

Description: Bristly-hairy, sticky stems grow from a
basal rosette, each long branch topped
by a flower head with *many narrow pale
pink or lavender rays* surrounding a
yellowish disk.

Flowers: heads 1½–2½″ (3.8–6.3 cm)
wide; about 100 rays; bracts shaggy-
hairy.

Leaves: to 5″ (12.5 cm) long, broadly
spatula-shaped, sometimes with teeth
on the edges near the top, tapered to a
broad, flat stalk.

Fruit: seed-like, with numerous fragile,
fine bristles at top.

Height: 4–16″ (10–40 cm).

Flowering: April–August.

Habitat: Coastal bluffs, hills, and old dunes.

Range: Oregon to southern California.

Comments:   Succulence is a common feature of
seaside plants, and this Daisy is unusual
in its genus, for it, too, is slightly
succulent.

### 479   Philadelphia Fleabane
(*Erigeron philadelphicus*)
Sunflower Family (Asteraceae)

Description:   A plant covered with sparse, long,
spreading hairs, the single leafy stem
branched mostly in the upper half, the
end of each branch with a flower head
bearing *150–400 very slender white or
pink rays.*
Flowers: heads ½–1" (1.3–2.5 cm)
wide, with *bracts all about the same length
and mostly lined up side by side,* not
overlapping like shingles; rays, each
¼–½" (6–10 mm) long, surround a
yellow disk.
Leaves: up to 6" (15 cm) long, *spatula-
shaped,* the bases on most continuing
around the point of attachment and
*clasping the stem;* those at the bottom of
the plant taper to stalks.
Fruit: seed-like, with numerous fragile,
fine bristles at top.
Height: 8–28" (20–70 cm).

Flowering:   May–September.

Habitat:   Most commonly in moist, often partly
shaded sites where the soil has been
disturbed.

Range:   Throughout the United States and most
of Canada.

Comments:   In this especially pretty species, the
many thread-like rays form a delicate
fringe around the head. The name
Fleabane comes from the old belief that
these plants repelled fleas. Fleabanes are
very similar to Asters, but species of
*Aster* usually bloom late in the season
and have bracts on the head of different
lengths, overlapping like shingles.

### 480 Showy Daisy
(*Erigeron speciosus*)
Sunflower Family (Asteraceae)

Description: A leafy stem branches near the top into
leafless stalks, each with one flower
head at the end, with *many narrow pink,
lavender or white rays* surrounding a
yellow disk.
Flowers: heads 1½–2" (3.8–5 cm)
wide, with *bracts all about the same length
and lined up side by side,* not overlapping
like shingles; rays ½–¾" (1.3–2 cm)
long.
Leaves: lower 3 to 6" (7.5–15 cm)
long, lanceolate, smooth, commonly
with 3 veins, the bases joined to the
stem about halfway around and
therefore slightly clasping.
Fruit: seed-like, with fragile, fine
bristles at top.
Height: 1–3' (30–90 cm).
Flowering: June–September.
Habitat: Openings in woods or in lightly
wooded areas at moderate elevations in
the mountains.
Range: From southern British Columbia to
Baja California; east to New Mexico,
South Dakota, and Montana.
Comments: This *Erigeron* has one of the showiest
heads, reflected in the species name,
*speciosus,* which means "pretty." The
similar Hairy Showy Daisy (*E.
subtrinervis*) has spreading hairs over
most of the stem and leaves.

### 252 Golden Yarrow
(*Eriophyllum lanatum*)
Sunflower Family (Asteraceae)

Description: A *grayish, woolly, leafy plant* with
several branched stems ending in short
leafless stalks and *golden-yellow flower
heads.*
Flowers: heads 1½–2½" (3.8–6.3 cm)
wide, with broadly lanceolate bracts
prominently ridged on back, and 8–12

broad rays, each ½–¾″ (1.3–2 cm)
long, around the disk.
Leaves: 1–3″ (2.5–7.5 cm) long,
irregularly divided into narrow lobes.
Fruit: seed-like, narrow, smooth, with
a low crown of scales at top.
Height: 4–24″ (10–60 cm).

Flowering: May–July.

Habitat: Dry thickets and dry open places.

Range: British Columbia to southern California
and western Nevada; east to
northeastern Oregon and western
Montana.

Comments: This common and variable species often
colors banks along roads with a blaze of
yellow in drier portions of the West.
The plant's white hairs, by reflecting
heat and reducing air movement across
the leaf's surface, conserve water.

241 **Woolly Daisy**
(*Eriophyllum wallacei*)
Sunflower Family (Asteraceae)

Description: A tiny, *gray, woolly tufted plant* with
small *golden-yellow flower heads*.
Flowers: heads about ¼″ (6 mm) wide,
with 5–10 oval rays, each about ⅛″ (3
mm) long, around a few disk flowers.
Leaves: to ¾″ (2 cm) long, ovate,
tapering to short stalks.
Fruit: seed-like, narrow, black, topped
by a few short scales.
Height: ½–4″ (1.3–10 cm).

Flowering: March–June.

Habitat: Sandy desert soil.

Range: Southeastern California to southwestern
Utah and northwestern Arizona.

Comments: In desert annuals, such as Woolly
Daisy, seed production is vital for
yearly survival. During drought plants
often grow only about ¼″ (6 mm)
before producing one head, ensuring at
least some seeds. Under moister
conditions plants repeatedly branch
near the base, producing taller stems,
many heads, and abundant seed.

### 394 Indian Blanket; Firewheel; Gaillardia
(*Gaillardia pulchella*)
Sunflower Family (Asteraceae)

Description: Branched stems, mostly leafy near the base, have showy flower heads with *rays red at base, tipped with yellow, each with 3 teeth at broad end.*
Flowers: head 1½–2½" (3.8–6.3 cm) wide; disk reddish-maroon, dome-like, with *bristly scales* among the flowers; rays ½–¾" (1.3–2 cm) long.
Leaves: to 3" (7.5 cm) long, oblong, toothed or plain on edges.
Fruit: seed-like, with tapered, white, translucent scales at tip.
Height: 1–2' (30–60 cm).
Flowering: May–July.
Habitat: Sandy plains and desert, common along roadsides.
Range: Arizona to Texas; north to southeastern Colorado and Nebraska; south into Mexico.
Comments: Frequent along roadsides in the Southwest, these wildflowers stand like hundreds of showy Fourth of July pinwheels at the top of slender stalks. Varieties are popular in cultivation, for they tolerate heat and dryness. Among several species in the Southwest, some flowers are entirely yellow.

### 254 Desert Sunflower
(*Gerea canescens*)
Sunflower Family (Asteraceae)

Description: A slender, hairy plant with a few leaves and, at the ends of the several branches, *golden-yellow flower heads.*
Flowers: heads about 2" (5 cm) wide; 10–20 oblong rays, each ¾" (2 cm) long, surround the disk; bracts have long, stiff white hairs on edges.
Leaves: to 3" (7.5 cm) long, lanceolate or ovate, often with a few teeth.
Fruit: seed-like, flat, each tightly

enfolded by a parchment-like bract, the surface of the fruit hairy, the top with 2 pointed scales, the edges with a strong white margin.
Height: 1–3′ (30–90 cm).

Flowering: February–May and, depending upon rains, October–November.

Habitat: Sandy, barren, flat desert.

Range: Southeastern California to southwestern Utah; south to western Arizona and northwestern Mexico.

Comments: *Gerea* comes from the Greek *geraios* ("old man"), referring to the white hairs on the fruits. After adequate rain, these plants may line mile after mile along hot, dry, desolate roadsides.

## 259 Curlycup Gumweed
(*Grindelia squarrosa*)
Sunflower Family (Asteraceae)

Description: A dark green leafy plant, openly branched in the upper parts, with many *yellow flower heads. Tips of bracts around head strongly rolled back.*
Flowers: heads about 1½″ (3.8 cm) wide, with 25–40 rays around a small disk.
Leaves: to 3″ (7.5 cm) long, oblong, clasping the stem at bases, the edges with sharp teeth pointing forward.
Fruit: seed-like, plump, brownish, usually with 4 angles and with several narrow scales at top which easily drop off.
Height: 1–3′ (30–90 cm).

Flowering: July–September.

Habitat: Dry, open places, often in old fields and waste places.

Range: Probably native mostly east of the Continental Divide on the Great Plains, but now frequent through much of the arid West.

Comments: The toxicity of Gumweeds (*Grindelia*), especially Curlycup Gumweed, depends upon the soil in which it grows. When it absorbs the element selenium, it becomes poisonous and poses considerable problems for ranchers. However, species have been used medicinally for centuries. Influenced by magical numbers, Spanish New Mexicans boiled three times three buds of flowers in three pints of water until only one pint remained, and drank a glassful three times daily for kidney disorders. Extracts were used for a wide variety of complaints, from skin irritations to rheumatic pains.

349 **Snakeweed; Matchweed; Matchbush; Broomweed; Turpentine Weed**
(*Gutierrezia sarothrae*)
Sunflower Family (Asteraceae)

Description: *Many slender green branches form a round shrublet* with *hundreds of tiny yellow flower heads* in loose clusters.
Flowers: heads narrow, ⅛–¼″ (3–6 mm) long, with 3–7 ray flowers, each about ⅛″ (3 mm) long, and 2–6 tiny disk flowers.
Leaves: ¼–2½″ (6–63 mm) long and very narrow, less than ⅛″ (3 mm) wide, resinous.
Fruit: seed-like, hairy, plump, with low scales at top.
Height: 6–36″ (15–90 cm).

Flowering: August–September.

Habitat: In deserts, on plains, and among piñon and juniper.

Range: From eastern Oregon and southern Idaho to southern California; east to Texas and the western Plains as far north as central Canada; also Mexico.

Comments: A very similar species, Little-head Snakeweed (*G. microcephala*), which may grow in the same area, has 1–3 ray flowers and 1–3 disk flowers. The names Matchweed and Matchbush refer to the match-like heads. As with many aromatic plants, this species was used medicinally, occasionally as a treatment

for snakebite; hence the name
Snakeweed. Bundled, dried stems made
primitive brooms, hence Broomweed.
This plant poses serious problems as a
range weed. More frequent under
improper range management, it now
covers thousands of square miles of once
good grassland. Poisonous, it
occasionally kills grazing livestock but
more commonly aborts fetuses.

238  **Stemless Golden Weed**
     (*Haplopappus acaulis*)
     Sunflower Family (Asteraceae)

Description:  *Dark green, erect, stiff leaves in dense tufts
or mats* from which grow numerous
nearly leafless stalks each with a *yellow
flower head.*
Flowers: heads about 1½" (3.8 cm)
wide, with 6–15 rays, each about ½"
(1.3 cm) long, around the disk, and
lanceolate *pointed bracts.*
Leaves: ½–2" (1.3–5 cm) long, with 3
veins.
Fruit: seed-like, with numerous pale
tan bristles at top.
Height: ½–6" (1.3–15 cm).

Flowering:  May–August.

Habitat:  Dry open places from foothills to fairly
high elevations.

Range:  Central Idaho to southeastern Oregon
and along the length of the eastern
slopes of the Sierra Nevada in
California; east to Colorado and
southwestern Montana; then northeast
to central Canada.

Comments:  The very similar Thrift Golden Weed
(*H. armerioides*), growing from Montana
to Arizona, New Mexico, and
Nebraska, can be distinguished by the
round tips on the bracts. Both species
are easily recognized in a genus of
notorious taxonomic difficulty.

## 236 Yellow Spiny Daisy
(*Haplopappus spinulosus*)
Sunflower Family (Asteraceae)

Description: A slender plant with small, weakly
bristly leaves and *yellow flower heads,*
each at the tip of one of the many upper
branches.
Flowers: heads about 1" (2.5 cm) wide,
with rays about ⅜" (9 mm) long
surrounding the disk.
Leaves: ⅛–¾" (3–20 mm) long,
narrow, the lowest sometimes with a
few lobes, angled upward or pressed
against the stem, the edges with a *spiny
bristle at tip of each tooth.*
Fruit: seed-like, densely covered with
short hairs, bearing at top numerous,
slender, pale tan bristles.
Height: 6–14" (15–35 cm).
Flowering: August–October.
Habitat: Open places in arid grassland, in
desert, and among piñon and juniper.
Range: Southern California and Arizona to
New Mexico; north through the Rocky
Mountain states to Alberta; on much of
the Plains; also northern Mexico.
Comments: This species has the fewest number of
chromosomes per cell known in any
plant, 4 instead of the more usual 20 or
so.

## 240 Orange Sneezeweed; Owlclaws
(*Helenium hoopesii*)
Sunflower Family (Asteraceae)

Description: One or several stout, leafy stems have
*drooping rays on orange-yellow flower heads*
at tops of nearly leafless stalks.
Flowers: heads 2–3" (5–7.5 cm) wide,
with a *nearly spherical disk* surrounded
by narrow rays ¾–1" (2–2.5 cm) long,
each with 3 teeth at tip.
Leaves: to 1' (30 cm) long, lanceolate,
progressively smaller higher on the
stem.
Fruit: seed-like, densely covered with

tan hairs and topped by several sharply
pointed scales.
Height: 2–4′ (60–120 cm).

Flowering: July–September.

Habitat: Wet places in mountain meadows.

Range: Southern Oregon and northern
California and along the Sierra Nevada;
east to New Mexico, Colorado, and
Wyoming.

Comments: The round, deep yellow heads with rays
hanging around the edge distinguish
Sneezeweeds, although the heads in
some species are much smaller and in
several the edges of leaves continue
down the stem as "wings." Orange
Sneezeweed, which has become
increasingly frequent in heavily grazed
areas, causes the sheep poisoning called
"spewing sickness." The name
Sneezeweed refers to the irritation the
pollen causes in people allergic to it.
Preparations made from the root have
been used to alleviate rheumatic pains,
treat stomach disorders, and cure colic
and diarrhea in infants.

---

247   **Common Sunflower; Mirasol**
(*Helianthus annuus*)
Sunflower Family (Asteraceae)

Description: A *tall, coarse, leafy plant* with a hairy
stem commonly branched in the upper
half and bearing several or many flower
heads, the *central maroon disk*
surrounded by many *bright yellow rays.*
Flowers: heads 3–5″ (7.5–12.5 cm)
wide; ovate bracts abruptly narrowed to
a slender tip, and stiff scales among
disk flowers.
Leaves: the lowest ovate, often heart-
shaped, the edges usually with irregular
teeth; the upper, smaller and narrower.
Fruit: seed-like, flattish but plump,
bearing above the 2 sharp edges 2 scales
which readily drop off.
Height: 2–13′ (60–390 cm).

Flowering: June–September.

Habitat: Dry open plains and foothills, now
especially common along roads and
edges of fields.

Range: Throughout most of the United States,
much of North America.

Comments: The state flower of Kansas. The heads
follow the sun each day, facing
eastward in the morning, westward at
sunset; the name in Spanish means
"looks at the sun." The plant has been
cultivated in the Americas since pre-
Columbian times; yellow dye obtained
from the flowers, and a black or dull
blue dye from the seeds, were once
important in Indian basketry and
weaving. In the United States and
Eurasia seeds from cultivated strains are
now used for cooking oil and livestock
feed. Many variants have been
developed, some with one huge head
topping a stalk 9–16' (3–5 m) tall,
others with maroon rays. Prairie
Sunflower (*H. petiolaris*), similar to the
wild forms of Common Sunflower, has
scales on the disk in the center of the
head tipped by white hairs, easily
visible when the central flowers are
spread apart.

270 **Alpine Gold; Alpine Hulsea**
(*Hulsea algida*)
Sunflower Family (Asteraceae)

Description: A low, tufted, densely glandular-hairy
plant with sparsely leafy stems, each
topped by a flower head with *25–50
short, narrow yellow rays* surrounding a
yellow disk.
Flowers: heads 2–3½" (5–8.8 cm)
wide, with a broad disk and narrow,
overlapping *bracts all about the same
length*.
Leaves: lower to 6" (15 cm), succulent,
lanceolate, often with scalloped or
lobed edges.
Fruit: seed-like, narrow, about ½" (1.3
cm) long, with 4 scales at top.

Height: 6–14" (15–35 cm).
ering: July–September.
Habitat: Sand or gravel, or rock crevices high in
the mountains.
Range: Idaho and southwestern Montana to
northeastern Oregon and the mountains
along the eastern edge of California.
Comments: The similar Dwarf Hulsea (*H. nana*),
from the mountains of Washington,
Oregon, and northern California, is
more compact, rarely more than 4" (10
cm) high, with a flower stalk that is
usually leafless, and a head with only
about 21 rays.

## 255 Stemless Hymenoxys
(*Hymenoxys acaulis*)
Sunflower Family (Asteraceae)

Description: From *tufted basal leaves* grow short
leafless flower stalks ending with one
*yellow flower head*.
Flowers: head 1–2" (2.5–5 cm) wide;
rays broad, with 3 teeth.
Leaves: to 3" (7.5 cm) long, ½" (1.3
cm) wide, hairy or smooth.
Fruit: seedlike, hairy, usually tipped by
a few pointed scales.
Height: 3–12" (7.5–30 cm).
Flowering: June–September.
Habitat: Open dry hillsides and dry plains.
Range: Southern Idaho to southeastern
California; eastward to Texas, Ohio,
North Dakota, and Central Canada.
Comments: This common species is highly variable,
reaching its greatest complexity in
Wyoming and western Colorado. A few
plants may lack rays, some are very
hairy, others nearly hairless, most have
no stems below the flower stalk, but
some do.

### 256 Old Man of the Mountain; Alpine Sunflower
(*Hymenoxys grandiflora*)
Sunflower Family (Asteraceae)

Description: A *whitish, hairy plant* with feather-like leaves mostly near the base, and one or several stout stems each bearing *one large yellow flower head*.
Flowers: head 3–4½" (7.5–11.3 cm) wide; with 20 or more rays surrounding a broad disk, and numerous very narrow, woolly bracts.
Leaves: 3–4" (7.5–10 cm), pinnately divided into very narrow segments.
Fruit: seed-like, 5-sided, densely hairy, narrow, with 5–8 stiff, narrow scales at top.
Height: 1–12" (2.5–30 cm).
Flowering: June–August.
Habitat: Rocky slopes, high meadows, and tundra.
Range: Central Idaho and southwestern Montana to Colorado and eastern Utah.
Comments: In a complicated genus of about 20 species in western North America, this has the largest and prettiest heads (*grandiflora* means "large-flowered").

### 263 Goldfields
(*Lasthenia chrysostoma*)
Sunflower Family (Asteraceae)

Description: A small, slender annual with reddish stems, *very narrow opposite leaves,* and a small *golden-yellow flower head* at the end of each branch.
Flowers: heads ¾–1" (2–2.5 cm) wide, with about 10 oblong rays surrounding a conical disk.
Leaves: ½–2½" (1.3–6.3 cm) long, stiffly hairy at base.
Fruit: seed-like, slender, with several narrow, brownish, pointed scales at top, or sometimes without scales.
Height: 4–10" (10–25 cm).
Flowering: March–May.

Habitat:   Open fields and slopes at low
elevations.
Range:   Southwestern Oregon to Baja California
and central Arizona.
Comments:   On open areas with poor soils, where
grass is sparse, this plant will form
carpets of gold if moisture is ample. It
is also sometimes placed in the genus
*Baeria*. Spring Gold (*Crocidium
multicaule*) looks very much like
Goldfields, but has most leaves in a
basal rosette. Those on the stem are
alternate, and have tufts of hair in the
axils.

### 533   Dotted Gayfeather
(*Liatris punctata*)
Sunflower Family (Asteraceae)

Description:   Several stems bear *narrow, crowded heads
with rose-lavender flowers arranged in
slender wands.*
Flowers: heads about ¾" (2 cm) long,
with 4–8 flowers, none of the ray type.
Leaves: 3–6" (7.5–15 cm) long, very
narrow, stiff, minutely dotted.
Fruit: seed-like, narrow, hairy, with
many small plumes at top.
Height: 6–32" (15–80 cm).
Flowering:   August–September.
Habitat:   Dry open places, on plains and among
piñon and juniper, often in sandy soil.
Range:   Central Canada; south along the eastern
base of the Rocky Mountains to western
Texas and northern Mexico; east to
Michigan, Iowa, and Arkansas.
Comments:   Rayless heads of purple flowers and
slender, often plume-like bristles on the
fruits generally identify this complex
genus of the eastern United States that
barely extends into the West.

## 271 Silvery Luina
### (*Luina hypoleuca*)
Sunflower Family (Asteraceae)

Description: A leafy plant with several *stems in a clump, covered with white wool* that is densest on stems and underside of leaves.
Flowers: heads in a branched cluster at tip of each stem, *dull yellowish and rayless,* nearly ⅜" (9 cm) long, with bracts all of the same length, side by side, and barely overlapping.
Leaves: 1–2½" (2.5–6.3 cm) long, broadly ovate.
Fruit: seed-like, with soft white bristles at top.
Height: 6–16" (15–40 cm).
Flowering: June–October.
Habitat: In rocky places and on cliffs.
Range: Central British Columbia to central California.
Comments: The leaves have a white underside, as the species name suggests, often contrasting with the upper surface, which may be darker. The plant must have reminded the botanist who named this genus of another, *Inula,* also white and woolly, for *Luina* is an obvious anagram.

## 481, 596 Sticky Aster
### (*Machaeranthera bigelovii*)
Sunflower Family (Asteraceae)

Description: Leafy, branched stems are topped by heads with *many narrow bright reddish-lavender or purple rays* that surround a yellow disk.
Flowers: heads about 1½" (3.8 cm) wide, with *glandular–hairy bracts,* pale and stiff at the base and green at the *bent or curled-back tip.*
Leaves: 2–4" (5–10 cm) long, oblong, with *sharp teeth on edges.*
Fruit: seed-like, with many slender bristles at top.

Height: 1–3′ (30–90 cm).
Flowering: August–October.
Habitat: Plains and openings in coniferous forests.
Range: Western Colorado to New Mexico and Arizona.
Comments: These wildflowers of late summer often color entire banks and roadsides vibrant purple. In the afternoon, as heads become shaded, the rays fold upward in the "sleep position." The Sticky Aster resembles true Asters but has spiny or divided leaves.

---

595  **Tahoka Daisy**
(*Machaeranthera tanacetifolia*)
Sunflower Family (Asteraceae)

Description: Branched stems with *fern-like leaves* end in *heads with many bright purple, very narrow rays* surrounding a *yellow disk.*
Flowers: heads 1¼–2½″ (3.1–6.3 cm) wide.
Leaves: 2–5″ (5–12.5 cm) long, pinnately divided, the main segments also pinnately divided.
Fruit: seed-like, covered with short hairs lying flat on the surface, the top with many slender bristles.
Height: 4–16″ (10–40 cm).
Flowering: May–September.
Habitat: Sandy open ground on plains or deserts.
Range: Alberta to Texas, Arizona, and Mexico.
Comments: The fern-like leaves of this beautiful species make it one of the easiest to identify in a complex group. False Tahoka Daisy (*M. parviflora*), similar but with smaller heads—disk only ¼–½″ (6–13 mm) wide—and less elaborately divided leaves, grows from Utah to Arizona, Texas, and Mexico.

### 476 Mojave Aster
(*Machaeranthera tortifolia*)
Sunflower Family (Asteraceae)

Description: Several grayish, leafy stems grow from a woody base, and have at their long, leafless ends flower heads with *many narrow pale lavender or pale violet rays* surrounding a yellow disk.
Flowers: heads about 2″ (5 cm) wide.
Leaves: 1–2½″ (2.5–6.3 cm) long, lanceolate or narrower, usually covered with *gray hairs,* bearing *spiny teeth along edges* and a spine at tip.
Height: 1–2½′ (30–75 cm).
Flowering: March–May, and again in October, depending on rains.
Habitat: Dry rocky desert slopes and washes.
Range: Southeastern California to southwestern Utah and western Arizona.
Comments: The rays' pastel hue seems unexpectedly delicate in this harsh environment. Plants occasionally line roadsides, but usually occur on rocky outwash fans. A similar species, Big Bend Aster (*M. wrightii*), grows in western Texas and nearby Mexico.

### 262 Common Madia
(*Madia elegans*)
Sunflower Family (Asteraceae)

Description: Slender, erect leafy stems have mostly *yellow flower heads* at the ends of branches in the upper part.
Flowers: heads 1¼–2″ (3.1–5 cm) wide, with about 13 *yellow rays* ½–¾″ (1.3–2 cm) long, each with *3 teeth* at broad end and often a maroon patch near base, and bracts that *completely enfold the adjacent fruit.* Among the disk flowers are erect hairs.
Leaves: to 8″ (20 cm) long, narrow.
Fruit: seed-like, flat, dark, produced only by ray flowers.
Height: 1–4′ (30–120 cm).
Flowering: July–September.

Habitat: Dry, open, usually grassy places, often along roadsides.

Range: Southwestern Washington to Baja California.

Comments: Species of *Madia* (a Chilean name for a species once grown for the oil in its seeds) are covered with sticky, glandular hairs and are often called Tarweed. The heads of many, including those of Common Madia, close at night.

## 258 Snakehead
(*Malacothrix coulteri*)
Sunflower Family (Asteraceae)

Description: Pale, smooth, branched stems with most leaves near the base, and at the tips *pale yellow flower heads.* Sap milky.
Flowers: heads 1–1½" (2.5–3.8 cm) wide, with only flowers of ray type, those in center smaller.
Leaves: those near base 2–4" (5–10 cm) long, lanceolate, the edges coarsely toothed; those on stem ovate, the bases "clasping" the stem.
Fruit: seed-like, narrow, pale greenish-brown, with 4 or 5 sharp angles and 2 fine lines between the angles, and topped with slender bristles, most of which break off easily.
Height: 4–20" (10–50 cm).

Flowering: March–May.

Habitat: Open flats and hills in grassland or desert.

Range: Central California to Baja California; east to southwestern Utah and southern Arizona.

Comments: The flower head's broad, round bracts have parchment-like edges and a purplish or greenish central band that resembles a serpent's scales, and the bud resembles a fanciful snake head, thus the common name. Among similar species, Tackstem (*Calycoseris parryi*), has small tack-shaped glands on the bracts and upper stem; Scalebud

(*Anisocoma acaulis*) has seed-like fruits with feathery bristles at the tip, the outer bristles half the length of the inner.

## 257 Desert Dandelion
(*Malacothrix glabrata*)
Sunflower Family (Asteraceae)

Description: A smooth plant with a *few pinnately divided leaves* and bright *pale yellow flower heads* on branched stems.
Flowers: heads 1–1½" (2.5–3.8 cm) wide; flowers all ray type.
Leaves: 2½–5" (6.3–12.5 cm) long, divided into a few thread-like lobes.
Fruit: seed-like, topped by several soft bristles, but only two of them not falling off.
Height: 6–14" (15–35 cm).
Flowering: March–June.
Habitat: Sandy desert, plains, and washes.
Range: Southwestern Idaho and eastern Oregon to southern California, much of Arizona, and northwestern Mexico.
Comments: In wet years this showy wildflower will form masses of yellow in sandy deserts.

## 65 Blackfoot Daisy
(*Melampodium leucanthum*)
Sunflower Family (Asteraceae)

Description: A low, round, bushy plant with flower heads of *8–10 broad white rays* surrounding a small yellow disk.
Flowers: heads about 1" (2.5 cm) wide, with *5 broad outer bracts* joined to one another for ½ or ⅔ their length.
Leaves: ¾–2" (2–5 cm) long, opposite, narrow.
Fruit: seed-like, with several narrow scales at tip.
Height: 6–20" (15–50 cm).
Flowering: March–November.
Habitat: Rocky soil in deserts and on dry plains.

Range: Arizona to Kansas; south to Mexico.
Comments: At first glance Blackfoot Daisy appears the twin of White Zinnia (*Zinnia acerosa*), but heads of that species have 4–6 broad white rays and a narrow base of several overlapping scales. Both may be found in the same habitat, the range of White Zinnia ending south of Oklahoma.

## 67 Mojave Desert Star
(*Monoptilon bellioides*)
Sunflower Family (Asteraceae)

Description: A small, low plant with flower heads composed of *white rays* often tinged with rose and a *yellow disk,* the longer branches tending to lie on the ground.
Flowers: heads ¾″ (2 cm) wide, with nearly 20 rays.
Leaves: to ½″ (1.3 cm) long, few, narrow, stiffly hairy.
Fruit: seed-like, plump, hairy, topped with *several short scales and longer bristles.*
Height: usually only 1–2″ (2.5–5 cm), but up to 1–10″ (2.5–25 cm) wide.
Flowering: January–May and again in September, depending on rains.
Habitat: Sandy or gravelly desert flats.
Range: Southern California to western Arizona and northwestern Mexico.
Comments: As is often characteristic of desert annuals, Mojave Desert Star's growth depends upon the amount of rainfall. If winter rains are ample, it and other spring wildflowers grow in profusion, even obscuring the surface of the ground; but if rainfall is scanty, the plant will be only a fraction of an inch tall, if it grows at all, with one head disproportionately large in comparison to the rest of the plant.

### 478 Showy Palafoxia
(*Palafoxia sphacelata*)
Sunflower Family (Asteraceae)

Description: A slender, erect, sparsely-leaved plant, usually glandular-hairy on the upper parts, with a few *pink flower heads* at the ends of upper branches.
Flowers: heads 1–1½" (2.5–3.8 cm) wide, with bracts all about the same length, and rays that have a narrow base and a *broad tip with 3 narrow lobes.*
Leaves: 1½–3" (3.8–7.5 cm) long, lanceolate.
Fruit: seed-like, narrow, topped by several *slender, pointed scales.*
Height: 1–2' (30–60 cm).
Flowering: May–October.
Habitat: Sandy plains, deserts, piñon and juniper rangeland, and dunes.
Range: Kansas to New Mexico, Texas, and Mexico.
Comments: A relative, Spanish Needles (*P. arida*), has only very pale lavender disk flowers. On top of the fruit are 4 slender, pointed scales (the "Spanish needles"). It is common on sandy flats and in washes from southeastern California to southwestern Utah and western Arizona.

### 235 Chinchweed
(*Pectis papposa*)
Sunflower Family (Asteraceae)

Description: Slender stems branch many times in a forked manner producing a low, small, leafy plant with *small yellow flower heads* in bundles at the ends of branches.
Flowers: heads about ½" (1.3 cm) wide, with 7–9 rays surrounding a small disk, and narrow bracts less than ¼" (6 mm) long, lined up side by side and not overlapping, each with 3–7 conspicuous *glands.*
Leaves: up to 1½" (3.8 cm) long, less than ⅛" (3 mm) wide, dotted with

glands, the leaf base broad, translucent, edges have a few lobes tipped by bristles.

Fruit: seed-like, narrow, topped with a low crown of a few scales, 1 or 2 sometimes much longer than the others.

Height: 2–8″ (5–20 cm).

Flowering: July–October.

Habitat: Open areas on arid plains or in deserts, especially on sandy soil, frequent along roadsides.

Range: Southern California to western Texas; south into Mexico.

Comments: On a hot summer afternoon where these plants are numerous, the air is saturated with a heavy, lemon odor. A look-alike, Lemonweed (*P. angustifolia*), often grows with Chinchweed but is denser and has only one gland at the tip of each bract.

---

### 373 Pericome
(*Pericome caudata*)
Sunflower Family (Asteraceae)

Description: Several branched, leafy stems produce large rounded masses of foliage, above which are *rayless yellow flower heads in branched clusters.*

Flowers: heads nearly ½″ (1.3 cm) wide, with numerous bracts lined up side by side.

Leaves: 2–5″ (5–12.5 cm) long, *shaped like arrowheads* but the *tip tapered to a long, slender "tail."*

Height: 2–5′ (60–150 cm).

Flowering: August–October.

Habitat: On slopes in coniferous forests.

Range: Southeastern Colorado to Arizona, western Texas, and northern Mexico.

Comments: A common late-season wildflower along mountain road banks, named by early Spaniards "Yerba de Chivato" (the "herb of the he-goat") because of its odor.

## 277 Turtleback; Desert Velvet
(*Psathyrotes ramosissima*)
Sunflower Family (Asteraceae)

Description: A *low compact, round, flat, gray, velvety plant* with a strong *turpentine odor.*
Flowers: rayless yellow heads about ¼" (6 mm) wide, held erect just above the leaves.
Leaves: to ¾" (2 cm) long, *thick, roundish,* with prominent veins and coarsely toothed edges.
Fruit: seed-like, densely silky-hairy, with yellow-brown bristles at top.
Height: 2–5" (5–12.5 cm).
Flowering: March–June.
Habitat: Desert flats and ledges.
Range: Southeastern California to southwestern Utah, western Arizona, and northwestern Mexico.
Comments: The plants form mounds resembling the shape of a turtle's shell, with the intermeshed leaves even fancied to represent its scales.

## 245 Paperflower
(*Psilostrophe cooperi*)
Sunflower Family (Asteraceae)

Description: Many well-branched leafy stems, woolly at the base, form a nearly *round plant covered with loose wool,* usually bearing only *one yellow flower head* at the end of each branch.
Flowers: heads ½–1" (1.3–2.5 cm) wide, with 3–5 *very broad rays,* each with 3 *shallow teeth* at end, surrounding a few small disk flowers.
Leaves: 1–2½" (2.5–6.3 cm) long, very narrow.
Fruit: seed-like, with several pointed scales at top.
Height: 4–20" (10–50 cm).
Flowering: April–October.
Habitat: Deserts or plains.
Range: Southeastern California to southwestern Utah and southwestern New Mexico;

south to Mexico.

Comments: Paperflower forms brilliant yellow globes. Its rays become dry and papery, remaining on the plant long after flowering. There are several closely related species, all poisonous to livestock and usually avoided.

## 76 Desert Chicory; Plumeseed
(*Rafinesquia neomexicana*)
Sunflower Family (Asteraceae)

Description: A smooth, sparsely-leaved, grayish-green plant with *white flower heads* at the ends of the few branches. Sap milky.
Flowers: heads 1–1½″ (2.5–3.8 cm) wide, with *flowers all of ray type,* often purplish on back side, the longest ones ⅝″ (15 mm) long, and short outer bracts with slender tips curling back.
Leaves: those at base 2–8″ (5–20 cm) long, pinnately divided into narrow lobes; upper leaves much smaller.
Fruit: seed-like, with a *slender, rigid stalk bearing feathery hairs at top,* the stalk not quite as long as the narrow fruit.
Height: 6–20″ (15–50 cm).
Flowering: March–May.
Habitat: Sandy or gravelly flats or slopes in deserts, often supported by shrubs.
Range: Southeastern California and southern Utah to the tip of western Texas; south to Mexico.
Comments: The genus name honors C. S. Rafinesque, an eccentric early naturalist. Two similar species in the same region are California Plumeseed (*R. californica*), with smaller heads and the stalk on the fruit longer than the body, and Tackstem (*Calycoseris wrightii*), with tack-shaped glands beneath the head.

### 265 Mexican Hat
(*Ratibida columnaris*)
Sunflower Family (Asteraceae)

Description: Branched and leafy in the lower part, with flower heads on long leafless stalks, 3–7 *yellow or yellow and red-brown rays* drooping around a *long red-brown disk.*

Flowers: heads 1–3″ (2.5–7.5 cm) long, with rays ½–¾″ (1.3–2 cm) long that may be yellow, yellow with red-brown base, or red-brown with small yellow tip; a bluntly conical disk ½–2½″ (1.3–6.3 cm) high and ½″ (1.3 cm) thick; and outer bracts about twice the length of the inner.

Leaves: 1–6″ (2.5–15 cm) long, pinnately cleft into a few very narrow segments.

Fruit: seed-like, with a fringe on one edge, the top of the fruit with a low crown and 2 tooth-like projections.

Height: 1–4′ (30–120 cm).

Flowering: July–October.

Habitat: Open, limestone soil, common along roadsides and on prairies.

Range: On most of the Great Plains, along the eastern base of the Rocky Mountains; west to Arizona; south to Mexico.

Comments: The colorful heads, resembling the traditional broad-brimmed, high-centered hat worn during Mexican fiestas, often bloom by the thousands. Prairie Coneflower (*R. tagetes*), has a spherical or oblong disk and leaves closer to the head.

### 264 Cutleaved Coneflower
(*Rudbeckia laciniata*)
Sunflower Family (Asteraceae)

Description: A tall, leafy plant whose erect branches end in large yellow flower heads with *downward-arching rays.*

Flowers: heads 3–6″ (7.5–15 cm) wide with a *cylindrical or conical brown disk* and 6—16 slender rays 1—2½" (2.5—6.3 cm) long.

Leaves: 3—8" (7.5—20 cm) long, deeply cut into 3, 5, or 7 variously cut and toothed lobes, lower ones on long stalks.

Fruit: seed-like, 4-sided, with a low crown at top.

Height: 2—7' (60—210 cm).

Flowering: July—October.

Habitat: Moist meadows, slopes, and valleys in the mountains.

Range: Canada; south through the Rocky Mountain region to Arizona and Texas; east to the Atlantic Coast.

Comments: These plants are mildly toxic to livestock. Blackeyed Susan (*R. hirta*), an eastern species introduced many places in the West, has a dark brown or brown-maroon hemispheric disk surrounded by orange-yellow, somewhat drooping rays. The lanceolate leaf blades sometimes have teeth, and there is no crown or ring of scales on the fruit.

---

### 313  Nodding Groundsel
(*Senecio bigelovii*)
Sunflower Family (Asteraceae)

Description: An erect, leafy stem has *rayless yellow flower heads* generally on bent individual stalks and *turned downward,* arranged in a narrow, branched cluster.

Flowers: heads ½" (1.3 cm) wide, with most bracts all of the same length, ½—¾" (1.3—2 cm) long, *side by side and not overlapping.*

Leaves: 4—8" (10—20 cm) long, lanceolate, with teeth on edges.

Fruit: seed-like, with a *tuft of fine white hairs at top.*

Height: 1—3' (30—90 cm).

Flowering: July—September.

Habitat: Rich, moist soil on grassy hillsides and in forests in the mountains.

Range: Western Colorado to Arizona and New Mexico.

Comments: *Senecio* is one of the largest genera of plants, with 2,000–3,000 species worldwide. Nearly 100 species occur in the West.

## 242 Threadleaf Groundsel
(*Senecio douglasii*)
Sunflower Family (Asteraceae)

Description: A *bluish-green, bushy, leafy plant covered with close white wool,* bearing *yellow flower heads* in branched clusters.
Flowers: heads about 1¼″ (3.1 cm) wide, with rays about ½″ (1.3 cm) long surrounding a narrow disk; most bracts about same length, *lined up side by side and not overlapping.*
Leaves: 1–5″ (2.5–12.5 cm) long, *divided into few very narrow lobes;* upper leaves often simply very narrow.
Fruit: seed-like, with a tuft of slender white hairs at top.
Height: 1–3′ (30–90 cm).
Flowering: April–September.
Habitat: Dry rocky plains, deserts, and piñon-juniper rangeland.
Range: Southern Colorado and Utah to Arizona, Texas, and Mexico.
Comments: One of the most toxic range plants to livestock, especially the tender new growth; because it is generally avoided, it tends to increase on overstocked ranges. Once used medicinally by southwestern Indians.

## 239 Arrowleaf Groundsel
(*Senecio triangularis*)
Sunflower Family (Asteraceae)

Description: *Broadly or narrowly triangular or arrowhead-shaped leaves, with many sharp teeth on edges,* grow on several leafy stems that bear *yellow flower heads* in a branched, flattish cluster at top.
Flowers: heads 1–1½″ (2.5–3.8 cm)

wide, with about 8 rays ½" (1.3 cm)
long surrounding the small disk, and
bracts mostly all the same length,
about ½" (1.3 cm) long, lined up side
by side and not overlapping.
Leaves: 2–8" (5–20 cm) long.
Fruit: seed-like, with a tuft of slender
white hairs at top.
Height: 1–5' (30–150 cm).

Flowering: June–September.

Habitat: Stream banks and other moist places in
the mountains.

Range: Alaska and western Canada; south to
southern California, Arizona, and New
Mexico.

Comments: As indicated by the common and
technical names, the triangular leaves
are distinctive.

### 308 Meadow Goldenrod
(*Solidago canadensis*)
Sunflower Family (Asteraceae)

Description: Tall, leafy, *finely hairy stem* has *tiny
yellow flower heads on arching branches* in a
long or flat-topped cluster at top.
Flowers: each head about ⅛" (3 mm)
long, with 3 short rays.
Leaves: 2–5" (5–12.5 cm) long,
lanceolate, finely hairy, with 3
prominent veins.
Fruit: seed-like, sparsely hairy, with
numerous pale bristles at top.
Height: 1–5' (30–150 cm).

Flowering: May–September.

Habitat: Meadows and open forest.

Range: Across Canada and throughout the
United States.

Comments: This handsome species produces showy
displays, usually late in the summer.
Although it and other Goldenrods are
commonly blamed for hay fever, this
discomfort is usually caused by pollen
from Ragweed (*Ambrosia* spp.), which
are less conspicuous plants with
greenish flowers that bloom at the
same time. Missouri Goldenrod

(*Solidago missouriensis*), is similar but
usually smaller, with smooth stems.

### 309 Narrow Goldenrod
(*Solidago spathulata*)
Sunflower Family (Asteraceae)

Description: Generally several stems in a clump with
largest leaves at the base and many
*small yellow flower heads in a narrow, long
cluster.*
Flowers: heads about ¼″ (6 mm) long,
with *5–10 (usually 8) rays* surrounding
the small disk.
Leaves: to 6″ (15 cm) long, lanceolate,
smooth, tapered to a smooth stalk-like
base.
Fruit: seed-like, topped with a tuft of
fine white bristles.
Height: 2–32″ (5–80 cm).
Flowering: June–September.
Habitat: Coastal sand dunes and open mountain
slopes and valleys.
Range: Across Canada south to the coast of
central California, and in mountains to
Arizona and New Mexico; also in
eastern United States.
Comments: These plants occupy a wide range of
habitats and are variable. Although
they occur well into the mountains, in
alpine regions they are replaced by
Alpine Goldenrod (*S. multiradiata*),
which is similar but with bristly hairs
on edges of the leaf stalks.

### 339 Northern Dune Tansy
(*Tanacetum douglasii*)
Sunflower Family (Asteraceae)

Description: A leafy, lightly hairy plant that grows
in patches; *leaves feathery,* aromatic
when crushed; stems topped by an *open
cluster of small, button-like yellow flower
heads.*
Flowers: heads about ½″ (1.3 cm) wide,

with disk and *inconspicuous ray flowers*.
Leaves: 2–8″ (5–20 cm) long, *pinnately divided, the lobes again pinnately divided* 1 or 2 times.
Fruit: seed-like, tipped with a minute crown of tiny scales.
Height: 8–24″ (20–60 cm).

Flowering: June–September.

Habitat: Sand dunes along the Pacific Coast.

Range: British Columbia to northern California.

Comments: This is closely related to the similar Camphor Dune Tansy (*T. camphoratum*), densely hairy and lacking rays, which grows only near the San Francisco Bay. Tansy (*T. vulgare*), with no hairs and a cluster of 20–200 heads, was widely used medicinally; it was brought from Europe to the New World, where it was planted in colonial gardens, from which it escaped into the wild. Tansy's poisonous oil caused abortions, whereas a tea made from its steeped leaves was used to prevent miscarriage, and crushed leaves were used to poultice sprains and bruises.

---

### 267  Common Dandelion
(*Taraxacum officinale*)
Sunflower Family (Asteraceae)

Description: A common weed, its yellow flower head topping a *hollow, leafless stalk* that rises from the center of a *rosette of toothed leaves*.
Flowers: heads ¾–1½″ (2–3.8 cm) wide, with *outer bracts short, curled back*, inner bracts longer, curling back when fruits mature; *flowers all of ray type*.
Leaves: 2–16″ (5–40 cm) long, lanceolate, broadest near tip, with jagged, backward-pointing lobes or teeth.
Fruit: seed-like, gray or olive brown, the body about ³⁄₁₆″ (4.5 mm) long, rough in upper portion, and tipped by a *stalk 2–4 times the length of body*,

bearing *white, feathery bristles* at the end.
Height: 2–20″ (5–50 cm).

Flowering: Mostly the winter months in the South; summer in the North.

Habitat: Lawns, pastures, fields, and roadsides.

Range: Throughout.

Comments: The popular name comes from *dent de lion,* French for "lion's tooth," referring to the teeth on the leaves. The young leaves may be used in salads and soups; wine is made from the heads. Several species, some native to high mountain meadows, are similar to the Common Dandelion but may have reddish-brown fruits and outer bracts that do not curl.

## 73 Stemless Daisy
(*Townsendia exscapa*)
Sunflower Family (Asteraceae)

Description: A *dwarf, tufted, nearly stemless plant* that has comparatively large flower heads nestled among *very narrow leaves,* and many *white or pinkish rays* surrounding a yellow disk.
Flowers: heads 1–2″ (2.5–5 cm) wide, with rays ½–¾″ (1.3–2 cm) long, bracts ½–⅝″ (1.3–1.5 cm) long.
Leaves: ¾–2″ (2–5 cm) long, erect, densely clustered.
Fruit: seed-like, flat, lightly hairy, bearing at top *rigid bristles* longer than the body.
Height: 1–2″ (2.5–5 cm).

Flowering: March–May.

Habitat: Dry open plains and barren places in open piñon and juniper woodland.

Range: Central Canada; south through Montana and North Dakota to western Texas; west to central and northern Arizona.

Comments: The several species of *Townsendia* are distinguished from the numerous, rather similar ones in *Erigeron* by the fine slender bristles atop the fruit.

### 269  Yellow Salsify
*(Tragopogon dubius)*
Sunflower Family (Asteraceae)

Description: Hollow stems, branched near the base,
have a few long, narrow, tapered leaves,
and at the top a *pale yellow head.* Sap
milky.
Flowers: heads 1½–2″ (3.8–5 cm)
wide, with flowers *all of ray type* about
½″ (1.3 cm) long, and 8–13 *bracts,
longer than the flowers.*
Leaves: 5–6″ (12.5–15 cm) long.
Fruit: seed-like, rough, brown, tapered
at both ends, topped with a slender
stalk tipped by *pale brown, feathery
bristles* nearly 1″ (2.5 cm) long.
Height: 16–32″ (40–80 cm).
Flowering: May–September.
Habitat: Roadsides, old lots, and fields.
Range: Throughout.
Comments: *Tragopogon,* Greek for "goat's beard,"
probably refers to the thin, tapering,
tufted, grass-like leaves. The
widespread Meadow Salsify (*T.
pratensis*) has yellow flowers and bracts
shorter than the flowers.

### 597  Salsify; Oyster Plant
*(Tragopogon porrifolius)*
Sunflower Family (Asteraceae)

Description: At the *swollen, hollow top* of a sparsely
leafy stem blooms a *purple flower head.*
Sap milky.
Flowers: heads 2–3″ (5–7.5 cm) wide,
with flowers *all of ray type,* outer about
¾″ (2 cm) long, and generally 8 or 9
tapered bracts.
Leaves: to 12″ (30 cm) long, narrow
and tapered.
Fruit: seed-like, brown, rough, tapered
at both ends, topped with a long stalk
tipped by *pale brown, feathery bristles*
about ¾″ (2 cm) long, like brown
parachutes arranged in a lacy
hemisphere 4–5″ (10–12.5 cm) wide.

Height: 20–48″ (50–120 cm).
Flowering: June–September.
Habitat: Fields, old lots, and roadsides.
Range: Throughout.
Comments: In the Mediterranean, Salsify has been cultivated for 2,000 years for the edible root, which has a flavor resembling that of an oyster or an artichoke. When a stalk bearing a bud is picked, milky sap oozes over the hollow cut end.

### 274 Yellow Head
(*Trichoptilium incisum*)
Sunflower Family (Asteraceae)

Description: A low, fragrant, lightly woolly plant with *small, rayless yellow flower heads* on stalks much taller than the *jagged leaves*.
Flowers: heads about ½″ (1.3 cm) wide, with a few *jagged, forward-pointing teeth on edges*.
Leaves: mostly near base, ¾–2″ (2–5 cm) long, lanceolate, tapered to a long stalk.
Fruit: seed-like, tipped with 5 white or pale tan scales with fringed edges.
Height: 2–8″ (5–20 cm).
Flowering: February–May, and October–November.
Habitat: Sandy or gravelly areas in deserts.
Range: Southeastern Arizona, southern Nevada, western Arizona, and northwestern Mexico.
Comments: *Trichoptilium* comes from Greek words meaning "hair" and "feather," referring to the fruit tip's dissected scales.

### 343 Trixis
(*Trixis californica*)
Sunflower Family (Asteraceae)

Description: A very leafy, branched shrub, often much broader than tall, with small, *yellow, rayless, flower heads among lanceolate leaves*.

Flowers: heads ¾″ (2 cm) long, each
corolla with 3 lobes, 2 lobes toward the
outside of the head narrow and curled,
1 toward the inside is broader, often
with 3 teeth at the tip; flowers
surrounded by leaf-like bracts, those
innermost long and narrow.
Leaves: ¾–2″ (2–5 cm) long, with
smooth edges or tiny teeth.
Fruit: seed-like, topped with straw-
colored bristles.
Height: 1–3′ (30–90 cm).
Flowering: February–October.
Habitat: Rocky slopes in deserts.
Range: Southern California to western Texas;
south to northern Mexico.
Comments: *Trixis,* from the Greek meaning
"threefold," refers to the 3-cleft corolla.

---

## 251 Cowpen Daisy
(*Verbesina encelioides*)
Sunflower Family (Asteraceae)

Description: A well-branched *grayish-green plant* with
mostly *opposite, toothed, nearly triangular
leaves* and *yellow flower heads.*
Flowers: heads 1½–2″ (3.8–5 cm)
wide, with *rays about ½″ (1.3 cm) long*
around the disk.
Leaves: 1–4″ (2.5–10 cm) long, with
coarse teeth on edges, the base
narrowed to a broad stalk.
Fruit: seed-like; those of disk flowers
with 2 slender, rigid bristles at tip;
none on fruit of ray flowers.
Height: 4–60″ (10–150 cm).
Flowering: June–September.
Habitat: Along roads, in pastures and on
rangeland, in washes, edges of fields.
Range: Central California to Arizona, New
Mexico, and Texas; north through
eastern Utah and Colorado to Montana;
east to Kansas and southeastern United
States; south into tropical America.
Comments: This plant, common on disturbed
ground and sometimes coloring acres or
miles of roadside solid yellow, was used

by Indians and early settlers to treat
skin ailments.

---

249 **Mule's Ears**
(*Wyethia amplexicaulis*)
Sunflower Family (Asteraceae)

Description: Plant seems *varnished with resin,* the
*stout leafy stems* growing from clumps of
*lanceolate leaves,* ending in several *large
deep yellow flower heads* on long stalks,
the central head largest.
Flowers: central head 3–5″ (7.5–12.5
cm) wide, with lanceolate bracts that
often extend past top of disk; about
13–21 rays and scales enfold bases of
disk flowers.
Leaves: those at base 8–24″ (20–60 cm)
long, with lanceolate blades on short
stalks; those on stem smaller, their
bases wrapped partly around the stem.
Fruit: seed-like, narrow, 4-sided, with
a low crown of scales at top.
Height: 12–32″ (30–80 cm).
Flowering: May–July.
Habitat: Open hillsides and meadows, open
woods, from foothills to moderate
elevations in mountains.
Range: Central Washington to western
Montana; south to northwestern
Colorado, northern Utah, and Nevada.
Comments: All species have leaves on the stem,
distinguishing them from *Balsamorhiza,*
which has all leaves at the base.

---

74 **White-rayed Mule's Ears**
(*Wyethia helianthoides*)
Sunflower Family (Asteraceae)

Description: *Stout, leafy, hairy stems* grow from a
cluster of basal leaves, and have at top a
flower head with *about 13 white or pale
cream rays* and a *yellow disk.*
Flowers: heads 2½–5″ (5–12.5 cm)
wide, with narrow bracts, hairy on

edges, and scales that enfold bases of flowers.

Leaves: those at base 3½–14″ (8.8–35 cm) long, elliptic, tapered to a short stalk; those on stem smaller.

Fruit: seed-like, narrow, 4-sided, with a crown of low scales at top.

Height: 6–32″ (15–80 cm).

Flowering: May–June.

Habitat: Moist meadows in mountains.

Range: From central Oregon to southwestern Montana, northwestern Wyoming, and northern Nevada.

Comments: This species, the only white-rayed *Wyethia,* often forms dense patches in low spots in valleys.

### 244 Little Golden Zinnia
(*Zinnia grandiflora*)
Sunflower Family (Asteraceae)

Description: Several short, leafy, slightly woody stems in a low, round clump have numerous small flower heads with 3–6 *nearly round yellow-orange rays.*

Flowers: *heads* 1–1½″ (2.5–3.8 cm) wide; disk flowers reddish or greenish; bracts overlap, with round, translucent tips.

Leaves: 1″ (2.5 cm) long, *very narrow, opposite,* with 3 veins at base.

Fruit: seed-like, usually with 1 or 2 spines at tip.

Height: 3–9″ (7.5–22.5 cm).

Flowering: June–October.

Habitat: Dry areas in desert and on plains.

Range: Eastern Arizona to southeastern Colorado and southwestern Kansas; south to Mexico.

Comments: The genus is named for Johann Zinn, an 18th century German professor, who collected seeds of *Z. elegans* (from which the garden *Zinnia* descends) in Mexico. There he was accosted by bandits who, after searching his bag, left him alone, believing him crazy and therefore unlucky.

## BARBERRY FAMILY
## (Berberidaceae)

Herbs or shrubs, with flowers in clusters or racemes and often with spiny leaves.
Flowers: radially symmetrical, single; sepals 4–6, often petal-like; petals 4–6; stamens 4–18, in two circles, with pollen sacs opening by little flaps.
Leaves: simple or compound.
Fruit: berry.
There are about 9 genera and nearly 600 species. A few Barberry species are cultivated as ornamentals. Common Barberry is a necessary host in the complex life cycle of wheat rust, a destructive parasitic fungus.

### 107 Vanilla Leaf; Deer Foot
(*Achlys triphylla*)
Barberry Family (Berberidaceae)

Description: *Pairs of low slender stalks grow in patches,* one stalk actually a petiole, having at its tip a round leaf blade with *3 broad, fan-shaped leaflets;* the other stalk ending in a narrow spike of *small white flowers.*
Flowers: spike 1–2″ (2.5–5 cm) long; the flowers without sepals or petals but with 6–13 white stamens, the outer ones swollen toward tip.
Leaves: leaflets 2–4″ (5–10 cm) long, with blunt teeth on ends, the central leaflet with 3–5 or up to 8 teeth.
Height: 10–20″ (25–50 cm).
Flowering: April–June.
Habitat: Woods.
Range: Southern British Columbia to near the coast of northern California; in California mostly outside the redwood region.
Comments: The large, 3-parted leaf is unusual, like that of its only close relative, California Vanilla Leaf (*A. californica*), found nearer the coast, but which generally

has 6–8 (rarely up to 12) teeth on the central leaflet.

## 348  Creeping Oregon Grape
(*Berberis repens*)
Barberry Family (Berberidaceae)

Description:  A plant with 2 or 3 *pinnately compound leaves with leathery, holly-like leaflets* on low, short stems ending in dense, branched clusters of *small yellow flowers.*
Flowers: about ½" (1.3 cm) wide; sepals 6, in 2 whorls; petals 6, also in 2 whorls, slightly shorter than sepals; 3 small bracts outside sepals; stamens 6, lying against petals and moving toward the single style when touched.
Leaves: 5–7 (occasionally 3 or 9) ovate spiny-margined leaflets 1¼–3" (3.1–7.5 cm) long, shiny on upper side.
Fruit: chalky-blue berry about ¼" (6 mm) wide.
Height: 4–8" (10–20 cm).

Flowering:  March–June.

Habitat:  Open pine forests.

Range:  Western Canada to northeastern California and southern Nevada; east to Colorado, western Texas, South Dakota, and western Montana.

Comments:  This plant grows from a creeping underground rhizome, its erect stems surfacing here and there in the woods. Another low-growing species, Cascade Oregon Grape (*B. nervosa*), found from southwestern British Columbia to central California, has 7–21 leaflets. A shrubby species, Tall Oregon Grape (*B. aquifolium*), is the state flower of Oregon. The berries are eaten by wildlife and make good jelly. Indians made a yellow dye from the bark and wood of shrubby species. Several are used as ornamentals; in the nursery trade those with pinnate leaves are known as Mahonia.

### 103 Northern Inside-out Flower
(*Vancouveria hexandra*)
Barberry Family (Berberidaceae)

Description: *Small, pointed white flowers* in open
clusters on smooth stalks supported by
leafless stems, and *leathery pinnately
compound leaves* that grow in patches.
Flowers: about ½" (1.3 cm) long; 6
*white sepals* (remaining on open flower;
more present earlier), sharply bent back
at base, but with tips arched outward;
6 white petals shorter than sepals, also
bent back. Pistil and 6 stamens form
point in center of flower.
Leaves: 4–16" (10–40 cm) long, *divided
2 or 3 times into 3-lobed leaflets* up to 1½"
(3.8 cm) long, nearly as broad.
Height: 6–20" (15–50 cm).

Flowering: May–July.

Habitat: Shady coniferous woods.

Range: Western Washington to northwestern
California.

Comments: This genus has only 3 species; in mild
climates they make excellent ground
cover for woodland gardens. Redwood
Inside-out Flower (*V. planipetala*), with
thick-edged leaflets and gland-tipped
hairs on the flower stalks, grows in
shady woods from southwestern Oregon
to central California, near the coast.
One, Golden Inside-out Flower (*V.
chrysantha*), has yellow flowers.

## TRUMPET CREEPER FAMILY
### (Bignoniaceae)

Trees, shrubs, or woody vines, occasionally herbs, with large, showy, clustered flowers.
Flowers: in clusters at ends of branches or at axils; bilaterally symmetrical; calyx 5-lobed; corolla funnelform, bell-shaped, or tubular, 5-lobed and often 2-lipped; stamens 2 or 4. All these parts attached at base of ovary.
Leaves: usually opposite, simple or pinnately or palmately compound.
Fruit: 2-valved capsule.
A tropical family of about 120 genera and 650 species, some used as handsome ornamentals.

---

### 575 Desert Willow
(*Chilopsis linearis*)
Trumpet Creeper Family (Bignoniaceae)

Description: A shrub or tree with narrow leaves and *large, pinkish bilateral flowers.*
Flowers: corolla, ¾–1½" (2–3.8 cm) long, 2-lipped with lower lip slightly longer than upper, varies from white blushed with pink, to pink or pale purple, usually with purple stripes and often with a yellow hue in the tube; 4 stamens have pollen sac, the fifth does not.
Leaves: willow-like, 4–12" (10–30 cm) long.
Fruit: pod, very slender, hanging, 6–12" (15–30 cm) long, containing numerous flat seeds with white membranous margins.
Height: 4–30' (1.2–9 m).
Flowering: April–September.
Habitat: Along desert washes, streams, and highways where water collects.
Range: Southern California to southern Texas; south into northern Mexico.
Comments: The habitat and resemblance of the leaves to those of the willow give the

common name, although there is no relationship between them. If allowed to grow, a stout shrub or small tree develops. The large flowers resemble those of the related Catalpa (*Catalpa*) and attract hummingbirds all season long.

## FORGET-ME-NOT OR BORAGE FAMILY (Boraginaceae)

Generally herbs, often covered with bristly hairs.

Flowers: radially symmetrical, often borne along one side of branch or stem tip in a coil like a fiddleneck; sepals 5, united at base; petals 5, united into a narrow tube and an abruptly flared top; around the small entry to the tube usually 5 small pads; stamens 5. All these parts attached near base of ovary.

Leaves: simple.

Fruit: separates into 4 hard seed-like sections (nutlets); or in a few species, fruit is a berry.

There are about 100 genera and 2,000 species, found mostly in warm or temperate regions. Forget-me-nots are grown as ornamentals.

---

### 372 Fiddleneck
(*Amsinckia retrorsa*)
Forget-me-not Family (Boraginaceae)

Description: *Coils of small yellow-orange flowers* grow at ends of branches; the leafy stems have both long, spreading, bristly hairs and very short, dense, downward-projecting ones.
Flowers: calyx with 5 narrow lobes; *corolla* about ⅛″ (3 mm) wide, all petals joined, forming a funnel with a narrow tube and an abruptly flared end.
Leaves: ¾–6″ (2–15 cm) long, narrowly or broadly lanceolate.
Fruit: divided into 4 grayish nutlets about ⅛″ (3 mm) long, somewhat wrinkled on the back and with a rough surface.
Height: 1–3′ (30–90 cm).
Flowering: April–May.
Habitat: Along roadsides, fields, and other dry, open places.
Range: Baja California to Arizona; north to Idaho and Washington.

Comments: The name Fiddleneck refers to the coiled inflorescence. As blooming proceeds the coil opens; maturing fruits are farther down the stem. The other western species have larger flowers.

---

### 566 Shrubby Coldenia
(*Coldenia greggii*)
Forget-me-not Family (Boraginaceae)

Description: A small, round, *gray shrub* with many twigs bearing *funnel-shaped pink or reddish-lavender flowers in small feathery clusters.*
Flowers: calyx with 5 very slender lobes of different lengths, about ⅜" (9 mm) long, with long hairs, feathery and purplish at maturity; corolla about ¼" (6 mm) long, with 5 round lobes.
Leaves: about ⅜" (9 mm) long, ovate, hairy.
Height: 4–20" (10–50 cm).
Flowering: March–August.
Habitat: Open limestone slopes.
Range: Southern New Mexico, western Texas, and northern Mexico.
Comments: The feathery calyx, surrounding and carrying the tiny one-seeded fruit, is blown by the wind.

---

### 312 Yellow Cryptantha
(*Cryptantha flava*)
Forget-me-not Family (Boraginaceae)

Description: A *hairy plant* with stems in clumps, the leaves at base largest, and with *coils of small yellow flowers* at the tips.
Flowers: corolla funnel-shaped, the narrow tube about ½" (1.3 cm) long, flaring abruptly into 5 lobes about ⅜" (9 mm) wide.
Leaves: ¾–4" (2–10 cm) long, narrowly lanceolate, those at base broadest.
Fruit: divided into 4 *smooth, glossy, gray*

*nutlets* about ³⁄₁₆″ (5 mm) long.
Height: 3–10″ (7.5–25 cm).
Flowering: April–August.
Habitat: Open sandy areas, common on plains and among juniper.
Range: Northeastern Arizona and northwestern New Mexico; north to southwestern Wyoming.
Comments: There are only two yellow species in the genus. The similar Mojave Popcorn Flower (*C. confertiflora*), occurs from central Utah and northwestern Arizona westward to the base of the Sierra Nevada.

### 644 Hound's Tongue
(*Cynoglossum grande*)
Forget-me-not Family (Boraginaceae)

Description: Several smooth stems with *large ovate leaves on long stalks* mostly near the base, and *loose clusters of deep blue flowers* on branches at the top.
Flowers: corolla about ½″ (1.3 cm) wide, with 5 petals joined into a funnel with *5 white, 2-lobed pads* around opening of tube.
Leaves: blades 3–16″ (7.5–40 cm) long, ovate, a few hairs on upper side, many on lower.
Fruit: divided into 4 hard, roundish nutlets ¼″ (6 mm) long, with *tiny barbed prickles* all over surface.
Height: 12–32″ (30–80 cm).
Flowering: March–June.
Habitat: Dry shaded places in woods.
Range: Southern California to western Washington.
Comments: The common name refers to the shape of the broad leaves. Indians used preparations from the root to treat burns and stomachaches. There are several species, all with blue or maroon flowers and large rough nutlets that stick to clothing.

### 578 Alpine Forget-me-not
(*Eritrichium nanum*)
Forget-me-not Family (Boraginaceae)

Description: A low, *cushion-like plant* with *deep blue flowers* just above the tufted leaves.
Flowers: corolla funnel-shaped, about ¼" (6 mm) wide, 5-lobed, with 5 yellow pads around the opening to the narrow tube.
Leaves: up to ½" (1.3 cm) long, lanceolate, covered with loose hairs.
Fruit: divided into 4 smooth nutlets.
Height: to 4" (10 cm).

Flowering: June–August.

Habitat: Open rocky places high in the mountains.

Range: Northern New Mexico to western Montana and northeastern Oregon; north to Alaska.

Comments: The genus name comes from the Greek *erion* ("wool") and *trichos* ("hair"), referring to the hairs on the plants, which on Howard's Alpine Forget-me-not (*E. howardii*) of western Montana and northern Wyoming are so dense they usually hide the leaf surface.

### 643 Many-flowered Stickseed; Wild Forget-me-not
(*Hackelia floribunda*)
Forget-me-not Family (Boraginaceae)

Description: *Small, pale blue, funnel-shaped flowers* grow in a long, open, branched cluster at top of one or a few leafy stems, *branches coiled at tips.*
Flowers: corolla about ¼" (6 mm) wide, with yellow pads around opening of the narrow tube.
Leaves: 1½–8" (3.8–20 cm) long, lanceolate, the lower with petioles, the upper without, becoming progressively smaller toward top of stem.
Fruit: divided into hard nutlets, *each with barbed prickles on edges* but none on back.

Height: 1–3′ (30–90 cm).
Flowering: June–August.
Habitat: Moist thickets and meadows, generally in coniferous forests.
Range: From Washington to northern California and southern Nevada; east to northern New Mexico, Colorado, and Montana.
Comments: It is the prickles on the nutlets that distinguish these plants from Forget-me-nots (*Myosotis*). The similar Jessica's Stickseed (*H. micrantha*), from the Sierra Nevada to Utah and Wyoming and northward into Canada, generally has several stems and several very small prickles on the back of each nutlet.

## 51 Sweet-scented Heliotrope
(*Heliotropium convolvulaceum*)
Forget-me-not Family (Boraginaceae)

Description: A hairy, sparsely-leaved plant with one erect, branched stem or many long, sprawling branches, the *fragrant, white, broadly funnel-shaped flowers* blooming in small coils along upper parts of stems.
Flowers: corolla ⅝–1″ (1.5–2.5 cm) wide, with 5 low lobes and, in the center, a yellow "eye" around the tiny opening of the narrow tube.
Leaves: up to 1½″ (3.8 cm) long, lanceolate or ovate, with short stalks.
Fruit: divided into 4 silky-hairy segments about ⅛″ (3 mm) long.
Height: 4–16″ (10–40 cm).
Flowering: March–October.
Habitat: Dunes and other sandy places in deserts and arid grasslands.
Range: Southeastern California to southern Utah, Wyoming, Nebraska, and western Texas; south to northern Mexico.
Comments: The fragrant flowers, largest of all Heliotropes in the West, open in the cool hours of the evening. The ornamental Common Heliotrope (*H. arborescens*), comes from Peru.

### 153 Quail Plant; Cola de Mico
(*Heliotropium curassavicum*)
Forget-me-not Family (Boraginaceae)

Description: *A fleshy, bluish-green, smooth plant,* with leafy stems mostly lying on the ground, usually with *paired coils of small white or purplish-tinged flowers.*
Flowers: corolla funnel-shaped, ³⁄₁₆–³⁄₈" (5–9 mm) wide, with 5 round lobes.
Leaves: ½–1½" (1.3–3.8 cm) long, spatula-shaped, sometimes broader toward the tip.
Fruit: divided into 4 small segments.
Height: creeper, the flowering branches up to 16" (40 cm) high, stems to 4' (1.2 m) long.
Flowering: March–October.
Habitat: Open alkaline or saline soil, often in sand or clay, common in beds of dried ponds.
Range: Western United States; east to the Great Plains and across southern United States; Mexico, South America.
Comments: In some parts of the West, it is named Quail Plant after the birds that feed on its fruits, but more frequently it has no common name. The Spanish name, meaning "monkey tail," describes the coiled flower cluster.

### 209 Fringed Gromwell; Puccoon
(*Lithospermum incisum*)
Forget-me-not Family (Boraginaceae)

Description: A hairy plant with several leafy stems in a clump, the *fringed, bright yellow, trumpet-shaped flowers* crowded in uppermost axils.
Flowers: corolla ½–1¼" (1.3–3.1 cm) long, with a narrow tube that abruptly flares into a 5-lobed top ½–¾" (1.3–2 cm) wide, the lobes finely and irregularly toothed.
Leaves: ¾–2½" (2–6.3 cm) long, narrowly lanceolate.
Fruit: divided into 4 *gray, shiny, hard*

nutlets about ⅛" (3 mm) long.
Height: 2–12" (5–30 cm).
Flowering: May–July.
Habitat: Dry open plains and foothills.
Range: British Columbia, western Montana,
Utah, and Arizona; east across Canada
to Ontario; south to Illinois and Texas.
Comments: The genus name means "stone seed,"
referring to the hard nutlets. This
species produces few fruits from the
showy flowers; instead, late in the
season inconspicuous flowers that
remain closed produce fruit in the lower
leaf axils. There are several species in
the West, one white-flowered, the rest
with shorter, yellow corollas.

331 **Wayside Gromwell; Puccoon**
(*Lithospermum ruderale*)
Forget-me-not Family (Boraginaceae)

Description: Several or many leafy stems in a clump
produce, in the upper axils, clusters of
*5-lobed light yellow flowers.*
Flowers: corolla funnel-shaped, ¼–½"
(6–13 mm) wide.
Leaves: 1¼–4" (3.1–10 cm) long,
numerous, lanceolate, hairy.
Fruit: divided into *4 shiny, gray nutlets,*
often only 1 or 2 produced, ⅛–¼" (3–
6 mm) long.
Height: 8–24" (20–60 cm).
Flowering: April–June.
Habitat: Open places in sagebrush, juniper, or
pine.
Range: Northeastern California to western
Colorado; north to western Canada.
Comments: Puccoon, an Indian word for plants
which yield dye, alludes to the purple
dye extracted from the roots of several
species.

### 290 Green-flowered Macromeria
(*Macromeria viridiflora*)
Forget-me-not Family (Boraginaceae)

Description: A *hairy, leafy plant* with several stout
stems in a clump, and *pale, hairy,
trumpet-shaped flowers in large coils* at the
ends of upper branches.
Flowers: corolla 1½" (3.8 cm) long,
pale greenish-yellow, with 5 pointed
lobes; 5 stamens protruding slightly.
Leaves: 2–5" (5–12.5 cm) long,
broadly lanceolate, largest near base and
progressively smaller toward the top.
Height: to 3' (90 cm).
Flowering: July–September.
Habitat: Rocky slopes and valleys in pine woods,
moderate to high elevations.
Range: Southern New Mexico and eastern
Arizona; south to Mexico.
Comments: The flowers are long for the family. Its
leaves and flowers were dried and mixed
with wild tobacco for Hopi "rain-
bringing" ceremonies.

### 648 Mountain Bluebell
(*Mertensia ciliata*)
Forget-me-not Family (Boraginaceae)

Description: A plant with clumps of leafy stems and
loose clusters of *narrowly bell-shaped,
blue flowers turning pink with age.*
Flowers: corolla 5-lobed, ½–¾" (1.3–2
cm) long, tubular part same length as
the bell-like end.
Leaves: 1¼–6" (3.1–15 cm) long,
tapered at base, the lower on long
petioles.
Fruit: divided into 4 small, wrinkled
segments.
Height: 6–60" (15–150 cm).
Flowering: May–August.
Habitat: Stream banks, seeps, and wet meadows.
Range: Central Idaho to central Oregon and the
Sierra Nevada; east to western
Montana, western Colorado, and
northern New Mexico.

Comments:    Mertensias are also called Lungworts,
after a European species with spotted
leaves which was believed to be a
remedy for lung disease. Similar species
differ in the proportions of the corolla.

152    **Popcorn Flower**
(*Plagiobothrys nothofulvus*)
Forget-me-not Family (Boraginaceae)

Description:    A slender, hairy plant with most leaves
in a basal tuft and *small white flowers in
a coil* at the ends of a few branches or
branchless stems.
Flowers: brownish-hairy calyx with 5
narrow lobes; 5-lobed corolla ¼″ (6
mm) wide, the flat top with 5 yellow
pads surrounding the narrow opening of
the short tube.
Leaves: those at base in tuft, ¾−4″ (2−
10 cm) long, spatula-shaped; those on
stem becoming progressively smaller
toward the top.
Fruit: divided into 4 small nutlets.
Height: 6−20″ (15−50 cm).
Flowering:    March−May.
Habitat:    Open places, commonly in grass.
Range:    South-central Washington to northern
Baja California.
Comments:    Open flowers are clustered at the top of
the coil, resembling pieces of popcorn.
Popcorn Flower is similar to
Cryptantha, but generally Popcorn
Flower is more softly hairy and grows
in moister places. Many species have a
purple dye in the stem and roots.
When they are pressed and dried in a
folded sheet of clean paper, a striking
mirror-image pattern results.

## MUSTARD FAMILY
### (Brassicaceae or Cruciferae)

Herbs, often with peppery sap.
Flowers: usually radially symmetrical,
in racemes; sepals 4, separate; petals 4,
separate, the base of each often long
and slender; stamens usually 6, with 2
outer shorter than the inner 4. All these
parts attached near base of ovary.
Leaves: usually simple, but sometimes
pinnately divided.
Fruit: pod, either long and narrow
(silique) or short and relatively broader
(silicle), divided into 2 chambers by
parchment-like partition.
There are about 375 genera and 3,200
species, found mostly in cooler regions
of the Northern Hemisphere. The
family is economically important,
providing vegetables, spices, and
ornamentals. Some species are
unwelcome weeds, a few poisonous to
livestock.

---

**333 Charlock**
(*Brassica kaber*)
Mustard Family (Brassicaceae)

Description: A hairy, leafy plant with *many racemes of
yellow flowers* at the ends of almost
leafless branches.
Flowers: petals 4, each ½" (1.3 cm)
long.
Leaves: largest at base, with stalks,
pinnately lobed, the blade with several
pairs of lobes, and teeth on edges;
progressing upward, leaves have shorter
stalks, less prominent lobes and finally
none of each.
Fruit: *slender, smooth, round pod,* 1¼–
2½" (3.1–6.3 cm) long, with a *solid,
pointed, flat beak* ½–1" (1.3–2.5 cm)
long at tip.
Height: 1–3' (30–90 cm).
Flowering: January–June.
Habitat: Fields, roadsides, and old lots.

Range: Throughout.
Comments: Occasionally seeds have been used for mustard, but table mustard comes mostly from Black Mustard (*B. nigra*).

---

## 157  Shepherd's Purse
(*Capsella bursa-pastoris*)
Mustard Family (Brassicaceae)

Description: *Flat, triangular pods* are attached by their pointed ends to fine stalks along the main stem of this small plant, which is topped by tiny white flowers.
Flowers: about ⅛″ (3 mm) wide, with 4 white petals.
Leaves: 1–2½″ (2.5–6.3 cm) long, lanceolate in outline, shallowly or deeply lobed.
Fruit: about ¼″ (6 mm) long, shallowly notched across broad end.
Height: 6–16″ (15–40 cm).
Flowering: Throughout the year, early in the South, later in the North.
Habitat: Gardens, lots, and edges of fields.
Range: Throughout.
Comments: *Capsella* means "little box," referring to the fruit, as does *bursa-pastoris* ("purse of the shepherd").

---

## 133  Heartleaved Bittercress
(*Cardamine cordifolia*)
Mustard Family (Brassicaceae)

Description: Several or many leafy stems with *white flowers* grow from an extensive system of underground runners.
Flowers: petals 4, ½–¾″ (1.3–2 cm) long.
Leaves: ¾–4″ (2–10 cm) wide, roundish blades with shallowly scalloped margins, indented at base; leaf stalks 2–5 times the length of blades.
Fruit: pods ¾–1½″ (2–3.8 cm) long, slightly flat, slender.

Height: 4–32" (10–80 cm).
Flowering: June–September.
Habitat: Along mountain stream banks, in streams and alpine meadows.
Range: British Columbia; south to northern California; east to New Mexico, Wyoming, and Idaho.
Comments: Some plants in this family were reputed to have medicinal qualities that were used in the treatment of heart ailments. Among the several species in the West, most have pinnately parted or lobed leaves.

## 159 Hoary Cress; White Top
(*Cardaria draba*)
Mustard Family (Brassicaceae)

Description: Patches of leafy stems, branched near the top and bearing *numerous tiny white flowers* in racemes, grow from an extensive underground system of runners. Leaves and stems grayish with dense hairs.
Flowers: petals 4, ⅛" (3 mm) long; 4 sepals drop upon opening.
Leaves: 1½–4" (3.8–10 cm) long, oblong, pointed at tip, edges with small teeth, *base of blade attached to stem in notch between 2 backward-projecting pointed lobes.*
Fruit: pod about ¼" (6 mm) wide, roundish, slightly flat, smooth, 2-lobed, 1 seed in each lobe.
Height: 8–20" (20–50 cm).
Flowering: April–August.
Habitat: Roadsides, fields, and old lots.
Range: Nearly throughout.
Comments: A second but less common species, Globepodded Hoary Cress (*C. pubescens*), is distinguished by its downy pod.

### 391  Desert Candle; Squaw Cabbage
(*Caulanthus inflatus*)
Mustard Family (Brassicaceae)

Description:  A *stout, swollen, hollow, yellow-green stem*
with a few leaves, mostly near the base,
and many narrow flowers in a raceme.
Flowers: about ½″ (1.3 cm) long; petals
4, narrow, white, crinkled near tip;
sepals 4, whitish or purplish-brown.
Leaves: 1¼–3″ (3.1–7.5 cm) long,
pointed, with 2 backward-projecting
lobes at base on each side of stem.
Fruit: pods 2½–4″ (6.3–10 cm) long,
narrow, erect.
Height: 1–2′ (30–60 cm).

Flowering:  March–May.

Habitat:  Sandy or gravelly soils on dry open
slopes in brush or deserts.

Range:  Southern California and southwestern
Nevada.

Comments:  These weird-looking plants resemble
candles. Wild Cabbage (*C. crassicaulis*),
is similar but lacks backward-projecting
lobes on leaves and its sepals and petals
are purplish or brownish; it generally
grows among sagebrush from western
Nevada to southern Idaho, western
Wyoming, and northwestern Colorado.

### 134  Spectacle Pod
(*Dithyrea wislizenii*)
Mustard Family (Brassicaceae)

Description:  A grayish, hairy plant, either branched
or unbranched, with pinnately lobed
leaves and *white flowers* in dense, thick
racemes.
Flowers: petals 4, about ½″ (1.3 cm)
long.
Leaves: at base up to 6″ (15 cm) long,
edges deeply pinnately lobed; those on
stem shorter and generally less deeply
indented.
Fruit: pod nearly ½″ (1.3 cm) wide,
*flat, with 2 round lobes*.
Height: to 2′ (60 cm).

Flowering: February–May and often again after summer rains.

Habitat: Open sandy soil in dry grassland and deserts.

Range: Western Oklahoma and western Texas to southern Utah, western Arizona, and northern Mexico.

Comments: The genus name means "two shields" in Greek and refers to the pod, which resembles a pair of spectacles. A second species, California Spectacle Pod (*D. californica*), which grows in western Arizona, southern Nevada, southern California, and northwestern Mexico, has shallowly lobed, yellowish-green leaves.

---

131 **Lance-leaved Draba**
(*Draba lanceolata*)
Mustard Family (Brassicaceae)

Description: Small *white flowers* in open racemes grow from densely velvety, grayish basal rosettes.
Flowers: petals 4, about ³⁄₁₆″ (5 mm) long, notched at tip.
Leaves: most in basal rosette ½–1¼″ (1.3–3.1 cm) long, their edges smooth or with small teeth; those on stem smaller, with teeth.
Fruit: pods ¼–½″ (6–13 mm) long, flat, lanceolate, generally slightly twisted.
Height: 2–10″ (5–25 cm).

Flowering: May–July.

Habitat: Dry open meadows and rock crevices high in the mountains.

Range: Central Colorado to Nevada; north to Alaska; east to the Atlantic Coast.

Comments: There are about 300 species in the family, distinguished mostly by technical features. Small, tufted, alpine plants with short, flat or swollen pods are likely to be *Draba*.

## 216  Comb Draba
(*Draba oligosperma*)
Mustard Family (Brassicaceae)

Description:  This small, grayish, hairy, *densely tufted plant* with basal leaves has small yellow flowers in racemes on leafless stalks. Entire surface of plant is covered with microscopic hairs that lie flat, each with a main axis and perpendicular branches on either side (similar to 2 combs back to back).
Flowers: petals 4, slightly more than ⅛" (3 mm) long.
Leaves: ⅛–½" (3–13 mm) long, very narrow.
Fruit: pods ⅛–⅜" (3–9 mm) long, flat, oval, smooth or bearing hairs similar to those on leaves.
Height: ½–4" (1.3–10 cm).

Flowering:  May–July.

Habitat:  Open slopes and ridges from moderate to high mountain elevations.

Range:  Western Canada; south to the central Sierra Nevada of California, western Nevada, Utah, and Colorado.

Comments:  This is one of many tufted species with yellow flowers, distinguished in part by technical characteristics of the hairs.

## 326  Plains Wallflower
(*Erysimum asperum*)
Mustard Family (Brassicaceae)

Description:  *Erect, leafy stems,* branched in upper part, have dense racemes of *bright yellow flowers at top.*
Flowers: ½–1" (1.3–2.5 cm) wide; petals 4, each with a long slender base and a broad tip spreading at right angles.
Leaves: 1–5" (2.5–12.5 cm) long, crowded, sometimes with teeth.
Fruit: very slender 4-sided pod 3–5" (7.5–12.5 cm) long, projecting upward at an angle from the stem, not pressed against it.

Height: 6–14″ (15–35 cm).
Flowering: April–July
Habitat: On open hills and plains.
Range: Central Canada to Texas, most frequent east of the Rocky Mountains, but found sporadically to the Cascades and Sierra Nevada.
Comments: This species is very closely related to Western Wallflower (*E. capitatum*), which is taller and has erect pods, and many botanists consider the two as one species, *E. asperum*.

### 367 Western Wallflower
(*Erysimum capitatum*)
Mustard Family (Brassicaceae)

Description: Erect stems, unbranched or branched in the upper parts, with narrow leaves, end in a dense raceme of *showy orange, burnt-orange, or orange-maroon, or yellow flowers*.
Flowers: about ¾″ (2 cm) wide, petals 4.
Leaves: 1–5″ (2.5–12.5 cm) long, in a basal rosette and all along stem except uppermost parts, narrowly lanceolate, with small teeth on edges.
Fruit: pod 2–4″ (5–10 cm) long, very slender, with 4 sides, held erect or nearly so.
Height: 6–36″ (15–90 cm).
Flowering: March–July.
Habitat: Dry stony banks, slopes, and open flats.
Range: British Columbia and Idaho; south to southern California and New Mexico.
Comments: This handsome and variable species intergrades with the more eastern Plains Wallflower (*E. asperum*). Pale Wallflower (*E. occidentale*), with flat pods, grows with sagebrush in eastern Washington and Oregon, southern Idaho and northern Nevada.

### 327  Menzies' Wallflower
(*Erysimum menziesii*)
Mustard Family (Brassicaceae)

Description:  A few short branches at base, and one
short erect stem, end in *dense, thick
racemes of bright orange-yellow flowers.*
Flowers: ½–¾″ (1.3–2 cm) wide;
petals 4.
Leaves: largest at base, 1¼–3½″ (3.1–
8.8 cm) long, spatula-shaped,
sometimes very shallowly lobed, blunt
at tip.
Fruit: slender pod 1½–3″ (3.8–7.5 cm)
long, flat, stiffly standing out from
stem.
Height: 1–8″ (2.5–20 cm).

Flowering:  Mostly March–May.

Habitat:  Coastal dunes.

Range:  Northern two-thirds of California.

Comments:  This lovely coastal wildflower will form
low, conical mounds of solid yellow-
orange when in full bloom. Several
other species grow along the Pacific
Coast.

### 325  Alpine Wallflower
(*Erysimum nivale*)
Mustard Family (Brassicaceae)

Description:  A low plant with several short stems
growing from *tufts of basal leaves* and
*yellow flowers* in compact racemes.
Flowers: ½–¾″ (1.3–2 cm) wide,
petals 4.
Leaves: 1¼–2½″ (3.1–6.3 cm) long,
very narrow, edges smooth, toothed, or
shallowly indented and with roundish
teeth.
Fruit: pods 1¼–3″ (3.1–7.5 cm) long,
erect or nearly so.
Height: 2–8″ (5–20 cm).

Flowering:  June–July.

Habitat:  Alpine tundra in mountains.

Range:  Colorado and eastern Utah.

Comments:  The scientific name *nivale* means "of
snow," referring to its habitat.

15 **Flatpod**
(*Idahoa scapigera*)
Mustard Family (Brassicaceae)

Description: A tiny plant with a basal rosette of leaves and several slender, leafless stems each tipped with *1 minute white flower* or a *round flat pod.*
Flowers: petals 4, about ⅛" (3 mm) long.
Leaves: blades ¼–⅝" (6–15 mm) long, ovate, on petioles up to 3 times as long.
Fruit: pod ¼–½" (6–13 mm) wide; green, often mottled with reddish brown.
Height: 1–5" (2.5–12.5 cm).
Flowering: February–April.
Habitat: Open places in grassland or among sagebrush, commonly where moist early in season.
Range: Northern California to eastern Washington, southern Idaho, and northern Nevada.
Comments: When the 2 sides of the pod fall away, the silvery partition remains attached to the tip of the flower stalk.

340 **Yellow Peppergrass**
(*Lepidium flavum*)
Mustard Family (Brassicaceae)

Description: Several stems, brittle at the joints, lie on the ground; only the *dense, short racemes of yellow flowers* are turned upward.
Flowers: petals 4, about ⅛" (3 mm) long.
Leaves: ¾–2" (2–5 cm) long, the larger ones pinnately lobed.
Fruit: pod, ⅛" (3 mm) long, flat, oval.
Height: creeper, the flower clusters about 2" (5 cm) high, stems 4–16" (10–40 cm) long.
Flowering: March–June.
Habitat: Low flats in deserts.
Range: Southeastern California and southern

Nevada to Baja California.

Comments: Yellow Peppergrass, often so common it colors broad expanses of the desert yellow, has seeds with a peppery flavor.

---

## 135  Western Peppergrass
(*Lepidium montanum*)
Mustard Family (Brassicaceae)

Description: Many slender branches form a round plant, each branch ending in a short, dense raceme of *minute white flowers*.
Flowers: petals 4, each ⅛″ (3 mm) long.
Leaves: at base about 1½–3″ (3.8–7.5 cm) long, deeply and sharply pinnately lobed; ones on stem smaller and often not lobed.
Fruit: pods ⅛″ (3 mm) long, ovate, flat, style at tip longer than tiny notch in which it grows.
Height: to 16″ (40 cm).

Flowering: March–June and sometimes again after summer rains.

Habitat: Dry open areas in deserts and rangeland, occurring with creosotebush, sagebrush, piñon, and juniper.

Range: Southeastern Oregon to southern California; east to western Texas, central Wyoming, and central Colorado.

Comments: There are at least 15 races of this species, but in this region any perennial rather bushy Mustard with small white flowers is likely to be Western Peppergrass. The showiest species is Fremont's Peppergrass (*L. fremontii*), from southeastern California to southwestern Utah, western Arizona, and northwestern Mexico. It has white flowers with petals ³⁄₁₆″ (5 mm) long and pods resembling broad hearts about ¼″ (6 mm) wide.

### 217 Fendler's Bladderpod
(*Lesquerella fendleri*)
Mustard Family (Brassicaceae)

Description: *Yellow flowers* bloom in loose, short
racemes at the ends of the stems of this
low, rather *tightly tufted, silvery-gray*
*perennial* whose surfaces are covered
with tiny star-like scales.
Flowers: petals 4, about ½" (1.3 cm)
wide.
Leaves: up to 4" (10 cm) long,
lanceolate or strap-shaped, those at base
sometimes with a few teeth on edges.
Fruit: nearly spherical pod, ¼–⅜"
(6–9 mm) long, smooth.
Height: 1–16" (2.5–40 cm).

Flowering: March–June and often again after
summer rains.

Habitat: Rocky or sandy soil, especially that
derived from limestone, in arid
grassland or deserts.

Range: Western Kansas to southern Utah;
south through eastern Arizona, New
Mexico, and western Texas to northern
Mexico.

Comments: One of the earliest plants to flower in
its area, its bright yellow is conspicuous
against the drab ground of early spring.
In the same region is the similar
Gordon's Bladderpod (*L. gordonii*),
which has several slender stems that lie
on the ground, turning up at the tips.
Unlike Fendler's Bladderpod, it is an
annual, not tufted, and also has a more
open appearance.

### 441 Honesty
(*Lunaria annua*)
Mustard Family (Brassicaceae)

Description: Leafy, freely branched stems with a few
*deep reddish-brown flowers* in racemes and
*hanging flat, oval pods.*
Flowers: about ¾" (2 cm) wide;
petals 4.
Leaves: 1½–4" (3.8–10 cm) long,

heart-shaped, the lower on long stalks, the upper without stalks.
Fruit: pod 1½–2″ (3.8–5 cm) long.
Height: 20–40″ (50–100 cm).
Flowering: May–June.
Habitat: Partly shaded moist areas.
Range: Central Washington to central California.
Comments: A native of Europe. When the sides of the pod fall away, the glistening white parchment-like partition between the halves remains, suggesting the genus name, from the Latin *luna* ("moon").

---

132 **Watercress**
(*Nasturtium officinale*)
Mustard Family (Brassicaceae)

Description: The leafy, branched stems of this plant mostly float in water or lie on mud, their *tiny white flowers blooming in short racemes* on the upturned tips.
Flowers: petals 4, about $\frac{3}{16}$″ (5 mm) long.
Leaves: 1½–5″ (3.8–12.5 cm) long, pinnate, leaflets ovate, terminal leaflet largest.
Fruit: slender pods, each ½–1″ (1.3–2.5 cm) long, gently curved, pointed upward.
Height: creeper, the flower stalks about 4″ (10 cm) high, stems to 24″ (60 cm) long.
Flowering: March–October.
Habitat: Quiet streams and freshwater ponds.
Range: Throughout.
Comments: Leaves add a mild peppery flavor to salads. *Nasturtium* comes from the Latin *nasi tortium* ("distortion of the nose"), referring to the plant's pungency. Although the large, orange-flowered garden Nasturtium (*Tropaeolum majus*) also has a sharp flavor, it is not related.

## 32 Velvety Nerisyrenia
(*Nerisyrenia camporum*)
Mustard Family (Brassicaceae)

Description: This *grayish, hairy plant* has clumps of leafy, branched stems and bears at the ends of branches *racemes of white or lavender flowers.*
Flowers: about ¾" (2 cm) wide; petals 4.
Leaves: ½–2½" (1.3–6.3 cm) long, lanceolate, toothed, with short stalks.
Fruit: pods ½–1½" (1.3–3.8 cm) long, narrow, 4-sided, and slightly flattened, held erect, the partition in center of pod perpendicular to broad sides.
Height: 8–24" (20–60 cm).
Flowering: February–October.
Habitat: Gravelly or rocky soils derived from limestone, or on limestone in deserts and arid grassland.
Range: Western Texas, southwestern New Mexico, and northern Mexico.
Comments: This is the most common species of Mustard with large white flowers in the region.

## 541 Dagger Pod
(*Phoenicaulis cheiranthoides*)
Mustard Family (Brassicaceae)

Description: Several short, smooth, somewhat shiny, unbranched stems grow from grayish basal tufts of leaves, ending in dense *racemes of pink or purplish flowers.*
Flowers: about ½" (1.3 cm) wide; petals 4.
Leaves: 1¼–6" (3.1–15 cm) long, lanceolate, broader above middle, tapered to a slender petiole.
Fruit: pods, each ¾–3" (2–7.5 cm) long, flat, narrow, pointed, *standing almost straight out from stem.*
Height: 2–8" (5–20 cm).
Flowering: April–June.
Habitat: Among sagebrush and in ponderosa pine woods.

Range:   Central Washington to northern
         California, northern Nevada, and
         southern Idaho.
Comments: This is the only species in this genus.
         When the pods dry, the entire
         flowering stem breaks at the base and is
         tumbled away by the wind.

## 328 Double Bladderpod
   (*Physaria didymocarpa*)
   Mustard Family (Brassicaceae)

Description:   *Silvery plants* with a basal rosette of
              leaves, stems lying on the ground, their
              turned-up tips with *dense racemes of
              yellow flowers.*
              Flowers: about ½" (1.3 cm) wide;
              petals 4.
              Leaves: ¾–3" (2–7.5 cm) long; blades
              roundish, often with a few small teeth,
              on long stalks.
              Fruit: pod ⅜–¾" (9–20 mm) long, at
              least as broad, with *2 round, swollen
              lobes.*
              Height: creeper, flowers about 3" (7.5
              cm) high, stems up to 7" (17.5 cm)
              long.
Flowering:   June–August.
Habitat:   Dry rocky or gravelly areas in foothills
           and in mountains, commonly with
           sagebrush or pine.
Range:   From Alberta south to Wyoming; west
         to northeastern Washington.
Comments: *Physaria* comes from Greek *physa*
         meaning "bellows," which refers to the
         swollen pod halves. There are 14
         species in the West, with most
         occurring in dry, mountain areas.

## 332 Hedge Mustard
   (*Sisymbrium officinale*)
   Mustard Family (Brassicaceae)

Description:   A hairy plant with most leaves in lower
              half, branches in upper part ending in

*racemes of small, pale yellow flowers.*
Flowers: petals 4, about ³⁄₁₆″ (5 mm) long.
Leaves: those near base to 8″ (20 cm) long, oblong, deeply pinnately cleft, with end lobe largest, and edges irregularly toothed; upper leaves much smaller, narrow, with a few narrow lobes.
Fruit: pods, each ³⁄₈–⁵⁄₈″ (9–15 mm) long, slender, tapered from base to tip, *erect and pressed against stem,* on which hairs stand out or point downward.
Height: 1–3′ (30–90 cm).

Flowering: March–September.
Habitat: Fields, roadsides, and vacant lots.
Range: Throughout, but more frequent west of the Sierra Nevada and the Cascade Mountains.
Comments: Originally from Europe. There are 2 other common weedy relatives: Tumblemustard (*S. altissimum*), with rigidly spreading pods, each 2–4″ (5–10 cm) long, and Loesel Tumblemustard (*S. loeselii*), with slender erect pods, each ³⁄₄–1¹⁄₂″ (2–3.8 cm) long, held away from stem.

---

### 136 Western Smelowskia
(*Smelowskia calycina*)
Mustard Family (Brassicaceae)

Description: A *gray, matted plant with white or purplish flowers* in dense racemes held well above thick clusters of basal leaves.
Flowers: petals 4, each about ¹⁄₄″ (4–8 mm) long.
Leaves: 1–2¹⁄₂″ (2.5–6.3 cm) long, oblong, *pinnately divided into narrow segments,* on stiffly hairy stalks as long as blades.
Fruit: pods, each ¹⁄₄–¹⁄₂″ (6–13 mm) long, lanceolate, held erect.
Height: 2–8″ (5–20 cm).

Flowering: May–August.
Habitat: Dry open slopes at high elevations.
Range: Western Canada; south in mountains to

Washington, northern Nevada, Utah, and central Colorado.

Comments: The genus name honors T. Smelowsky, an 18th-century Russian botanist. A second species, Alpine Smelowskia (*S. ovalis*), whose pods are each ⅛–¼" (3–6 mm) long and whose petioles lack stiff hairs, grows in mountains from central Washington to central Oregon, and in northeastern California.

## 307 Desert Plume; Golden Prince's Plume
(*Stanleya pinnata*)
Mustard Family (Brassicaceae)

Description: *Slender wands of yellow flowers* top tall, stout, smooth, bluish-green, leafy stems.
Flowers: *petals 4, yellow,* ⅜–⅝" (9–15 mm) long, densely hairy on inner side of brownish base; sepals 4, yellow.
Leaves: at base 2–6" (5–15 cm) long, pinnately divided, broadly lanceolate; those on stem smaller, often also pinnately divided.
Fruit: pod 1¼–2½" (3.1–6.3 cm) long, very slender, each on slender stalk ½–¾" (1.3–2 cm) long joined to slightly thicker stalk.
Height: 1½–5' (45–150 cm).

Flowering: May–July.

Habitat: Deserts and plains to lower mountains, often with sagebrush.

Range: Southeastern Oregon to southeastern California; east to western Texas; north to western North Dakota.

Comments: This is a conspicuous wildflower in the arid West, its flowers generally standing above any nearby shrubs. All other species have yellow flowers without hairs except White Desert Plume (*S. albescens*), which has hairs on the inside of its white petals. It occurs from northeastern Arizona to west-central Colorado and northwestern New Mexico.

### 315 Arizona Jewel Flower; Arizona Twist Flower
(*Streptanthus arizonicus*)
Mustard Family (Brassicaceae)

Description: A smooth, bluish-green plant with small *flask-shaped pale yellow or cream flowers* (sometimes purplish-tinged) in open racemes at the ends of the few erect branches.
Flowers: about ½" (1.3 cm) long; sepals 4; petals 4, narrow, crinkled.
Leaves: about 4" (10 cm) long, pinnately lobed or undivided, with backward-projecting lobes at base on each side of stem.
Fruit: pods, each 1¼–2½" (3.1–6.3 cm) long, slender, flat, held nearly erect.
Height: 1–2' (30–60 cm).
Flowering: January–April.
Habitat: Open gravelly or sandy areas from deserts to open piñon and juniper woodland.
Range: Central and southern Arizona to south-central New Mexico and northern Mexico.
Comments: A very similar species, Pecos Twist Flower (*S. carinatus*), with narrow petals but violet flowers, grows mostly on limestone from western Texas to southern Arizona.

### 316, 382 Mountain Jewel Flower
(*Streptanthus tortuosus*)
Mustard Family (Brassicaceae)

Description: A branched plant with heart-shaped or round leaves and green racemes of *flask-shaped pale yellow or cream to dark brownish-purple flowers*.
Flowers: ½" (1.3 cm) long, petals 4, crinkled, whitish with purple veins; sepals 4.
Leaves: ¾–3½" (2–8.8 cm) long, clasping, often slightly cupped, concave side downward.

Fruit: slender pod 2½–5″ (6.3–
12.5 cm) long, arched and spreading.
Height: 8–40″ (20–100 cm).
Flowering: May–August.
Habitat: Dry rocky slopes.
Range: Southern Oregon to southern
California, west of the Sierra Nevada.
Comments: One of the most widespread and
variable species in this western genus.
Heartleaf Jewel Flower (*S. cordatus*) is
very similar, but grows east of the
Sierra Nevada and Cascade Mountains.

## 156  Wild Candytuft
(*Thlaspi montanum*)
Mustard Family (Brassicaceae)

Description: From basal rosettes of leaves grow one
or several short, unbranched stems that
have small, arrow-shaped leaves and
end in *dense racemes of tiny white flowers.*
Flowers: petals 4, each ¼″ (6 mm)
long.
Leaves: at base ½–2½″ (1.3–6.3 cm)
long, with ovate blades which abruptly
taper to a slender petiole; those on stem
smaller, without petioles.
Fruit: pods ³⁄₁₆–½″ (5–13 mm) long,
flat, ovate, bluntly pointed at tip and
distinctly notched.
Height: 1¼–16″ (3.1–40 cm).
Flowering: February–August.
Habitat: Open slopes in mountains from
moderate to high elevations.
Range: British Columbia to northern
California; east to the Rocky Mountains
from Alberta to southern New Mexico
and western Texas.
Comments: Candytufts resemble some
Peppergrasses, but in each chamber of
Candytufts' tiny pods there are 2 seeds;
in Peppergrasses', 1.

# CACTUS FAMILY (Cactaceae)

Succulent, mostly leafless, commonly spiny herbs and shrubs.

Flowers: often showy, radially symmetrical, blooming singly on sides or near top of stem; many separate sepals, often petal-like; many separate petals, the bases of both may be fused into a long tube above the ovary; many stamens. All these parts attached near base of ovary.

Stems: varying from low and spherical to cylindrical or flat; in some genera divided into sections (joints) that may break off easily; raised ribs or nipples may be present.

Spines: needle-like or flat, in clusters or absent.

Fruit: berry-like, fleshy or dry, large or small, with many seeds.

About 140 genera have perhaps 2,000 species, mostly occurring in the warm parts of the Americas. In primitive, tropical species there are normal-looking leaves, but in dry, hot western habitats leaves of Cacti are very small and drop early, or are entirely absent. Reduction of leaves, along with the compact shape of the stem, is a water-conserving adaptation, for overall surface area is reduced. There are several other adaptations aiding survival in this harsh environment. Root systems are shallow, absorbing from brief showers water that is stored in the succulent stems. Pores (stomates) in the skin (epidermis) open during the cool night, allowing entry of carbon dioxide, which is chemically stored; during the day the carbon dioxide is used in photosynthesis. Spines discourage eating of the plants by animals in regions where there is little other green growth for food; they reflect light and heat, and also shade the surface, aiding to keep the plant cool. Many are grown as succulent novelties, and collecting of Cacti, a popular hobby, has brought some rarer species near extinction.

## 183  Saguaro; Giant Cactus
(*Cereus gigantea*)
Cactus Family (Cactaceae)

Description: *Tall, thick, columnar spiny stems* generally with several large erect or twisted branches; flowers white.
Flowers: 2½–3″ (6.3–7.5 cm) wide, funnel-shaped, in crown-like clusters near ends of branches, with many petals.
Stems: 8–24″ (20–60 cm) wide; 12–24 ribs.
Spines: stout, to 2″ (5 cm) long, in clusters on ribs, 10–25 in each cluster.
Fruit: fleshy, egg-shaped, 2½–3½″ (6.3–8.8 cm) long, green on outside, red inside.
Height: up to 50′ (15 m).
Flowering: May–June.
Habitat: Desert slopes and flats.
Range: Extreme southeastern California to southern Arizona and northern Sonora.
Comments: The Saguaro (pronounced *sah-wah'-ro*) is the state flower of Arizona, where, like all Cacti and many other plants, it is protected by law. It grows very slowly, the oldest plants are estimated to be 150–200 years old. Many are killed or injured by lightning during desert storms. Its slow growth and capacity to store great quantities of water allow it to flower each year regardless of drought. The fruits were an important source of food for Indians and are still used to some extent, the pulp eaten raw or preserved, the juice fermented to make an intoxicating drink, and the seeds ground into a butter. The woody ribs of the stems are used in building shelters. Its flowers open at night and are visited by nectar-feeding bats, moths, and a variety of insects.

181 **Night-blooming Cereus;**
**Queen of the Night**
(*Cereus greggii*)
Cactus Family (Cactaceae)

Description: With its *few angular, gray, thin, barely*
*spiny, twiggy stems,* this white-flowered
plant resembles a small dead bush.
Flowers: 2–3″ (5–7.5 cm) wide, 4–6″
(10–15 cm) long, very sweet-scented,
with many petals.
Stems: about 1″ (2.5 cm) wide; 4–6
ribs.
Spines: 11–13 in a cluster, about ⅛″
(3 mm) long, mostly lying flat.
Fruit: plump, bright red, with many
seeds.
Height: 1–3′ (30–90 cm).
Flowering: Usually June.
Habitat: Desert flats and washes.
Range: Southern Arizona to western Texas and
northern Mexico.
Comments: This Cactus is inconspicuous most of
the year. When in bloom, it is easily
spotted only in the evening and early
morning when its spectacular night-
blooming flowers are open. It is very
popular in desert rock gardens and in
the Cactus trade; when a population is
found, the large, turnip-like roots are
quickly dug out. It can be grown from
stem cuttings, the cut end allowed to
heal in shade for several weeks before it
is planted in dry sand.

471 **Cushion Cactus**
(*Coryphantha vivipara*)
Cactus Family (Cactaceae)

Description: *Small, nearly spherical to barrel-shaped*
*stems,* sometimes single, but often many
in a mound, have pink, red, lavender,
or yellow-green flowers near top.
Flowers: 1–2″ (2.5–5 cm) wide, with
many petals, each ¼–½″ (6–13 mm)
long.
Stems: to 3″ (7.5 cm) wide; nipples

1–1½" (2.5–3.8 cm) long, grooved on upper side.

Spines: in clusters; central ones 3–10, straight, tipped with pink, red, or black, each ½–¾" (1.3–2 cm) long, surrounded by 12–40 white ones, slightly shorter.

Fruit: plump, green, smooth, ½–1" (1.3–2.5 cm) long, with brown seeds.

Height: 1½–6" (3.8–15 cm).

Flowering: May–June.

Habitat: Rocky desert slopes and rocky or sandy soil among piñon, juniper, and ponderosa pine.

Range: Central Canada to Minnesota and southeastern Oregon; south to southeastern California, western Texas, and northern Mexico.

Comments: The genus name comes from the Greek *koryphe* ("cluster") and *anthos* ("flower"). Nipple Cactus (*C. missouriensis*), is very similar, differing in having 1 central spine in each cluster, greenish-white flowers, and reddish fruit with black seeds; it occurs mostly east of the Rocky Mountains but grows westward to central Idaho, western Colorado, southern Utah, and northern Arizona.

## 233 Rainbow Cactus; Comb Hedgehog
(*Echinocereus pectinatus*)
Cactus Family (Cactaceae)

Description: From the top to the bottom, this low, cylindrical cactus is girdled by *bands of colorful spines,* pink, gray, pale yellow, brown, or white. Flowers pink, rose, lavender, or yellow.

Flowers: 1 or a few, 2½–5½" (6.3–13.8 cm) wide; many petals.

Stems: to 4" (10 cm) wide; 15–22 ribs.

Spines: up to ½" (1.3 cm) long, slender, in close clusters; point at which they attach is a vertical oval.

Fruit: plump, greenish, with spines that eventually drop.

Height: 4–12" (10–30 cm).

Flowering: June–August.
Habitat: Rocky slopes and flats, commonly on limestone.
Range: Central and southern Arizona to western Texas; northern Mexico.
Comments: The banded colors of spines explain the name "rainbow." The strikingly beautiful flowers seem far too large for the plant.

### 423 Claret Cup Cactus; King's Cup Cactus; Strawberry Cactus
(*Echinocereus triglochidiatus*)
Cactus Family (Cactaceae)

Description: *Brilliant scarlet flowers* bloom atop spiny cylindrical stems, in old plants many stems in a hemispherical clump.
Flowers: 1¼–2″ (3.1–5 cm) wide, with many petals.
Stems: 3–4″ (7.5–10 cm) thick; 5–12 ribs.
Spines: in clusters of 2–16; on ribs.
Fruit: ½–1″ (1.3–2.5 cm) long, plump, red, with a few clusters of spines that eventually drop.
Height: 2–12″ (5–30 cm).
Flowering: April–May.
Habitat: Rocky desert slopes, or dry woodland in mountains.
Range: Southeastern California; east to southern Utah, central Colorado, and western Texas; south into northern Mexico.
Comments: Among the most beautiful Cacti, large plants with many stems in full flower make breathtaking mounds of scarlet. Stems are highly variable, often with two strikingly different forms growing in the same area.

5 **Green Pitaya**
(*Echinocereus viridiflorus*)
Cactus Family (Cactaceae)

Description: A small Cactus with 1 cylindrical stem
or several in a clump; flowers
yellowish-green or magenta.
Flowers: near top of stem, ¾–1″ (2–
2.5 cm) wide; many petals.
Stems: 4″ (10 cm) wide; 6–14 ribs.
Spines: ½–1″ (1.3–2.5 cm) long, red,
brownish, white, gray, or greenish-
yellow, making bands of color on stem.
Fruit: green, with spines that
eventually drop.
Height: 1–10″ (2.5–25 cm).

Flowering: May–July.

Habitat: Dry plains and hills.

Range: Southeastern Wyoming and western
South Dakota; south to eastern New
Mexico and western Texas.

Comments: Pitaya (pronounced *pee-tah'-yah*) is the
phonetic spelling of the original
Spanish *pitahaya,* a name given to
species of *Echinocereus* but more broadly
applied to a number of Cacti which
produce sweet, edible fruit.

234 **Barrel Cactus**
(*Ferocactus acanthodes*)
Cactus Family (Cactaceae)

Description: *1 large columnar or barrel-shaped stem;*
flowers yellow or reddish near base of
petals.
Flowers: 1½–2½″ (3.8–6.3 cm) wide,
in a crown near top of stem.
Stems: 1–1½′ (30–45 cm) in diameter;
18–27 stout ribs.
Spines: *stout, reddish or yellowish* in dense
clusters along ribs, almost hiding
stem's surface, *4 in center of cluster* in the
form of a cross, curved, surrounded by
12–20 similarly stout ones.
Fruit: fleshy, yellow, scaly.
Height: 3–10′ (90–300 cm).

Flowering: April–May.

Habitat: Along washes, on gravelly slopes, and on canyon walls in deserts.

Range: Southern California to south-central Arizona.

Comments: The genus name comes from the Latin *ferox* ("fierce"), commonly applied to very spiny plants. Candy Barrel Cactus or Fishhook Barrel Cactus (*F. wislizenii*), which grows from southern Arizona to western Texas and northern Mexico, is used for making cactus candy. It has in each cluster a large spine oriented upward, then sharply curved downward at the tip, and other central spines much stouter than the slender surrounding spines.

---

469 **Peyote**
(*Lophophora williamsii*)
Cactus Family (Cactaceae)

Description: *Low, gray, spineless, nearly hemispherical stems* grow singly or in broad, dense clumps, with several pink flowers at the top.
Flowers: ½–1" (1.3–2.5 cm) wide; petals many, pink.
Stems: 2–3" (5–7.5 cm) wide; about 8 low ribs.
Spines: none; in their place are tufts of hair on the ribs.
Fruit: ½–¾" (1.3–2 cm) long, fleshy, red.
Height: 1–3" (2.5–7.5 cm).

Flowering: May–September.

Habitat: Limestone soil in desert.

Range: Southern Texas to northern Mexico.

Comments: Cut, dried "buttons" of Peyote, when chewed, produce color hallucinations and are important in certain Indian religious ceremonies. A federal permit is required to possess any part of the plant. In Texas the Cactus has almost been eliminated, but in areas of Mexico it is still very common.

### 470  **Fishhook Cactus**
(*Mammilaria microcarpa*)
Cactus Family (Cactaceae)

Description:   A low, cylindrical cactus with 1 or
several stems and *many hooked spines;
flowers pink or lavender.*
Flowers : ¾–1″ (2–2.5 cm) wide near
top of stem; petals many, each about
½″ (12–15 mm) long.
Stems: 1½–3″ (3.8–7.5 cm) wide.
Spines: about ¼–½″ (6–13 cm) long,
in clusters at tips of "nipples"; central
one ½″ (1.3 cm) long, hooked,
surrounded by 18–28 shorter, straight,
light tan or brownish-pink ones.
Fruit: ½–1″ (1.3–2.5 cm) long,
broadest above middle, smooth, red.
Height: to 6″ (15 cm).

Flowering:   April–May.

Habitat:   Dry gravelly places in deserts or arid
grassland.

Range:   Southeastern California to western
Texas and northern Mexico.

Comments:   The genus name *Mammilaria* refers to
the nipple-like projections on the
stems. Similar species of *Mammilaria*
and *Coryphantha* are distinguished by
the position of the flower relative to the
cluster of spines. In *Coryphantha* older
nipples have a groove on the upper
side. Both genera have some species
with hooked spines.

### 473  **Beavertail Cactus**
(*Opuntia basilaris*)
Cactus Family (Cactaceae)

Description:   Flat, grayish-green, *leafless, jointed stems*
in a clump, *lack large spines* and have
*vivid rose or reddish-lavender flowers* on
upper edge of joint.
Flowers: 2–3″ (5–7.5 cm) wide, with
many petals.
Stems: joints oval, widest above middle,
2–13″ (5–32.5 cm) long, 1–6″ (2.5–
12.5 cm) wide, ½″ (1.3 cm) thick.

Spines: ⅛–¼" (3–6 mm) long, red-brown, in many small clusters.
Fruit: 1¼" (3.1 cm) long, egg-shaped, grayish-brown, dry, with many seeds.
Height: 6–12" (15–30 cm), with the clump of stems 6' (1.8 m) wide.

Flowering: March–June.

Habitat: Dry, rocky, desert flats or slopes.

Range: Southeastern California to southwestern Utah and western Arizona; south to Sonora.

Comments: The gray-green stems, low growth, and brilliant flowers, which often nearly cover the plant, make this a popular ornamental in hot, dry climates. The bristles can irritate the skin but do not pose the danger of species with long, rigid spines, such as the Plains Pricklypear (*Opuntia polyacantha*). It need not be dug up; a joint broken from a plant will quickly root in dry sand. *Opuntia* with flat joints are called Pricklypear; in the Southwest, if the fruits are juicy and edible, they are called *tuna* by people of Spanish-American heritage.

6 **Teddybear Cholla; Jumping Cholla**
(*Opuntia bigelovii*)
Cactus Family (Cactaceae)

Description: A miniature tree, the upper half with *short, stubby branches densely covered with pale golden spines*. Flowers green or yellow, the petals often streaked with lavender.
Flowers: 1–1½" (2.5–3.8 cm) wide, near ends of joints.
Stems: joints cylindrical, 3–10" (7.5–25 cm) long.
Spines: ½–1" (1.3–2.5 cm) long.
Fruit: about ¾" (2 cm) long, yellow, egg-shaped, knobby.
Height: 3–9' (30–270 cm).

Flowering: March–April.

Habitat: Hot, dry, rocky slopes in deserts.

Range: Southeastern California to western Arizona; south to northwestern Mexico.

Comments:   Though the branches resemble the arms and legs of a fuzzy teddy bear, this plant is far from cuddly: its spines stick instantly and hold tightly by means of minute, backwardly directed barbs. It is one of the most formidable and respected Cacti of the Southwest. When a joint (which seems to "jump" when detached by a light touch or bump) is severely stuck, the victim's best solution is to cut the spines with scissors or nippers and pull them from the flesh with pliers.

### 231  Fragile Pricklypear; Brittle Cactus
(*Opuntia fragilis*)
Cactus Family (Cactaceae)

Description:   The entire plant forms a *low, matted, clump of spiny jointed stems.* Flowers yellow or greenish.
Flowers: 1½–2" (3.8–5 cm) wide, blooming near upper ends of joints.
Stems: joints broadest above middle, slightly flat, ¾–2" (2–5 cm) long, readily detached.
Spines: ½–1" (1.3–2.5 cm) long, white or pale gray; 1–9 in each cluster.
Fruit: about ½" (1.3 cm) long, egg-shaped, tan when ripe.
Height: 8–10" (20–25 cm), with the clump 1–3' (30–90 cm) wide.
Flowering:   May–June.
Habitat:   Dry open areas.
Range:   Western Washington and southern British Columbia; south on the east side of the Cascade Mountains to northern California and northern Arizona; east to northern Texas and southern Michigan.
Comments:   This is one of the most common low Pricklypears. Most have flatter stems.

474 **Tree Cholla; Cane Cholla**
(*Opuntia imbricata*)
Cactus Family (Cactaceae)

Description: *A small, spiny, leafless tree or bush* with
cylindrical, jointed branches, the *deep,
reddish-lavender flowers* blooming near
ends.
Flowers: 2–3" (5–7.5 cm) wide; many
petals.
Stems: joints 5–16" (12.5–40 cm)
long, ¾–1¼" (2–3.1 cm) wide, with
sharply raised, spine-bearing knobs.
Spines: ½–1" (1.3–2.5 cm) long, 10–
30 per cluster.
Fruit: 1–2" (2.5–5 cm) long, yellow,
egg-shaped, fleshy.
Height: 3–7' (90–210 cm).

Flowering: May–July.

Habitat: Plains, deserts, and among piñon and
juniper.

Range: Southern Colorado and Kansas to
Arizona, New Mexico, Texas, and
northern Mexico.

Comments: This is the first bush-like or tree-like
Cholla (pronounced *choy'-yah*)
encountered when traveling from the
East to the Southwest. Near the Rio
Grande other species appear, and in
Arizona there are many, making
identification more difficult. Once the
flesh has weathered away, their woody
stems are hollow, with many holes, and
are popular souvenirs.

429 **Desert Christmas Cactus**
(*Opuntia leptocaulis*)
Cactus Family (Cactaceae)

Description: *Many spiny, intertangled, slender branches*
form a small bush. Flowers greenish,
yellow, or bronze.
Flowers: ½–1" (1.3–2.5 cm) wide,
along stem.
Stems: branched, about ¼" (6 mm)
thick.
Spines: 1–2½" (2.5–6.3 cm) long, tan

or gray, 1 from each raised cluster of tiny reddish bristles.

Fruit: about ½″ (1.3 cm) long, fleshy, bright red, on stem through most of winter.

Height: to 3′ (90 cm).

Flowering: May–June.

Habitat: Flats, slopes, and along washes in deserts and grassland.

Range: Western Arizona to southern Oklahoma; south to northern Mexico.

Comments: This plant has the most slender stems of all southwestern Chollas. During winter its bright red fruits add attractive color to the brown desert.

---

### 232  Plains Pricklypear
(*Opuntia polyacantha*)
Cactus Family (Cactaceae)

Description: *Low mound of spiny, flat, nearly oval joints* has bright yellow or sometimes bright magenta flowers.

Flowers: 2–3″ (5–7.5 cm) wide, with many petals on upper edge of joints.

Stems: joints bluish-green, 2–4″ (5–10 cm) long.

Spines: 2–3″ (5–7.5 cm) long, 6–10 per cluster, mostly bent down.

Fruit: ¾–1½″ (2–3.8 cm) long, egg-shaped, tan when ripe.

Height: 3–6″ (7.5–15 cm), with clumps of stems 1–10′ (30–300 cm) wide.

Flowering: May–July.

Habitat: Open areas on plains, in deserts, and among piñon and juniper.

Range: Southern British Columbia to eastern Oregon and northern Arizona; east to western Texas, Missouri, and central Canada.

Comments: This Cactus is a nuisance on rangeland, becoming more frequent as grass is grazed away. The spiny pads often break off and stick in the noses and throats of livestock.

## 472 Simpson's Hedgehog Cactus
(*Pediocactus simpsonii*)
Cactus Family (Cactaceae)

Description: *1 or a few spiny, nearly spherical stems*
have several white, rose, or yellow
flowers near top.
Flowers: 1–1½" (2.5–3.8 cm) wide.
Stems: 2–3" (5–7.5 cm) wide.
Spines: ⅜–¾" (9–20 mm) long,
straight, brownish; in clusters of 5–11
on low tubercles, spreading in all
directions from center, and surrounded
by 15–30 white or cream ones, each
about ¼" (6 mm) long.
Fruit: about ¼" (6 mm) long, tan and
dry when mature.
Height: 2–8" (5–20 cm).
Flowering: May–July.
Habitat: Powdery soils among sagebrush and
piñon and juniper.
Range: Eastern Washington to west-central
Nevada and northern Arizona; east to
northern New Mexico, western
Colorado, western South Dakota, and
western Montana.
Comments: This Cactus is fairly popular with
collectors. Other species of the genus
are rare. Mass collecting of Cacti is
inexcusable, but even the person who
digs only one has a detrimental effect,
for if many take only "their share"
eventually entire plant populations are
depleted.

## BLUEBELL FAMILY
### (Campanulaceae)

Usually herbs, rarely trees or shrubs, commonly with blue, lavender, or white flowers, solitary or clustered. Flowers: radially symmetrical, with corolla tubular or bell-shaped, having 5 lobes; or bilaterally symmetrical, with corolla conspicuously 2-lipped; stamens 5. All these parts attached at top of ovary.
Leaves: alternate, simple, sometimes deeply divided.
Fruit: berry or capsule.
There are about 35 genera and 900 species, widely distributed in tropical and temperate regions. Many are used as ornamentals.

---

611 **Bluebell; Harebell; Bluebell of Scotland**
(*Campanula rotundifolia*)
Bluebell Family (Campanulaceae)

Description: *Blue-violet bell-shaped flowers hang* along the top parts of slender, mostly unbranched stems that grow in small patches.
Flowers: corolla ½–1″ (1.3–2.5 cm) long with 5 pointed lobes that gently curve back; style about as long as corolla.
Leaves: those along stem ½–3″ (1.3–7.5 cm) long, very narrow; those at base with round blades, but usually withered by flowering time.
Height: 4–40″ (10–100 cm).

Flowering: June–September.
Habitat: Meadows and rocky slopes at moderate or high elevations.
Range: In nearly all the high western mountains except the Sierra Nevada.
Comments: The genus name, from the Latin *campana* ("bell"), means "little bell." The name Harebell may allude to an association with witches, who were

believed able to transform themselves
into hares, portents of bad luck when
they crossed a person's path. In
Scotland, another old name for this
plant was Witches' Thimble.

### 631 Southwestern Blue Lobelia
(*Lobelia anatina*)
Bluebell Family (Campanulaceae)

Description: Usually only one slender, erect stem has
a few sparse, *deep blue-violet bilaterally
symmetrical flowers blooming in an open
raceme* at top.
Flowers: ½–1" (1.3–2.5 cm) long;
tubular portion of corolla slit only on
top, 3 corolla lobes spreading sideways
and downward, 2 bent upward, their
tips touching above the flower; 2
anthers have a tuft of white hairs, 3
hairless.
Leaves: 1–3" (2.5–7.5 cm) long,
lanceolate, often with low, blunt teeth.
Height: 8–28" (20–70 cm).
Flowering: July–October.
Habitat: Moist places in meadows, along
streams, and in marshes.
Range: Southern Arizona and southern New
Mexico to northern Mexico.
Comments: This slender little Lobelia is one of
several bluish-flowered species in the
West.

### 419 Cardinal Flower; Scarlet Lobelia
(*Lobelia cardinalis*)
Bluebell Family (Campanulaceae)

Description: Erect leafy stems, often in clusters,
with *racemes of flowers resembling flaming
red spires*.
Flowers: corolla 1–1½" (2.5–3.8 cm)
long, bilaterally symmetrical, with 2
small upper lobes and 3 larger lower
lobes, the tubular base slit along top
and sides.

Leaves: 2–5" (5–12.5 cm) long, narrowly lanceolate, with fine teeth on edges.
Height: 1–3' (30–90 cm).

Flowering: July–October.

Habitat: Moist shady slopes and sunny stream banks.

Range: Southern California to southern Utah and western Texas; north to eastern Colorado; east across most of eastern United States.

Comments: One of the West's most handsome wildflowers, it attracts hummingbirds, which feed on the nectar, pollinating the flowers. In southern Arizona, Sierra Madre Lobelia (*L. laxiflora*) is also found; its corolla is red with yellow lobes or all yellow.

629 **Venus' Looking Glass**
(*Triodanis perfoliata*)
Bluebell Family (Campanulaceae)

Description: Erect, bristly-hairy, leafy stems have, in axils of upper leaves, 1 or a few nearly *flat blue or white flowers.*
Flowers: ½–¾" (1.3–2 cm) wide, with 5 narrow, sharp sepals; corolla usually with 5 bluntly pointed lobes.
Leaves: ½–1¼" (1.3–3.1 cm) long, broadly ovate, attached to stem in notch base, edges generally scalloped.
Height: 6–24" (15–60 cm).

Flowering: April–July.

Habitat: Rocky banks, dry woods, plains, often where soil has been disturbed.

Range: Southern British Columbia; south to northern California and southern Arizona; east across the continent; also Mexico and South America.

Comments: Some of the flowers are small, inconspicuous and do not open; pollination occurs entirely within them. Such flowers generally have only 3 or 4 sepals.

## CAPER FAMILY (Capparaceae)

Commonly herbs in the United States but mostly trees or shrubs in tropical regions.

Flowers: radially or bilaterally symmetrical, usually in racemes; sepals 4, separate; petals 4, separate, each commonly with a slender, stalk-like base; stamens 4 to many. All these parts attached at the base of a stalk beneath the ovary.

Leaves: alternate, simple or often palmately compound.

Fruit: 1-chambered capsule, berry, or drupe.

About 45 genera and 800 species occur in warm regions of the world. A few are grown as ornamentals; the flower buds of Capers are used as a seasoning.

---

### 321 Yellow Bee Plant
(*Cleome lutea*)
Caper Family (Capparaceae)

Description: A branched plant with *palmately compound leaves* and racemes of *small yellow flowers* at the tops.
Flowers: petals 4, about ¼" (6 mm) long; stamens 6, long.
Leaves: palmately compound, 3–7 leaflets, each ¾–2½" (6–6.3 cm) long, lanceolate.
Fruit: pod ½–1½" (1.3–3.8 cm) long, slender, on *long arched stalks, jointed at middle.*
Height: 1½–5' (45–150 cm).
Flowering: May–September.
Habitat: Desert plains and lower valleys in mountains, commonly near water or areas formerly filled with water.
Range: Eastern Washington to eastern California; east to southern Arizona, northern New Mexico, western Nebraska, and Montana.
Comments: The genus name was used by the Greek philosopher Theophrastus for a plant

resembling Mustard, and while the flowers resemble those of Mustards, the ovary on a jointed stalk and palmately compound leaves distinguish this as Capparaceae. The similar Golden Spider Flower (*C. platycarpa*), from eastern Oregon, southwestern Idaho, and adjacent portions of California and Nevada, has hairs on stems and leaves tipped with glands.

---

530  **Rocky Mountain Bee Plant**
(*Cleome serrulata*)
Caper Family (Capparaceae)

Description:  Branched stems have *palmately compound leaves* and, in racemes at ends of branches, *pink or reddish-purple flowers* (sometimes white).
Flowers: ½″ (1.3 cm) long; petals 4; stamens 6, long; ovary on a long, protruding stalk.
Leaves: 3 lanceolate leaflets, each ½–3″ (1.3–7.5 cm) long.
Fruit: pod 1½–2½″ (3.8–6.3 cm) long, slender, on *long, arched stalks jointed at middle.*
Height: ½–5′ (15–150 cm).

Flowering:  June–September.

Habitat:  Plains and rangeland, foothills of lower mountains.

Range:  Eastern Washington to northern California; east on most of the Great Plains; south to central Arizona, central New Mexico, and northern Texas; introduced elsewhere.

Comments:  Flowers produce copious nectar and attract bees, hence the common name. Indians boiled the strong leaves for food and as a stomachache remedy. In times of drought early Spanish-Americans made tortillas from the barely palatable but nourishing seeds.

## 16, 350 Bladderpod
(*Isomeris arborea*)
Caper Family (Capparaceae)

Description: *Yellow flowers* bloom in many short
racemes on this *strong-smelling, dense,
round shrub with palmately compound
leaves.*
Flowers: about 1″ (2.5 cm) wide; petals
4; stamens 6, long.
Leaves: 3 oblong leaflets, each ½–1½″
(1.3–3.8 cm) long.
Fruit: pod 1–2″ (2.5–5 cm) long,
plump, pointed, hanging down on *long
stalk jointed at middle.*
Height: 2–8′ (60–240 cm).
Flowering: January–November.
Habitat: Among brush, along washes, especially
in alkaline soil.
Range: Southern California and Baja California
from western edge of desert to coast.
Comments: The genus name comes from the Greek
*isos* ("equal") and *meris* ("part"),
possibly describing the equal halves of
the pod.

## 166 Clammyweed
(*Polanisia dodecandra*)
Caper Family (Capparaceae)

Description: *Sticky short hairs* cover this strong-
smelling, branched plant which has
*palmately compound leaves and racemes of
white or cream flowers.*
Flowers: petals 4, ¼–¾″ (6–20 mm)
long, notched at tip and tapered at base
to slender stalk; 6–20 long, *pink or
purple stamens* of unequal length.
Leaves: 3 broadly lanceolate leaflets,
each ½–1½″ (1.3–3.8 cm) long.
Fruit: pod ¾–3″ (2–7.5 cm) long,
plump, cylindrical, held erect.
Height: 4–32″ (10–80 cm).
Flowering: May–October.
Habitat: Sandy slopes and flats, common along
washes, in deserts, on plains, and
among piñon and juniper.

Range:    Southeastern Oregon; east across
          northern states to Minnesota; south to
          northeastern California, southern
          Arizona, northern Mexico, and most of
          Texas.

Comments: The common name, Clammyweed,
          refers to the sticky, moist glands on the
          surface of this plant.

---

324 **Jackass Clover**
    (*Wislizenia refracta*)
    Caper Family (Capparaceae)

Description: An often densely branched plant with
             *palmately compound leaves* and many *tiny
             yellow flowers in dense racemes.*
             Flowers: petals 4, about ⅛″ (3 mm)
             long; stamens 6.
             Leaves: 3 elliptic leaflets, each ½–1¼″
             (1.3–3.1 cm) long.
             Fruit: pod about ⅛″ (3 mm) long, with
             *2 round lobes side by side,* a pointed style
             between, the *stalk of pod sharply bent in
             middle at joint.*
             Height: 16–28″ (40–70 cm).

Flowering: April–September.

Habitat:   Low sandy or alkaline soil in deserts
           and in arid grassland, especially
           frequent along roads and washes.

Range:     Central Valley of California to southern
           Nevada and western Texas; south into
           Mexico.

Comments:  Malodorous and poisonous to livestock,
           but probably distasteful and rarely
           eaten. The 3 leaflets give it a
           resemblance to Clover, but there is no
           relationship. The origin of the name
           "jackass" is unknown.

# HONEYSUCKLE FAMILY
## (Caprifoliaceae)

Mostly shrubs, sometimes vines or
herbs, commonly with showy flowers.
Flowers: radially or bilaterally
symmetrical, usually in a branched or
forked cluster; sepals 5, small; corolla
with 5 petals united into a slender
tube, flared into a trumpet-shaped end
or forming an upper and lower lip;
stamens usually 5. All these parts
attached at top of ovary.
Leaves: opposite, simple or compound.
Fruit: berry, drupe, or capsule.
There are about 15 genera and 400
species in north temperate regions and
in tropical mountains. Snowberries,
Honeysuckles, and Elderberries are
grown as ornamentals, and the fruit of
Elderberries are also eaten or made into
jelly or wine.

## 507 Twinflower
(*Linnaea borealis*)
Honeysuckle Family (Caprifoliaceae)

Description: A matted plant with erect, short,
leafless, forked stalks from whose tops
hang *2 pink flowers like narrow bells*.
Flowers: about ½" (1.3 cm) long;
corolla with 5 round lobes.
Leaves: ¼–1" (6–25 mm) long,
opposite, broadly elliptic, sometimes
with a few shallow teeth on edges.
Height: creeper, the flower stalks less
than 4" (10 cm) high.
Flowering: June–September.
Habitat: Moist woods and brush.
Range: Throughout the western mountains,
south to northern California, northern
Arizona, and New Mexico; east to
western South Dakota.
Comments: Named for Carolus Linnaeus, the father
of systematic botany, this charming
plant makes a good ground cover in the
woodland garden.

## PINK OR CARNATION FAMILY
(Caryophyllaceae)

Herbs with swollen nodes on the stems
and flowers blooming singly or in a
branched or forked cluster.
Flowers: sepals 5, free from one another
or united; petals 5, each often with a
slender portion at base and fringed or
toothed at end; stamens 5 or 10. All
these parts attached at base of ovary.
Leaves: simple, opposite.
Fruit: usually capsule.
There are about 80 genera and 2,000
species, primarily occurring in the
Northern Hemisphere, especially in
cool regions.

## 462 Corn Cockle
(*Agrostemma githago*)
Pink Family (Caryophyllaceae)

Description: The few branches on this slender, finely
hairy, *stiffly erect plant form narrow forks*
and are tipped with *1 deep reddish-
lavender flower.*
Flowers: about 1″ (2.5 cm) wide; sepals
5, ¾–1½″ (2–3.8 cm) long, with
narrow tips, joined at base to form a
broad hard tube with 10 ribs; petals 5,
shorter than sepals.
Leaves: 2–6″ (5–15 cm) long, opposite,
narrowly lanceolate, held nearly erect
against stem.
Fruit: capsule with 5 styles.
Height: 1–3′ (30–90 cm).
Flowering: May–July.
Habitat: Roadsides and other disturbed areas.
Range: Throughout, but most frequent in
Washington, Oregon, and California's
interior valleys.
Comments: In England, where "corn" generally
means wheat, Corn Cockle was a weed
in grain fields; before the advent of
machine harvesting, the separation of
its poisonous seeds from the wheat was
a tedious procedure.

## 38 Beautiful Sandwort
*(Arenaria capillaris)*
Pink Family (Caryophyllaceae)

Description: A single *small, white, star-like flower*
blooms at the end of each of *many
slender, forked branches* that grow on a
main stalk above a leafy, matted base
up to 8″ (20 cm) wide.
Flowers: petals 5, ¼–½″ (6–13 mm)
wide; sepals 5, bluntly pointed with
translucent edges.
Leaves: ½–2½″(1.3–6.3 cm) long,
very narrow, opposite, most on lower
fourth of stem.
Fruit: capsule, with 3 styles and many
seeds.
Height: 2–12″ (5–30 cm).

Flowering: June–August.
Habitat: From sagebrush plains to rocky
mountain slopes.
Range: From Alaska to northern Oregon,
northern Nevada, and western
Montana.
Comments: The genus name comes from the Latin
*arena* ("sand"), referring to the
preferred soil of many species. Several
similar species, distinguished by
technical characteristics, generally may
be recognized by white flowers with 5
petals, 3 styles on the ovary, and very
narrow, opposite leaves.

## 39 Fendler's Sandwort
*(Arenaria fendleri)*
Pink Family (Caryophyllaceae)

Description: *Tufted plant* with many slender stems,
very narrow leaves, and *numerous small
white flowers* in open, branched clusters.
Flowers: about ½″ (1.3 cm) wide;
petals 5; sepals 5, pointed, glandular.
Leaves: ¾–3″ (2–7.5 cm) long,
opposite, almost thread-like, sharply
pointed.
Fruit: small 1-chambered capsule that
has 6 teeth at top when open.

Height: 4–12″ (10–30 cm).
Flowering: July–September.
Habitat: On cliffs, ledges, and rocky banks in the mountains.
Range: Wyoming to Arizona, New Mexico, and western Texas.
Comments: This common southern Rocky Mountain species gives the impression of numerous white stars in an airy tuft. There are a number of species of Sandwort, some forming tight, sometimes prickly, mats, others tall and open but with flowers in tight heads.

## 18   Meadow Chickweed
(*Cerastium arvense*)
Pink Family (Caryophyllaceae)

Description: A plant with several stems leaning on the ground, and a *white flower* blooming at the end of each of the few branches of the nearly leafless flower cluster. Below the point where leaves attach the stem are downward-pointing hairs, those in flower cluster tipped with glands.
Flowers: nearly 1″ (2.5 cm) wide; sepals 5; petals 5, about ½″ (1.3 cm) long, *deeply notched at tip;* styles 5; bracts surrounding flower cluster with stiff, translucent edges.
Leaves: ½–1½″ (1.3–3.8 cm) long, opposite, narrowly lanceolate.
Fruit: cylindrical capsule with 10 teeth at tip after it opens.
Height: 2–20″ (5–50 cm).
Flowering: April–August.
Habitat: Open, generally grassy areas from near the coast to high in the mountains.
Range: Northern Hemisphere; south in the West to northern California, northern Arizona, and southern New Mexico.
Comments: *Cerastium,* from the Greek *keras* ("horn"), refers to the capsule, which is tapered and, in some species, bent slightly like a cow's horn. The very similar Mountain Chickweed

(*C. beeringianum*), which grows at high elevations in America's western mountains, has green-edged bracts in the flower cluster.

## 450 Grass Pink; Deptford Pink
(*Dianthus armeria*)
Pink Family (Caryophyllaceae)

Description: 1 or several stiffly erect stems, prominently swollen where leaves attach, with several *pink or red flowers*. Flowers: about ½" (1.3 cm) wide in a tight, forked, hairy, flower cluster; calyx narrow, tubular, about ½" (1.3 cm) wide, with 5 pointed lobes; petals 5, ¾–1" (2–2.5 cm) long, their bases long and slender, upper ends broad, and with teeth on outer edges. Leaves: 1½–4" (3.8–10 cm) long, opposite, very narrow, those on stem held erect.
Fruit: capsule with 2 styles.
Height: 8–24" (20–60 cm).
Flowering: June–August.
Habitat: Roadsides, lots, and old fields.
Range: Washington, Oregon, Idaho, and Montana.
Comments: This relative of the Carnation (*D. caryophyllus*) once grew in fields near Deptford, now an industrial section of London, hence one of its common names.

## 34 White Campion; Evening Lychnis
(*Lychnis alba*)
Pink Family (Caryophyllaceae)

Description: Several erect stems, covered with glandular hairs, forked in the flower cluster, have *white flowers* at the end of each branch, and leaves mostly on lower half of plant.
Flowers: about ¾" (2 cm) wide; calyx narrow, tubular, about ¾" (2 cm) long

when flower blooms, swelling as fruit matures; petals 5, about 1″ (2.5 cm) long, each divided by several small scales near middle into an upper part deeply notched at tip and a long, slender lower part. Some plants have flowers with stamens only; others have flowers with ovaries only.
Leaves: to 4″ (10 cm) long, opposite, lanceolate, broader above middle.
Height: 1½–4½′ (45–135 cm).

Flowering: June–August.

Habitat: Roadsides, old fields, and brushy areas.

Range: A weed in northern California, northern Idaho, eastern Utah, and western Colorado, but to be expected elsewhere.

Comments: White Campion is often confused with Night Flowering Catchfly (*Silene noctiflora*), which has stamens and ovary in the same flower.

## 154  Bouncing Bet
(*Saponaria officinalis*)
Pink Family (Caryophyllaceae)

Description: Leafy, unbranched *stems grow in patches* and bear near the top many sweetly scented *white or pink flowers* in fairly dense clusters.
Flowers: about 1″ (2.5 cm) wide; calyx tubular, with 5 pointed teeth; petals 5, the broad upper part about ½″ (1.3 cm) long, the slender lower part as long as calyx; styles 2.
Leaves: 1½–5″ (3.8–12.5 cm) long, opposite, broadly lanceolate.
Height: 1–3′ (30–90 cm).

Flowering: June–September.

Habitat: Mostly moist places at low or moderate elevations, especially where cool.

Range: Most frequent in California, Oregon, and Washington.

Comments: An old-fashioned ornamental native to Europe. The genus name, from the Latin *sapo*, meaning "soap," refers to the juice, which contains saponins that

produce a lather when mixed in water.
Saponins are poisonous when ingested.

---

### 431 Moss Pink
(*Silene acaulis*)
Pink Family (Caryophyllaceae)

Description: *Pink flowers* bloom on short stems barely
above *thick moss-like mats.*
Flowers: about ½″ (1.3 cm) wide; calyx
tubular, pinkish, ⅛–⅜″ (3–9 mm)
long, with 10 veins and 5 pointed
lobes; 5 petals, the broad upper part
usually notched at tip, the slender
lower part as long as calyx; 3 styles on
ovary.
Leaves: ¼–⅝″ (6–15 mm) long,
opposite, most at base, very narrow.
Height: 1–2½″ (2.5–6.3 cm), with
mats to 1′ (30 cm) wide.

Flowering: June–August.

Habitat: Moist areas above timberline, often in
rock crevices.

Range: Throughout Northern Hemisphere; in
North America south in the mountains
to Oregon, northern Arizona, and
northern New Mexico and New
Hampshire.

Comments: A beautiful alpine wildflower that has
adopted a low form as protection from
frigid, drying winds. Moss Pink
resembles other tufted alpine plants
with pink flowers, such as Purple
Saxifrage (*Saxifraga oppositifolia*), with
ovate leaves and only 2 styles, and
species of *Phlox*, whose petals join into
a tube.

---

### 393 Indian Pink
(*Silene californica*)
Pink Family (Caryophyllaceae)

Description: *Flowers with fringed bright red petals
resemble brilliant pinwheels* at the ends of
branches on erect or trailing leafy stems.

Flowers: 1–1½″ (2.5–3.8 cm) wide; a calyx broad, tubular, ⅝–1″ (1.5–2.5 cm) long, with 5 pointed teeth; petals 5, divided by small scales in middle, the broad upper part with deep notches at end, the slender lower part as long as calyx.

Leaves: 1¼–3″ (3.1–7.5 cm) long, opposite, ovate.

Fruit: capsule, not longer than calyx.

Height: 6–16″ (15–40 cm).

Flowering: May–July.

Habitat: Rocky open woods.

Range: Northern two-thirds of California into southwestern Oregon.

Comments: One of the showiest of western wildflowers, which, although widespread, is usually not numerous. Mexican Campion (*S. laciniata*), from the southern third of California eastward to western Texas, is similar, though it has erect stems 16–40″ (40–100 cm) high and capsules longer than the calyx.

## 33 Bladder Campion
(*Silene cucubalis*)
Pink Family (Caryophyllaceae)

Description: Several *white flowers, each with a large, swollen calyx,* bloom in an open, forked cluster on this usually smooth plant.

Flowers: about ½″ (1.3 cm) wide; petals 5, deeply notched at the tip, with a long stalk-like base; calyx smooth, like a deep cup with 5 points on rim, enlarging as fruit matures and becoming up to ¾″ (2 cm) long; styles 3.

Leaves: 1¼–3″ (3.1–7.5 cm) long, opposite, broadly lanceolate.

Fruit: 3-celled capsule.

Height: to 3′ (90 cm).

Flowering: June–August.

Habitat: A weed of vacant lots, fields, roadsides.

Range: Throughout.

Comments: The swollen mature calyx of Bladder

Campion, often tinged with purple,
resembles a tiny decorative paper
lantern. Sticky Cockle, (*S. noctiflora,*)
another weedy species, has a hairy
calyx. Both differ from White
Campion, (*Lychnis alba,*) by having
stamens and pistil in the same flower.

77, 459 **Stringflower**
(*Silene hookeri*)
Pink Family (Caryophyllaceae)

Description: A hairy gray plant with many short,
spreading stems in a cluster and, on a
few branches at the ends, several flowers
with *fringed petals.*
Flowers: 1–2″ (2.5–5 cm) wide, with a
tubular calyx ½–¾″ (1.3–2 cm) long,
with 5 teeth; *petals 5, white, pink, or
purple,* divided into upper and lower
parts by scales near middle, upper part
fan-shaped, ½–1″ (1.3–2.5 cm) long,
deeply divided into narrow lobes, lower
part slender and as long as calyx;
styles 3.
Leaves: 1½–2½″ (3.8–6.3 cm) long,
opposite, lanceolate, widest above
middle.
Height: 2–6″ (5–15 cm).
Flowering: May–June.
Habitat: Dry rocky ground in brush and open
coniferous forests.
Range: Northwestern California and
southwestern Oregon.
Comments: The name Stringflower best applies to
the race with white petals divided into
4 narrow, string-like lobes.

## ROCKROSE FAMILY (Cistaceae)

Herbs or shrubs with flowers borne
singly or in a branched cluster.
Flowers: radially symmetrical; calyx
usually with 3 large sepals and 2
smaller ones, or small ones absent;
petals 5, separate, sometimes fewer,
occasionally none; stamens many. All
these parts attached at base of ovary.
Leaves: alternate or opposite, simple.
Fruit: leathery or woody capsule with 3
or more chambers.
There are about 8 genera and 200
species, with most occurring in dry,
sunny locations, often in chalky or
sandy soil. The family is found
in northern temperate regions,
with a few species in South America.

221 **Rock Rose; Sun Rose**
(*Helianthemum scoparium*)
Rockrose Family (Cistaceae)

Description: A low plant that forms a tuft with *many
spreading branches* and has *very narrow
leaves* that soon drop off; in each upper
axil there is a *yellow flower.*
Flowers: about 1″ (2.5 cm) wide; sepals
5, about ¼″ (6 mm) long, the 2 outer
ones much narrower and shorter than
the inner 3; petals 5, broadly ovate,
⅜–½″ (9–13 mm) long; stamens
many.
Leaves: ½–1¼″ (1.3–3.1 cm) long.
Height: 8–12″ (20–30 cm).

Flowering: March–July.

Habitat: Dry sandy flats near the coast and
inland on rocky slopes and ridges.

Range: Northern California south to Baja
California.

Comments: The name, from the Greek *helios*
("sun") and *anthemon* ("flower"), refers
to its flowers, which open only in sun.
Bicknell's Rock Rose (*H. bicknellii*),
from South Dakota eastward, has
similar flowers, but broom-like stems.

## SPIDERWORT FAMILY
### (Commelinaceae)

Herbs with more or less swollen nodes; flowers arranged in clusters enveloped by boat-shaped bracts.

Flowers: radially symmetrical; sepals 3; petals 3; stamens 6, the stalks often with colored hairs. All these parts attached at base of ovary.

Leaves: alternate, simple, the base of each forming a tubular sheath around the stem.

Fruit: capsule with 3 chambers.

About 40 genera and 600 species are known, found mostly in tropical and subtropical regions. Dayflower, Wandering Jew, and Moses-in-a-Boat are cultivated as ornamentals.

---

### 601 Western Dayflower
(*Commelina dianthifolia*)
Spiderwort Family (Commelinaceae)

Description: Flowers with *3 broad blue petals protrude from a broad folded leaf* at the top of a leaning or erect branched stem with narrow leaves.
Flowers: about ¾″ (2 cm) wide; petals 3, on short stalks, lower slightly smaller; stamens 6.
Leaves: to 6″ (15 cm) long, narrow, forming a sheath around stem at base; spathe 1–3″ (2.5–7.5 cm) long, including a long, narrow tip.
Height: to 20″ (50 cm).

Flowering: July–September.
Habitat: Rocky soil among piñon and juniper or in pine woods.
Range: Western Texas to south-central Colorado and eastern half of Arizona; south throughout most of Mexico.
Comments: Called Dayflower because 1 flower appears outside the sheath every 1–4 days, opening near dawn and wilting by midday.

### 600 Small-bracted Dayflower; Hierba de Pollo
(*Commelina erecta*)
Spiderwort Family (Commelinaceae)

Description: Flowers with *2 large, ear-like, blue petals* and one smaller petal bloom in small clusters, in a bract, at the top of several erect branches.
Flowers: about 1″ (2.5 cm) wide; petals 2, blue, on very slender stalks, the third, lowest petal very small and white; flower cluster borne in a boat-like bract ½–1½″ (1.3–3.8 cm) long.
Leaves: to 6″ (15 cm) long, very narrow to lanceolate, the base forming a sheath around stem.
Height: creeper, with branches usually only about 1′ (30 cm) high, but stems long and reclining, to 3′ (90 cm).

Flowering: May–October.

Habitat: In sandy or rocky soil in grassy areas, in open woods, or where weedy.

Range: Southern Arizona to eastern Colorado and Wyoming; south to New Mexico and Texas; eastern United States.

Comments: This is a highly variable species. The Spanish name means "herb of the (cooked) chicken."

### 646 Pine Spiderwort
(*Tradescantia pinetorum*)
Spiderwort Family (Commelinaceae)

Description: Clusters of *blue-purple flowers with 3 petals* bloom at the top of several lightly but roughly hairy stems that are mostly unbranched and erect, but often bent and leaning at the knee-like nodes.
Flowers: less than ¾″ (2 cm) wide; petals broad.
Leaves: 2–5″ (5–12.5 cm) long, sometimes much longer, very narrow.
Height: 8–20″ (20–50 cm).

Flowering: August–September.

Habitat: Open brush and in open woods.

Range: Southern Arizona and southern New

Mexico to northern Mexico.

Comments: This species and Western Spiderwort (*T. occidentalis*), were used by Indians as a cooked vegetable. Western Spiderwort, which grows from Arizona to Montana and east to North Dakota and Texas, has smooth stems with several joints and bright blue to nearly rose-colored flowers. Wright's Spiderwort (*T. wrightii*), on limestone slopes from central New Mexico to western Texas, has smooth stems in tufts, only about 6″ (15 cm) tall, and a few glandular hairs on the sepals and individual flower stalks.

## MORNING GLORY FAMILY
### (Convolvulaceae)

Trees, shrubs, vines, or herbs,
commonly with handsome, funnel-
shaped flowers.
Flowers: radially symmetrical; sepals 5;
corolla of 5 united petals, almost
unlobed on the rim; stamens 5. All
these parts attached at base of ovary.
Leaves: alternate, simple.
Fruit: capsule, berry, or nut.
About 50 genera and 1,400 species
occur, mostly in temperate and tropical
regions. Some species are cultivated for
their handsome flowers—and one, the
Sweet Potato, for its edible
underground fleshy stems.

---

468 **Beach Morning Glory**
(*Calystegia soldanella*)
Morning Glory Family (Convolvulaceae)

Description: *Trailing stems* growing from deep
rootstocks have *thick, kidney-shaped
leaves* and *funnel-shaped, pink or rose
flowers* on short stalks from axils.
Flowers: corolla 1½–2½″ (3.8–6.3 cm)
wide, with 5 short, blunt points. 2
bracts about ½″ (1.3 cm) long partially
hide calyx.
Leaves: 1–2″ (2.5–5 cm) wide.
Height: creeper, with branches to 3″
(7.5 cm) high, and stems to 20″ (50
cm) long.
Flowering: April–September.
Habitat: Common on beach sands.
Range: Along the Pacific Coast from British
Columbia to southern California.
Comments: This fleshy plant does not seem very
similar to the garden Morning Glory,
but the resemblance of its flower is
unmistakable. In the cool, humid,
coastal climate it remains open most of
the day.

### 173 Bindweed; Field Bindweed; Possession Vine
(*Convolvulus arvensis*)
Morning Glory Family (Convolvulaceae)

Description: Long *trailing and twining stems* with rather triangular leaves have, on short stalks, *white or pinkish, funnel-shaped flowers.*
Flowers: about 1″ (2.5 cm) wide; corolla with 5 veins leading to low lobes on edge; *2 narrow bracts* about ¼″ (6 mm) long on stalk well below calyx.
Leaves: ¾–1½″ (2–3.8 cm) long, generally triangular, but sometimes arrow-shaped or ovate; short stalk.
Height: 1–3′ (30–90 cm).
Flowering: May–October.
Habitat: Fields, lots, gardens, and roadsides.
Range: Throughout.
Comments: Bindweed's very deep roots make it a troublesome weed, difficult to eradicate. A common and very similar genus is *Calystegia,* which has the typical funnel-shaped corollas of Morning Glories, often white or cream, but the lobes at the end of the style are oblong and blunt rather than narrow and pointed. Hedge Bindweed (*Calystegia sepium*), in moist places throughout much of the United States, has 2 large bracts concealing the calyx and white to cream flowers.

### 582 Arizona Blue-eyes
(*Evolvulus arizonicus*)
Morning Glory Family (Convolvulaceae)

Description: This plant has grayish hairs, slender, erect stems, and a *shallow, bowl-shaped blue flower* on a slender stalk in each upper leaf axil.
Flowers: corolla ½–¾″ (1.3–2 cm) wide, with 5 round lobes; stamens 5.
Leaves: ¾–1″ (2–2.5 cm) long, lanceolate.
Height: to 1′ (30 cm).

Flowering: April–October.
Habitat: Open areas in deserts, grassland, and among piñon and juniper.
Range: Southern Arizona, southwestern New Mexico, and northern Mexico.
Comments: This has the largest, prettiest flowers of several southwestern species of *Evolvulus*.

### 397 Scarlet Creeper; Star Glory
*(Ipomoea cristulata)*
Morning Glory Family (Convolvulaceae)

Description: These leafy vines have *scarlet trumpet-shaped flowers*.
Flowers: corolla ¾–1½" (2–3.8 cm) long, with 5 pointed lobes; sepals ¼" (6 mm) long.
Leaves: 1¼–3" (3.1–7.5 cm) long, about as wide, with 3 angular lobes.
Height: vine, with stems to 3–7' (90–210 cm) long.
Flowering: May–October.
Habitat: Brushy hillsides and canyons.
Range: Western Texas to Arizona and Mexico.
Comments: Very similar to the cultivated Scarlet Creeper, (*I. coccinea*), a southeastern species sometimes found in waste places in the Southwest. This large tropical genus includes vines, shrubs and trees.

### 467 Bush Morning Glory
*(Ipomoea leptophylla)*
Morning Glory Family (Convolvulaceae)

Description: Smooth, erect, leafy stems, sometimes leaning on the ground at the base, form a roundish plant; in the upper axils are flowers with *pinkish-lavender or purplish-red, funnel-shaped corollas* with darker centers.
Flowers: 2–2½" (5–6.3 cm) wide; sepals 5, of different lengths, joined at base.
Leaves: 1¼–3½" (3.1–8.8 cm) long,

narrowly lanceolate.
Height: to 4' (1.2 m).

Flowering: May–July.
Habitat: Sandy or disturbed soil in prairies.
Range: Eastern Montana and western South
Dakota; south to northeastern New
Mexico and western Texas.
Comments: This beautiful wildflower is
representative of several species of
*Ipomoea* that, unlike garden Morning
Glories, are not vines.

### 573 Morning Glory
(*Ipomoea purpurea*)
Morning Glory Family (Convolvulaceae)

Description: Flowers with large, *funnel-shaped corollas*
bloom from the axils of broad, often
heart-shaped leaves on these *vines*.
Flowers: corolla 1½–2½" (3.8–6.3 cm)
wide, *blue-violet, red, or white;* sepals 5,
stiffly hairy on backs, joined at base,
about ½" (1.3 cm) long, their narrow
green tips about as long as body of
sepal.
Leaves: 1¼–6" (3.1–15 cm) long, vary
from heart-shaped to 3-lobed (if lobed,
2 at base point outward and backward).
Height: vine, with stems 3–10'
(30–300 cm) long.
Flowering: June–November.
Habitat: Fields, lots, and roadsides.
Range: California to Texas.
Comments: Grown in much of the West as an
ornamental and occasionally found in
waste places, established as a weed. The
name Morning Glory comes from the
showy flowers that open in the morning
and wilt by late afternoon. Of two
similar species in the Southwest, both
with the common name Morning
Glory, *I. hederaceae* has narrow sepal
tips that curve outward and are longer
than the body of the sepal; *I. nil,* from
which many varieties of the garden
Morning Glory derive, has narrow,
straight sepal tips.

## DOGWOOD FAMILY (Cornaceae)

Mostly trees or shrubs, rarely herbs, commonly with tiny flowers surrounded by petal-like bracts, so as to resemble a single large flower.
Flowers: bisexual or unisexual, radially symmetrical; sepals 4 or 5, small; petals 4 or 5; stamens 4 or 5. All these parts attached at top of ovary.
Leaves: alternate or opposite, simple.
Fruit: berry or stone fruit.
About 12 genera and 100 species are known, mostly in temperate regions. Many are grown as ornamentals.

---

### 36 Bunchberry; Dwarf Cornel; Puddingberry
(*Cornus canadensis*)
Dogwood Family (Cornaceae)

Description: Stems grow in extensive low patches, with *1 whorl of leaves at top* and, just above, a cluster of *tiny greenish flowers surrounded by 4 ovate white or pinkish bracts.* The *flower cluster resembles a single large flower* held on a short stalk above leaves.
Flowers: bracts to 4" (10 cm) wide; small flowers in center of head have 4 sepals and 4 petals.
Leaves: ¾–3" (2–7.5 cm) long, narrowly ovate.
Fruit: bright red, round, berries in a tight cluster.
Height: 2–8" (5–20 cm).
Flowering: June–August.
Habitat: Moist woods.
Range: Across northern North America; south near the coast and in the mountains to northern California, Idaho, and northern New Mexico.
Comments: Among the smallest of a genus of mostly shrubs and trees, Bunchberry makes an excellent ground cover in the moist woodland garden, and is equally attractive in flower or fruit.

180 **Pacific Dogwood; Mountain
Dogwood; Western Flowering
Dogwood**
(*Cornus nuttallii*)
Dogwood Family (Cornaceae)

Description: A shrub or tree that *seems to have many
large white flowers* but actually has round
heads of small greenish flowers
surrounded by *4–7 conspicuous, broadly
ovate white bracts.*
Flowers: bracts to 4″ (10 cm) wide;
small flowers in center of head
have 4 sepals and 4 petals.
Leaves: 1½–4″ (3.8–10 cm) long,
broadly lanceolate, opposite.
Fruit: red berries about ½″ (1.3 cm)
long form tight clusters.
Height: 6–65′ (1.8–19.5 m).
Flowering: April–June.
Habitat: Open or fairly dense forest.
Range: British Columbia to southern
California; also in western Idaho.
Comments: In dense forests this is often an
understory tree. Open and lacy, its
broad white bracts seem to glitter in
the filtered light. In the fall, it is one of
the few western trees with red foliage.

## SEDUM FAMILY (Crassulaceae)

Succulent herbs or small shrubs, commonly with star-like flowers in branched clusters.

Flowers: sepals 4 or 5; petals 4 or 5, free or united, with a scale-like gland at the base of each; stamens as many, or twice as many, as petals; pistils 4 or 5.

Leaves: simple, alternate or opposite, fleshy.

Fruit: tiny pod.

There are about 35 genera and 1,500 species. Many are cultivated as ornamentals or succulent novelties, including Jade Trees, Stonecrops, and Air Plants. Vegetative reproduction is common in the family, and in some members little plantlets grow along the leaves, drop to the ground, and root.

### 402 Canyon Dudleya
(*Dudleya cymosa*)
Sedum Family (Crassulaceae)

Description: 1 or a few reddish flower stalks, with *red to yellow flowers* in a flat-topped, branched, dense flower cluster, grow from a *basal rosette of thick, succulent, grayish-green leaves.*
Flowers: about ½" (1.3 cm) long; sepals 5, fleshy, joined at base; petals 5, erect, yellow to red, joined near base; flowers on individual stalks ¼–¾" (6–20 mm) long along branches of cluster.
Leaves: 2–4" (5–10 cm) long, broadly lanceolate, those on flower stalk much smaller.
Height: 4–8" (10–20 cm).
Flowering: April–June.
Habitat: On rock in brush and open woods.
Range: Much of California in the Sierra Nevada and Coast Ranges.
Comments: The many species of *Dudleya* in California, fewer in Arizona, may hybridize, adding to the difficulty of

identification. They resemble *Sedum,* but the latter generally have flower stalks growing from the center of the rosette or the tip of stem rather than from leaf axils, and do not have petals joined near the base.

## 278 Powdery Dudleya
*(Dudleya farinosa)*
Sedum Family (Crassulaceae)

Description: Whitish flower stalks and *clusters of yellow flowers* grow from *dense rosettes of ovate, succulent leaves* often covered with whitish powder.
Flowers: about ⅜" (9 mm) wide, narrow; sepals 5, short, triangular; petals 5, narrow; flowers erect on individual stalks ¼–½" (6–13 mm) long on main branches of cluster.
Leaves: 1–2½" (2.5–6.3 cm) long, pointed, those on flower stalk much smaller.
Height: 4–14" (10–35 cm).
Flowering: May–September.
Habitat: On bluffs near the Pacific Coast.
Range: Southern Oregon to southern California.
Comments: This plant often grows in large mat-like clusters. In the northern part of its range it is the only coastal species; to the south there are several.

## 335 Sierra Sedum
*(Sedum obtusatum)*
Sedum Family (Crassulaceae)

Description: *Pale yellow flowers* bloom on branched clusters atop reddish stalks that grow from *dense basal rosettes of succulent, often reddish-tinged leaves.*
Flowers: sepals 5, blunt; petals 5, narrow, pointed, united in their lower fourth, about ⅜" (9 mm) long, yellow

at first, but fading to white or pinkish.

Leaves: ¼–1″ (6–25 mm) long, broadest in upper half, rounded or slightly indented at tip; leaves on flower stalk much smaller.

Height: 1–7″ (2.5–17.5 cm).

Flowering: June–July.

Habitat: Rocky slopes at moderate to high elevations.

Range: Southern Oregon to the southern Sierra Nevada.

Comments: *Sedum,* from the Latin *sedere,* "to sit," here refers to the tendency of many species to grow low to the ground. In all plants, open pores in the leaves let in carbon dioxide to be used in the food-making process called photosynthesis. However, this allows stored water to escape, a critical problem in arid environments. Many succulents reduce water loss by opening their pores at night; the carbon dioxide that enters is stored for use in daylight, when the pores are closed.

## 385 Roseroot; King's Crown
(*Sedum rosea*)
Sedum Family (Crassulaceae)

Description: A *succulent, leafy plant* with erect, clustered stems and *small brownish-purple or maroon flowers* in head-like bunches at the top.

Flowers: about ⅛″ (3 mm) long; sepals 4, fleshy; petals 4, fleshy; stamens 8; no ovaries on some plants, 4 ovaries and no stamens on others. Sometimes there are more parts.

Leaves: ¼–1″ (6–25 mm) long, broadly lanceolate, crowded but equally spaced along stem.

Height: 1¼–12″ (3.1–30 cm).

Flowering: June–August.

Habitat: Open areas high in the mountains.

Range: Across northern North America; south in the mountains to southern

California, Nevada, Utah, and northern New Mexico.

Comments: The root has a Rose-like fragrance, giving one of its common names. A similar species, Red Orpine or Rose Crown (*S. rhodanthum*), has deep pink to nearly white flowers, petals ⅜–½" (9–13 mm) long, and each flower has stamens and ovaries; it generally grows in wet places from moderate to high elevations from south-central Montana to northern Arizona and southern New Mexico.

## CUCUMBER FAMILY
### (Cucurbitaceae)

Herbs, often trailing or climbing by coiled tendrils.
Flowers: radially symmetrical; sepals 5; petals 5, united; some flowers have 5 stamens and no ovary; others have an ovary with all parts attached at the top, but lack stamens.
Leaves: alternate, varying from not lobed to deeply palmately lobed.
Fruit: berry with a leathery rind.
About 100 genera and 850 species occur in warm regions of the world. Melons, Cucumbers, Squash, and Pumpkins are economically important members of the family.

345 **Melon Loco**
(*Apodanthera undulata*)
Cucumber Family (Cucurbitaceae)

Description: A bad-smelling, grayish, hairy plant with *long, coarse, prostrate stems* that have tendrils, *kidney-shaped leaf blades,* and *yellow, funnel-shaped flowers.*
Flowers: 1½" (3.8 cm) wide; petals 5, joined at base; some with 3 stamens and no functional ovary, others with an ovary and no stamens.
Leaves: 2–6" (5–15 cm) wide, attached to stalk at indented side, edges shallowly toothed, lobed, or wavy.
Fruit: 2½–4" (6.3–10 cm) long, oval, ribbed.
Height: creeper, the leaves up to 8" (20 cm) high, the stems to 10' (3 m).
Flowering: May–September.
Habitat: Sand dunes, gravelly flats, and slopes.
Range: Southern Arizona to western Texas; south to Mexico.
Comments: Plants with the name "loco" are usually poisonous to some degree; several have toxins that produce madness.

### 344 Buffalo Gourd; Calabacilla Loca
(*Cucurbita foetidissima*)
Cucumber Family (Cucurbitaceae)

Description: A malodorous plant with *large, gray-green, triangular leaves growing along long, prostrate stems.* Mostly hidden under leaves are *funnel-shaped orange to yellow flowers.*
Flowers: 2–3" (5–7.5 cm) wide; some with stamens, others only with an ovary; corolla with 5 lobes.
Leaves: to 1' (30 cm) long, rough.
Fruit: 3" (7.5 cm) in diameter, spherical, hard, striped, pale and dark green when immature, lemon yellow when ripe.
Height: creeper, with leaves reaching about 1' (30 cm) high, on trailing stems to 20' (6 m).
Flowering: April–July.
Habitat: Open areas on plains and deserts.
Range: Southern California to eastern Colorado; east to Missouri; south into Mexico.
Comments: The fruits are easily dried and often brightly painted for decorative use. They are foul-tasting, inedible, and when mature somewhat poisonous. Massive roots of large specimens may weigh several hundred pounds.

### 3 Globe Berry
(*Ibervillea lindheimeri*)
Cucumber Family (Cucurbitaceae)

Description: *Shiny, spherical berries resembling scarlet marbles* hang on these small climbing vines. The tiny flowers are yellowish-green.
Flowers: about ½" (1.3 cm) wide, with only stamens on some plants, and only an ovary on others.
Leaves: 1–5" (2.5–12.5 cm) long, about as wide, deeply divided into 3 or 5 narrow lobes, at least ½" (1.3 cm) wide, which may also be lobed.
Fruit: berry 1–1½" (2.5–3.8 cm) wide.

|  |  |
|---|---|
| | Height: vine, to 4' (1.2 m) long. |
| Flowering: | June—August. |
| Habitat: | Along draws and on rocky slopes in deserts. |
| Range: | South-central Texas to southern Oklahoma. |
| Comments: | Female plants make handsome ornamentals where low vines are desired, but male plants must also be planted nearby for fruits to grow. This species barely enters the southeastern range of this book. More common is Cut-leaved Globe Berry (*I. tenuisecta*), from southeastern Arizona to western Texas and northern Mexico. Its leaf divisions are much narrower, its berry only ⅝" (1.5 cm) in diameter. |

## SEDGE FAMILY (Cyperaceae)

Herbs of wet sites, often grass-like,
with stems commonly 3-sided.
Flowers: bisexual or unisexual, radially
symmetrical, nestled in the axil of a
bract, aggregated into small compact
spikes arranged in raceme-like, dense or
openly branched clusters; sepals and
petals are bristles or scales, or entirely
absent; stamens 3 or 6. Floral parts
attached at base of the ovary.
Leaves: long, narrow, with sheaths at
base enclosing stem; in some, the leaf
blade is absent.
Fruit: seed-like, lens-shaped or 3-sided.
There are about 90 genera and 4,000
species occurring nearly throughout the
world. Cotton Grass, Bulrush, and
Tule are members of this family.

### 96 Cotton Grass
*(Eriophorum polystachion)*
Sedge Family (Cyperaceae)

Description: Extensive patches of erect stems with
grass-like leaves, topped by *2–8 white,
cottony heads in a cluster.*
Flowers: cluster of heads 2–3" (5–
7.5 cm) wide; small brownish or
blackish scales around base of each
individual head in cluster, each scale
with a midrib that does not reach tip.
Leaves: 6–20" (15–50 cm) long.
Height: 8–40" (20–100 cm).

Flowering: July–August.

Habitat: Cold swamps and bogs.

Range: Throughout the Northern Hemisphere,
south to central Oregon, Idaho,
northeastern Utah, and northern New
Mexico.

Comments: The name comes from the Greek *erion*
("wool") and *phoros* ("bearing"). The
slender bristles of "cotton" are actually
modified sepals and petals of minute
flowers. There are several similar
species.

## TEASEL FAMILY (Dipsacaceae)

Herbs with flowers in dense heads.
Flowers: bilaterally symmetrical, each
associated with 2 united bracts forming
a calyx-like structure; sepals 5; petals 5,
united; stamens 4. All these parts
attached at top of ovary.
Leaves: simple or deeply divided,
opposite.
Fruit: seed-like.
There are about 10 genera and 270
species, natives of the Old World.
Bluebuttons and Pincushion Flower are
grown as ornamentals, and the weedy
Teasel is used in dried flower
arrangements.

---

### 615 Teasel
(*Dipsacus sylvestris*)
Teasel Family (Dipsacaceae)

Description: Angular, prickly, erect stems end in
*oval heads with many small, sharp bracts.*
Flowers: heads 1¼–2″ (3.1–5 cm)
wide, beneath which curve upward a
few long, narrow bracts, each associated
with a *small, pale purple flower.*
Leaves: to 1″ (2.5 cm) long, lanceolate,
opposite, bases of a pair joined, prickly
on midvein on underside.
Height: 1½–7′ (45–210 cm).

Flowering: April–September.

Habitat: Moist places, frequent on grassy
hillsides.

Range: Throughout; especially frequent west of
the Cascade Mountains and Sierra
Nevada.

Comments: *Dipsacus,* presumably coming from the
Greek *dipsa,* meaning "thirst," refers to
the water accumulated in the cup-like
bases of joined leaves. Fuller's Teasel
(*D. fullonum*), occasionally found in the
West, has small bracts with hooked
tips, a characteristic which prompted
cloth cleaners to use its dried heads to
raise the nap after beating and cleaning.

## SUNDEW FAMILY (Droseraceae)

Carnivorous herbs, mostly of acidic
bogs, with flowers in a raceme or
openly branched clusters.
Flowers: radially symmetrical; sepals 5,
united; petals 5, separate; stamens 5.
All these parts attached at base of
ovary.
Leaves: covered with sticky glandular
hairs on which insects become trapped.
Fruit: capsule with 2–5 chambers.
There are 4 genera and about 100
species, which generally grow in very
poor soil, so that extra nutrients
obtained from digested organisms may
be devoted mostly to seed production.

### 27 Roundleaved Sundew
(*Drosera rotundifolia*)
Sundew Family (Droseraceae)

Description: *White or pinkish flowers* bloom near the
bent end of a slender stalk that grows
from a *small basal rosette of leaves*.
Flowers: about ⅜" (9 mm) wide; petals
4–8 (usually 5).
Leaves: 1–4" (2.5–10 cm) long, with
long stout stalks, spreading, the round
blades ¼–½" (6–13 mm) wide, *covered
with reddish stalked glands*.
Height: to 10" (25 cm).

Flowering: June–September.

Habitat: Swamps and bogs.

Range: In the Sierra Nevada and northward;
east from Washington across northern
Montana and North Dakota.

Comments: The genus name, Greek for "dewy,"
refers to the moist, glistening drops on
the leaves, to which small organisms
stick. Longer-stalked glands near the
edge of a leaf slowly bend inward,
securing and placing an entrapped
organism in the digestive area of
stalkless glands. Narrowleaf Sundew
(*D. anglica*) has erect leaves with long,
narrow blades.

## HEATH FAMILY (Ericaceae)

Usually shrubs or woody perennial herbs, sometimes trees, often with showy flowers blooming singly or in clusters.

Flowers: radially or bilaterally symmetrical; sepals 4 or 5, united; petals 4 or 5, united, often taking the shape of a miniature Chinese lantern; stamens twice as many as petals, each anther usually opening by a terminal pore. All these parts attached either at base or at top of ovary.

Leaves: simple, usually alternate, often leathery.

Fruit: capsule, berry, or drupe.

There are at least 50 genera and up to 2,500 species, mostly occurring on acid soils in temperate regions. Numerous handsome ornamentals, including the spectacular Rhododendrons and Azaleas, come from this family, as do several edible fruits such as blueberries, huckleberries, and cranberries.

---

**428, 558 Kinnikinnick; Bearberry**
(*Arctostaphylos uva-ursi*)
Heath Family (Ericaceae)

Description: A low, matted plant with smooth, *red-brown, woody trailing stems, leathery, dark green leaves,* and small, *pink, lantern-shaped flowers* in racemes on short branches.
Flowers: corolla ¼" (6 mm) long, with 5 lobes around small opening.
Leaves: ¼–1¼" (1.3–3.1 cm) long, oblong, widest near blunt tips.
Fruit: bright red berry ⅜" (9 mm) wide.
Height: creeper, the leaves and flower clusters about 6" (15 cm) high, the stems to 10′ (3 m) long.
Flowering: March–June.
Habitat: Open places near the coast or high in the mountains.

Range:      Coastal northern California north to
            Alaska; east from Oregon and
            Washington to the Rocky Mountains,
            and then south to New Mexico.
Comments:   Kinnikinnick, an Indian word for many
            tobacco substitutes, is most frequently
            applied to this species, which also had
            many medicinal uses, including the
            alleged control of several sexually
            transmitted diseases. In Greek *arctos* is
            "bear" and *staphyle* "grape," whereas in
            Latin *uva* is "a bunch of grapes" and
            *ursus* is "bear." The berries are indeed
            eaten by bears, as the name redundantly
            indicates. A similar species found in the
            Cascade Mountains and Sierra Nevada,
            Pinemat Manzanita (*A. nevadensis*), has
            a tiny sharp point at the tip of the leaf.

## 174 White Heather; Mountain Heather
(*Cassiope mertensiana*)
Heath Family (Ericaceae)

Description:  *Flowers like small white bells* hang from
              the tips of slender stalks that grow from
              the axils near the ends of the branches
              on this matted plant.
              Flowers: corolla ¼" (6 mm) long, with
              5 bluntly pointed lobes.
              Leaves: ⅛"–¼" (3–6 mm) long, *very
              narrow*, angled upward, opposite and
              *arranged in 4 rows that hide stem*.
              Fruit: 4- or 5-chambered capsule that
              opens along back of each chamber.
              Height: 2–12" (5–30 cm).
Flowering:    July–August.
Habitat:      Open slopes near and above the
              timberline.
Range:        Alaska and Canada south to central
              California, northern Nevada, and
              western Montana.
Comments:     The white flowers, somewhat star-like,
              may have inspired the genus name of
              this plant, for in Greek mythology
              Cassiopeia was set among the stars as a
              constellation. Firemoss Cassiope
              (*C. tetragona*), near the Canadian

border, has a prominent groove on the
lower side of each leaf. Starry Cassiope
(*C. stelleriana*), which grows in bogs
from Mount Rainier northward, has
alternate, spreading leaves.

---

574  **Salal**
(*Gaultheria shallon*)
Heath Family (Ericaceae)

Description:  Shrub-like, with spreading or erect
hairy stems, often in large, dense
patches, the *pale pink, urn-shaped flowers*
hanging along *reddish or salmon racemes*
in upper axils.
Flowers: corolla hairy, ⅜″ (9 mm) long,
with 5 pointed lobes around opening.
Leaves: 2–4″ (5–10 cm) long, ovate,
with many minute teeth on edges.
Fruit: dark purple berry ¼–½″
(6–13 mm) in diameter.
Height: 4–48″ (10–120 cm).
Flowering:  May–July.
Habitat:  Woods or brush.
Range:  Southern California to British
Columbia.
Comments:  The berries are a source of food for
wildlife, and were once also eaten by
coastal Indians. The leaves are often
used in floral arrangements.

---

560  **Alpine Laurel**
(*Kalmia microphylla*)
Heath Family (Ericaceae)

Description:  Several *deep pink, bowl-shaped flowers* face
upward on slender stalks growing near
the top of the leafy stems of this low,
matted plant.
Flowers: corolla ½″ (1.3 cm) wide,
with 5 lobes, and 10 little pouches that
hold the 10 stamens, which spring up
suddenly as corolla expands or is bent
back.
Leaves: ½–1½″ (1.3–3.8 cm) long,

opposite, lanceolate, smooth and *dark green on upper side, gray and hairy on lower,* edges often curled downward. Height: 4–20″ (10–50 cm).

Flowering: June–September.

Habitat: Bogs and wet mountain meadows.

Range: Canada and Alaska; south to southern California and central Colorado.

Comments: Leaves, in spite of the name, are not to be used as a seasoning as they are suspected of being poisonous. The smaller Western Swamp Laurel (*K. occidentalis*), from lowlands of Alaska to Oregon, has flowers ⅝–¾″ (1.5–2 cm) wide.

---

177 **Trapper's Tea**
(*Ledum glandulosum*)
Heath Family (Ericaceae)

Description: *White flowers bloom in roundish clusters* at ends of branches of this *shrub.*
Flowers: about ½″ (1.3 cm) wide; petals 5, white; stamens 5–12, the lower part of the stalks hairy.
Leaves: ½–2½″ (1.3–6.3 cm) long, closely placed on stem, ovate or elliptic, with white, felt-like hairs beneath.
Fruit: roundish 5-chambered capsule.
Height: 2–7′ (60–210 cm).

Flowering: June–August.

Habitat: Wet places in the mountains.

Range: British Columbia; south to the Sierra Nevada of California, northeastern Oregon, central Idaho, and northwestern Wyoming.

Comments: As with many shrubby species in this family, Trapper's Tea is poisonous. Labrador Tea (*L. groenlandicum*) grows across Canada, and occurs in the West from Alaska to the coast of Oregon. It has a rusty hue to the woolly underside of the leaf.

### 559  Pink Mountain Heather
(*Phyllodoce empetriformis*)
Heath Family (Ericaceae)

Description:  A low, matted shrub with *short, needle-like leaves* and *deep pink, bell-shaped flowers* that hang at the ends of slender stalks in upper leaf axils.
Flowers: corolla about ¼" (6 mm) long, with 5 lobes tightly curled back; stamens 10, shorter than corolla.
Leaves: ⅜–⅝" (9–15 mm) long, with deep groove on lower side.
Fruit: 5-chambered capsule that splits open along the walls between chambers.
Height: 4–16" (10–40 cm).
Flowering:  June–August.
Habitat:  Open rocky slopes or in forests high in the mountains.
Range:  Alaska to northern California, Idaho, and Colorado.
Comments:  Brewer Mountain Heather (*P. breweri*), from the California mountains, has pink flowers and stamens longer than the corolla. Cream Mountain Heather (*P. glandulifera*), growing in the mountains from Oregon and Wyoming northward, has glandular hairs on a yellowish or greenish-white corolla.

### 179  White Rhododendron
(*Rhododendron albiflorum*)
Heath Family (Ericaceae)

Description:  A shrub with *1–4 white, bowl-shaped flowers clustered in leaf axils along the stem.*
Flowers: corolla ⅝–¾" (1.5–2 cm) wide, with 5 round lobes; stamens 10, hairy near base.
Leaves: 1½–4" (3.8–10 cm) long, broadly lanceolate, with short petioles.
Height: 3–7' (90–210 cm).
Flowering:  June–August.
Habitat:  Wet places in the mountains.
Range:  British Columbia; south to Oregon; east to western Montana.

Comments: This species does not produce the spectacular brilliant flowers that many of its relatives do, yet its dainty clusters of mildly citrus-scented white flowers and bright green leaves are delightful. The genus name comes from the Greek *rhodon* ("rose") and *dendron* ("tree").

## 572 Western Azalea
(*Rhododendron occidentale*)
Heath Family (Ericaceae)

Description: Large *white to deep pink, very fragrant flowers* bloom in large clusters at ends of stems on this shrub.
Flowers: corolla 1½–2½" (3.8–6.3 cm) wide, with narrow, tubular base and 5 wavy, pointed lobes, the upper lobe with yellow-orange patch; stamens 5, with hairy stalks.
Leaves: 1¼–3½" (3.1–8.8 cm) long, thin, bright green, elliptic.
Height: 4–17' (1.2–5.1 m).

Flowering: April–August.

Habitat: Moist places, in open areas near the coast, otherwise where partly shaded.

Range: Southern California to southwestern Oregon.

Comments: Flower variations include mixtures of pale pink, deep pink, and yellow-orange. The evergreen, pink-flowered native relative, California Rosebay (*R. macrophyllum*), grows from California to Canada and makes a choice ornamental.

## SPURGE FAMILY (Euphorbiaceae)

Usually herbs with milky sap; also shrubs or trees in the tropics.
Flowers: unisexual; radially symmetrical; calyx and corolla each with 5 separate parts, or corolla absent, or both calyx and corolla absent; stamens 1–10 or more. All these parts attached at base of ovary.
Leaves: simple or compound, alternate or opposite.
Fruit: round, 3-lobed, divided into 3 one-seeded sections.
There are about 290 genera and 7,500 species, mostly occurring in warm or hot regions. Among the valuable products of the family are rubber, castor and tung oils, and tapioca. Some are grown as ornamentals in tropical areas. Most members of the family are poisonous, and their milky sap will irritate the membranes of the eyes and mouth.

---

23 **Rattlesnake Weed**
(*Euphorbia albomarginata*)
Spurge Family (Euphorbiaceae)

Description: *Dense, thin mats of small, roundish opposite leaves* and slender stems have *milky sap,* and have *many tiny white flower-like cups.*
Flowers: attached to a cup less than ⅛" (3 mm) wide, 1 at each node; 4 or 5 small white appendages resembling petals, with a maroon pad at the base of each; nearly spherical, smooth ovary on stalk in center, with 3 lobes.
Leaves: ⅛–⅜" (3–9 mm) long, round or oblong, the stalks of the 2 leaves on opposite sides of stem connected by a single white scale on either side.
Fruit: tiny, plump, triangular capsule that splits into 3 sections, each section containing one pale brown seed with a white coat.
Height: creeper, with branches barely

½" (1.3 cm) high, and stems 2–10" (5–25 cm) long.

Flowering: April–November.

Habitat: Open areas in deserts, arid grassland, and piñon and juniper woodland.

Range: Southeastern California and southern Utah to Oklahoma; south to Mexico.

Comments: One of the showiest of the low Spurges, it was once thought useful for treatment of snakebite; hence its common name. The cup-like structure has many simple flowers: those producing pollen have only 1 stamen; those producing seeds consist of just an ovary. Around the edge of the cup are several glands which may or may not have petal-like appendages. The entire structure mimics a single flower, whose structure is typical of many species of *Euphorbia*. Most are poisonous, some dangerously so.

## PEA OR BEAN FAMILY
## (Fabaceae or Leguminosae)

Trees, shrubs, herbs, or vines with compound leaves and flowers in clusters.

Flowers: 3 distinct kinds: the one most commonly described in this book, the "pea flower," has a broad upper petal (banner or standard), two lateral petals (wings), and two bottom petals (keel) joined and shaped like the prow of a boat; usually has 9 stamens joined and 1 free, surrounding the ovary and hidden inside the keel. The two other kinds of flowers are those of Acacias, radially symmetrical and with conspicuous stamens, and those of Sennas, bilaterally symmetrical, but without a distinct banner and keel.

Leaves: pinnately or palmately compound; or sometimes simple by evolutionary loss of leaflets.

Fruit: 1-chambered pod that usually opens along one or two seams.

This enormous family has tremendous economic importance, encompassing such products as peas, beans, soybeans, peanuts, and lentils. Alfalfa and Clover provide forage for domestic livestock, but many other species are poisonous range weeds. Exotic hardwoods and gum arabic are provided by tropical trees belonging to the family, and numerous members are cultivated as handsome ornamentals.

---

557 **Field Milkvetch**
(*Astragalus agrestis*)
Pea Family (Fabaceae)

Description:  This soft, green plant tends to grow in patches, the weak stems often leaning on other vegetation; *lavender or purple "pea flowers" are crowded in short heads.*
Flowers: about ¾" (2 cm) wide; calyx with short, black hairs.

Leaves: *pinnately compound,* narrow, with
13–21 broadly lanceolate or oval
leaflets ¼–¾" (6–20 mm) long.
Fruit: pod about ½" (1.3 cm) long,
erect, 3 sides, the lowest with a groove.
Height: 2–12" (5–30 cm).

Flowering: May–August.

Habitat: Commonly in moist meadows and
prairies or on cool brushy slopes.

Range: Across much of Canada; south to
northeastern California, southern Utah,
central New Mexico, Kansas, and Iowa.

Comments: Representative of many of the low
*Astragalus* with lilac or purple flowers,
of which the hundreds in the West are
difficult to identify. The poisonous
species are known as "Locoweeds;"
apparently this species is not toxic.

---

490 **Crescent Milkvetch**
(*Astragalus amphioxys*)
Pea Family (Fabaceae)

Description: A *tufted, grayish, hairy plant* with
*pinnately compound leaves* and *lavender or
red-violet "pea flowers"* in short racemes.
Flowers: ¾–1" (2–2.5 cm) long.
Leaves: 7–21 ovate leaflets, each ⅛–¾"
(3–20 mm) long.
Fruit: pod ¾–2" (2–5 cm) long,
crescent-shaped or straight, tapered at
both ends, sharply pointed at the tip.
Height: 2–10" (5–25 cm).

Flowering: March–June.

Habitat: Sandy or gravelly soil in deserts, arid
grassland, or among piñon and juniper.

Range: Southern Nevada to western Colorado,
central New Mexico, and extreme
western Texas.

Comments: Crescent Milkvetch can be
distinguished from many similar species
by its pod, which has only one chamber
and has a lower seam that lies in a
groove rather than forming a prominent
ridge.

318 **Canada Milkvetch**
(*Astragalus canadensis*)
Pea Family (Fabaceae)

Description: Many *whitish to pale yellow "pea flowers"*
hang down slightly in dense racemes
atop leafy stems that often grow in
clusters.
Flowers: ½–¾" (1.3–2 cm) long.
Leaves: 2½–6" (6.3–15 cm) long,
*pinnately compound,* with 13–29 broadly
lanceolate leaflets.
Fruit: pod ½–¾" (1.3–2 cm) long,
erect, pointed, commonly grooved on
the lower (outer) side.
Height: 12–32" (30–80 cm).
Flowering: June–September.
Habitat: Open meadows and clearings in
coniferous forests, along roadside
ditches, and near creeks and lakeshores.
Range: Western Canada south to the central
Sierra Nevada of California, central
Nevada, southern Utah, and central
New Mexico.
Comments: The first *Astragalus* from North
America to be scientifically described.
Representative of many species with
white corollas, several notoriously
poisonous, the Canada Milkvetch has
toxic compounds but seems not to be a
serious pest.

401 **Crimson Woolly Pod**
(*Astragalus coccineus*)
Pea Family (Fabaceae)

Description: Long, *red "pea flowers"* angle upward in
loose heads above tufted, white,
woolly, pinnately compound leaves.
Flowers: 1½" (3.8 cm) long.
Leaves: 7–15 broad leaflets, each ⅛–
⅝" (3–15 mm) long.
Fruit: pod 1–1½" (2.5–3.8 cm) long,
covered with woolly white hairs,
plump, often bending the stem with
their weight and lying on the ground.
Height: 4–8" (10–20 cm).

Flowering: March—June.
Habitat: Open gravelly ridges and benches with piñon, juniper, or sagebrush.
Range: Southeastern California to western Arizona and northern Baja California.
Comments: Of the several low, tufted western *Astragalus* species with plump, woolly pods, this is the most spectacular. The unusually long red flowers, a rare color in the genus, are positioned to be easily accessible to hummingbirds.

### 489 Bent Milkvetch
(*Astragalus inflexus*)
Pea Family (Fabaceae)

Description: A low, *grayish-hairy plant, commonly forming small mats,* with pinnately compound leaves and rose-pink bilateral "pea flowers" on very short stalks.
Flowers: ¾–1¼" (2–3.1 cm) long, the upper petal (banner) arched upward, hairy on back; calyx has 5 very slender teeth at least half as long as tubular part; 6–19 flowers in each raceme.
Leaves: 13–29 oval to ovate leaflets ¼–¾" (6–20 mm) long.
Fruit: pod, plump, 1-chambered, silky—hairy.
Height: creeper, with flowering branches 1–4" (2.5–10 cm) high, and prostrate stems to 20" (50 cm) long.
Flowering: April—July.
Habitat: Dry hillsides and sagebrush deserts.
Range: Central Washington to northern Oregon; east to western Montana.
Comments: When in full flower, this species forms conspicuous, bright pink tufts or pads. There are many similar species distinguished by technical features. One, Pursh's Milkvetch (*A. purshii*), common throughout much of the West, has densely matted stems rarely longer than 4" (10 cm), and flowers varying from cream to deep reddish-purple, the narrowly lanceolate calyx teeth less than half the length of the tube.

### 430 Freckled Milkvetch
(*Astragalus lentigenosus*)
Pea Family (Fabaceae)

Description:   A more or less succulent plant with
stems that vary from erect to prostrate
and *whitish, pinkish, or purplish "pea
flowers" in racemes.*
Flowers: ⅜–¾" (9–20 mm) long,
spreading or erect.
Leaves: 11–19 broadly ovate or
roundish leaflets ⅜–⅝" (9–15 mm)
long, smooth or lightly hairy on upper
surface.
Fruit: pod ½–1½" (1.3–3.8 cm) long,
swollen and leathery-walled or bladdery
and thin-walled, 2-chambered, the end
flattened sideways into a prominent
upcurved beak.
Height: 4–16" (10–40 cm) long.
Flowering:   May–July.
Habitat:   From deserts and salt flats to open
slopes high in the mountains.
Range:   Western Canada; south through most of
the West to northwestern Mexico.
Comments:   One of the most variable of western
plants, with numerous types differing
in height, flowers, and pods. The
common name refers to the red-mottled
pod of many races.

### 567 Fairy Duster
(*Calliandra eriophylla*)
Pea Family (Fabaceae)

Description:   *Pinkish puffs* made by *many showy, deep
pink stamens* decorate this low, densely
branched shrub.
Flowers: in dense heads nearly 2" (5 cm)
wide, on short stems; tiny reddish calyx
with 5 teeth; petals 5, reddish, only
about ¼" (6 mm) long; stamens about
¾" (2 cm) long, projecting outward;
style red, slightly longer than
stamens.
Leaves: twice pinnately compound, 2–4
pairs of main divisions each bearing

5–10 pairs of oblong leaflets, each ³⁄₁₆″
(5 mm) long.
Height: 8–20″ (20–50 cm).
Flowering: February–May.
Habitat: Sandy washes and slopes in deserts or
arid grassland.
Range: Southern California to southwestern
New Mexico; south into northwestern
Mexico.
Comments: This little shrub is an inconspicuous
part of the arid landscape most of the
year, but in spring the exquisite
clusters of flowers with their many long
stamens form delicate, pink balls,
giving the plant a fluffy pink
appearance in full bloom. It belongs to
a group of mostly tropical woody plants
that includes Acacias and Mimosas.

## 194 Twinleaf
(*Cassia bauhinioides*)
Pea Family (Fabaceae)

Description: A low plant with few stems and *1–3
slightly bilateral yellow flowers* on short
stalks in axils of grayish leaves with
only 2 leaflets.
Flowers: ½″ (1.3 cm) wide; sepals 5,
narrow; petals 5, round, with upper
petal forward of others; stamens 10,
brown, the 3 upper ones very small.
Leaves: leaflets ¾–2″ (2–5 cm) long.
Fruit: pod ¾–1½″ (2–3.8 cm) long,
hairy.
Height: 4–16″ (10–40 cm).
Flowering: April–August.
Habitat: Hills and flats in arid grassland and
deserts.
Range: Central Arizona to western Texas; south
to northern Mexico.
Comments: This large genus, many species of
which are trees or shrubs, is found
primarily throughout the world's
tropics.

### 353  Blue Palo Verde
(*Cercidium floridum*)
Pea Family (Fabaceae)

Description:  This round tree has *smooth, blue-green bark,* is *leafless most of the year,* and when in bloom is covered with *yellow flowers in loose clusters* hanging from the leaf axils.
Flowers: about ¾" (2 cm) wide, slightly bilateral; petals 5, ⅜" (9 mm) long.
Leaves: ½–¾" (1.3 cm) long, few, each with 1 pair of ovate leaflets; smaller branches often spiny.
Fruit: pods 1½–3" (3.8–7.5 cm) long.
Height: to 33' (9.9 m).
Flowering:  March–May.
Habitat:  Washes and low sandy places.
Range:  Southern California, southern Arizona, and northwestern Mexico.
Comments:  Palo Verde is Spanish for "green tree," and even when leafless, the trees are conspicuously green in the brown desert. Photosynthesis occurs mostly in the bark, rather than the leaves—a mechanism for conserving water through a reduction in surface area. Little Leaf Palo Verde (*C. microphyllum*), growing in the same area and more frequent on gravelly slopes, has yellow-green bark, 4–8 pairs of leaflets on each leaf, and pale yellow flowers, the uppermost petal often whitish.

### 568  Western Redbud
(*Cercis occidentalis*)
Pea Family (Fabaceae)

Description:  The many erect stems of this shrub are leafless when they bloom, the *numerous small, rose-pink bilateral flowers in clusters* along the branches and nearly hiding the rest of the plant.
Flowers: ½" (1.3 cm) long; petals 5, the 2 lower cupped, facing one another and enclosing 1 pistil and 10 stamens,

the uppermost central, in front of lateral 2.

Leaves: 1¼–3½" (3.1–8.8 cm) wide, roundish, *kidney-shaped or broadly heart-shaped,* smooth, glossy.

Fruit: pods 1½–3½" (3.8–8.8 cm) long, flat, hang on shrub until late in season.

Height: 6–17' (1.8–5.1 m).

Flowering: February–April.
Habitat: Dry brushy slopes.
Range: Most of California; east to southern Utah and central Arizona.
Comments: One of the most handsome shrubs of the western foothills; commonly used as an ornamental. In spring the entire plant is covered with bright rose-pink flowers; the dense foliage is dark green in summer, reddish in the fall. Indians made baskets from the shredded bark, and extracts from the bark were used medicinally.

354 **Scotch Broom; Common Broom**
(*Cytisus scoparius*)
Pea Family (Fabaceae)

Description: A *shrub with many small, strongly angled branches and bright yellow "pea flowers"* usually blooming singly on stalks from the leaf axils; when in full flower the plant is a mass of yellow.

Flowers: about ¾" (2 cm) long.

Leaves: those near base of branches with 3 leaflets about ½" (1.3 cm) long; upper leaves with only 1 leaflet.

Fruit: pod 2–3" (5–7.5 cm) long, slender, hairy only on edges.

Height: to 10' (3 m).

Flowering: April–June.
Habitat: Road banks, open woods, and fields.
Range: Washington to California.
Comments: This handsome ornamental, a native of Europe, has proven to be a pesty shrub, filling in many areas that were once open prairies and sparse woods.

### 491 Feather Peabush; Feather Plume
(*Dalea formosa*)
Pea Family (Fabaceae)

Description: A low, scraggly shrub with *tiny pinnately compound leaves,* and "pea flowers" in short, head-like racemes, the *petals yellow and vivid reddish-lavender.*
Flowers: about ½" (1.3 cm) wide; upper petal broad and yellow, the remaining 4 bright purple; long, slender teeth of calyx have silky hairs and resemble little feathers.
Leaves: less than ½" (1.3 cm) long, divided into 7 or 9 plump, folded little leaflets.
Height: 1–3' (30–90 cm).
Flowering: March–May, often again in September.
Habitat: Scrubby vegetation on high plains and in deserts.
Range: Western Oklahoma to central Arizona; south to northern Mexico.
Comments: One of many shrubby species of *Dalea,* its dark bark, contorted branches, and small leaves make it an excellent candidate for bonsai. This and other shrubby *Dalea* species are hosts of a very strange flowering parasite, Thurber's Pilostyles (*Pilostyles thurberi*), which remains under the bark most of the year, then produces tiny, inconspicuous, yellowish-brown flowers that burst through and bloom early in the summer.

### 666 Smoke Tree
(*Dalea spinosa*)
Pea Family (Fabaceae)

Description: An *intricately branched, ashy-gray tree* with spine-tipped branches and *deep-blue-purple bilateral flowers* in numerous short spikes.
Flowers: "pea-like," nearly ½" (1.3 cm) long; calyx dotted with glands.
Leaves: ½–¾" (1.3–2 cm) long,

oblong, notched at tip, dropping from plant soon after they grow.
Fruit: tiny pod barely ¼" (6 mm) long, dotted with amber-colored glands.
Height: 4–26' (1.2–7.8 m).

Flowering: June–July.

Habitat: Sandy desert washes.

Range: Southeastern California to southwestern Arizona and northwestern Mexico.

Comments: From a distance, Smoke Tree looks gray and fluffy, like a puff of smoke. Its seeds will not sprout until the hard coat is scratched deeply enough to allow water to enter, usually by tumbling in turbid water and gravel during a heavy flow in the washes.

## 425 Western Coral Bean; Indian Bean; Chilicote
(*Erythrina flabelliformis*)
Pea Family (Fabaceae)

Description: A *shrub or small tree,* leafless much of the year, with *prickly stems and leafstalks,* and *long, bright red flowers* in racemes near ends of the branches.
Flowers: to 3" (7.5 cm) long, basically "pea-like," but modified so that the upper petal (banner) is straight and beak-like, nearly hiding 4 lower petals; calyx waxy white, nearly without lobes.
Leaves: compound, with 3 leaflets, each to 3" (7.5 cm) long.
Fruit: pod, with several large, scarlet, bean-like seeds.
Height: to 15' (4.5 m), but usually much shorter.

Flowering: March–May, also September.

Habitat: Rocky hillsides among oaks, juniper, and brush.

Range: Southern Arizona and southwestern New Mexico to northwestern Mexico.

Comments: This plant, though handsome in flower, is leafless and unattractive most of the year. The bright seeds, often used in Mexican necklaces, are deadly poisonous.

### 512   Western Sweetvetch
(*Hedysarum occidentale*)
Pea Family (Fabaceae)

Description:   The stems of this plant are bunched, with papery brown sheaths at base, *pinnately compound leaves,* and *deep pink or pinkish-purple spires of nodding "pea flowers"* in dense racemes.
Flowers: about ¾" (2 cm) long; upper 2 calyx lobes broader but shorter than lower 3.
Leaves: divided into 9−21 ovate leaflets, each ½−1¼" (1.3−3.1 cm) long, with *minute brown dots on upper surface.*
Fruit: pod, constricted into *1−4 oval segments* ¼−½" (6−13 mm) wide, flat, the sides with a light network of veins.
Height: 16−32" (40−80 cm).

Flowering:   June−September.
Habitat:   High elevations in the mountains, in meadows or in open forests.
Range:   Washington to Montana; south to Colorado.
Comments:   Attractive plants of the western mountains and northern plains; in the West, only 4 species of *Hedysarum* represent this northern genus of about 100 species.

### 314   Hog Potato; Camote de Raton
(*Hoffmanseggia glauca*)
Pea Family (Fabaceae)

Description:   A low plant in patches, with *pinnately compound leaves,* and *bilateral yellow-orange flowers* in glandular racemes.
Flowers: about ¾" (2 cm) wide; petals with narrow glandular stalks, upper petal speckled and blotched with orange near base; stamens 10.
Leaves: divided into 5−11 main sections, these divided into 5−11 pairs of oblong leaflets, each ⅛−⅜" (3−9 mm) long.
Fruit: pod ¾−1½" (2−3.8 cm) long,

flat, curved, glandular.
Height: 4–12″ (10–30 cm).

Flowering: March–September.
Habitat: In open alkaline areas, common along roads and as an agricultural weed.
Range: Southern California to southern Colorado and Texas; south to Mexico.
Comments: Hog Potato has small, edible swellings on the roots that provide good nourishment for many animals.
The Spanish name means "mouse's sweet potato." They also provided food for Indians.

## 556 Silky Beach Pea
(*Lathyrus littoralis*)
Pea Family (Fabaceae)

Description: This *silky-hairy, gray plant* grows in low patches, with *pink and white "pea flowers"* in dense racemes among pinnately compound leaves.
Flowers: ¾″ (2 cm) long; upper petal usually rose-pink, the lower ones white or pale pink.
Leaves: 2–10 broadly lanceolate leaflets, each ¼–¾″ (6–20 mm) long.
Fruit: pod about 1¼″ (3.1 cm) long.
Height: 8–24″ (20–60 cm).

Flowering: April–June.
Habitat: Sand dunes along the Pacific Coast.
Range: Washington to central California.
Comments: This beautifully colored plant forms dense patches among yellow and pink Sand Verbenas and Beach Morning Glories, adding to the spectacular natural garden of coastal dunes. A relative, Beach Pea or Sand Pea (*L. japonicus*), differs in having smooth stems and leaves, 2–8 flowers, each ¾–1¼″ (2–3.1 cm) long, with reddish-purple petals; it grows on sand dunes from northern California to Alaska.

### 285  Snub Pea
(*Lathyrus sulphureus*)
Pea Family (Fabaceae)

Description:  Several sprawling or clambering angular
stems bear *pinnately compound leaves,* and
yellowish "pea flowers" turned to one
side in racemes growing from leaf
axils.
Flowers: about ½" (1.3 cm) long;
corolla at first cream, but deepening
from *tan-yellow to dull orange,* the broad
upper petal often with rose veins, its
base as broad as or broader than turned-
up end.
Leaves: 6–12 leaflets, each ¾–2½"
(2–6.3 cm) long, tipped with clinging
tendrils.
Fruit: pod 1½–3" (3.8–7.5 cm) long,
narrow.
Height: 2–3' (60–90 cm).

Flowering:  April–June.

Habitat:  Slopes in chaparral and open forests.

Range:  Southwestern Oregon and the northern
two-thirds of California.

Comments:  The unusually broad base and the
barely upturned end of the banner
produce a stubby flower, hence the
common name. Del Norte Pea
(*L. delnorticus*), which grows near the
border of California and Oregon, differs
by having wing-like ridges on the
stem.

### 337  Bird's Foot Trefoil
(*Lotus corniculatus*)
Pea Family (Fabaceae)

Description:  Stems trail on the ground and root,
their tips turning upward, and in the
axils of pinnately compound leaves
grow stalks with *loose heads of yellow "pea
flowers."*
Flowers: ⅜–⅝" (9–15 mm) long;
petals 5, bright yellow, tinged
increasingly with red as they age.

Leaves: leaflets each ¼–¾" (6–20 mm) long, 3 grouped near tip, 2 placed at junction of leafstalk and stem.
Fruit: pod ¾–1½" (2–3.8 cm) long, slender, projecting mostly horizontally from flower stalk.
Height: creeper, the erect stem tips 3–12" (7.5–30 cm) high.

Flowering: May–September.

Habitat: Meadows, wet low places, and lawns.

Range: Washington and Idaho to northern California.

Comments: The spreading, slender pods of Bird's Foot Trefoil resemble a bird's foot; hence the common name.

### 293 Hill Lotus
(*Lotus humistratus*)
Pea Family (Fabaceae)

Description: A hairy, matted plant with many *small, yellow "pea flowers,"* each nestled in the axil of a *pinnately compound leaf.*
Flowers: about ¼" (6 mm) long, with petals that become reddish with age.
Leaves: 3–5 leaflets, each ¼–½" (6–13 mm) long.
Fruit: pod ¼–½" (6–13 mm) long, hairy.
Height: creeper, the flowers and leaves barely 2" (5 cm) high, but stems 4–18" (10–45 cm) long.

Flowering: March–June.

Habitat: Disturbed ground, roadsides, riverbanks, gullies, trails, old fields, and vacant lots.

Range: Most of California from low to moderate elevations; east to southwestern New Mexico.

Comments: This is a common weed in California, rather attractive when covered with hundreds of deep yellow flowers. A similar species, Chile Lotus (*L. subpinnatus*), has almost no hairs and grows in California's dry grassy slopes. It is one of nearly 100 western plants also found in Chile and Argentina, but not in the intervening thousands of miles, a natural distribution still not satisfactorily explained.

---

### 284 Deer Weed; California Broom
(*Lotus scoparius*)
Pea Family (Fabaceae)

Description: The *bunched, erect, tough, green stems* have small, pinnately compound leaves and *1–4 yellow "pea flowers" in clusters* in the upper leaf axils.
Flowers: about ⅜" (9 mm) long; petals 5, often developing a reddish hue as they age.
Leaves: *3 oblong leaflets,* each ¼–½" (6–13 mm) long.
Fruit: pod, slender, curved, with a narrow, *knife-like beak* and only 2 seeds.
Height: 1–3' (30–90 cm).
Flowering: March–August.
Habitat: Dry brushy slopes.
Range: Most of California to northern Baja California.
Comments: This is one of the many species of flowering plants that thrive after fire has ravaged chaparral-covered slopes. It vigorously persists for several years, although it is choked out of most areas by the thick brush that eventually returns. By taking advantage of the open habitat and quickly covering exposed slopes, it helps reduce erosion, which would be far greater if the soil depended for cover on the slower-growing brush. Like most other members of the Pea Family, it has the capacity to enrich the soil with nitrogen.

### 292 Wright's Deer Vetch
(*Lotus wrightii*)
Pea Family (Fabaceae)

Description: A dark green plant with several erect
stems, *stalkless pinnately compound leaves,*
and on slender stalks growing from leaf
axils 1 or a few *deep yellow "pea flowers."*
Flowers: ½" (1.3 cm) long; petals 5,
usually becoming reddish with age.
Leaves: 3–5 *crowded leaflets,* each ¼–½"
(6–13 mm) long.
Fruit: pod about 1" (2.5 cm) long,
slender.
Height: 8–16" (20–40 cm).

Flowering: April–August.

Habitat: Rocky slopes, mainly among piñon and
juniper.

Range: Southeastern California to southern
Utah and Colorado; south to New
Mexico and Arizona.

Comments: Wright's Deer Vetch is a favored
browse for deer and domestic livestock.
Like many species of the Pea Family, it
has an intricate method of pollination
that generally requires the aid of insects.

### 299 Tree Lupine; Yellow Bush Lupine
(*Lupinus arboreus*)
Pea Family (Fabaceae)

Description: A large, round, bushy plant with
*palmately compound leaves* and showy,
sweet-scented, *cone-like racemes of usually
yellow "pea flowers"* held just above the
foliage at ends of short branches.
Flowers occasionally violet or blue.
Flowers: over ½" (1.3 cm) long, in
dense racemes 4–12" (10–30 cm) long;
top petal (banner) hairless on back.
Leaves: 6–12 leaflets, each to 2½"
(6.3 cm) long, arranged like wheel
spokes.
Height: 2–9' (60–270 cm).

Flowering: March–June.

Habitat: Sandy areas and canyons near the Pacific
Coast.

Range: Along the coast of the northern two-thirds of California; introduced as a sand binder in Oregon and Washington.

Comments: Lupines were once believed to be "wolf-like," devouring soil nutrients (the genus name comes from Latin *lupus,* meaning wolf). In fact, they "prefer" poor soil, which they do not further deplete. Tree Lupine, one of the most handsome species in the genus, grows rapidly, and its deep roots make it an effective and beautiful stabilizer of shifting coastal dunes; portions of San Francisco that were once unstable sand were reclaimed by Tree Lupine.

## 636 Miniature Lupine
(*Lupinus bicolor*)
Pea Family (Fabaceae)

Description: A usually small, grayish, hairy, branched plant with *palmately compound leaves* and *blue-violet and white "pea flowers" arranged in whorls* in short, thick, conelike racemes.
Flowers: about ⅜" (9 mm) long, the central part of the top petal white and dotted with black, and the upper edge of the 2 lower petals (keel) with a few hairs near the tip; stalks of individual flowers only about ⅛" (3 mm) long.
Leaves: 5–7 leaflets, each ½–1¼" (1.3–3.1 cm) long, arranged like wheel spokes.
Fruit: pods about ¾" (2 cm) long, less than ¼" (6 mm) wide, hairy.
Height: 4–16" (10–40 cm).

Flowering: March–May.

Habitat: Mostly in open, often grassy, places from sea level to moderate elevations.

Range: Southern British Columbia to southern California.

Comments: The Miniature Lupine and the California Poppy (*Eschscholtzia californica*), are common companions, the blue cast given to fields by the Lupine complementing perfectly the fiery orange of the Poppy. There are many other annual Lupines. The oldest known viable seeds, discovered in 1967 frozen in a lemming burrow, are from an arctic Lupine, estimated at 10,000 years old; when planted they germinated in 48 hours.

### 514 Stinging Lupine
(*Lupinus hirsutissimus*)
Pea Family (Fabaceae)

Description: Erect, leafy plants with *yellow stinging bristles* on stems and leaves, and *reddish-lavender "pea flowers"* in racemes.
Flowers: slightly more than ½″ (1.3 cm) long.
Leaves: palmately compound, with 5–8 leaflets, each ¾–2″ (2–5 cm) long, arranged like wheel spokes.
Height: 8–40″ (20–100 cm).
Flowering: March–May.
Habitat: Woods and thickets and open places at the edges of deserts.
Range: Southern half of California and northern Baja California.
Comments: In a genus of lovely wildflowers this is an unpleasant exception. Its stiff yellow hairs sting like nettles.

### 302 Butter Lupine
(*Lupinus luteolus*)
Pea Family (Fabaceae)

Description: *Yellow "pea flowers" crowded in whorls* in long racemes grow on branched stems.
Flowers: ½″ (1.3 cm) long; sometimes pale lilac when young, turning to yellow; the lower 2 petals (keel) hairy on both edges near base.
Leaves: palmately compound, with 7–9

leaflets, each ¾–1¼" (2–3.1 cm) long,
arranged like wheel spokes.
Fruit: pod ½–¾" (1.3–2 cm) long,
harshly hairy.
Height: 12–32" (30–80 cm).

Flowering: May–August.

Habitat: Dry slopes and flats in open forests or
on grassy slopes.

Range: Southern Oregon to southern
California.

Comments: As the pod matures and dries, its walls
become elastic and finally burst open,
instantly curling and throwing the
seeds some distance. On a warm
afternoon these opening pods can be
heard softly popping, and a person
standing in a patch of mature Lupines
may be hit by flying seeds.

### 638  Blue-pod Lupine
(*Lupinus polyphyllus*)
Pea Family (Fabaceae)

Description: 1 or several, mostly unbranched, stout,
hollow stems have *violet or blue-violet*
*"pea flowers"* in dense, long racemes.
Flowers: about ½" (1.3 cm) long.
Leaves: palmately compound, generally
with 9–13 leaflets, each 1½–4" (3.8–
10 cm) long, smooth on upper surface,
arranged like wheel spokes.
Height: 2–5' (60–150 cm).

Flowering: June–August.

Habitat: Moist meadows and forests, along
streams, from lowlands to mountains.

Range: British Columbia to the Coast Ranges
of central California; east to Colorado,
Montana, and Alberta.

Comments: This somewhat succulent Lupine is one
of the tallest and lushest western
species. It has been crossed with other
Lupines, particularly Yellow Bush
Lupine (*L. arboreus*), for beautiful
horticultural hybrids. Along with
several other Lupine species, it is
known to be toxic to livestock.

### 637 Coulter's Lupine
(*Lupinus sparsiflorus*)
Pea Family (Fabaceae)

Description: Slender, erect, branched stems have *pale blue or blue-lilac "pea flowers"* in open racemes.
Flowers: ½" (1.3 cm) long; top petal (banner) usually with white or pale yellow center; 2 bottom petals (keel) usually hairy on lower edge near base, and with a slender point at tip.
Leaves: palmately compound, with 5–9 leaflets, each ½–1½" (1.3–3.8 cm) long, usually only about ⅛" (3 mm) wide, arranged like wheel spokes.
Height: 8–16" (20–40 cm).

Flowering: January–May.

Habitat: Open fields, slopes, and deserts.

Range: Southern California and northern Baja California, southern Nevada and southwestern New Mexico.

Comments: In a "good year" with ample fall and winter rains, Coulter's Lupine carpets the floor of the southern Arizona desert, competing for attention with Globemallows (*Sphaeralcea* spp.) and Desert Marigold (*Baileya multiradiata*), providing mile after mile of blue-violet, brick red, and brilliant yellow. Found only in the Big Bend region of Texas is the similar Chisos Bluebonnet (*L. havardii*), with dark blue-violet petals.

### 513 Harlequin Lupine; Stiver's Lupine
(*Lupinus stiversii*)
Pea Family (Fabaceae)

Description: Racemes of *3-colored "pea flowers," rose, yellow, and white,* bloom on this freely branched plant.
Flowers: slightly more than ½" (1.3 cm) long; upper petal (banner) yellow, side petals (wings) rose, lower petals (keel) white.
Leaves: palmately compound, with 6–8 leaflets, each ½–1½" (1.3–3.8 cm)

long, arranged like wheel spokes.
Height: 4–18″ (10–45 cm).
Flowering: April–July.
Habitat: Open sandy or gravelly places in oak
and pine woodland.
Range: Western slope of the Sierra Nevada to
the mountains of southern California.
Comments: The unusual coloration of the flower
immediately distinguishes this species,
and accounts for one of its common
names.

## 119 White Sweet Clover
(*Melilotus alba*)
Pea Family (Fabaceae)

Description: A tall, widely branched, leafy plant
with *tiny, white "pea flowers" in numerous
slender racemes.*
Flowers: racemes 1½–5″ (3.8–12.5 cm)
long; individual flowers less than
¼″ (6 mm) long.
Leaves: divided into 3 lanceolate
leaflets, each ¾–1¼″ (2–3.1 cm) long,
with teeth on edges.
Fruit: pod ³⁄₁₆″ (5 mm) long, usually
only 1-seeded.
Height: 2–10′ (60–300 cm).
Flowering: May–October.
Habitat: A weed along roadsides, riverbanks, in
old fields, wherever the ground has
been disturbed, often forming very
dense patches.
Range: Throughout; especially common from
Washington to California.
Comments: Sweet Clover's scent, which resembles
that of newly mown hay, is especially
noticeable on a warm, still day. There
are two similar species with yellow
petals: Yellow Sweet Clover (*M.
officinalis*), especially common in the
Rocky Mountain region, has flowers
³⁄₁₆–¼″ (5–6 mm) long and usually
grows more than 3′ (90 cm) tall. Sour
Clover (*M. indicus*), less common, has
flowers ⅛″ (3 mm) long and rarely
exceeds 3′ (90 cm) in height.

### 516 Purple Loco; Lambert's Loco; Colorado Loco
(*Oxytropis lambertii*)
Pea Family (Fabaceae)

Description: A tufted plant, usually covered with silvery hairs, with *dense racemes of bright reddish-lavender "pea flowers"* held just above the basal leaves by long stalks.
Flowers: ½–1" (1.3–2.5 cm) long; 2 lower petals (keel) with a common slender point projecting forward at the tip.
Leaves: 3–12" (8–30 cm) long, pinnately compound, with leaflets ¼–1½" (6–38 mm) long.
Fruit: pod ¾–1¼" (2–3.1 cm) long, erect, plump, pointed, with a groove on side toward stem.
Height: 4–16" (10–40 cm).

Flowering: June–September.

Habitat: Plains and open areas in pine forests.

Range: On the Great Plains from Canada to Texas; west to the eastern base of the Rocky Mountains in Montana and Wyoming; through the mountains to central Utah and Arizona.

Comments: One of the most dangerously poisonous plants on western ranges, it is lethally toxic to all kinds of livestock. The single feature that distinguishes Purple Loco from other American *Oxytropis* species is the hairs attached by their middle to a short stalk forming a miniature teeter-totter, a feature seen only with a lens and even then sometimes escaping notice.

### 124 White Loco; Silky Loco; Silverleaf Locoweed
(*Oxytropis sericea*)
Pea Family (Fabaceae)

Description: A densely tufted, grayish, hairy plant with *racemes of white or cream "pea flowers"* held just above the basal leaves on long stalks.

Flowers: ¾–1″ (2–2.5 cm) long; the 2 lower petals (keel) with a common slender point that projects forward and is often purplish.
Leaves: 2–12″ (5–30 cm) long, pinnately compound, with lanceolate leaflets ½–1½″ (1.3–3.8 cm) long.
Fruit: pod ½–1″ (1.3–2.5 cm) long, erect, plump, with a groove on side toward stem, and thick, fleshy walls that become hard when dry.
Height: 3–16″ (8–40 cm).

Flowering: May–September.

Habitat: Prairies, mountain meadows, and open mountain slopes.

Range: Western Canada; south to southern Idaho, northeastern Nevada, southern Utah, central New Mexico, and western Oklahoma.

Comments: White Loco has been implicated in the poisoning of domestic livestock. In some areas it has purple petals, the result of hybridization with Purple Loco (*O. lambertii*), but the hairs on the hybrid's leaves are attached by the base rather than by a bisecting stalk.

### 515 Showy Loco
(*Oxytropis splendens*)
Pea Family (Fabaceae)

Description: A tufted plant covered with *silky, white hairs,* with dense spikes of *deep pink to lavender "pea flowers"* held on long stalks just above the basal leaves.
Flowers: about ½″ (1.3 cm) long; 2 bottom petals (keel) with a tip with a narrow point that projects forward.
Leaves: compound, with *clusters of 2–4 leaflets,* each ⅛–¾″ (3–20 mm) long, in 7–15 whorls along main stalk.
Height: 4–16″ (10–40 cm).

Flowering: June–August.

Habitat: Open areas on road banks, riverbanks, and meadows.

Range: Alaska; south to northern New Mexico; east to Minnesota.

Comments: One of the showiest of *Oxytropis,* the bright deep pink to lavender petals are beautifully set off by the unusual silvery foliage.

---

93 **White Prairie Clover**
(*Petalostemon candidum*)
Pea Family (Fabaceae)

Description: A plant with several branched stems; smooth, bright green leaves, and *dense spikes of white bilateral flowers.*
Flowers: less than ¼" (6 mm) long, in clusters to 2½" (6.3 cm) long, petals 5, the upper broader and slender stalks; stamens 5; calyx with glands just beneath the 5 teeth.
Leaves: pinnately compound, with 5–9 oblong leaflets, each ½–1¼" (1.3–3.8 cm) long, minutely dotted with glands on the lower side.
Fruit: pod ⅛" (3 mm) long, with glands on walls.
Height: 1–2' (30–60 cm).

Flowering: May–September.
Habitat: Plains, arroyos, along roads, and among piñon and juniper.
Range: Central Canada; south, mostly along the eastern slope of the Rocky Mountains, to Colorado; west to Utah and Arizona; east across the plains to Illinois and Alabama; south into Mexico.
Comments: The genus is closely related to *Dalea* and by one expert recently included within it. White Dalea (*D. albiflora*), from Arizona, southwestern New Mexico, and Mexico, resembles White Prairie Clover, but has 10 stamens. Species of *Petalostemum* always have 5, *Dalea,* 10.

### 496 Purple Prairie Clover
(*Petalostemon purpureum*)
Pea Family (Fabaceae)

Description: A fairly slender plant varying from nearly smooth to grayish-woolly, with *pinnately compound leaves* and *dense, hairy spikes of deep reddish-lavender bilateral flowers*.
Flowers: spikes ¾–3" (2–7.5 cm) long and about ½" (1.3 cm) thick; individual flowers about ¼" (6 mm) long, the upper petal broader and protruding less than the others; calyx densely hairy; stamens 5, with golden-orange pollen sacs.
Leaves: usually 5 narrow leaflets, each ½–1" (1.3–2.5 cm) long.
Fruit: pod, tiny, plump, usually with 1 seed.
Height: 1–3' (30–90 cm).
Flowering: May–August.
Habitat: Open prairies and foothills.
Range: Central Canada; south along the eastern slope of the Rocky Mountains northern Arizona, New Mexico, and western Texas; on the eastern side of the range reaching Illinois and Alabama.
Comments: The flower is unusual. Probably the upper petal is the only true petal, the other 4 being modified stamens.

### 569 Chaparral Pea
(*Pickeringia montana*)
Pea Family (Fabaceae)

Description: A *spiny dark green shrub*, often forming impenetrable thickets, with bright *reddish-lavender "pea flowers"* near the ends of branches.
Flowers: about ¾" (2 cm) long.
Leaves: 3 leaflets, less than ½" (1.3 cm) long, stiff, broadly lanceolate.
Fruit: pod 1¼–2" (3.1–5 cm) long, flat, straight.
Height: to 7' (2.1 m).
Flowering: May–August.

Habitat: Dry hillsides in chaparral.

Range: Central to southern California.

Comments: The only species in a genus confined to California, Chaparral Pea contributes to the state's unique flora. Rarely reproducing from seed, it grows new stems from roots that spread, especially after fires.

## 300 Yellow Pea; Golden Pea; Buck Bean; False Lupine
(*Thermopsis montana*)
Pea Family (Fabaceae)

Description: A plant with one or several hollow stems, slightly or not at all hairy, and *yellow "pea flowers"* in long racemes in upper leaf axils.
Flowers: ¾–1" (2–2.5 cm) long; stamens 10, none joined together by their stalks.
Leaves: compound, with *3 broadly lanceolate leaflets,* each 2–4" (5–10 cm) long; a pair of broadly ovate, leaf-like stipules occur where leafstalk joins stem.
Fruit: pod 1½–3" (3.8–7.5 cm) long, slender, erect, hairy.
Height: 2–4' (60–120 cm).

Flowering: May–August.

Habitat: Meadows or openings in coniferous forests, in dry or moist soil.

Range: British Columbia to northern California; east to Montana and Colorado.

Comments: This genus resembles the Lupines, but *Thermopsis* has only 3 leaflets on each leaf; *Lupinus* has more. Yellow Peas, while handsome plants, are suspected of being poisonous. Among the several western species, some quite hairy, Prairie Thermopsis (*T. rhombifolia*), which grows on the eastern slopes of the Rocky Mountains and on the northwestern plains, has pods that spread outward from the curve or coil.

90  **Sour Clover; Bull Clover; Puff Clover**
(*Trifolium fucatum*)
Pea Family (Fabaceae)

Description:   A Clover with several stout, hollow stems that may lean or lie on the ground, and *usually swollen "pea-flowers,"* clustered in heads.
Flowers: clusters 1–2″ (2.5–5 cm) wide; petals 5, at first *white, pink,* or *yellow,* becoming very large, swollen, and deeper pink or purplish with age; beneath head a papery collar with 5–9 lobes.
Leaves: compound, 3 broad leaflets ¼–1¼″ (6–31 mm) long, with small teeth on edges.
Height: 4–32″ (10–80 cm).
Flowering:   April–June.
Habitat:   Grassy slopes, roadsides, moist fields, and somewhat brackish areas.
Range:   Southern Oregon and most of California.
Comments:   The enlargement of the corolla into a papery bladder is unusual, but occurs also in two other species that have smaller flowers, Bladder Campion (*T. amplectens*) and Balloon Clover (*T. depanpuratum*).

416  **Bighead Clover**
(*Trifolium macrocephalum*)
Pea Family (Fabaceae)

Description:   An unusual low clover with large round heads of *red to deep pink "pea flowers."*
Flowers: heads 1¼–2″ (3.1–5 cm) wide; calyx teeth feathery.
Leaves: palmately compound, with 3–9 leaflets, each ¼–1″ (6–25 mm) long, thick, leathery, with teeth on edges.
Height: 4–12″ (10–30 cm).
Flowering:   April–June.
Habitat:   Sagebrush deserts and pine woods.
Range:   Eastern Washington to east-central California, western Nevada and Idaho.

Comments: The large red heads of two-tone flowers make this one of the prettiest of Clovers. The name *Trifolium,* referring to the trio of leaflets, is contradicted in this species, which usually has 6–9.

## 499 Red Clover
(*Trifolium pratense*)
Pea Family (Fabaceae)

Description: A softly but sparsely-haired, fairly tall Clover with several stems in a clump and *deep pink "pea flowers" in round or egg-shaped heads.*
Flowers: heads 1–1½" (2.5–3.8 cm) wide.
Leaves: compound, with 3 broad leaflets, each ¾–2½" (2–6.3 cm) long; upper 2 leaves usually close to head, but no collar around stem beneath it.
Height: 1–3' (30–90 cm).
Flowering: June–August.
Habitat: Fields, roadsides, riverbanks, vacant lots, and where the soil has been disturbed.
Range: Throughout.
Comments: Like many Clovers, this does not make good hay. If cut late in the season and fed in quantity to livestock it is debilitating, for reasons not entirely known.

## 89 White Clover
(*Trifolium repens*)
Pea Family (Fabaceae)

Description: A plant with creeping stems and *white or very pale pink round heads of tiny, clustered "pea flowers,"* held barely above the leaves on long, leafless stalks.
Flowers: heads about ½" (1.3 cm) wide; calyx has no hairs; no collar (involucre) beneath head.
Leaves: compound, with 3 broad leaflets ½–¾" (1.3–2 cm) long, with tiny

teeth on edges.
Height: creeper, the flower stalks 4–
24″ (10–60 cm) high.

Flowering: April–September.

Habitat: Pastures, meadows, vacant lots, lawns, and along roadsides.

Range: Throughout.

Comments: This is the common Clover in lawn-seed mixes. The similar Alsike Clover (*T. hybridum*) is distinguished by its pinker corollas and tufts of hair at the base of calyx lobes. Animals pastured on it are likely to develop extreme skin sensitivity to sunlight.

---

### 498 Cow Clover
(*Trifolium wormskjoldii*)
Pea Family (Fabaceae)

Description: The several stems on this plant are erect, or lean on the ground, and bear *round heads of clustered reddish-lavender "pea flowers."*
Flowers: heads ¾–1¼″ (2–3.1 cm) wide; petals usually with very pale or white tips; beneath the head is a collar with jagged edges.
Leaves: compound, with leaflets ½–1¼″ (1.3–3.1 cm) long, hairless, rather narrow, with tiny teeth on edges.
Height: 4–32″ (10–80 cm).

Flowering: May–September.

Habitat: Coastal dunes, mountain meadows, and stream banks.

Range: Idaho, Utah, Colorado, and New Mexico; west to the Pacific Coast; north to British Columbia; south into Mexico.

Comments: This Clover is one of the most common wild species. The relatively large flowers with white-tipped petals and the jagged-edged collar are distinctive features.

### 506 American Vetch
#### (*Vicia americana*)
#### Pea Family (Fabaceae)

Description: A slender, climbing plant that clings to
other vegetation or structures by
slender *coiling tendrils* at the end of each
leaf. Loose racemes of 4–10 *deep reddish-
lavender "pea flowers"* grow on stalks
arising from leaf axils.
Flowers: ½–1¼" (1.3–3.1 cm) long;
petals become bluish with age.
Leaves: pinnately compound, with 8–
12 leaflets, each ½–1½" (1.3–3.8 cm)
long.
Height: 2–4' (60–120 cm).
Flowering: May–July.
Habitat: Open places in woods, on road banks,
along fences.
Range: Throughout.
Comments: With showy flowers unusually large for
the genus, it resembles many species of
*Lathyrus,* but can be distinguished by
the distribution of the hairs at the tip
of the style. In *Vicia,* the hairs
surround the tip, resembling a shaving
brush; in *Lathyrus,* they are on the
upper side, like a little hairbrush. The
seeds of some contain compounds
producing toxic levels of cyanide when
digested.

### 519 Bird Vetch; Tufted Vetch; Cat Peas;
### Tinegrass
#### (*Vicia cracca*)
#### Pea Family (Fabaceae)

Description: *Climbing plants* that cling to structures,
other vegetation, or their own stems by
*coiling tendrils* at the end of each leaf.
Growing from stalks in the leaf axils are
racemes of 20–70 closely packed
*reddish-lavender "pea flowers."*
Flowers: ½–¾" (1.3–2 cm) long.
Leaves: pinnately compound, with 19–
29 leaflets ¾–1½" (2–3.8 cm) long.
Fruit: pod about ¾" (2 cm) long.

Height: 4–7′ (1.2–2.1 m).
Flowering: May–July.
Habitat: On road banks, along fencerows, and in fields.
Range: Throughout.
Comments: As with most Vetches, this is a native of Europe. Another similar species with racemes of many lavender to purple flowers is Hairy Vetch (*V. villosa*), which differs by having longer hairs.

## OCOTILLO FAMILY
### (Fouquieriaceae)

Unusual shrubs and trees covered with
spines, with red or white flowers in
clusters at ends of branches.
Flowers: radially symmetrical; sepals 5,
separate; petals 5, united into a tube;
stamens 10–15. All these parts
attached at base of ovary.
Leaves: simple, mostly in little clusters
in axils of spines.
Fruit: capsule.
One or two genera and about 11 species
are known, all but one restricted to
Mexico. The Boojum Tree of Baja
California is in this family.

## 426 Ocotillo
*(Fouquieria splendens)*
Ocotillo Family (Fouquieriaceae)

Description: A funnel-shaped plant with several
woody, almost unbranched, *spiny,
commonly straight stems* leafless most of
the year, and a tight *cluster of red flowers*
at tip of each branch.
Flowers: corolla tubular, ⅝–1″ (1.5–
2.5 cm) long, the 5 short lobes curled
back; in clusters to 10″ (25 cm) long.
Leaves: to 2″ (5 cm) long, narrowly
ovate, broader above middle, almost
without stalks, in bunches above spines.
Height: to 30′ (9 m).
Flowering: March–June, sometimes later.
Habitat: Open stony slopes in deserts.
Range: Western Texas to southeastern
California; northern Mexico.
Comments: The family consists of about 11 species,
mostly Mexican, with Ocotillo
(pronounced *o-ko-tee′-yo*) the most
northern, and perhaps the Boojum Tree
(*F. columnaris*) of Baja California the
most unusual. Leaves appear only after
rain and wither when the soil dries, a
cycle commonly repeated several times
during the warm season.

## FUMITORY FAMILY (Fumariaceae)

Leafy herbs with succulent stems and
flowers in racemes.
Flowers: bilaterally symmetrical; calyx
has 2 small sepals that drop off; corolla
has 2 different pairs of petals that are
partially united, one pair often spurred
or sac-like at base; stamens 4 and
separate, or 6 and united into 2 groups
of 3. All these parts attached at base of
the ovary.
Leaves: alternate or in rosettes, with
blades several times compound or
divided.
Fruit: long, single-chambered capsule
or, rarely, hard and nut-like.
There are 16 genera and 450 species
that are chiefly distributed in north
temperate regions of Eurasia.

---

317 **Golden Smoke; Scrambled Eggs**
   (*Corydalis aurea*)
   Fumitory Family (Fumariaceae)

Description: A soft plant, the stems weakly erect or
   supported by vegetation or rocks, with
   *bilateral yellow flowers in racemes* shorter
   than the leaves.
   Flowers: ½–¾″ (1.3–2 cm) long, with
   2 tiny sepals that drop off; 4 very
   different petals: uppermost, as long as
   the flower, forms a hollow spur behind
   and an arched hood in front; lowest
   forms a scoop in front; inner 2 face
   one another and enclose 6 stamens and
   1 pistil.
   Leaves: 3–6″ (7.5–15 cm) long, each
   pinnately divided into 5–7 main
   divisions again divided, those divisions
   lobed, soft, succulent but thin.
   Fruit: pod ¾–1″ (2–2.5 cm) long,
   narrow, curved.
   Height: 4–24″ (10–60 cm).
Flowering: February–September.
Habitat: Gravelly hillsides among rocks or
   brush, and flats along creek bottoms

under trees.
Range: Throughout, except in most of California.
Comments: Believed poisonous to livestock if consumed in quantity.

---

### 118 Case's Fitweed
(*Corydalis caseana*)
Fumitory Family (Fumariaceae)

Description: A rather *soft, almost succulent, tall plant* with leafy, hollow stems, *large fern-like leaves,* and *dense racemes of 50–200 bilaterally symmetrical pinkish-white flowers.*
Flowers: ¾–1" (2–2.5 cm) long, with 2 tiny sepals that drop off; petals 4, very different, pink or white, purplish at tip: uppermost, as long as the flower, curves upward at front and forms a straight spur behind; lowest forms a scoop in front; inner 2 face one another and enclose 6 stamens and 1 pistil.
Leaves: 12–20" (30–50 cm) long, triangular in outline, pinnately divided 3 times, with leaflets each ½–2" (1.3–5 cm) long, ovate.
Fruit: pod ½" (1.3 cm) long, plump, hanging.
Height: 2–7' (60–210 cm).
Flowering: June–August.
Habitat: Mountains, in shady moist places.
Range: Northeastern Oregon, Idaho, and Colorado to the central Sierra Nevada of California.
Comments: Contains alkaloids poisonous to livestock, particularly sheep, since cattle rarely graze where it grows. The pods of this and other species have elastic walls which when touched instantly curl back and explosively eject seeds. Scouler Corydalis (*C. scouleri*), from British Columbia south to northern Oregon, is similar, but has only 15–35 flowers in the largest racemes, the petals rarely purple at the tips.

## 311 Golden Ear-drops
### (*Dicentra chrysantha*)
Fumitory Family (Fumariaceae)

Description:   Peculiar *bilateral yellow flowers,* with 2
petals bent at midlength and sticking
out sideways, bloom in open branched
clusters at tops of several stems with
*fern-like leaves.*
Flowers: about ½″ (1.3 cm) long; at
base 2 small sepals that drop off; petals
4, in 2 pairs: outer 2 with pouch at
base, tips bent outward, and inner 2
facing one another, with a crinkled
crest on back, enclosing 6 stamens and
1 pistil.
Leaves: 6–12″ (15–30 cm) long,
pinnately compound, with leaflets
sharply divided into narrow lobes,
smooth, bluish green.
Fruit: pod ¾–1″ (2–2.5 cm) long.
Height: 1½–5′ (45–150 cm).

Flowering:   April–September.

Habitat:   Dry, often brushy slopes.

Range:   Southern two-thirds of California to
northern Baja California.

Comments:   Most common in disturbed areas;
frequent after burns in chaparral.

## 505 Western Bleeding Heart
### (*Dicentra formosa*)
Fumitory Family (Fumariaceae)

Description:   *Pink, heart-shaped flowers hang* in small,
branched clusters above *soft, fern-like,
bluish-green leaves at base.*
Flowers: about ¾″ (2 cm) long; at base
2 small sepals that drop off; petals 4,
pale pink or rose, in 2 pairs: outer 2
with pouch at base, forming outline of
heart, with spreading tips, and inner 2
facing one another, with a wavy crest
on back, enclosing 6 stamens and 1
pistil.
Leaves: with long stalks, 9–20″ (22.5–
50 cm) long, elaborately pinnately
compound, leaflets ¾–2″ (2–5 cm)

long, oblong, cut into divisions about
⅛″ (3 mm) wide, soft.
Fruit: pod ½–¾″ (1.3–2 cm) long,
plump.
Height: 8–18″ (20–45 cm).

Flowering: March–July.

Habitat: Damp shaded places or, in wetter
climates, open woods.

Range: Southern British Columbia to central
California.

Comments: One of the nursery-trade species.
Bleeding Heart (*D. spectabilis*), from
Japan, has larger, rosy-red or white
flowers, about 1″ (2.5 cm) long.

## 483 Steer's Head
(*Dicentra uniflora*)
Fumitory Family (Fumariaceae)

Description: A tiny plant with leaves and flower
stalks growing separately, each attached
to the root cluster deep beneath the
surface. Each flower stalk ends in *1 pink
or white bilateral flower resembling a steer's
skull with horns.*
Flowers: ½–⅝″ (1.3–1.5 cm) long; 2
small sepals at base; petals 4, in 2 pairs:
outer 2 with pouch at base, their
narrow tips curving backward
("horns"), and inner 2 facing and
joining one another, enclosing 6
stamens and 1 pistil.
Leaves: 1–4″ (2.5–10 cm), about as tall
as flower stalks, divided into 3 main
segments, each divided into narrow
lobes.
Height: 1–4″ (2.5–10 cm).

Flowering: February–June.

Habitat: Open, well-drained ground, commonly
among sagebrush in foothills to open
woods at high elevations in mountains.

Range: Northern California to Washington;
east to Idaho, western Wyoming, and
northern Utah.

Comments: Though common, these low plants
bloom early and are usually obscured by
the surrounding sagebrush.

## GENTIAN FAMILY (Gentianaceae)

Leafy herbs, commonly with showy
bell- or trumpet-shaped flowers
blooming in a branched cluster.
Flowers: radially symmetrical; sepals
4 or 5, free or united; petals 5, united;
stamens as many as petals. All these
parts attached at base of ovary.
Leaves: simple, opposite.
Fruit: usually capsule, rarely berry.
There are about 70 genera and 1,100
species that occur in many different
habitats in temperate and subtropical
regions. Some Gentians are cultivated
as ornamentals.

### 451 Centaury; Rosita
(*Centaurium calycosum*)
Gentian Family (Gentianaceae)

Description: An erect, sparsely-leaved plant with
*pink, trumpet-shaped flowers* in small
clusters at ends or in forks of the many
branches.
Flowers: ⅜–½" (9–13 mm) wide; calyx
with 5 very slender lobes pressed
against the tube of corolla; corolla with
5 abruptly flared ovate lobes as long as
its tube; stamens 5, with spirally
twisted anthers.
Leaves: ½–2½" (1.3–6.3 cm) long,
opposite.
Height: 5–24" (12.5–60 cm).
Flowering: April–June.
Habitat: Moist, open areas along streams,
prairies, and meadows, on hillsides.
Range: Southeastern California to southern
Utah and central Texas; south to
northern Mexico.
Comments: The brilliant pink corolla resembles
that of *Phlox*, which has 3 branches on
the style, whereas the *Centaurium* style
ends with a small knob or 2 short
branches.

## 612 Prairie Gentian; Tulip Gentian; Bluebell
(*Eustoma grandiflorum*)
Gentian Family (Gentianaceae)

Description: Erect stems, with *evenly spaced opposite leaves,* grow in small clumps; at their tops bloom small clusters of *large, erect, bell-shaped, usually bluish flowers.*
Flowers: 1¼–1½″ (3.1–3.8 cm) long; calyx to 1¼″ (3.1 cm) long, with 5 needle-like lobes; bluish-purple, pinkish, white, white and purplish- or yellowish-tinged corolla with a short broad tube and 5 broad lobes 1¼–1½″ (3.1–3.8 cm) long.
Leaves: to 3″ (7.5 cm) long, ovate, with 3 conspicuous veins.
Height: 10–28″ (25–70 cm).
Flowering: June–September.
Habitat: Moist places in prairies and fields.
Range: Eastern Colorado to Nebraska; south to eastern New Mexico and Texas.
Comments: One of the most handsome prairie wildflowers. *Eustoma,* from the Greek *eu* ("good") and *stoma* ("mouth"), refers to the large opening into the flower's "throat" where the corolla lobes join. A closely related species, Catch-fly Gentian (*E. exaltatum*), has corolla lobes 1″ (2.5 cm) long or less, and is found from Florida to southern California, and southward.

## 4 Monument Plant; Deer's Ears
(*Frasera speciosa*)
Gentian Family (Gentianaceae)

Description: A narrowly cone-shaped plant with 1 stout, tall, erect stem, large leaves in evenly spaced whorls, and clusters of *4-lobed, yellowish-green corollas* in axils of upper leaves and leaf-like bracts.
Flowers: 1–1½″ (2.5–3.8 cm) wide; corolla with pointed lobes joined at base, spotted with purple, with 2 oblong glands in the lower central

part of each lobe; stamens 4.
Leaves: at base 10−20″ (25−50 cm) long, lanceolate, 3−4 in a whorl; on stem equally spaced, progressively smaller; veins of leaves parallel.
Height: 4−7′ (1.2−2.1 m).

Flowering: May−August.
Habitat: Rich soil in woodland openings, from moderate to high elevations.
Range: Eastern Washington to central California; east to western Texas, eastern Wyoming, and Montana; also northern Mexico.
Comments: The broad leaves are shaped like the ears of a deer, giving one of its common names, and are also a good browse for deer.

### 603 Northern Gentian
(*Gentiana amarella*)
Gentian Family (Gentianaceae)

Description: A leafy plant with angled, erect stem, commonly with erect branches, and *small, trumpet-shaped, purplish or bluish flowers from near base to top.*
Flowers: corolla ½−¾″ (1.3−2 cm) wide, the 5 lobes flared only slightly from the tube, a fringe of hairs inside at base of lobes; corolla varies from pale yellowish and lightly blue-tinged to clear blue, lavender, purplish, or dark bluish-purple; calyx has sepals joined at base.
Leaves: ¼−1½″ (6−38 mm) long, oblong, opposite, without stalks.
Height: 2−16″ (5−40 cm).

Flowering: June−September.
Habitat: Meadows and moist areas, mostly in the mountains.
Range: Throughout.
Comments: This is one of the smaller, less showy Gentians, but it often grows in dense, colorful patches.

## 609 Explorer's Gentian
(*Gentiana calycosa*)
Gentian Family (Gentianaceae)

Description: Several leafy stems in a clump bear at
the top *1–3 blue, broadly funnel-shaped
flowers*.
Flowers: 1–1½″ (2.5–3.8 cm) long;
corolla varies from blue to yellowish
green and also often has greenish
streaks; 5 pointed, nearly erect lobes,
between which are plaits cut into fine
segments at end. Bell-shaped calyx
with 5 lobes, with a membranous
lining.
Leaves: ½–1¼″ (1.3–3.1 cm) long,
opposite, broadly ovate, bases of lower
leaves joined, forming sheath around
stem.
Height: 2–12″ (5–30 cm).

Flowering: July–October.
Habitat: Mountain meadows and stream banks.
Range: British Columbia south to the Sierra
Nevada of California; east to the Rocky
Mountains of Montana and Canada.

Comments: Gentians are among the most lovely of
mountain wildflowers and are rock-
garden favorites. The genus honors
King Gentius of Illyria, ruler of an
ancient country on the east side of the
Adriatic Sea, who is reputed to have
discovered medicinal virtues in
Gentians.

## 610 Fringed Gentian
(*Gentiana detonsa*)
Gentian Family (Gentianaceae)

Description: Several clumped stems have a few leaves
at base, 2–4 pairs of leaves on the
stem, and, on leafless stalks at end of
stem or in upper axils, a few *bell-shaped,
deep blue or blue-violet flowers*.
Flowers: 1¼–2″ (3.1–5 cm) long;
corolla with 4 lobes fringed on broad
end; calyx ½–1″ (1.3–2.5 cm) long,
with bell-shaped base and 4 pointed

lobes; stamens 4.
Leaves: ½–2″ (1.3–5 cm) long,
opposite, narrowly lanceolate.
Height: 4–16″ (10–40 cm).
Flowering: July–August.
Habitat: Meadows, bogs, and moist ground.
Range: Throughout most of the western
mountains.
Comments: Many forms of this wide-ranging
species are fairly different. The
Rocky Mountain race has been called
*G. thermalis,* for the hot springs in
Yellowstone National Park, where it is
the park flower, but in the Sierra
Nevada it is known as Tufted Gentian
(*G. holopetala*). Many botanists now
consider these to be geographic
variations of a single species.

### 592   Felwort; Star Swertia
(*Swertia perennis*)
Gentian Family (Gentianaceae)

Description: Several erect stems, with most leaves at
base, and *star-like, pale bluish-purple
flowers* with greenish or white spots in
an open, branched, but narrow cluster
at the top.
Flowers: about ¾″ (2 cm) wide; corolla
with 5 pointed lobes joined at base;
2 fringed glands at base of each lobe;
very short, thick style.
Leaves: at base 2–8″ (5–20 cm) long,
the lanceolate blades tapered to a
slender stalk; 1 or 2 pairs of smaller
leaves on stem.
Height: 2–20″ (5–50 cm).
Flowering: July–September.
Habitat: Meadows and moist places at high
mountain elevations.
Range: Alaska to the southern Sierra Nevada of
California; east to New Mexico; north
through the Rocky Mountains to
Canada.
Comments: The genus is named for E. Sweert, a
16th-century Dutch gardener and
author.

## GERANIUM FAMILY (Geraniaceae)

Leafy herbs with showy white, pink, or
purple flowers in clusters.
Flowers: usually radially symmetrical;
sepals 5, free or slightly united at base;
petals 5, free; stamens 5, 10, or 15,
with stalks sometimes united at base.
Leaves: alternate or opposite, simple or
pinnately or palmately lobed or
compound.
Fruit: develops from a long-beaked
pistil with 5 united chambers at its
base, each chamber with a long style
attached to the central core and coiling
away from it at maturity, thus lifting
the chambers of the ovary upward and
aiding in the dispersal of seeds.
There are about 11 genera nearly
800 species, with many occurring
frequently in the north temperate zone.
The cultivated Geranium is
*Pelargonium,* a tropical genus especially
well developed in South Africa.

---

452 **Filaree; Clocks; Redstem Storksbill**
(*Erodium cicutarium*)
Geranium Family (Geraniaceae)

Description: Usually reddish stems leaning or lying
on the ground, small fern-like leaves,
*2–10 small, deep reddish-lavender flowers*
in a loose cluster, and long, slender,
pin-like fruits that stick straight up.
Flowers: about ½" (1.3 cm) wide;
petals 5.
Leaves: 1¼–4" (3.1–10 cm) long,
pinnately divided, with each segment
further divided; stalk less than ¼ the
length of blade.
Fruit: ¾–2" (2–5 cm) long, including
slender center, with 5 lobes at base.
Height: creeper, some branches to 1'
(30 cm) high, others 20" (50 cm) long.
Flowering: February–June.
Habitat: Open areas, often where the soil is
disturbed.

Range:     Throughout.
Comments:  This is one of the earliest flowers to
           bloom in the spring. Texas Storksbill
           (*E. texanum*), has flowers nearly 1″
           (2.5 cm) wide; and ovate, deeply lobed
           leaves. It is found on prairies and desert
           from southeastern California to central
           Texas and southwestern Oklahoma; also
           in northern Mexico.

---

43  **Richardson's Geranium; Crane's Bill**
    (*Geranium richardsonii*)
    Geranium Family (Geraniaceae)

Description:  This plant's several stems have
              *palmately cleft leaves on long stalks,* most
              near the base, and bear a few *white or
              pale pink flowers* in a branched cluster.
              Flowers: about 1″ (2.5 cm) wide; petals
              5, ½–¾″ (1.3–2 cm) long with
              purplish veins, the petals hairy on
              upper side on at least lower half;
              stamens 10. Branches of flower cluster
              have purplish-tipped glandular hairs.
              Leaves: 1½–6″ (3.8–15 cm) wide,
              nearly round blades cleft into 5–7 main
              segments, each with a few pointed
              lobes.
              Fruit: about 1″ (2.5 cm) long,
              including slender, pointed center, with
              5 lobes at base.
              Height: 8–32″ (20–80 cm).
Flowering:    June–August.
Habitat:      Partial shade in woods, from lowlands
              into the mountains.
Range:        Southeastern British Columbia; south
              through eastern Washington and
              Oregon to southern California; east to
              New Mexico, South Dakota, and
              Saskatchewan.
Comments:     One of the most widespread western
              Geraniums, it frequently hybridizes
              with other species, often making
              identification difficult. The genus
              name, from the Greek *geranos* ("crane"),
              refers to the fruit's beak.

### 456 Sticky Geranium; Crane's Bill
(*Geranium viscosissimum*)
Geranium Family (Geraniaceae)

Description: A lightly-haired plant with several stems, *leaves on long stalks,* most near the base, and a few *pink-lavender to purplish flowers* in an open cluster near the top.
Flowers: about 1″ (2.5 cm) wide; petals 5, broad, ½–¾″ (1.3–2 cm) long, hairy on upper side on no more than lower third; stamens 10. Branches of flower cluster have glandular hairs.
Leaves: 1½–5″ (3.8–12.5 cm) wide, palmately cleft and deeply divided into 5–7 segments with sharp teeth on ends and edges.
Fruit: slender, pointed column 1–2″ (2.5–5 cm) long, with 5 lobes at base.
Height: 1–3′ (30–90 cm).
Flowering: May–August.
Habitat: Open woods and meadows from lowlands to well into the mountains.
Range: Southern British Columbia; south through eastern Washington and Oregon to northern California; east to western Colorado, western South Dakota, and Saskatchewan.
Comments: This is one of several western Geraniums with pinkish-purple flowers; all are similar, distinguished only by technical features. Dove's Foot Geranium (*G. molle*), with small pink flowers, is a common weed on lawns and in vacant lots.

## BUCKEYE FAMILY
## (Hippocastanaceae)

Trees or shrubs with large, hanging
leaves and flowers in showy clusters.
Flowers: slightly bilateral; calyx with 5
unequal joined sepals; petals 4 or 5,
unequal in size, with slender stalk at
base; stamens 5 to 8, long and slender.
All these parts attached at base of ovary.
Leaves: opposite, palmately compound.
Fruit: leathery, round capsule, usually
with one large, brown, shining seed.
There are 2 genera and 15 species, some
grown as handsome ornamentals.

---

## 176 California Buckeye; California Horse–chestnut
*(Aesculus californica)*
Buckeye Family (Hippocastanaceae)

Description:  A large, round bush or small tree, with
large leaves and many *cone-shaped clusters
of whitish flowers*.
Flowers: clusters 4–8″ (10–20 cm)
long; flowers slightly bilateral, with
petals 5, each crinkled ½″ (1.3 cm)
long, white or blushed with pale rose;
stamens 5–7, and style 1, sweeping
downward and projecting from front.
Leaves: palmately compound, with 5–7
leaflets 2–6″ (5–15 cm) long,
lanceolate, with teeth on edges.
Fruit: about 1½″ (3.8 cm) wide, pear-
shaped, with thick rind and 1 large,
glossy, brown seed.
Height: to 40′ (12 m).

Flowering:  May–June.

Habitat:  Dry slopes and canyons.

Range:  Northern to southern California.

Comments:  A unique western tree, a remnant of
ancient times when wetter summers
prevailed in western North America.
Poisonous seeds were pulverized by
Indians and thrown into dammed
streams in order to stupefy fish, thereby
making them easier to catch.

## HYDRANGEA FAMILY
(Hydrangeaceae)

Usually small trees or shrubs,
sometimes herbs, with flowers often in
roundish or flattish clusters, sometimes
in heads.
Flowers: radially symmetrical; sepals 4–
10; petals 4–10; stamens 4 to many.
All these parts attached at top of ovary.
Leaves: usually simple, opposite.
Fruit: capsule with 2–5 chambers.
There are about 10 genera and 115
species that occur in north temperate
and subtropical regions and in South
America. Hydrangeas are popular
ornamental shrubs.

---

### 178 Mockorange; Lewis' Syringa; Indian Arrowhead
(*Philadelphus lewisii*)
Hydrangea Family (Hydrangeaceae)

Description: A *loosely branched shrub,* covered in the
spring by many *white flowers.*
Flowers: ¾–1¼" (2–3.1 cm) wide; in
clusters at ends of short branches; petals
4 or 5; stamens many.
Leaves: 1¼–3" (3.1–7.5 cm) long,
opposite, on short stalks, ovate, smooth
or minutely toothed on edges.
Fruit: woody capsule.
Height: 4–10' (1.2–3 m).

Flowering: May–July.

Habitat: Rocky slopes and open banks in open
pine woods and mixed woodland.

Range: British Columbia to central California;
east to western Montana.

Comments: Idaho's state flower; when in full bloom
the flowers scent the air with a
delightfully sweet fragrance reminiscent
of orange blossoms. The genus is
named for the Egyptian king Ptolemy
Philadelphus, and the species name
(and one of its common names) honors
the scientist-explorer Meriwether
Lewis, who first discovered and

collected it during his exploration of
the Louisiana Purchase. Indians used its
straight stems in making arrows.

---

162  **Yerba de Selva**
(*Whipplea modesta*)
Hydrangea Family (Hydrangeaceae)

Description:  From long, trailing, rooting stems
grow many erect shoots, each tipped
with a *small head of white flowers.*
Flowers: 4–6 petals about ⅛" (3 mm)
long, spatula-shaped; twice as many
stamens.
Leaves: ½–1" (1.3–2.5 cm) long,
opposite, elliptic.
Height: creeper, the erect, leafy,
flowering branches 4–8" (10–20 cm)
high.

Flowering:  April–June.

Habitat:  In open or light woods, usually in dry
and rocky areas.

Range:  Western Washington to central
California near the Pacific Coast.

Comments:  These plants often form dense, low
patches on rocky banks or in open,
mixed woods of broadleaf trees and
conifers. The Spanish name means
"herb of the forest."

# WATERLEAF FAMILY
# (Hydrophyllaceae)

Usually herbs, rarely shrubs, often bristly or glandular, with flowers often arranged along one side of the branches, or at the tip of the stem, in coils like fiddlenecks.

Flowers: radially symmetrical; sepals 5, united; corolla has 5 united petals, varying from nearly flat to bell- or funnel-shaped; stamens 5, often protruding. All these parts attached at base of ovary.

Leaves: simple or pinnately compound, alternate or opposite, often in basal rosettes.

Fruit: capsule.

There are about 20 genera and 270 species occurring nearly worldwide; the western United States is the main center of diversity.

---

## 207 Whispering Bells
(*Emmenanthe penduliflora*)
Waterleaf Family (Hydrophyllaceae)

Description: *Pale yellow, bell-shaped flowers hang* from very slender stalks in a branched cluster; the delicate, erect, branched stems are covered with sticky hairs that exude a pleasant, somewhat medicinal odor.
Flowers: about ½″ (1.3 cm) long; corolla has 5 round lobes; stamens 5, hidden within.
Leaves: 1–4″ (2.5–10 cm) long, narrowly oblong, pinnately lobed.
Fruit: capsule with many seeds.
Height: 6–20″ (15–50 cm).
Flowering: March–July.
Habitat: Brushy hills and desert washes.
Range: Central California south to Baja California.
Comments: The corolla remains on the plant long after it dries, a tissue-paper-like bell that rustles in gentle breezes. In the

hills of southern California there is a form with a pink corolla.

## 22   Dwarf Hesperochiron
### (*Hesperochiron pumilus*)
Waterleaf Family (Hydrophyllaceae)

Description:   A low plant with *leaves in a rosette* from which grows a slender stalk topped by *1–5 white, saucer-shaped flowers.*
Flowers: corolla ⅝–1¼″ (1.5–3.1 cm) wide, 5 ovate lobes with fine purplish lines, short corolla tube has dense hairs inside; stamens 5; style with 2 branches.
Leaves: 1–3″ (2.5–7.5 cm) long, lanceolate.
Height: 1–2″ (2.5–5 cm).
Flowering:   April–June.
Habitat:   Moist meadows, flats, and slopes.
Range:   Eastern Washington to southern California and northern Arizona; east to western Montana.
Comments:   The one other species, California Hesperochiron (*H. californicus*), which grows in the same region, has a funnel-shaped corolla with lobes about as long as the tube.

## 614   Dwarf Waterleaf
### (*Hydrophyllum capitatum*)
Waterleaf Family (Hydrophyllaceae)

Description:   A low plant with *round heads of small, white or pale purple flowers* on short stalks among *pinnately divided leaves.*
Flowers: heads about 1¼″ (3.1 cm) wide; flowers ¼–⅜″ (6–9 mm) long, with 5 round lobes at end of corolla, and 5 projecting stamens.
Leaves: to 4″ (10 cm) wide and 6″ (15 cm) long, triangular, divided into 7–11 segments which may have 2 or 3 large *teeth on ends, but none on edges;* some leaves with long stalks attached

below ground.
Height: 4–16″ (10–40 cm).

Flowering: March–July.

Habitat: Brushy areas and open woods.

Range: Southern British Columbia; south through eastern Washington and Oregon to central California; east to western Colorado, northern Utah, Idaho, and Alberta.

Comments: In the northeastern United States plants of this genus were cooked for greens by Indians and settlers. A form of Dwarf Waterleaf in northern Oregon and south-central Washington has flower heads on long stalks above leaves.

## 165 Fendler's Waterleaf; Squaw Lettuce
(*Hydrophyllum fendleri*)
Waterleaf Family (Hydrophyllaceae)

Description: A fairly coarse plant with 1 stem that has downward-projecting hairs, a *few, large, pinnately divided leaves,* and *white or lavender, bell-shaped flowers* in a loose, branched cluster at the top or on stalks growing from leaf axils.
Flowers: ¼–⅜″ (6–9 mm) wide; corolla with 5 round lobes at end; stamens 5, projecting.
Leaves: to 10″ (25 cm) long, with 7–15 lanceolate segments bearing 4–8 sharp teeth on each edge; stalks long or short.
Height: 8–32″ (20–80 cm).

Flowering: May–August.

Habitat: Moist places in brush and open areas from low to high elevations.

Range: Southern British Columbia to northern California; east to New Mexico, southeastern Utah, southern Wyoming, and central Idaho.

Comments: This is a common, rather plain-looking, woodland plant. Pacific Waterleaf (*H. tenuipes*), which grows west of the Cascade Mountains and the Sierra Nevada from British Columbia to Northern California, has leaves barely longer than wide, divided into 5–9

segments. California Waterleaf
(*H. occidentale*) has blunt points on the
leaf segments, unlike the long, tapered
points of Fender's Waterleaf, and only
2–4 teeth on each edge.

### 540  Purple Mat
(*Nama demissum*)
Waterleaf Family (Hydrophyllaceae)

Description:  Mats of slender, hairy *stems that lie on
the ground, and are leafy toward the ends,*
with several *bell-shaped, deep reddish-
lavender flowers* growing from leaf
axils.
Flowers: ⅜" (9 mm) wide; corolla with
5 round lobes at end; stamens 5,
hidden within.
Leaves: 1½" (3.8 cm) long, sticky,
narrowly spatula-shaped or ovate.
Height: creeper, flower clusters 1–3"
(2.5–7.5 cm) high, stems to 8" (20 cm)
long.
Flowering:  March–May.
Habitat:  Desert flats and washes.
Range:  Southeastern California to southwestern
Utah, central Arizona, and
northwestern Mexico.
Comments:  *Nama* in Greek means "spring." There
are many species, both perennials and
showy annuals, that carpet the desert
floor with purple after adequate rainfall.
Hispid Nama (*N. hispidum*), with erect,
bush-branched stems and very narrow
leaves, is another low species common
in deserts from southern California to
western Texas and northern Mexico.

### 579  Baby Blue Eyes
(*Nemophila menziesii*)
Waterleaf Family (Hydrophyllaceae)

Description:  A low plant with *pale or clear blue, bowl-
shaped flowers* that bloom singly on
slender stalks growing near the ends of

slender, leaning, branched stems.
Flowers: ½–1½″ (1.3–3.8 cm) wide;
corolla with 5 broad, pale or bright
blue petals, often paler near base,
generally with small black spots;
stamens 5; style with 2 branches at tip.
Leaves: ¾–2″ (2–5 cm) long, opposite,
oblong, pinnately divided into
segments with teeth along edges.
Height: 4–12″ (10–30 cm).

Flowering: March–June.

Habitat: Grassy hillsides and among brush.

Range: Central Oregon to southern California.

Comments: One of the most charming and best-
known spring wildflowers in California,
it is often included in commercial
wildflower seed mixtures and has been
cultivated in England for more than a
century. Closely related is the equally
delightful Five Spot (*N. maculata*) of
central California, with white petals,
each with a large blue-violet spot at the
base.

## 652 Desert Bell
(*Phacelia campanularia*)
Waterleaf Family (Hydrophyllaceae)

Description: Stiff, erect, leafy, glandular-hairy plant
with *dark blue, bell-like flowers in loose
coils* at the end of a branched, open
flower cluster.
Flowers: ¾–1½″ (2–3.8 cm) long,
with 5 round lobes, the tubular part
not constricted at base of lobes;
expanded stamen bases hairless.
Leaves: ¾–3″ (2–7.5 cm) long, ovate,
the edges shallowly lobed and sharply
toothed.
Height: 8–30″ (20–75 cm).

Flowering: February–April.

Habitat: Dry sandy or gravelly places in deserts.

Range: Southern California.

Comments: In a spring following a wet winter,
thousands of these plants will bloom,
forming masses of deep, rich blue. The
similar California Bell (*P. minor*), from

southern California and northern Baja California, has a violet corolla with a cream spot on each lobe, the opening slightly constricted, and hair on the expanded stamen bases.

---

650   **Wild Heliotrope; Common Phacelia**
(*Phacelia distans*)
Waterleaf Family (Hydrophyllaceae)

Description:   A finely-haired, branched plant, glandular in the upper parts, with *fern-like leaves* and *coils of broadly bell-shaped, blue flowers.*
Flowers: ¼″ (6 mm) wide; calyx with 5 unequal lobes; 5 round lobes on corolla; stamens 5, barely projecting.
Leaves: ¾–4″ (2–10 cm) long, once or twice pinnately divided into segments that are pinnately lobed.
Height: 8–32″ (20–80 cm).
Flowering:   March–June.
Habitat:   Fields, brushy slopes, and washes.
Range:   Northern California to Baja California; east to southern Nevada and eastern Arizona.
Comments:   Plants mature rapidly as the soil dries in the late spring. Although called "Heliotrope," this species is not related to those Heliotropes grown in the garden.

---

651   **Silverleaf Phacelia**
(*Phacelia hastata*)
Waterleaf Family (Hydrophyllaceae)

Description:   Many tight *coils of small, white or pale purple flowers,* on short branches at ends of leafy stems, bristly hairy because of *harsh hairs on calyx* lobes.
Flowers: corolla ¼″ (6 mm) long, bell-shaped, with 5 round lobes at end; stamens 5, protruding.
Leaves: 1¼–2½″ (3.1–6.3 cm) long, lanceolate, with *prominent, nearly*

*parallel veins,* dense silvery hairs that lie flat, and 2 small lobes occasionally on edges at base.
Height: 8–20″ (20–50 cm).

Flowering: May–July.

Habitat: Dry, rocky places among sagebrush and in coniferous forests.

Range: Southern British Columbia to northern California; east to western Nebraska, Colorado, and Alberta.

Comments: This species belongs to a complex group of closely related plants of dry, rocky mountain habitat, all with whitish flowers. They are distinguished from other Phacelias by their leaf veins.

---

**649 Scalloped Phacelia**
(*Phacelia integrifolia*)
Waterleaf Family (Hydrophyllaceae)

Description: Glandular, bad-scented, sticky, commonly stout, leafy stems with *purplish-lavender or bluish-purple flowers in coils* at ends of upper branches.
Flowers: corolla about ¼″ (6 mm) wide, funnel-shaped, with 5 round lobes at end; stamens 5, protruding.
Leaves: to 3″ (7.5 cm) long, narrowly ovate, scalloped or shallowly lobed.
Fruit: capsule, with only 4 dark seeds, each with 2 grooves on inner side, no wrinkles in grooves as in similar species.
Height: 6–30″ (15–75 cm).

Flowering: March–September.

Habitat: Rocky or sandy places in deserts and among piñon and juniper.

Range: Southern Utah to western Oklahoma; south to western Texas, New Mexico, Arizona, and northern Mexico.

Comments: A large, mostly western American genus that is distinguished by bluish or purplish corollas in coils and protruding stamens. Identification of individual species is determined by technical features such as seed details.

### 546  Threadleaf Phacelia
*(Phacelia linearis)*
Waterleaf Family (Hydrophyllaceae)

Description: Slender, commonly branched, erect
stems are topped with *reddish-lavender
flowers in loose coils.*
Flowers: corolla ⅜–¾″ (9–20 mm)
wide, broadly bell-shaped, with
5 round lobes; stamens 5, barely
protruding.
Leaves: ½–4″ (1.3–10 cm) long,
narrowly lanceolate, hairy, sometimes
with 1–4 pairs of small lobes in lower
half.
Fruit: small capsule; 6–15 seeds with
pitted surfaces.
Height: 4–20″ (10–50 cm).
Flowering: April–June.
Habitat: Among brush and in open grassy areas
in foothills and on plains.
Range: Southern British Columbia to northern
California; east across much of Utah
and Idaho to western Wyoming.
Comments: A common, showy species,
distinguished from other Phacelias by
its comparatively large, broad corolla
and narrow leaves.

### 642  Purple Fringe; Alpine Phacelia
*(Phacelia sericea)*
Waterleaf Family (Hydrophyllaceae)

Description: A cluster of several erect stems with
most leaves near the base, covered with
dense hairs that have a silvery-gray hue.
*Purple or dark blue-violet flowers are in
many dense, short coils in a tight
cylindrical cluster,* which, because of
long, protruding stamens, appears
fringed.
Flowers: corolla about ¼″ (6 mm) long,
bell-shaped with 5 round lobes.
Leaves: 1–4″ (2.5–10 cm) long,
broadly lanceolate, pinnately cleft into
many narrow lobes.
Height: to 16″ (40 cm).

Flowering: June—August.

Habitat: Open or wooded rocky places in the mountains, often at high elevations.

Range: Southern British Columbia to northeastern California; east to Alberta; south in the mountains to Colorado.

Comments: A common mountain wildflower easily distinguished from other Phacelias by its cylindrical inflorescence.

## ST. JOHNSWORT FAMILY
(Hypericaceae)

Herbs or shrubs with leaves that have
numerous, often black, dots.
Flowers: bisexual, radially symmetrical,
usually yellow or orange, borne in
branched clusters; sepals 5; petals 5;
stamens numerous, usually united into
several bunches by the bases of the
stalks. All these parts attached at base
of ovary.
Leaves: opposite or whorled, simple.
Fruit: usually capsule, sometimes berry.
There are 3 genera and about 300
species that occur in temperate and
tropical regions. Some are grown as
ornamentals. The family is commonly
combined with the Clusiaceae
(Guttiferae), a tropical family of mostly
trees and shrubs.

### 202 Tinker's Penny
(*Hypericum anagalloides*)
St. Johnswort Family (Hypericaceae)

Description: Prostrate stems form leafy mats; at ends
of short, erect branches bloom *small,
golden-yellow or salmon-yellow flowers.*
Flowers: about ¼" (6 mm) wide; petals
5; sepals 5, slightly shorter to slightly
longer than petals; stamens 15–25,
about as long as petals; styles 3, atop
ovary.
Leaves: ³⁄₁₆–⅝" (4.5–15 mm) long,
opposite, ovate.
Height: creeper, branches to 3"
(7.5 cm) high, stems to 8" (20 cm)
long.
Flowering: June–August.
Habitat: Wet places from the coast to high
elevations.
Range: British Columbia to Baja California;
east to Montana.
Comments: Some *Hypericum* species are known as
St. Johnswort. Their flowers bloom
around June 24, the feast day of St.

John the Baptist. For centuries the plants had the reputation of warding off evil; when hung about the house or kept in pockets they were thought to guard against thunder and witches.

211 **Klamath Weed**
(*Hypericum perforatum*)
St. Johnswort Family (Hypericaceae)

Description: Several erect stems, especially leafy and branched near the top, where *bright yellow, star-like flowers* bloom in an open, round-topped flower cluster.
Flowers: nearly 1″ (2.5 cm) wide; petals 5, longer than sepals, sometimes with black dots near tips; many stamens in 3–5 bunches.
Leaves: ½–1½″ (1.3–3.8 cm) long, *opposite*, elliptic, with black dots that when held to the light reveal numerous translucent dots resembling pinpricks.
Height: 1–3′ (30–90 cm).
Flowering: June–September.
Habitat: Roadsides and pastures.
Range: In the West especially common from California to western Washington.
Comments: First discovered in the eastern United States in 1793, it appeared in California near the Klamath River about 1900 and by 1940 had made 250,000 acres of California rangeland worthless. After 1945 it was quickly controlled by two European beetles that feed only on this species.

## IRIS FAMILY (Iridaceae)

Herbs growing from rhizomes, bulbs, or corms, with narrow basal leaves, and showy flower clusters at the tops of long stalks.
Flowers: usually radially symmetrical; sepals 3, petal-like; petals 3; stamens 3. All these parts attached at top of ovary.
Leaves: simple, alternate, folded and overlapping one another at the base, and aligned in two rows.
Fruit: capsule.
There are about 60 genera and 1,500 species that occur in temperate and tropical regions. Among them, Iris, Freesia, Gladiolus, Bugle Lily, and Montbretia are popular ornamentals. Saffron dye is obtained from Crocus, and "essence of violets," used in perfumes, is extracted from the rhizomes of an Iris.

---

608 **Douglas' Iris**
(*Iris douglasiana*)
Iris Family (Iridaceae)

Description: *Large, reddish-purple, pinkish, white or cream flowers* (with lilac veins) bloom on stout, branched stalks rising from *clumps of sword-shaped leaves.*
Flowers: 3–4″ (7.5–10 cm) wide; sepals 3, long, resembling petals, curved downward; petals 3, erect, about same length as sepals and slightly narrower; sepals and petals join to form a tube at base ½–1″ (1.3–2.5 cm) long. Pair of bracts beneath flower grow nearly opposite one another, bases not separated by space on stem.
Leaves: to 3′ (90 cm) long, usually shorter, ¾″ (2 cm) wide, flexible, tough.
Height: 6–32″ (15–80 cm).
Flowering: March–May.
Habitat: Grassy slopes and open brush.
Range: Coast Ranges from southern Oregon to

central California.

Comments: A common Iris in the redwood region. *Iris,* Greek for "rainbow," refers to the variegated colors of the flowers. A member of Juno's court and goddess of the rainbow, Iris so impressed Juno with her purity that she was commemorated with a flower that blooms with the rainbow colors of her robe.

---

281 **Ground Iris; Bowl-tubed Iris**
(*Iris macrosiphon*)
Iris Family (Iridaceae)

Description: *Large, deep golden yellow, cream, pale lavender, or deep blue-purple flowers* (usually with distinct veins) bloom on short stalks among *sword-shaped leaves.*
Flowers: 2½–4" (6.3–10 cm) wide; sepals 3, resembling petals, curved down; petals 3, erect, slightly narrower and shorter than sepals; sepals and petals join to form a *tube at base 1½–3" (3.8–7.5 cm) long.*
Leaves: to 10" (25 cm) long, about ¼" (6 mm) wide, flexible, tough.
Height: 6–8" (15–20 cm).
Flowering: April–May.
Habitat: Grassy or open wooded slopes.
Range: The Central Valley of California.
Comments: The range in coloration may be due partly to hybridization with other native species, common among western Irises.

---

606 **Rocky Mountain Iris; Western Blue Flag**
(*Iris missouriensis*)
Iris Family (Iridaceae)

Description: Large, delicate, *pale blue or blue-violet flowers,* often with purple veins, bloom at the top of *stout, leafless (or with 1 short leaf) stalks* that grow from dense clumps

of *flexible, tough, sword-shaped leaves.*
Flowers: 3–4″ (7.5–10 cm) wide;
sepals 3, resembling petals, curved
downward; petals 3, erect.
Leaves: 8–20″ (20–50 cm) long, ¼–½″
(6–13 mm) wide.
Height: 8–20″ (20–50 cm).

Flowering:   May–July.

Habitat:   Meadows and stream banks, always
where moisture is abundant until
flowering time.

Range:   British Columbia to southern
California, east of the Cascade
Mountains and Sierra Nevada (and on
islands in Puget Sound); east to
southern New Mexico, Colorado, and
North and South Dakota.

Comments:   The only native species east of the
Cascade Mountains and the Sierra
Nevada, it often forms dense, large
patches in low spots in pastures, where
the tough leaves are avoided by cattle.
It is suspected of being poisonous.

---

**607   Tough-leaved Iris**
(*Iris tenax*)
Iris Family (Iridaceae)

Description:   *Large, delicate, lavender to deep purple*
(*sometimes white, rarely yellow*) *flowers,*
commonly with dark violet veins, grow
at top of short stalks in *dense clumps of
narrow, tough leaves* about the same
height.
Flowers: 3–4″ (7.5–10 cm) wide;
sepals 3, resembling petals, curved
downward; petals 3, erect, slightly
shorter than sepals; sepals and petals
join to form a tube at base ¼–½″ (6–
13 mm) long; bracts beneath flower
joined to stem at distinctly different
levels.
Leaves: to 16″ (40 cm) long.
Height: to 16″ (40 cm).

Flowering:   April–June.

Habitat:   Pastures, fields, and open areas in
forests.

Range: Southwestern Washington to northwestern California, west of the Cascade Mountains.

Comments: In the Willamette Valley of Oregon these handsome flowers provide brilliant color displays along highways. *Tenax,* Latin for "tenacious," refers to the tough leaves; Indians used fibers from the edges of the leaves of some western species to make strong, pliable rope and cord.

### 583 Blue-eyed Grass
(*Sisyrinchium angustifolium*)
Iris Family (Iridaceae)

Description: Several *delicate, blue or deep blue-violet flowers* in 2 broad bracts top a *flat stem,* generally only 1 flower at a time in bloom; stems taller than the clusters of narrow, sword-shaped leaves near base.
Flowers: ½–1½" (1–3.8 cm) wide; 6 petal-like segments, each with a fine point on the otherwise blunt or notched tip.
Leaves: 2–10" (5–25 cm) long, ⅛–¼" (3–6 mm) wide.
Height: 4–20" (10–50 cm).

Flowering: April–September.

Habitat: Moist places (at least early in the season), generally in the open, from lowlands well into the mountains.

Range: Throughout.

Comments: One of the most perplexing groups of plants, with many, often intergrading, variants named as species.

### 464 Grass Widow
(*Sisyrinchium inflatum*)
Iris Family (Iridaceae)

Description: A few *reddish-lavender or purple, bowl-shaped flowers* bloom at the top of stems that grow from clumps of narrow, sword-like leaves.

Flowers: 1¼–2″ (3.1–5 cm) wide; 6 pointed petal-like segments, broadest in upper half; stamens 3, joined, forming a globe at base.
Leaves: usually about 4″ (10 cm) long, the lower half sheathing stem.
Height: 4–12″ (10–30 cm).

Flowering: March–June.

Habitat: Grassy areas in sagebrush and open woods.

Range: Southern British Columbia to northern California, mostly east of the Cascade Mountains; east to northern Utah and Idaho.

Comments: The flowers of this species are occasionally white. Douglas' Grass Widow (*S. douglasii*), from southern British Columbia to northern California, mostly west of the Cascade Mountains, has more intensely colored flowers, rarely white, and only a slight swelling at the base of its stamens.

## RATANY FAMILY (Krameriaceae)

Small intricately branched shrubs or
perennial herbs, usually with reddish-
purple flowers in leaf axils or racemes.
Flowers: bilaterally symmetrical; sepals
4–5, unequal, often petal-like; corolla
with 5 petals, the upper 3 with stalks
at the base, the lower 2 thick and short;
stamens 3 or 4. All these parts attached
at base of ovary.
Leaves: simple, alternate.
Fruit: single-chambered, bristly globe,
with one large seed.
There is only one genus with 25
species, restricted to warm parts of the
Americas.

### 565 Range Ratany
(*Krameria glandulosa*)
Ratany Family (Krameriaceae)

Description: A low, grayish, *intricately branched, very
twiggy shrub* with bilaterally
symmetrical *reddish-lavender flowers*.
Flowers: about ¾" (2 cm) wide, each on
a *slender stalk bearing many gland-tipped
hairs;* sepals 5, reddish-lavender inside;
upper 3 petals much smaller than
sepals, reddish-lavender, joined at base;
lower 2 petals resembling small,
greenish pads.
Leaves: ¼–½" (6–13 mm) long, very
narrow, grayish, hairy.
Fruit: pod about ¼" (6 mm) wide,
roundish, with long reddish prickles,
each with scattered barbs near tip.
Height: 6–24" (15–60 cm).

Flowering: March–October.

Habitat: Desert slopes, flats, and dry plains.

Range: Southeastern California to western
Texas; northern Mexico.

Comments: This species is commonly found among
creosotebush. Similar species lack
glands beneath flowers and have
different barb arrangements on prickles
of fruit.

## MINT FAMILY (Lamiaceae)

Aromatic herbs or shrubs, rarely trees or vines, usually with stems square in cross section, 4-sided, and flowers in long clusters, heads, or interrupted whorls on the stem.

Flowers: bilaterally symmetrical; sepals 5, united; petals 5, united, usually arranged so as to form an upper and lower lip; stamens 2 or 4. All these parts attached at base of ovary.

Leaves: usually simple, opposite or whorled.

Fruit: lobes 4, each forming a hard, single-seeded nutlet; rarely stone-fruit.

There are about 180 genera and 3,500 species occurring nearly worldwide. The Mediterranean region, the chief area of diversity, has produced many spices and flavorings; various mints, oregano, marjoram, thyme, sage, and basil. Catnip and Lavender are in the family.

---

529 **Nettleleaf Horsemint**
(*Agastache urticifolia*)
Mint Family (Lamiaceae)

Description: Numerous leafy, *4-sided stems have opposite leaves* and, near the top, *pale lavender, bilaterally symmetrical flowers* in dense circles crowded into *tight spikes*.
Flowers: spikes 1¼–6″ (3.1–15 cm) long; corolla about ½″ (13 mm) long, the upper and lower lobes bent back from the opening; stamens 4, protruding, the upper 2 longer than, and bent down between the lower 2.
Leaves: 1¼–3″ (3.1–7.5 cm) long, ovate, toothed, smooth on lower surface.
Height: 1–5′ (30–150 cm).
Flowering: June–August.
Habitat: Open slopes in woods.
Range: Southeastern British Columbia and eastern Washington to southern

California; east to western Colorado and western Montana.

Comments: *Agastache,* from the Greek *agan* ("much") and *stachys* ("ear of grain"), refers to the flower clusters. The spikes, short corolla lobes, and protruding stamens are distinctive.

### 618 Creeping Charlie; Ground Ivy
(*Glecoma hederacea*)
Mint Family (Lamiaceae)

Description: The weak, creeping, *4-sided stems bear opposite leaves* and a *few bilateral lavender to blue-violet flowers* in *clusters in each axil.*
Flowers: ½–1" (1.3–2.5 cm) long; corolla spotted with purple, lower lobe with a broad central portion and 2 small lobes at side, upper lobe arching outward like a hood, notched at tip, hiding 2 stamens; other 2 stamens in corolla tube.
Leaves: ½–1¼" (1.3–3.1 cm) long, round or kidney-shaped, scalloped margins, on long stalks.
Height: creeper, with stem tips 4–16" (10–40 cm) high.

Flowering: March–June.
Habitat: Moist woods and thickets.
Range: Throughout.
Comments: In many areas this native of Europe is now considered a lawn weed. In large amounts it is toxic to horses.

### 487 Common Henbit; Common Dead Nettle
(*Lamium amplexicaule*)
Mint Family (Lamiaceae)

Description: Small plants with several *4-sided stems* leaning on ground at base, tips erect, the few *reddish-lavender bilaterally symmetrical flowers in clusters in opposite bracts.*

Flowers: ½–¾" (1.3–2 cm) long, with a long, narrow tube; lower lip notched at tip, strongly constricted at base; upper lip only ¼" (6 mm) long, like a hood, hiding the 4 stamens, its upper side with deep purple hairs.
Leaves: ¾–1¼" (2–3.1 cm) long, roundish, scalloped on edges, without stalks.
Height: 3–6" (7.5–15 cm).

Flowering: February–October.
Habitat: A weed of fields and gardens.
Range: Throughout.
Comments: Two other species, also introduced from Eurasia, occur in our range; both have stalks on all leaves. Spotted Henbit (*L. maculatum*) has upper corolla lobe ¼–½" (7–13 mm) long. Red Henbit (*L. purpureum*) has flowers about the same size of Common Henbit.

### 653  Field Mint
(*Mentha arvensis*)
Mint Family (Lamiaceae)

Description: A branched, minty-smelling plant with stems in patches and, in leaf axils, *dense whorls of small, pale pink or lavender flowers nearly hidden by the opposite leaves.*
Flowers: corolla barely ¼" (6 mm) long, nearly radially symmetrical, the upper lobe broader and notched at tip.
Leaves: ¾–3" (2–7.5 cm) long, broadly lanceolate, sharply toothed.
Height: 8–32" (20–80 cm).

Flowering: July–September.
Habitat: Moist places, especially along streams.
Range: Throughout.
Comments: The clusters of flowers along the stem distinguish this species from many others which have flowers in slender spikes at the stem tips or in upper axils. The genus name *Mentha* comes from Mintho, mistress of Pluto, ruler of Hades. His jealous queen, Proserpine, upon learning of Mintho, trampled her, transforming her into a lowly plant

forever to be walked upon. Pluto made this horrible fate more tolerable by willing that the more the plant was trampled, the sweeter it would smell.

### 410 Red Monardella
(*Monardella macrantha*)
Mint Family (Lamiaceae)

Description: A generally low plant with *aromatic leaves* all along the several stems, which bear at the top tight clusters of *bright red, slightly bilaterally symmetrical tubular flowers.*
Flowers: 1¼–2″ (3.1–5 cm) long; corolla lobes 5, pointed, 2 closer together than the other 3; stamens 4.
Leaves: ½–1¼″ (1.3–3.1 cm) long opposite, ovate.
Height: 4–20″ (10–50 cm).
Flowering: June–August.
Habitat: Dry slopes in chaparral or pine forests.
Range: Southern California to Baja California.
Comments: The bright red flowers attract hummingbirds, which carry pollen from flower to flower while they seek nectar. Most Monardellas have much smaller, whitish or lavender corollas.

### 616 Coyote Mint
(*Monardella odoratissima*)
Mint Family (Lamiaceae)

Description: A grayish, aromatic plant with erect, bunched, leafy stems bearing *opposite leaves,* and *small, whitish or pale purple flowers in a dense head* at the top.
Flowers: corolla ⅝″ (1.5 cm) long; bilaterally symmetrical, with 5 lobes, 2 closer together than the other 3; stamens 4, protruding. Broadly ovate bracts of head are purplish and membrane-like.
Leaves: to 1¼″ (3.1 cm) long, lanceolate.

Height: 6–14″ (15–35 cm).

Flowering: June–September.

Habitat: Dry slopes and rocky banks, from low elevations to well into the mountains.

Range: Eastern Washington to northern Idaho; south to California, Arizona, and New Mexico.

Comments: Coyote Mint has many races in the West, varying in density of foliage hairs, breadth of heads, and relative length of bracts and calyx.

---

### 617 Bladder Sage
(*Salazaria mexicana*)
Mint Family (Lamiaceae)

Description: On this grayish-green shrub with spine-tipped twigs, it is usually the *papery bladders* scattered over the surface that attract attention.
Flowers: ¾″ (2 cm) long, in loose racemes; *calyx bladder-like, pale orange or greenish,* swelling to ¾″ (2 cm) wide, corolla bilaterally symmetrical, with a deep blue-violet upper lip and a pale tube and lower lip.
Leaves: about ½″ (1.3 cm) long, opposite, broadly lanceolate.
Height: 2–3′ (60–90 cm).

Flowering: March–June.

Habitat: In deserts, commonly in washes.

Range: Southern California to southern Utah, western Arizona, southwestern Texas, and northern Mexico.

Comments: The bladder-like calyx may be blown by the wind, thus dispersing seeds to new areas.

---

### 563 Thistle Sage
(*Salvia carduacea*)
Mint Family (Lamiaceae)

Description: A handsome, *whitish woolly plant* with *vivid lavender bilaterally symmetrical flowers in a stacked series of prickly, round*

*clusters* near the top of a leafless stem.
Flowers: ¾–1″ (2–2.5 cm) long;
corolla with upper and lower lobes
fringed; stamens 2, with the 2 pollen
sacs of a single stamen at ends of long,
slender stalks joined near base.
Leaves: 1–6″ (2.5–15 cm) long, in a
basal rosette, lanceolate, irregularly
indented, prickly.
Height: 4–20″ (10–50 cm).

Flowering: March–June.
Habitat: Sandy or gravelly open places.
Range: Central California to Baja California.
Comments: One of the most beautiful native Sages,
the brilliant flowers contrast strikingly
against the pale foliage, the vermilion
pollen sacs providing color accent.

---

### 654 Chia
(*Salvia columbariae*)
Mint Family (Lamiaceae)

Description: At intervals near the top of a *4-sided
stem* bloom small, *very deep blue
bilaterally symmetrical flowers* in a few
*dense, round clusters,* beneath which are
purplish bracts, each tipped with a
spine.
Flowers: corolla about ½″ (1.3 cm)
long, with prominent upper and lower
lips; stamens 2.
Leaves: to 4″ (10 cm) long, mostly at
base, oblong, irregularly divided.
Height: 4–20″ (10–50 cm).

Flowering: March–June.
Habitat: Open places in chaparral and in deserts.
Range: Southern half of California to Baja
California; east to southwestern Utah,
Arizona, and southwestern New
Mexico.
Comments: Chia (pronounced *chee′-ah*) is the
common name for several *Salvia* species
from which Indians made pinole; a
meal ground from parched seeds. When
steeped in water the seeds also produced
a thick, mucilaginous drink.

### 664 Gray-ball Sage; Desert Sage
(*Salvia dorrii*)
Mint Family (Lamiaceae)

Description: A *broad bush* with many rigid, spine-
tipped branches, *silvery leaves, and bright
blue to blue-violet bilaterally symmetrical
flowers.*
Flowers: about ½" (1.3 cm) long; lower
lip with a very broad, spreading middle
lobe bent downward and 2 small outer
lobes at side of opening to tube; upper
lip with 2 short, ear-like lobes; 2
stamens and 1 style arch out in front of
flower; bracts among flowers purple.
Leaves: ½–1½" (1.3–3.8 cm) long,
broadly lanceolate, broadest near tip,
tapered to a stalk-like base, opposite,
often clustered along the stem.
Height: 8–32" (20–80 cm).

Flowering: May–July.
Habitat: Dry flats and slopes, often associated
with sagebrush.
Range: East of the Cascade Mountains and
Sierra Nevada from Washington to
southern California; east to central
Arizona, Utah, and southwestern
Idaho.
Comments: It is this Sage, not sagebrush, that is
referred to in Zane Grey's classic
western *Riders of the Purple Sage.* It is a
handsome plant, pretty in leaf as well
as in flower.

### 663 Death Valley Sage
(*Salvia funerea*)
Mint Family (Lamiaceae)

Description: A compact, densely branched, *ghostly
white-woolly shrub with deep bluish-violet
to violet bilaterally symmetrical flowers.*
Flowers: about ½" (1.3 cm) long with
corolla protruding from each densely
woolly calyx.
Leaves: ½–¾" (1.3–2 cm) long, ovate,
thick and leathery, spine-tipped,
covered with white wool.

Height: 1½–4′ (45–120 cm).
Flowering: March–May.
Habitat: Hot rocky washes and canyon walls.
Range: Mountains around Death Valley,
California, and adjacent Nevada.
Comments: This plant's conspicuous white wool
probably serves to reflect heat and
reduce the effect of the strong, drying
winds that sweep through the hot
canyons much of the year. It is
protected by law and should not be
picked.

### 570 Autumn Sage
(*Salvia greggii*)
Mint Family (Lamiaceae)

Description: A shrub with many branches, a minty
odor, and a few *reddish-lavender,
bilaterally symmetrical flowers* in each
leafless raceme.
Flowers: corolla 1–1¼″ (2.5–3.1 cm)
long, the tubular portion swollen, but
abruptly narrowed near the opening,
lower lip about as long as lightly
glandular-hairy upper lip.
Leaves: ½–1″ (1.3–2.5 cm) long,
elliptic, leathery, on short stalks.
Height: to 3′ (90 cm).
Flowering: March–May.
Habitat: Rocky soil on brushy slopes.
Range: Western and central Texas to Mexico.
Comments: The bright, vibrant, nearly red flowers
make this species a favorite of all who
visit the Big Bend region.

### 408 Crimson Sage
(*Salvia henryi*)
Mint Family (Lamiaceae)

Description: A slender plant covered with soft gray
hairs, with *bright red bilaterally
symmetrical flowers* in pairs at intervals
near top of a *4-sided stem.*
Flowers: 1½″ (3.8 cm) long; corolla

tube expands abruptly just past tip of
calyx, lower lip with 3 lobes, bent
downward, and upper lip projecting
forward; stamens 2.
Leaves: 1–2½″ (2.5–6.3 cm) long,
opposite, pinnately divided, with end
segment largest.
Height: to 20″ (50 cm).

Flowering: April–September.

Habitat: Rocky slopes and canyons, often among
piñon and juniper.

Range: Southern Arizona to western Texas;
south to northern Mexico.

Comments: The gray foliage complements the
brilliant flowers, making this plant
particularly attractive in its arid,
sometimes barren, habitat.

517  **Lemmon's Sage**
(*Salvia lemmonii*)
Mint Family (Lamiaceae)

Description: An aromatic, leafy-branched plant,
somewhat woody near base, with
*upward-angled, bilaterally symmetrical
deep pink to crimson flowers* in raceme-like
clusters at ends of stems.
Flowers: 1–1½″ (2.5–3.8 cm) long,
the upper lip projecting forward like a
visor, the lower lip very broad, bent
downward; usually 2 flowers grow
opposite one another in a long cluster.
Leaves: 1–2″ (2.5–5 cm) long, ovate,
with stalks.
Height: 1–3′ (30–90 cm).

Flowering: July–October.

Habitat: In dry woods on rocky slopes and in
canyons.

Range: Southern Arizona and northern Mexico.

Comments: This handsome plant has the long,
tubular reddish flowers typical of those
visited by hummingbirds.

### 143 Yerba Buena
(*Satureja douglasii*)
Mint Family (Lamiaceae)

Description: Long, slender, trailing stems with
1 *white or pale purplish bilaterally
symmetrical flower* in each upper leaf axil.
Flowers: corolla about ¼″ (6 mm) long,
short upper lip projecting forward,
with a shallow notch at tip, longer
3-lobed lower lip bent down;
stamens 4.
Leaves: ½–1″ (1.3–2.5 cm) long,
opposite, roundish.
Height: creeper, the erect stems to
1′ (30 cm) high, trailing stems to 2′
(60 cm) long.
Flowering: April–October.
Habitat: Shaded woods.
Range: Southern British Columbia to northern
Idaho; south on the western side of the
Cascade Mountains and Sierra Nevada
to Baja California.
Comments: The name Yerba Buena, Spanish for
"good herb," has been applied to
several species of Mint, especially
Spearmint (*Mentha spicata*), but in the
West generally refers to *S. douglasii*.
The mild and delightful tea made from
the leaves of this delicately fragrant
plant has been used to treat many
ailments and to alleviate the pain of
childbirth.

### 619 Austin's Skullcap
(*Scutellaria austinae*)
Mint Family (Lamiaceae)

Description: Pairs of *deep violet-blue, bilaterally
symmetrical flowers angle upward* from the
top of this low plant's erect stems.
Flowers: 1–1½″ (2.5–3.8 cm) long,
with a slender tube curved upward at
the base; upper lip arched forward like
a small helmet, lower lip bent down,
with a hump near opening to tube;
calyx broad and bell-shaped, 2-lipped,

the upper side with a crescent-shaped
ridge or crest.
Leaves: ½–1″ (1.3–2.5 cm) long,
nearly erect, lanceolate, broadest well
above the middle, without stalks.
Height: 4–12″ (10–30 cm).

Flowering: May–July.

Habitat: In gravelly or rocky places among pines
and brush.

Range: Most of California.

Comments: The species is representative of several
with dark blue-violet flowers.
Narrowleaf Skullcap (*S. angustifolia*),
which grows from British Columbia to
central California, east to Idaho, has
leaves with definite stalks and a corolla
⅞–1¼″ (2.1–3.1 cm) long.
Snapdragon Skullcap (*S. antirrhinoides*),
from southern Idaho to southern
Oregon, northern California, central
Nevada, and Utah, has flowers only ½–
⅞″ (1.3–2.1 cm) long.

---

### 620  Marsh Skullcap
(*Scutellaria galericulata*)
Mint Family (Lamiaceae)

Description: Grows in patches, with *blue bilaterally
symmetrical flowers, 1 blooming in each
axil of the upper leaves.*
Flowers: ½–¾″ (1.3–2 cm) long, with
upper lobe of corolla helmet-shaped,
lower lobe bent downward; upper and
lower lips of calyx without teeth, and
across top of upper lip is a raised crest.
Leaves: ¾–2″ (2–5 cm) long, opposite,
lanceolate, faintly scalloped on edges.
Height: 4–32″ (10–80 cm).

Flowering: June–September.

Habitat: Wet meadows, swamps, and along
streams at moderate elevations.

Range: Throughout, extending south in the
West to central California, northern
Arizona, and northern New Mexico.

Comments: In the West, where many species prefer
dry sites, this is one that prefers a moist
habitat.

411 **Texas Betony; Scarlet Hedge Nettle**
(*Stachys coccinea*)
Mint Family (Lamiaceae)

Description: A stout, erect, leafy plant, covered with soft hairs, with *scarlet bilaterally symmetrical flowers in whorls at intervals in a spike* at top of 4-sided stem.
Flowers: ¾–1″ (2–2.5 cm) long; corolla with a faint, but abrupt, constriction in tube near base; upper lip bent upward, 3-lobed lower lip bent downward.
Leaves: to 3″ (7.5 cm) long, opposite, nearly triangular with teeth on edges.
Height: to 3′ (90 cm).
Flowering: March–October.
Habitat: Moist, rich soil in rock crevices on steep, stony slopes.
Range: Western Texas to central Arizona; south to northern Mexico.
Comments: *Stachys* has no stinging hairs, as do true Nettles, but resembles Nettles in other ways, especially before flowering. In the Old World, some grow near hedges; hence the name Hedge Nettle. Its scarlet color distinguishes this species from other western ones, which are pink or purplish. If cultivated, it should be grown from seed.

518 **Great Hedge Nettle**
(*Stachys cooleyae*)
Mint Family (Lamiaceae)

Description: Stout, *4-sided, leafy stems* grow in patches and have *deep reddish-lavender bilaterally symmetrical flowers in whorls at intervals* in a spike at top.
Flowers: corolla ⅝–1″ (1.5–2.5 cm) long, upper lip projecting like a short hood, lower lip 3-lobed, much longer, bent downward.
Leaves: 2½–6″ (6.3–15 cm) long, opposite, all with stalks, broadly lanceolate, bearing blunt teeth on margins.

Height: 2–5' (60–150 cm).
Flowering: June–August.
Habitat: Swamps and moist low ground from sea
level to moderate elevations.
Range: Southern British Columbia to southern
Oregon, from the eastern slope of the
Cascade Mountains to the Pacific Coast.
Comments: The moist habitat is typical for Hedge
Nettles. Other western species may
have smaller, paler flowers and middle
and upper leaves without stalks.

### 640 Vinegar Weed; Common Blue Curls
(*Trichostema lanceolatum*)
Mint Family (Lamiaceae)

Description: Tall, leafy, *unpleasant smelling plant* with
*pale blue bilaterally symmetrical flowers* in
long clusters in leaf axils.
Flowers: about ½" (1.3 cm) long;
corolla with a narrow tube strongly
bent upward near the base of the 5
narrow lobes; stamens 4, long, with the
style projecting from between 2 upper
corolla lobes, bent toward back of
flower, then arching up and forward.
Leaves: ¾–3" (2–7.5 cm) long,
narrowly lanceolate, opposite, usually
much longer than section of stem
between pairs of leaves.
Height: 2–5' (60–150 cm).
Flowering: July–October.
Habitat: Dry slopes and fields.
Range: Northwestern Oregon to Baja
California.
Comments: The genus name comes from Greek
words *trichos* ("hair") and *stemon*
("stamen"), referring to the long,
slender stamens, characteristic of the
genus. Of the several other species, the
pleasantly aromatic shrub called Woolly
Blue Curls, or Romero (*T. lanatum*),
which grows in southern California,
might be the most handsome. The blue
flowers grow in dense terminal clusters
covered with violet wool.

## BLADDERWORT FAMILY
### (Lentibulariaceae)

Herbs of moist or aquatic habitats,
usually carnivorous, with flowers
solitary or in racemes.
Flowers: bilaterally symmetrical; sepals
2–5, united; petals 5, united forming
an upper and lower lip, the lower with
a spur projecting backward; stamens 2.
All these parts attach at base of ovary.
Leaves: alternate or in rosettes, simple
or highly divided.
Fruit: 1-chambered capsule, with a
central column to which the seeds
attach.
There are about 4 genera and possibly
200–300 species that occur worldwide.

---

**585 Common Butterwort**
(*Pinguicula vulgaris*)
Bladderwort Family (Lentibulariaceae)

Description: A small plant with stalkless, *broadly
lanceolate leaves in a basal rosette* and a
*single bilaterally symmetrical lavender or
purple flower* (rarely white) on a leafless
stalk.
Flowers: about ⅝" (15 mm) wide;
corolla with 2-lobed upper lip, 3-lobed
lower lip, and backward-projecting
spur about ³⁄₁₆–⅜" (5–9 mm) long.
Leaves: ¾–2" (2–5 cm) long, fleshy,
densely studded with microscopic
glands that give a greasy feel to the
upper surface.
Height: 2–6" (5–15 cm).
Flowering: April–August.
Habitat: Bogs and wet soil, rocks, or banks.
Range: Alaska to northwestern California; east
across the northern states and Canada.
Comments: The genus name means "greasy little
one" referring to the slimy upper
surface and fatty texture of the soft,
fleshy leaves. Small organisms that stick
to the leaves are digested by the plant.

## 283 Common Bladderwort
(*Utricularia vulgaris*)
Bladderwort Family (Lentibulariaceae)

Description: *Small floating plant with 6–20 bilaterally symmetrical yellow flowers,* in each rather stout, erect raceme.
Flowers: corolla about ½–¾″ (1.3–2 cm) long, with a spur curving forward and downward from near base.
Leaves: ½–2″ (1.3–5 cm) long, repeatedly and finely divided into almost hair-like segments, with bladders up to ⅛″ (3 mm) wide.
Height: aquatic, flower stalks 2½–8″ (6.3–20 cm) above water surface.
Flowering: June–August.
Habitat: Ponds or slowly moving water.
Range: Throughout.
Comments: Of possibly 5 species in the West, several difficult to distinguish, this has the largest flowers. Another species easy to identify is Mountain Bladderwort (*U. intermedia*), with bladders on special branches distinct from the leaves. The bladders are elaborate traps. When a small organism brushes hairs near a bladder pore, its tiny door opens inward, and water, carrying the organism with it, rushes inside. The door quickly closes, the trapping process taking $\frac{1}{460}$ second. Enzymes digest the victim. Comparatively large organisms such as mosquito larvae may be caught in the door, and if the door is repeatedly "triggered," they are then digested little by little.

## LILY FAMILY (Lilaceae)

Mostly perennial herbs from rhizomes, bulbs, or corms, some rather woody and treelike, and often with showy flowers in racemes or branched racemes.
Flowers: usually bisexual and radially symmetrical; sepals 3, commonly resembling petals; petals 3; petals and sepals may be united into a tube; stamens 6, or rarely 3. All these parts attach at base of ovary.
Leaves: alternate or basal, simple, usually narrow.
Fruit: 3-chambered capsule or berry.
The family is extremely complex and botanists estimate that it includes nearly 250 genera and 4,000–6,000 species. Many, including Tulips and Day Lilies, are handsome ornamentals. Asparagus, Sarsaparilla, Onions, and the medicinally useful Aloë are from the family. A few species are poisonous.

---

### 551 Hooker's Onion
(*Allium acuminatum*)
Lily Family (Liliaceae)

Description: An *umbel of pink or deep pink flowers* grows at the top of a leafless stalk. Plant has a strong onion odor.
Flowers: about ½″ (1.3 cm) long; 6 petal-like segments, each with a long point, inner 3 segments slightly taller than outer 3, edges with very small, almost microscopic teeth; 2 papery, pointed bracts, beneath umbel.
Leaves: 4–6″ (10–15 cm) long, 2 or 3, basal, very narrow.
Height: 4–12″ (10–30 cm).
Flowering: May–July.
Habitat: Open, often rocky slopes, among brush and pines.
Range: British Columbia to central California and southern Arizona; east to southern Wyoming and western Colorado.

Comments:   One of the most common of the many
western Wild Onions, all of which have
edible bulbs, though some are
extremely potent or unpalatable. In the
early days of the West, Indians saved at
least one exploration party from scurvy
by alerting the ill explorers to the
curative properties of Wild Onions.

### 550   Nodding Onion
(*Allium cernuum*)
Lily Family (Liliaceae)

Description:   A long, erect stalk, bent like a
shepherd's crook, grows from a basal
cluster of several long, narrow leaves; *at
the tip hangs an umbel of many pink or
white flowers.*
Flowers: about ¼″ (6 mm) long;
6 ovate, petal-like segments; 2 papery
bracts beneath umbel drop by flowering
time.
Leaves: 2–10″ (5–25 cm) long.
Height: 4–20″ (10–50 cm).
Flowering:   June–October.
Habitat:   Moist soils in cool mountain forests.
Range:   Across northern North America; south
to southern Oregon, Arizona, New
Mexico, and Texas; in the eastern
mountains to Georgia; also in Mexico.
Comments:   The "nodding" umbel distinguishes
this species from all others in the West.

### 368   Amber Lily
(*Anthericum torreyi*)
Lily Family (Liliaceae)

Description:   *Star-like, yellowish-orange flowers* bloom
in a narrow open cluster at top of a
leafless stalk that grows from a basal
cluster of several grass-like leaves.
Flowers: about 1″ (2.5 cm) wide;
6 narrow petal-like segments spread
from the base, each with 3–5 greenish
or brownish veins down the center.

Leaves: usually less than ¼" (6 mm) wide, from half to as long as stem.
Height: to 3' (90 cm).

Flowering: June–November.

Habitat: Rich soil in canyons, on hills among piñon and juniper, and in pine forests.

Range: North-central Arizona to central Texas; south into Mexico.

Comments: Of the approximately 300 species of *Anthericum* in the world, only 1 grows in the West. The similar California Bog-asphodel (*Narthecium californicum*), which grows in springs and bogs in northern California and southern Oregon, has yellow or yellowish-orange flowers about ½" (1.3 cm) wide and hairy stamen stalks.

### 319 Golden Stars
(*Bloomeria crocea*)
Lily Family (Liliaceae)

Description: An *umbel of yellow to orange, star-like flowers* blooms atop a stem with a narrow, grass-like leaf at base.
Flowers: ½–1" (1.3–2.5 cm) wide; 6 petal-like segments, each free from the other, have dark lines down the middle; stamens 6, each with a cup-like flap at base of stalk, notched at tip.
Leaves: 4–12" (10–30 cm) long, ³⁄₁₆–½" (5–13 mm) wide; one only.
Height: 6–24" (15–60 cm).

Flowering: April–June.

Habitat: On dry flats and hills, in grass, brush, and oak woodland.

Range: Southern one-third of California to Baja California.

Comments: The golden, star-like flowers with separate petal-like parts distinguish this genus. The one other species, Cleveland's Golden Stars (*B. clevelandii*), has several leaves less than ⅛" (3 mm) wide, and the flap at the base of each stamen is not notched.

### 657　Elegant Brodiaea
(*Brodiaea elegans*)
Lily Family (Liliaceae)

Description:　An *umbel of several violet or blue-violet,
 *funnel-shaped flowers* at top of a leafless
 stalk with a few long, very narrow basal
 leaves that are usually withered by
 flowering time.
 Flowers: 1–1½" (2.5–3.8 cm) long; 6
 narrow petal-like segments; inside,
 alternating with 3 stamens, are flat,
 white scales separated from, and shorter
 than, stamens.
 Leaves: 4–16" (10–40 cm) long.
 Height: 4–16" (10–40 cm).

Flowering:　April–July.

Habitat:　Dry plains and grassy hillsides.

Range:　Northern Oregon to southern
 California.

Comments:　This plant begins to flower as fields dry
 out in the early summer. Several species
 of Brodiaea (pronounced *bro-dee'-ah*),
 are similar. In Harvest Brodiaea
 (*B. coronaria*), from British Columbia to
 southern California, the scales between
 the stamens are concave on their inner
 side, longer than the stamens and lean
 toward them. One of the most
 handsome is Wally Basket, Grass Nut,
 or Ithuriel's Spear (*Trileleia laxa*),
 which grows on heavy soils in grassland
 or brush from southern Oregon to
 southern California; it reaches a height
 of up to 28" (70 cm) and has many
 flowers in a large umbel, with 6
 stamens and beneath the ovary a stalk
 2–3 times its length.

### 87　White Globe Lily
(*Calochortus albus*)
Lily Family (Liliaceae)

Description:　*Egg-shaped, white flowers* hang in an
 open, branched cluster.
 Flowers: about 1" (2.5 cm) long; sepals
 3, greenish white, often purplish-

tinged, lanceolate; petals 3, broad, satiny white.
Leaves: those on branched stems 2–6" (5–15 cm) long, the one at base 8–20" (20–50 cm) long.
Height: 1–2' (30–60 cm).
Flowering: April–June.
Habitat: Shaded, often rocky places, in open woods and brush.
Range: Southern two-thirds of California.
Comments: The several *Calochortus* species with egg-shaped flowers are generally called Globe Lilies, whereas those with more open flowers are known as Mariposa and Star Tulips. Other common names of this species include White Fairy Lantern, Snowdrops, Indian Bells, and Satin Bells. The Rose Globe Lily (*C. amoenus*), grows on the western slopes of the Sierra Nevada in the San Joaquin Valley.

## 279 Yellow Globe Lily; Golden Fairy Lantern
(*Calochortus amabilis*)
Lily Family (Liliaceae)

Description: Deep, *clear yellow, egg-shaped flowers* hang in an open branched cluster.
Flowers: about 1" (2.5 cm) long; sepals 3, lanceolate, about ¾" (2 cm) long; petals 3, broad, slightly longer than sepals, finely fringed on edges and bearing on inner surface a crescent-shaped gland covered by yellow hairs.
Leaves: those on branched stem ¾–8" (2–20 cm) long, the one at base to 20" (50 cm) long, narrow.
Height: 8–20" (20–50 cm).
Flowering: April–June.
Habitat: Dry slopes in brush and open woods.
Range: Northern California.
Comments: The nodding yellow flowers are a delight to behold, as indicated by the species name, which means "lovable beautiful grass."

**47   Elegant Cat's Ears; Star Tulip**
(*Calochortus elegans*)
Lily Family (Liliaceae)

Description:   A small plant with slender, bent stems and a *few white flowers* in a branched cluster shorter than the *single grass-like leaf.*
Flowers: about 1″ (2.5 cm) wide; sepals 3, lanceolate; petals 3, broad, slightly longer than sepals, densely hairy on surface, often with a purple crescent near base above the gland, on whose lower side is a fringed membrane.
Leaves: 4–8″ (10–20 cm) long.
Height: 2–8″ (5–20 cm).
Flowering:   May–June.
Habitat:   Grassy hillsides and open coniferous woods.
Range:   Southeastern Washington and northeastern Oregon to western Montana.
Comments:   The name Star Tulip refers to the flower's shape and Cat's Ears to the petal's resemblance to a kitten's ear. Similar species are distinguished by characteristics of the gland and pod.

**225, 362   Desert Mariposa Tulip**
(*Calochortus kennedyi*)
Lily Family (Liliaceae)

Description:   In an umbel-like cluster on top of short stems bloom 1–6 handsome *bell-shaped, vermilion, orange, or yellow flowers.*
Flowers: 1–2″ (2.5–3.8 cm) wide; sepals 3, lanceolate; petals 3, broad, fan-shaped, each with a dark maroon blotch near base and a round, depressed gland surrounded by a fringed membrane; near the gland are a few hairs with enlarged tips.
Leaves: 4–8″ (10–20 cm) long, few, narrowly lanceolate.
Height: 4–20″ (10–50 cm).
Flowering:   March–June.
Habitat:   Heavy soil in open or brushy areas from

creosotebush deserts to piñon and juniper rangeland.

Range: Southern California to central Arizona; south into northwestern Mexico.

Comments: One of the most brilliant of the Mariposa Tulips. In California, vermilion flowers are most frequent; orange flowers are more common eastward. The yellow phase is found throughout the range, especially at higher elevations.

## 226 Yellow Mariposa Tulip
(*Calochortus luteus*)
Lily Family (Liliaceae)

Description: The slender stems of this plant bear a few narrow leaves and at the top *1—4 large, deep yellow, bell-shaped flowers* in an umbel-like cluster.
Flowers: 1—1½" (2.5—3.8 cm) wide; sepals 3, lanceolate; petals 3, broad, fan-shaped, long, usually with fine red-brown lines on lower portion and also often with a central red-brown blotch; gland near base of petals broadly crescent-shaped, covered with short, matted hairs.
Leaves: 4—8" (10—20 cm) long.
Height: 8—24" (20—60 cm).

Flowering: April—June.

Habitat: Heavy soil in grassland and open forests at low elevations.

Range: California Coast Ranges and western foothills of the Sierra Nevada.

Comments: This species and some others frequently reproduce asexually by means of small "bulblets" in the leaf axils, which drop to the ground and grow into new plants.

461   **Sagebrush Mariposa Tulip**
      (*Calochortus macrocarpus*)
      Lily Family (Liliaceae)

Description:   At top of stout, erect, generally
              unbranched stems bloom *1–3 handsome,*
              *bell-shaped, lilac flowers* in a loose umbel-
              like cluster.
              Flowers: 1½–2½ (3.8–6.3 cm) wide;
              sepals 3, narrowly lanceolate, slightly
              longer than petals; petals 3, broad, fan-
              shaped, each with a greenish stripe
              down middle; oblong gland near base of
              each petal is surrounded by a fringed
              membrane and often marked above by a
              deep lilac, crescent-shaped patch.
              Leaves: 2–4″ (5–10 cm) long, several
              on the stem, very narrow, usually
              curled at tip.
              Height: 8–20″ (20–50 cm).
Flowering:    May–August.
Habitat:      Loose, dry soil on plains, among
              sagebrush, and in yellow pine forests.
Range:        The eastern side of the Cascade
              Mountains from southern British
              Columbia to northern California; east to
              northern Nevada and across central and
              northern Idaho to western Montana.
Comments:     One of the most frequent Mariposa
              Tulips in the arid Northwest. A white
              phase with a reddish stripe on each
              petal occurs in southeastern
              Washington and adjacent west-central
              Idaho.

48   **Sego Lily**
     (*Calochortus nuttallii*)
     Lily Family (Liliaceae)

Description:   Erect, unbranched stems with a few
              leaves are topped by *1–4 showy, white,*
              *bell-shaped flowers* in an umbel-like
              cluster.
              Flowers: 1–2″ (2.5–5 cm) wide; sepals
              3, lanceolate, slightly shorter than
              petals; petals 3, broad, fan-shaped;
              yellow around the gland at base,

marked with reddish brown or purple above the gland; gland circular, surrounded by a fringed membrane.
Leaves: 2–4″ (5–10 cm) long, narrow, the edges rolled upward.
Height: 6–18″ (15–45 cm).

Flowering: May–July.

Habitat: Dry soil on plains, among sagebrush, and in open pine forests.

Range: Eastern Montana and western North Dakota; south to eastern Idaho and northwestern Nebraska; across Utah and western Colorado to northern Arizona and northwestern New Mexico.

Comments: Occasionally petals are magenta or tinged with lilac. This is Utah's state flower; the Ute Indians called it "sago," and taught Mormon settlers to eat the bulbs in times of scarcity.

### 630 Common Camas
(*Camassia quamash*)
Lily Family (Liliaceae)

Description: *Light to deep blue-violet, star-shaped flowers* in a raceme; several narrow, grass-like leaves grow mostly near the base.
Flowers: 1½–2½″ (3.8–6.3 cm) wide; slightly bilaterally symmetrical; 6 narrow petal-like segments, lower ones tend to curve out from the stem more strongly than do upper ones.
Leaves: to 2′ (60 cm) long.
Height: 12–20″ (30–50 cm).

Flowering: April–June.

Habitat: Moist meadows.

Range: Southern British Columbia to northern California; east to northern Utah, Wyoming, and Montana.

Comments: This species is sometimes so frequent as to color entire meadows blue-violet. Indians pit-roasted the bland bulbs with other leaves, and also boiled them, which yielded a good syrup. Another similar species is Leichtlin's Camas (*C. leichtlinii*), which grows only west of the Cascade Mountains, from southern British Columbia to the southern portion of California's Sierra Nevada, and has radially symmetrical flowers.

---

### 79  Wavy-leaved Soap Plant; Amole
(*Chlorogalum pomeridianum*)
Lily Family (Liliaceae)

Description: Delicate, *star-like, white flowers* bloom in a *large, freely and openly branched cluster.*
Flowers: 1–1½″ (2.5–3.8 cm) wide; 6 narrow petal-like segments curve backward.
Leaves: to 2′ (60 cm) long, several, narrow, grass-like, with wavy edges, mostly all at base.
Height: 2–10′ (60–300 cm).

Flowering: May–August.

Habitat: Dry open hills and plains, often in open brush or woods.

Range: Southwestern Oregon to southern California.

Comments: By day this plant appears ungainly, the branches stark and unattractive, but toward the evening, or on cloudy days, the delicate flowers open, resembling thistledown caught among the twigs. Indians used bulbs crushed and rubbed with water to produce a lather for cleaning clothing and baskets. Roasted bulbs produced a substance used to glue feathers to arrow shafts, and to treat rashes caused by poison oak.

---

### 422, 561  Red Clintonia; Andrew's Clintonia
(*Clintonia andrewsiana*)
Lily Family (Liliaceae)

Description: An *umbel-like cluster of red or reddish-lavender, narrowly bell-shaped flowers* blooms at the top of a nearly leafless stalk, growing from a basal rosette.

Beneath main flower cluster, there may be smaller clusters with only a few flowers.
Flowers: 6 narrow petal-like segments about ½" (1.3 cm) long.
Leaves: 6–10" (15–25 cm) long, usually 5 or 6, broadly elliptic.
Fruit: deep blue berry to ½" (1.3 cm) long.
Height: 10–20" (25–50 cm).

Flowering: May–July.
Habitat: Shaded damp forests near the coast.
Range: Central California to southwestern Oregon.
Comments: One of the few wildflowers that grow in the dim light of the Pacific Coast redwood forests. The genus is named for DeWitt Clinton, naturalist and governor of New York in the early 19th Century.

## 40 Queen's Cup; Bride's Bonnet
(*Clintonia uniflora*)
Lily Family (Liliaceae)

Description: *1 (rarely 2) white, star-like flower* blooms on a short leafless stalk that grows from a basal cluster of 2 or 3 oblong or elliptic, shiny leaves.
Flowers: 1–1½" (2.5–3.8 cm) wide; 6 lanceolate petal-like segments form a broad bell.
Leaves: 2½–6" (6.3–15 cm) long.
Fruit: lustrous deep blue berry ¼–½" (6–13 mm) long.
Height: 2½–6" (6.3–15 cm).

Flowering: May–July.
Habitat: Coniferous forests, often where moist.
Range: Alaska to northern California and inland to the southern Sierra Nevada; east to eastern Oregon and western Montana.
Comments: Generally there are several clusters of leaves in a patch, for the plant produces an extensive system of underground stems.

### 185 Sotol; Desert Spoon
(*Dasylirion wheeleri*)
Lily Family (Liliaceae)

Description: *Thousands of tiny, greenish-white flowers in a long, narrow cluster* that grows from a dense bunch of *many slender, spiny leaves.*
Flowers: cluster 5–8' (1.5–2.4 m) long; 6 petal-like segments.
Leaves: to 3' (90 cm) long, ½–1" (1.3–2.5 cm) wide, with teeth on edges that curve forward.
Height: flower stalk 6–17' (1.8–5.1 m), atop a trunk to 3' (90 cm).

Flowering: May–July.

Habitat: Rocky desert slopes.

Range: Western Texas to southern Arizona.

Comments: Plants may be treated in the same manner as Agaves to produce food and liquor (sotol). The tough leaves are woven into mats and baskets and used for thatching. The broad, spoon-like base is often used in dried floral arrangements. The smaller Smooth-leaved Sotol (*D. leiophyllum*), which grows on limestone in southern New Mexico, western Texas, and northern Mexico, has teeth that curve toward the leaf base.

### 655 Forktooth Ookow
(*Dichelostemma congestum*)
Lily Family (Liliaceae)

Description: *A head of blue-violet flowers* blooms at the top of a long stalk with a few basal grass-like leaves.
Flowers: ½–¾" (1.3–2 cm) long; 6 petal-like segments join to form a broad tube not, or only barely, constricted just below opening; stamens 3, hidden within tube; 3 forked scales project from tube.
Leaves: 1–3' (30–90 cm) long, ¼–½" (6–13 mm) wide.
Height: 1–3' (30–90 cm).

Flowering: April–June.

Habitat: Open grassy hills.

Range: Western Washington to central California.

Comments: These wildflowers begin to bloom as grasses mature and begin to brown, signaling the onset of summer. Roundtooth Ookow (*D. multiflorum*), which grows from southern Oregon to central California, has round ends on the 3 scales projecting from the center of the flower. Blue Dicks (*D. pulchellum*), southern Oregon to northwestern Mexico, east to southern Utah and southern New Mexico, has 6 stamens hidden within the floral tube and no projecting scales.

## 412 Firecracker Flower
(*Dichelostemma ida-maia*)
Lily Family (Liliaceae)

Description: *Tubular, red flowers hang in an umbel* at the top of a leafless stalk that commonly has 3 long, narrow, grass-like leaves at its base.
Flowers: 1–1½″ (2.5–3.8 cm) long; 6 short, yellow-green lobes curled back at end of the red tube, from whose center protrude 3 short, pale yellow scales and 3 cream stamens.
Leaves: 12–20″ (30–50 cm) long.
Height: 1–3′ (30–90 cm).

Flowering: May–July.

Habitat: Grassy slopes in openings in forests, at low or moderate elevations.

Range: Northwestern California to southwestern Oregon.

Comments: The brilliant red flowers resemble loose clusters of firecrackers tied together by the ends of their fuses. One of the most charming and unusual of California wildflowers, the species name is said to have been suggested by a stagecoach driver who showed the plant to an early collector; it honors the driver's niece, Ida May.

## 81  **Wartberry Fairybell**
(*Disporum trachycarpum*)
Lily Family (Liliaceae)

Description:  This beautiful woodland plant, with
stems branched in a forked manner, has
1 or 2 small, *creamy white, narrowly bell-
shaped flowers hanging beneath the leaves* at
the ends of branches.
Flowers: ⅜–⅝" (9–15 mm) long;
6 petal-like segments; style lacks hairs.
Leaves: 1½–5" (3.8–12.5 cm) long,
many, all along stem, ovate, round or
indented at base, smooth on upper
surface; hairs on edges stick straight
out.
Fruit: round berry about ⅜" (9 mm)
wide, at first yellow, becoming red.
Height: 1–2' (30–60 cm).

Flowering:  May–July.

Habitat:  Wooded areas, often near streams.

Range:  British Columbia to northeastern
Oregon; east to eastern North Dakota;
south through the Rocky Mountain
region to southern Arizona and western
New Mexico.

Comments:  The regularly forked branches of these
attractive and orderly plants bear leaves
that are mostly oriented horizontally.
There are 3 western species. Smith's
Fairybell (*D. smithii*), which grows in
moist woods on the western side of the
Cascade Mountains and the Sierra
Nevada from British Columbia to
central California, has the largest
flowers, ⅝–1" (1.5–2.5 cm) long.
Hooker's Fairybell (*D. hookeri*), which
occurs from British Columbia south to
northwestern Oregon, east to Alberta
and western Montana, is very similar to
Wartberry Fairybell, but the style is
usually hairy, as are the upper surfaces
of the leaves, and the hairs on the leaf
edges point forward.

### 130 Lonely Lily
(*Eremocrinum albomarginatum*)
Lily Family (Liliaceae)

Description: A few *white, star-like flowers* in a dense
raceme top a flower stalk that grows
from a basal cluster of long, narrow
leaves.
Flowers: ¾–1″ (2–2.5 cm) wide; 6
broadly lanceolate petal-like segments.
Leaves: to 1′ (30 cm) long.
Height: 6–12″ (15–30 cm).

Flowering: June.

Habitat: Sandy soil.

Range: Southern Utah and northern Arizona.

Comments: The genus name is from the Greek
*eremos* ("lonely") and *krinon* ("lily"); the
only species in the genus, it occurs in
one of the most sparsely populated parts
of the country.

### 280 Yellow Fawn Lily
(*Erythronium grandiflorum*)
Lily Family (Liliaceae)

Description: *1–5 pale to golden yellow flowers hang* at
end of a stalk that grows from between
*2 broadly lanceolate basal leaves.*
Flowers: 6 lanceolate petal-like
segments 1–2″ (2.5–5 cm) long that
curve back behind base of flower;
stamens 6, protruding from center.
Leaves: 4–8″ (10–20 cm) long,
gradually tapered to a broad stalk.
Fruit: swollen 3-sided capsule.
Height: 6–12″ (15–30 cm).

Flowering: March–August.

Habitat: Sagebrush slopes and mountain forest
openings, often near melting snow.

Range: Southern British Columbia to northern
Oregon; east to western Colorado,
Wyoming, and western Montana.

Comments: This species often blooms as snow
recedes. A form with white or cream
petal-like segments with a band of
golden yellow at the base grows in
southeastern Washington and adjacent

Idaho. A second species with bright
yellow flowers, Mother Lode Fawn Lily
(*E. tuolumnense*), grows in woodland at
low elevations on the western slope of
the Sierra Nevada in central California.

---

**55   Avalanche Lily; Glacier Lily**
(*Erythronium montanum*)
Lily Family (Liliaceae)

Description:   *1—5 showy white flowers nod at end of a*
*stalk that grows from between 2 broadly*
*lanceolate basal leaves.*
Flowers: about 2½″ (5 cm) wide; 6
petal-like segments that curve back,
white except for a yellow band at base,
becoming pink with age; stamens 6,
protruding from center.
Leaves: 4—8″ (10—20 cm) long,
abruptly tapered to a distinct stalk.
Height: 6—10″ (15—25 cm).
Flowering:   June—September.
Habitat:   Alpine or subalpine meadows and
forests.
Range:   British Columbia to northern Oregon.
Comments:   This mountain species blooms just after
the snow melts, often carpeting
meadows with its white flowers. There
are a number of western species, some
with cream or yellow flowers, others
with pinkish ones.

---

**378   Mission Bells, Checker Lily**
(*Fritillaria lanceolata*)
Lily Family (Liliaceae)

Description:   On an erect stem, leafy in the upper
part, leafless below, bloom several
*nodding, greenish-brown, deeply bowl-*
*shaped flowers.*
Flowers: ¾—1½″ (2—3.8 cm) long;
6 lanceolate petal-like segments,
brownish, mottled green or yellow.
Leaves: 1½ to 6″ (3.1—15 cm) long,
lanceolate, generally less than 10 times

as long as wide, in several whorls on the stem.

Height: 1–4′ (30–120 cm).

Flowering: February–June.

Habitat: Grassy or brushy flats and slopes, or in open woods.

Range: Southern British Columbia to southern California; eastward to northern Idaho.

Comments: The genus name comes from Latin *fritillus,* meaning "dice box," in reference to the short, broad capsule characteristic of the genus. There are several species similar to Mission Bells. Spotted Mountain Bells (*F. atropurpurea*), also called Checker Lily throughout much of the West, has flowers ½–¾″ (1.3–2 cm) long, and leaves at least 15 times as long as wide. Black Lily or Kamchatka Fritillary (*F. camchatensis*), from northwestern Washington to Alaska, has dark purplish-brown flowers. Chocolate Lily (*F. biflora*), from the Coast Ranges of California, has dark brownish, unmottled flowers, and all leaves on the lower part of the stem.

502 **Adobe Lily**
(*Fritillaria pluriflora*)
Lily Family (Liliaceae)

Description: In an open raceme above the leaves bloom *1–7 nodding, pinkish-lavender, bell-shaped flowers.*

Flowers: 1–1½″ (2.5–3.8 cm) long; 6 petal-like segments; stamens 6, hidden inside; style longer than stamens.

Leaves: to 5″ (12.5 cm) long, narrowly lanceolate, clustered near base.

Height: 1–18″ (2.5–45 cm).

Flowering: February–April.

Habitat: Heavy soil in grassland and in brush.

Range: Interior hills of the North Coast Ranges of California; north to Oregon.

Comments: This is one of the prettiest species of *Fritillaria*. They are rarely common;

only a few scattered plants are generally
seen. Candy Bells (*F. striata*), in the
hills at the southern end of the San
Joaquin Valley, has white or pink
flowers, often with red stripes, and a
style not longer than the stamens.
Fragrant Fritillary (*F. liliacea*), which
grows near the coast in brush or forest
in central California, has white flowers
with pale green stripes.

## 282 Yellow Bell
(*Fritillaria pudica*)
Lily Family (Liliaceae)

Description: This dainty little plant has *1 yellow,
narrowly bell-shaped flower* hanging at the
top of the flower stalk.
Flowers: ½–1″ (1.3–2.5 cm) long;
6 petal-like segments.
Leaves: 2–8″ (5–20 cm) long, 2 or
several borne near middle of stem.
Height: 4–12″ (10–30 cm).

Flowering: March–June.

Habitat: Grasslands, among sagebrush, and in
open coniferous woods.

Range: British Columbia; south on the eastern
side of the Cascade Mountains to
northern California; east to Utah,
western North Dakota, Wyoming,
western Montana, and Alberta.

Comments: A charming, modest Lily that can be
mistaken for no other; the narrow
yellow bell becomes rusty red or
purplish as the flower ages.

## 395 Scarlet Fritillary
(*Fritillaria recurva*)
Lily Family (Liliaceae)

Description: A smooth, gray-green plant with most
leaves near the middle of the stem and,
hanging in an open raceme at top,
*1–9 scarlet, narrowly bell-shaped flowers.*
Flowers: ¾–1¼″ (2–3.1 cm) long,

tinged on the outside with purple,
inside checkered with yellow; 6 petal-
like segments with tips curved
backward.
Leaves: 1–4″ (2.5–10 cm) long,
narrow.
Height: 1–3′ (30–90 cm).

Flowering: March–July.

Habitat: Dry brushy or wooded hillsides.

Range: Southern Oregon to central California
and western Nevada.

Comments: One of the few red Lilies in the West
and the only red Fritillary. *Recurva*
refers to the recurved tips of the petal-
like segments. However, in the inner
parts of the northern Coast Ranges of
California there occurs a brilliant red-
flowered form whose petal-like segment
tips are not recurved.

## 54 Desert Lily
(*Hesperocallis undulata*)
Lily Family (Liliaceae)

Description: *Large, white, funnel-shaped flowers* bloom
in a stout raceme above long, narrow,
*basal leaves with wavy edges.*
Flowers: to 2½″ (6.3 cm) long; 6 petal-
like segments, each with a bluish-green
band on back.
Leaves: 8–20″ (20–50 cm) long.
Height: 1–6′ (30–180 cm).

Flowering: March–May.

Habitat: Sandy desert flats and gentle slopes.

Range: Southeastern California, western
Arizona, and northwestern Mexico.

Comments: Conspicuous and easily seen as one
drives desert roads, it seems at first
glance an Easter Lily out of place. The
bulbs of this species, the only one in its
genus, were once used by Indians for
food.

### 53 Sand Lily; Star Lily; Mountain Lily; Star of Bethlehem
(*Leucocrinum montanum*)
Lily Family (Liliaceae)

Description:  A low plant with several *star-like, white flowers blooming in a basal rosette of narrow, grass-like leaves.*
Flowers: about 1¼″ (3 cm) wide; 6 lanceolate petal-like segments join at base, forming a long slender tube that attaches underground.
Leaves: to 8″ (20 cm) long.
Fruit: capsule, below ground.
Height: to 8″ (20 cm).

Flowering:  April–June.

Habitat:  Among sagebrush and in open coniferous forests.

Range:  Central Oregon to northern California; east to northern New Mexico, Colorado, and western portions of North and South Dakota.

Comments:  With its flowers nestled among the leaves, this distinctive little Lily is unmistakable. This is the only species.

### 359 Tiger Lily; Columbia Lily; Oregon Lily
(*Lilium columbianum*)
Lily Family (Liliaceae)

Description:  A plant with *large, showy, mostly orange, nodding flowers* at top of a leafy stem.
Flowers: 2–3″ (5–7.5 cm) wide; 6 petal-like segments, each long, strongly curved back behind base of flower, yellow-orange to red-orange, spotted with deep red or purple; stamens 6, with anthers less than ¼″ (6 mm) long.
Leaves: 2–4″ (5–10 cm) long, narrowly lanceolate, in several whorls, or not in whorls but evenly scattered along length of stem.
Fruit: plump, 3-sided capsule.
Height: 2–4′ (60–120 cm).

Flowering:  May–August.

Habitat:  Prairies, thickets, and open forests.

Range: Southern British Columbia to northwestern California; east to northern Nevada and northern Idaho.

Comments: This is one of the most popular western wildflowers, often dug for the garden, and in some areas now uncommon. The similar Leopard Lily or Panther Lily (*L. pardalinum*), which grows along forest streams or near springs over most of California, has bright orange-red flowers with anthers ⅜–⅝" (9–15 mm) long.

## 399 Rocky Mountain Lily; Wood Lily; Red Lily
(*Lilium philadelphicum*)
Lily Family (Liliaceae)

Description: A plant with *1–3 mostly red funnel-shaped flowers* at top of an erect, leafy stem.
Flowers: 2–2½" (5–6.3 cm) wide; 6 lanceolate petal-like segments, red or red-orange near the gently outwardly curved tips, yellowish and with purple spots at base.
Leaves: 2–4" (5–10 cm) long, narrowly lanceolate, the lower ones scattered on stem, upper ones in 1 or 2 whorls.
Height: 12–28" (30–70 cm).

Flowering: June-August.

Habitat: Meadows and forests, commonly in aspen groves.

Range: British Columbia to Saskatchewan; south along the eastern edge of the Rocky Mountains to southern New Mexico; east to Michigan and Ohio.

Comments: Once much more common than now. It is too often picked by visitors to the mountains. It also disappears rapidly from intensively grazed meadowland.

### 56  Cascade Lily; Washington Lily
(*Lilium washingtonianum*)
Lily Family (Liliaceae)

Description:  The several *large, fragrant, trumpet-shaped flowers, delicate, waxy white or pale pink, often dotted with minute purple spots,* bloom at top of a stout leafy stem.
Flowers: 3–4″ (7.5–10 cm) wide, with 6 petal-like segments.
Leaves: 2–4″ (5–10 cm) long, lanceolate, scattered on lower portion of stem, in several whorls on upper part.
Height: 2–7′ (60–210 cm).

Flowering:  June–July.

Habitat:  Brush or open forests.

Range:  Northern Oregon to the mountains of northern California and the southern Sierra Nevada.

Comments:  Northern races tend to be more deeply colored. Near Mount Shasta, in northern California, there is a race of this species called the Shasta Lily that has more narrow spaces between the petal-like segments. Chaparral Lily, Lilac Lily, Redwood Lily, or Chamise Lily (*L. rubescens*), which grows in brush or woods in the Coast Ranges of central and northern California, has smaller flowers, 1½–2½″ (3.8–6.3 cm) long, that are at first white with purple spots but age to a rich wine color.

### 50  Alpine Lily
(*Lloydia serotina*)
Lily Family (Liliaceae)

Description:  A small Lily with usually only *1 broadly funnel-shaped, whitish flower* that blooms at top of a stem about as tall as the *very narrow basal leaves.*
Flowers: about ¾″ (2 cm) wide; 6 oblong petal-like segments, mostly white, yellowish at base, purplish on the outside, the veins pale green or purple.
Leaves: 2–8″ (5–20 cm) long, mostly at

base, several, very narrow.
Height: 2–6" (5–15 cm).
Flowering: June–July.
Habitat: Gravelly ridges and in rock crevices high in the mountains.
Range: Alaska; south to northwestern Oregon, northern Nevada, northern Utah, and along the Rocky Mountains to northern New Mexico.
Comments: Of the 10 or 12 species in the genus, this is the only native one; the rest are Eurasian.

109 **False Lily of the Valley**
(*Maianthemum dilatatum*)
Lily Family (Liliaceae)

Description: Grows in low patches and has *slender racemes of tiny white flowers* held stiffly erect just above *heart-shaped leaves*.
Flowers: 4 petal-like segments about ⅛" (3 mm) long; stamens 4.
Leaves: 2–4½" (5–11.3 cm) long, usually only 2 on each stem.
Fruit: red berry ¼" (6 mm) wide.
Height: 6–14" (15–35 cm).
Flowering: May–June.
Habitat: Moist or shaded places in woods.
Range: Alaska to the North Coast Ranges of California.
Comments: The genus name, from the Greek *maios* ("May") and *anthemon* ("flower"), refers to time of flowering. This plant, which spreads by underground roots, makes an attractive ground cover in woodland gardens.

186 **Parry's Nolina**
(*Nolina parryi*)
Lily Family (Liliaceae)

Description: A *very dense cluster of tiny, whitish flowers* grows from a *rosette of many long leaves atop a short trunk-like stem*.
Flowers: cluster about 2' (60 cm) long,

almost as wide, on a stalk 3–5' (1–
1.5 m) tall; individual flowers about ¼"
(6 mm) long.
Leaves: 2–3' (60–90 cm) long, less
than ¾" (2 cm) wide, flexible, concave
on the upper surface.
Height: to 10' (3 m).

Flowering: April–June.

Habitat: Dry, brushy slopes.

Range: Southern California.

Comments: This is one of the largest, showiest of
25 species in this Southwestern genus.
Many are much smaller, resembling
thick tufts or coarse grass on dry
hillsides, and are often called Sacahuista
(pronounced sac-ah-wee'-stah), the
Indian name for this plant. The leaves
were woven into baskets or mats, and
the young stems were prepared as food.
Bear Grass is another common name for
this species.

---

### 377   Fetid Adder's Tongue; Slink Pod; Slink Lily; Brownies
(*Scoliopus bigelovii*)
Lily Family (Liliaceae)

Description: A peculiar little plant with 3–12
leafless, *3-sided flower stalks,* each with
one *dull reddish-brown and green flower* at
the tip, which grow inbetween *2 basal
leaves mottled with maroon patches.*
Flowers: about 1" (2.5 cm) wide; sepals
3, lanceolate, spreading, greenish with
maroon veins; petals 3, erect, horn-
like, maroon; stamens 3.
Leaves: 2½–8" (6.3–20 cm) long,
broadly lanceolate.
Fruit: 3-angled pod.
Height: to 8" (20 cm).

Flowering: February–March.

Habitat: Moist woods.

Range: Coast Ranges of northern California.

Comments: The genus name, from the Greek *skolios*
("crooked") and *pous* ("foot"), and the
common name Slink Pod refer to the
way the flower stalk bends and sprawls

on the ground as the pods mature. The flowers' unpleasant odor, which probably attracts flies as pollinators, gives the name Fetid Adder's Tongue. The smaller Hall's Fetid Adder's Tongue (*S. hallii*), grows in western Oregon.

---

### 110 False Solomon's Seal
(*Smilacina racemosa*)
Lily Family (Liliaceae)

Description: Commonly with several leaning, leafy stems, each tipped with a *branched, dense, cluster of many tiny, white flowers*.
Flowers: 6 ovate petal-like segments about ⅒" (2.5 mm) long; stamens 6, slightly longer.
Leaves: 2½–8" (6.3–20 cm) long, ovate, clasping stem at base.
Fruit: reddish berries, ¼" (6 mm) long.
Height: 1–3' (30–90 cm).
Flowering: March–July.
Habitat: Moist woods from near sea level to moderate mountain elevations.
Range: Throughout.
Comments: "True" Solomon's Seal (*Polygonatum* spp.), Lilies from the eastern United States, are similar in leaf arrangement, but differ by having flowers in the leaf axils. A second western species, Star Solomon's Seal, or Star Flower (*S. stellata*), has up to 20 flowers loosely assembled in a zigzag raceme, each appearing as a dainty, white, 6-pointed star about ¼" (6 mm) wide.

---

### 380 Stenanthium
(*Stenanthium occidentale*)
Lily Family (Liliaceae)

Description: *Pale greenish-bronze or purplish-green flowers resembling dainty bells* hang in open racemes above several narrow, grass-like, basal leaves.

Flowers: ½–¾″ (1.3–2 cm) long; 6 narrow petal-like segments, the tip of each curved back.
Leaves: 4–12″ (10–30 cm) long.
Height: 4–20″ (10–50 cm).

Flowering: June–August.

Habitat: Wet cliffs and banks, moist mountain meadows and forests.

Range: British Columbia to northern California and western Montana.

Comments: Flowers tend to turn to one side of the inflorescence and resemble miniature strings of bells, reminiscent of those once decorating horse-drawn sleighs.

---

### 379  Rosy Twisted-stalk
(*Streptopus roseus*)
Lily Family (Liliaceae)

Description: *Small, bell-shaped, pinkish-brown flowers hang on twisted stalks along leafy stems.*
Flowers: ¼–½″ (6–13 mm) long; 6 petal-like segments, pale greenish-brown and spotted or streaked with deep pink.
Leaves: 1¼–4″ (3.1–10 cm) long, broadly lanceolate.
Height: 6–16″ (15–40 cm).

Flowering: June–July.

Habitat: Moist woods and streambanks.

Range: Alaska to Oregon.

Comments: The arching stems and orderly arrangement of leaves resemble those of Fairy Bell (*Disporum*) and False Solomon's Seal (*Smilacina*). However, *Streptopus,* meaning "twisted foot" in reference to the contorted flower stalk, seems to break a botanical rule. Flowers seem not to grow from axils of leaves as usual. Actually they do, but the base of the stalk is fused to the stem up to the level of the next leaf.

### 113  Sticky Tofieldia
(*Tofieldia glutinosa*)
Lily Family (Liliaceae)

Description:  Leafy only in the lower part, glandular
in the upper part, with many *tiny, white
flowers in a dense, often interrupted, cluster*
at top.
Flowers: 6 spreading petal-like
segments ⅛–¼″ (3–6 mm) long, and
stamens 6, that lie against them.
Leaves: 2–8″ (5–20 cm) long, erect,
narrow, sheathing stem at base.
Height: 4–20″ (10–50 cm), sometimes
to 32″ (80 cm).

Flowering:  June–August.

Habitat:  Wet places, meadows, and alpine
ridges.

Range:  Across Canada; south to central
California, Idaho, and Wyoming in the
West.

Comments:  The species name *glutinosa* refers to the
sticky, glandular hairs on the stem
beneath the flower clusters.

### 49  Western Wake Robin; Trillium
(*Trillium ovatum*)
Lily Family (Liliaceae)

Description:  A low plant with *1 white flower on a
short stalk* that grows from the center of
a *whorl of 3 broad, ovate leaves* at top of
an otherwise leafless stem.
Flowers: 1½–3″ (3.8–7.5 cm) wide;
petals 3, ovate, becoming pink or
reddish with age.
Leaves: 2–8″ (5–20 cm) long, without
stalks at base.
Height: 4–16″ (10–40 cm).

Flowering:  February–June.

Habitat:  Along stream banks and on the floor of
open or deep woods, from low to rather
high elevations.

Range:  British Columbia to central California;
east to northwestern Colorado,
Montana, and Alberta.

Comments:   The name Wake Robin indicates that
the flowers bloom in early spring, about
the time the robin arrives. Only one
other species in the West has a stalk
between the flower and the leaves,
Klamath Trillium (*T. rivale*), of
northwestern California and
southwestern Oregon. Giant Wake
Robin (*T. chloropetolum*), which grows
in dense patches west of the Cascade
Mountains and in the Sierra Nevada,
has no stalks at the base of the mottled
leaves. Its petals vary from white to
maroon; if maroon, usually with a
white base. Roundleaf Trillium
(*T. petiolatum*), from eastern
Washington and Oregon, has long
stalks on the leaves and dark red-brown
petals.

---

### 656  Douglas' Triteleia
(*Triteleia douglasii*)
Lily Family (Liliaceae)

Description:   *Pale or deep blue, narrowly bell-shaped
flowers bloom in an umbel* at the top of a
leafless stem that has one or two grass-
like basal leaves.
Flowers: about ¾" (2 cm) wide; 6 petal-
like segments joined at base to form a
broad tube about ½" (1.3 cm) long, the
inner 3 segments strongly ruffled and
nearly closing the opening; stamens 6,
attached to tube at different levels,
with stalks about as thick as broad.
Leaves: to 20" (50 cm) long.
Height: 8–28" (20–70 cm).

Flowering:   April–July.

Habitat:   In grassy areas, among sagebrush, or in
pine forests.

Range:   Southern British Columbia south on the
east side of the Cascade Mountains to
southeastern Oregon; eastward to
western Montana, western Wyoming,
and northern Utah.

Comments:   The ruffled, petal-like segments make
this flower unusual. Howell's Triteleia,

(*T. howellii*), from southern British Columbia to northern Oregon near the Cascade Mountains, has much shorter flower stalks and only slightly ruffled petal-like segments that vary from white to blue.

---

### 150 White Hyacinth
(*Triteleia hyacinthina*)
Lily Family (Liliaceae)

Description: *White, or rarely pale blue, bowl-shaped flowers bloom in an umbel* at the top of a stem that has long, narrow, grass-like leaves at base.
Flowers: about ½" (1.3 cm) wide; 6 petal-like segments, joined at base, each have a greenish midvein.
Leaves: 4–16" (10–40 cm) long.
Height: 10–28" (25–70 cm).

Flowering: May–August.

Habitat: Grassy flats, especially in low spots that are moist in the spring, or in open areas in brush and forests.

Range: Southern British Columbia to the northern two-thirds of California; eastward to northern Nevada, eastern Oregon and Idaho.

Comments: Its delicate, white, bowl-shaped flowers are unusual among the Triteleias and serve to distinguish this species.

---

### 320 Pretty Face
(*Triteleia ixioides*)
Lily Family (Liliaceae)

Description: *Yellow, funnel-shaped flowers bloom in an umbel* at the top of a leafless stalk that has a few, long, narrow, grass-like leaves at base.
Flowers: about ¾" (2 cm) wide; 6 lanceolate, petal-like segments are joined at the broad base; stamens 6, attached all at the same level to cup-like base of flower; on back of each

stamen is a scale with 2 teeth at tip.
Leaves: 6–16" (15–40 cm) long.
Height: 4–18" (10–45 cm).
Flowering: March to August.
Habitat: Grassy open areas or in open woods from low to high elevations.
Range: Southern Oregon to southern California.
Comments: Some variants have cream, straw-colored or dull yellow flowers, and in some races flowers become purplish with age.

---

**115 California Corn Lily; Skunk Cabbage; False Hellebore**
(*Veratrum californicum*)
Lily Family (Liliaceae)

Description: A *long, branched, dense cluster of relatively small, whitish or greenish flowers* top the stout, leafy stem of this tall plant.
Flowers: 6 petal-like segments ½–¾" (1.3–2 cm) long, each with a V-shaped green gland at base.
Leaves: 8–12" (20–30 cm) long, numerous, broad, ovate, plaited, without stalks, angled upward.
Height: 4–8' (1.2–2.4 m).
Flowering: June–August.
Habitat: Swamps and creek bottoms, wet meadows and moist forests.
Range: Western Washington to southern California; east to New Mexico, Colorado, Wyoming, and Montana.
Comments: California Corn Lily is extremely poisonous. Sheep that eat the plant in the early weeks of gestation produce lambs with deformed heads; the flowers are even poisonous to insects and may cause serious losses among honeybees.

### 116 Bear Grass; Indian Basket Grass
(*Xerophyllum tenax*)
Lily Family (Liliaceae)

Description: At the top of a stout stalk that grows
from a *massive bunch of basal leaves*
bloom many tiny flowers in a *dense,
broad, white raceme.*
Flowers: flat petal-like segments about
⅜" (9 mm) long.
Leaves: basal, approximately 1–2½'
(30–75 cm) long, very narrow.
Height: to 5' (1.5 m).
Flowering: May–August.
Habitat: Open woods and clearings.
Range: British Columbia to central California;
east to Idaho and Montana.
Comments: Indians used the leaves to weave
garments and baskets and ate the
roasted rootstock. Other common
names are Squaw Grass, Elk Grass,
Turkey Beard, Bear Lily, and Pine Lily.

### 188 Blue Yucca; Banana Yucca; Datil
(*Yucca baccata*)
Lily Family (Liliaceae)

Description: *Rigid, spine-tipped leaves* in 1 or several
rosettes, and a long cluster of *large
whitish flowers* on a stalk about as tall as
the leaves.
Flowers: 6 petal-like segments, each 2–
4" (5–10 cm) long, white or cream and
often also purplish-tinged, waxy.
Leaves: to about 3' (90 cm) long, edges
with a few whitish fibers.
Fruit: pod 2½–10" (6.3–25 cm) long,
fleshy, cylindrical, round at ends.
Height: to 5' (1.5 m), the trunks up to
20" (50 cm).
Flowering: April–July.
Habitat: Rocky soil in deserts, grasslands, and
open woods.
Range: Southeastern California across southern
Nevada and Utah to southwestern
Colorado; south through much of
Arizona, all of New Mexico, and

western Texas to northern Mexico.

Comments: The baked fruit of Blue Yucca tastes
somewhat like sweet potato. Yucca
flowers are still eaten by Mexican
Indians to such an extent that some
species now rarely show mature pods.
Identification of the many Yucca species
is often difficult. Those with broad
leaves are sometimes called Spanish
Daggers, a name generally applied to
the tree-like species of western Texas.
Plain's Yucca (*Y. angustifolia*), common
from the eastern edge of the Rocky
Mountains eastward almost throughout
the plains and prairies of the central
United States, is a small species with
narrow, gray-green leaves.

### 187   Mojave Yucca
(*Yucca schidigera*)
Lily Family (Liliaceae)

Description: Rosettes of *stiff, narrow, spine-tipped
leaves* grow on branched or unbranched
trunks, topped by long, broad clusters
of *many cream, bell-like flowers.*
Flowers: 1¼–2½" (3.1–6.3 cm) long,
nearly spherical, with 6 petal-like
segments.
Leaves: 1–5' (30–150 cm) long, with
pale fibers peeling and curling on the
edges.
Height: trunk 4–15' (1.2–4.5 m);
flower stalk and cluster to 4' (1.2 m).
Flowering: April–May.
Habitat: Brushy slopes, flats, and open deserts.
Range: Southern California to Baja California;
east to southern Nevada and
northwestern Arizona.
Comments: This is a common Yucca on the Mojave
Desert, often growing with Joshua Tree
(*Y. brevifolia*), a tree-like species that
often forms "forests." Its stiff leaves are
8–14" (20–35 cm) long.

### 184 Our Lord's Candle
(*Yucca whipplei*)
Lily Family (Liliaceae)

Description: On a stout stalk growing from a *dense basal rosette of gray-green, rigid, spine-tipped leaves* bloom, in a long, massive cluster, *several thousand white or cream flowers* often tinged with purple.
Flowers: 6 petal-like segments, each 1–1½" (2.5–3.8 cm) long form a bell.
Leaves: 3' (90 cm) long.
Height: 4–11' (1.2–3.3 m).

Flowering: April–May.
Habitat: Stony slopes in chaparral.
Range: Southern California and northern Baja California.

Comments: Showiest of the Yuccas. Hundreds in bloom provide a spectacular sight on brushy slopes. After flowering, the plants die. All Yuccas have a reciprocal relationship with the Yucca moth. After gathering pollen from a flower and rolling the pollen into a little ball, the moth lays its eggs in the ovary of another flower and then packs the pollen into holes on the stigma, thus both pollinating the flower and ensuring seed-set. The moth's larvae feed on some of the developing seeds, then burrow out of the fruit when mature.

### 129 Elegant Camas; Alkali Grass
(*Zigadenus elegans*)
Lily Family (Liliaceae)

Description: A plant with long, basal, grass-like leaves and *cream or greenish-white, bowl-shaped flowers* in a raceme or branched flower cluster.
Flowers: about ¾" (2 cm) wide; 6 broad, petal-like segments, each with a greenish, heart-shaped gland at base; flower parts attached around sides of ovary rather than at base.
Leaves: 6–12" (15–30 cm) long.

Height: 6–28″ (15–70 cm).

Flowering: June–August.

Habitat: Mountain meadows, rocky slopes, and forests.

Range: Western Canada; south to western Washington, eastern Oregon, Arizona, New Mexico, and Texas.

Comments: Camases are among the most infamous western plants, poisoning many livestock, especially sheep. Indians and early settlers were also poisoned whenever they mistook the bulbs for those of edible species, such as the Camas Lily (*Camassia*). The highly poisonous Death Camas (*Z. venenosus*) grows throughout most of the western United States. It has petal-like segments about ¼″ (6 mm) long, the inner 3 slightly longer and with a short stalk at the base, and stamens about as long as the segments.

## FALSE MERMAID FAMILY
### (Limnanthaceae)

Delicate, leafy herbs of moist places
with usually white or yellow flowers on
long slender stalks growing from leaf
axils.
Flowers: radially symmetrical; sepals
3 or 5, separate; petals 3 or 5, separate;
stamens 6 or 10, forming 2 circles. All
these parts attached at base of ovary.
Leaves: alternate, pinnately divided.
Fruit: 3 or 5 hard, one-seeded nutlets.
There are 2 genera and about 12 species
restricted to North America, primarily
California.

## 19, 196 Douglas' Meadow Foam
### (*Limnanthes douglasii*)
False Mermaid Family (Limnanthaceae)

Description: The broadly bell-shaped flowers of this
delicate, branched plant usually have a
*yellow center with a white rim,* or are all
yellow, and bloom on slender stalks in
upper leaf axils.
Flowers: about ¾" (2 cm) wide; petals
5, broad, notched at tip; stamens 10,
each about ¼" (6 mm) long.
Leaves: 2–5" (5–12.5 cm) long,
divided into jagged segments.
Fruit: divides into 5 smooth or slightly
warty, seed-like sections.
Height: 4–16" (10–40 cm).
Flowering: March–May.
Habitat: Low, moist places in grassland and
open woodland.
Range: Southern Oregon to southern California.
Comments: A form with all-yellow petals grows on
Point Reyes in northern California; in
the Coast Ranges, the flower may have
white petals often with dark purple
veins, whereas in and around the
Central Valley, petals may be white,
with rose veins, becoming all pink with
age.

## FLAX FAMILY (Linaceae)

Herbs, rarely shrubs or trees, with flowers borne in a forked cluster.
Flowers: radially symmetrical; sepals 5, separate; petals 5, separate, each with a narrow base and readily dropping off the flower; stamens 10, joined by bases of their stalks. All these parts attached at base of ovary.
Leaves: alternate or opposite, simple.
Fruit: 5-chambered capsule, rarely a stone-fruit.
There are about 12 genera and almost 300 species distributed nearly throughout the world. Linen and linseed oil are obtained from this family.

---

589 **Wild Blue Flax; Western Blue Flax**
(*Linum perenne*)
Flax Family (Linaceae)

Description: An open plant with mostly *unbranched leafy stems* and *delicate blue flowers* blooming on slender stalks near the top.
Flowers: ¾–1½" (2–3.8 cm) wide; petals 5, broad; stamens 5; styles 5, longer than stamens.
Leaves: ½–1¼" (1.3–3.1 cm) long, narrow, with only 1 vein.
Height: 6–32" (15–80 cm).

Flowering: March–September.

Habitat: Well-drained soil in prairies, meadows, open mountain slopes and ledges.

Range: Alaska to southern California; east to western Texas, central Kansas, and Saskatchewan; also northern Mexico.

Comments: Several Indian tribes used Wild Blue Flax for making cordage. Common Flax (*L. usitatissimum*), from which linen is made and linseed oil is obtained, often grows in the wild, "escaping" from cultivation. It has blue petals about ½" (1.3 cm) long and leaves with 3 veins. Narrow-leaved Flax (*L. angustifolium*), found from western Oregon to coastal central California, also has 3 leaf veins but its petals are only about ⅜" (9 mm) long.

### 229 Chihuahua Flax
(*Linum vernale*)
Flax Family (Linaceae)

Description: Very slender, erect plants with *yellow-orange, bowl-shaped flowers, each with a maroon center.*
Flowers: about ¾" (2 cm) wide; petals 5, fan-shaped; style with 5 branches at tip; sepals lanceolate, with gland-tipped teeth on edges.
Leaves: about ½" (1.3 cm) long, very narrow.
Fruit: 5-chambered capsule, walls between chambers open at top, fringed at opening.
Height: 4–20" (10–50 cm).
Flowering: March–October.
Habitat: Rocky, limestone soil in deserts.
Range: Southern New Mexico, western Texas, and northern Mexico.
Comments: A common species in parts of the Chihuahua Desert. Only the very bases of the petals are joined, and when the corolla falls from the flower, breezes may blow it across the ground like a fragile saucer. It is representative of a number of western yellow-flowered species, most slender and wiry, many without maroon centers in flowers.

## STICK-LEAF FAMILY (Loasaceae)

Mostly herbs with barbed, bristly, or stinging hairs, pale stems, and showy yellow flowers usually in a branched cluster.

Flowers: radially symmetrical; sepals 5, separate; petals 5, but the outer stamens often broad, flat, and sterile, resembling additional petals; stamens 5 or many, when many often bunched in 5 clusters. All these parts attached at base of ovary.

Leaves: alternate or opposite, simple or deeply pinnately lobed.

Fruit: 1-chambered capsule.

There are about 15 genera and 250 species, with most occurring in the warm and dry parts of the Americas.

### 203 Desert Rock Nettle
(*Eucnide urens*)
Stick-leaf Family (Loasaceae)

Description: A rounded, bushy plant, generally much broader than tall, with *stinging bristly hairs* and *large cream or pale yellow flowers* in branched clusters that nearly obscure foliage.
Flowers: 1–2" (2.5–5 cm) wide; petals 5, broad, translucent; 5 clusters of many stamens joined to base of petals.
Leaves: ¾–2½" (2–6.3 cm) long, ovate, coarsely toothed, covered with harsh hairs.
Height: 1–2' (30–60 cm).
Flowering: April–June.
Habitat: Dry rocky places in deserts, often on cliffs.
Range: Southeastern California to southwestern Utah and western Arizona; south into Baja California.
Comments: The lovely flowers invite picking, but the hairs sting viciously.

### 224 White-bracted Stick-leaf
(*Mentzelia involucrata*)
Stick-leaf Family (Loasaceae)

Description: A low, leafy plant with satiny, white
stems and narrow, *translucent, pale
yellow flowers* at ends of branches.
Flowers: 1–1¼" (2.5–3.1 cm) long;
petals 5, erect; stamens many; 3 lobes
on style; white bracts, with green,
toothed margins beneath flowers.
Leaves: 1–3" (2.5–7.5 cm) long,
lanceolate, sharply and irregularly
toothed, rough to the touch.
Height: 6–12" (15–30 cm).

Flowering: March–May.

Habitat: Dry desert hillsides, flats, and washes.

Range: Southeastern California and western
Arizona to northwestern Mexico.

Comments: This spring wildflower has showy
whitish bracts that are distinctive.

### 212 Blazing Star
(*Mentzelia laevicaulis*)
Stick-leaf Family (Loasaceae)

Description: *Many large, star-like, lemon-yellow flowers*
bloom on branches at the top of a stout,
*satiny, white stem.*
Flowers: 2–5" (2.5–12.5 cm) wide;
petals 5, lanceolate; stamens numerous,
long, with 1 between each pair of petals
having a broad, petal-like stalk.
Leaves: 4–12" (10–30 cm) long,
narrowly lanceolate, very rough, the
edges with large, irregular teeth.
Height: 1–3' (30–90 cm).

Flowering: June–September.

Habitat: Gravelly or sandy slopes and plains,
mostly in arid regions.

Range: Southeastern British Columbia to
southern California; east to Utah,
Wyoming; west to Montana.

Comments: There are many species of *Mentzelia* in
the West, called Stick-leaf because of
the leaves' barbed hairs that readily
cling to fabric.

## LOOSESTRIFE FAMILY
(Lythraceae)

Herbs, shrubs, or trees with flowers borne in racemes or branched clusters.
Flowers: radially or bilaterally symmetrical; sepals 4–6, joined at the base to form a tube to which petals and stamens attach; as many separate petals as there are sepals, often crumpled like crepe paper, or petals may be absent; usually twice as many stamens as sepals, in 2 series of different lengths; all joined to a tube that is attached at base of ovary.
Leaves: simple, usually opposite or whorled.
Fruit: a capsule with 2–6 chambers.
There are about 25 genera and 550 species nearly throughout the world. A few species yield dyes; some are grown as ornamentals.

### 535 Purple Loosestrife
(*Lythrum salicaria*)
Loosestrife Family (Lythraceae)

Description: Leafy, angular stems have *crowded spikes of brilliant pinkish-lavender flowers* at top. Plant grows in dense patches.
Flowers: petals 5, nearly ½" (1.3 cm) long, attached to a purplish calyx-like tube with several pointed teeth.
Leaves: 1¼–4" (3.1–10 cm) long, narrow, opposite, notched at base.
Height: 2–7' (60–210 cm).
Flowering: August–September.
Habitat: Marshes.
Range: Western Washington; eastern United States.
Comments: In late summer this species, mixed with Cattails at the water's edge, forms a spectacular color display around the shores of Lake Washington and other marshy areas in the region.

## MALLOW FAMILY (Malvaceae)

Herbs, shrubs, or rarely small trees, often velvety with starlike or branched hairs, the flowers borne singly or in branched clusters.

Flowers: usually bisexual, radially symmetrical; sepals 3–5, partly united; petals 5, separate; stamens many, joined by their stalks into a tube. All these parts attached at base of ovary.

Leaves: alternate, simple, often palmately veined and lobed.

Fruit: 5 to many chambers in a ring that separate from one another, or that form a capsule or berry.

There are about 85 genera and 1,500 species, many in tropical America. Rose-of-Sharon and other Hibiscus, and Hollyhocks are grown as ornamentals. Okra is the edible fruit of one species of Hibiscus, and the hairs of seed of *Gossypium* provide the fiber cotton.

---

## 214 Desert Rosemallow
(*Hibiscus coulteri*)
Mallow Family (Malvaceae)

Description: A shrubby plant with rough hairs, undivided lower leaves, *divided upper leaves,* and *large, cup-shaped, whitish to yellow flowers,* often tinged with red.
Flowers: 1–2″ (2.5–5 cm) wide; petals 5, broad; many stamens joined at bases, forming a tube around style.
Leaves: lower ovate, about 1″ (2.5 cm) wide; upper divided into 3 narrow, coarsely toothed lobes.
Height: to 4′ (1.2 m).

Flowering: April–August, or throughout the year in warm areas.

Habitat: Brushy desert hills and canyons.

Range: Southern Arizona to western Texas and northern Mexico.

Comments: A humble relative of the brilliant tropical Hibiscus plants, members of a genus that contains almost 300 species.

### 463 **Pale Face; Rock Hibiscus**
(*Hibiscus denudatus*)
Mallow Family (Malvaceae)

Description:  A scraggly, *pale plant* covered with whitish hairs. *Bowl-shaped, white to pinkish-lavender flowers,* more deeply colored in the center, bloom in upper leaf axils and along the ends of *leafless, erect branches.*
Flowers: 1–1½" (2–3.8 cm) wide; petals 5; stamens many, joined at bases, forming a tube around style.
Leaves: ½–1" (1.3–2.5 cm) long, very few, ovate.
Height: 1–3' (30–90 cm).

Flowering:  February–October.
Habitat:  Rocky slopes in deserts.
Range:  Southern California to western Texas and northern Mexico.
Comments:  These plants seem to have too few leaves. The delicate flowers are small for the genus and lack the flamboyance of ornamental species.

### 230 **Flower-of-an-Hour**
(*Hibiscus trionum*)
Mallow Family (Malvaceae)

Description:  A hairy, leafy plant with some stems lying on the ground, others more upright, with *1 pale yellow flower, blackish-maroon in the center,* blooming on stalk growing from each leaf axil.
Flowers: about 1½" (3.8 cm) wide; petals 5; stamens many, joined at base, forming a tube around style.
Leaves: ¾–1¼" (2–3.1 cm) wide, palmately divided into 3 or 5 divisions.
Fruit: 5 papery, bristly sepals, with many dark veins, grow and form a bladder around a capsule that divides into 5 sections.
Height: 1–2' (30–60 cm).

Flowering:  August–September.
Habitat:  Open places, commonly where the ground has been disturbed.

Range: Southern half of the West.
Comments: Flowers close in the shade, hence its common name. Sometimes grown as an ornamental, this central African plant is now rapidly spreading and becoming a garden nuisance.

510 **Mountain Globemallow; Streambank Globemallow**
(*Iliamna rivularis*)
Mallow Family (Malvaceae)

Description: A stout plant with *large, maple-like leaves* and *showy pink or pinkish-lavender flowers* in long, loose racemes at top of stem, and in shorter racemes in upper leaf axils.
Flowers: 1–2″ (2.5–5 cm) wide; petals 5; many stamens joined at base, forming a tube around branched style, each branch ending in a tiny knob.
Leaves: 2–8″ (5–20 cm) wide, nearly round, 5 or 7 triangular lobes.
Fruit: many segments in a ring, each containing 3 or 4 seeds.
Height: 3–7′ (90–210 cm).
Flowering: June–August.
Habitat: Springs and along mountain streams.
Range: British Columbia through eastern Washington to eastern Oregon; east to Montana; south to Utah and Colorado.
Comments: The several western Globemallow species are commonly found in wet places, recognizable by their maple-like leaves and pink or rose petals, and distinguished from other members of the Mallow Family by having more than one seed in each ovary segment.

465 **Desert Five Spot**
(*Malvastrum rotundifolium*)
Mallow Family (Malvaceae)

Description: *Flowers form purplish-pink or lilac globes,* each open at top and have a deep

reddish center, on short branches near
the top of this erect, sparsely-leaved
plant.
Flowers: ¾–1¼″ (2–3.1 cm) wide;
petals 5; stamens many, joined at base,
forming a tube around style.
Leaves: ¾–2″ (2–5 cm) wide, few,
round, toothed.
Height: 4–24″ (10–60 cm).

Flowering: March–May.
   Habitat: Desert washes and flats.
     Range: Southeastern California, southern
            Nevada, and western Arizona.
Comments: The pinkish, spherical corollas are
            distinctive and, when light passes
            through them, they resemble glowing
            lanterns.

---

125  **White Checkermallow; Wild
      Hollyhock**
      (*Sidalcea candida*)
      Mallow Family (Malvaceae)

Description: Narrow, leaning, handsome *sprays of
            many white or cream flowers* bloom at the
            top of this leafy plant.
            Flowers: about 1″ (2.5 cm) wide; petals
            5; stamens many, joined at base,
            forming a tube around style, whose
            slender branches have no knobs at tip.
            Leaves: lowest to 4″ (10 cm) wide,
            nearly round, the 7 lobes with coarse
            teeth; upper are smaller, palmately
            divided into usually 7 narrow lobes.
            Height: 1½–3′ (45–90 cm).

Flowering: June–September.
   Habitat: Along streams and in moist mountain
            meadows.
     Range: Nevada to Wyoming; south to southern
            New Mexico.
Comments: One of the few Checkermallows with
            white corollas. "Mallow," from a Greek
            word meaning "soft," may refer to the
            soft, fuzzy leaves characteristic of so
            many plants in the family, or to the
            sticky, soothing juice obtained from the
            roots of some species. Marshmallow

candies were once prepared from the root juice of Marsh Mallow (*Althaea officinalis*).

## 509 Checkermallow
(*Sidalcea neomexicana*)
Mallow Family (Malvaceae)

Description: Many *deep pink flowers crowded in narrow, leaning sprays* top the leafy stems.
Flowers: 1–1½" (2.5–3.8 cm) wide; petals 5; stamens many, joined at base, forming a tube around style, whose slender branches have no knobs at tip.
Leaves: lowest to 4" (10 cm) wide, nearly round, 5–7 shallow lobes with coarse teeth; upper are smaller, palmately divided into usually 7 lobes.
Height: 1–3' (30–90 cm).

Flowering: June–September.

Habitat: Moist, often heavy soil, in mountain valleys and along streams and ponds at lower elevations.

Range: Eastern Oregon to southern California; east to New Mexico, Colorado, and Wyoming; also northern Mexico.

Comments: The many Checkermallows with pink flowers, from coastal marshes to moderate elevations in the mountains, are difficult to distinguish and differentiated only by technical characteristics.

## 398 Desert Globemallow; Desert Hollyhock
(*Sphaeralcea ambigua*)
Mallow Family (Malvaceae)

Description: A *grayish plant* often with many stems, and *bright orange-red flowers* in clusters with erect branches.
Flowers: ½–1½" (1.3–3.8 cm) wide; petals 5; stamens many, joined into a tube.
Leaves: ¾–2½" (2–6.3 cm) long,

about as wide, ovate, shallowly 3-lobed, the edges scalloped.
Height: 20–40" (50–100 cm).

Flowering: March–June.
Habitat: Desert slopes and flats, and among piñon and juniper.
Range: Southern California to southwestern Utah, central Arizona, and northwestern Mexico.
Comments: One of the largest-flowered, most drought-tolerant species of Globemallow. In wet years it forms spectacular displays in the low, hot southwestern deserts. In some forms petals are pale purplish-pink.

### 366 Scarlet Globemallow; Red False Mallow
(*Sphaeralcea coccinea*)
Mallow Family (Malvaceae)

Description: *Red-orange or brick-red flowers* bloom in narrow clusters and in upper axils on these leafy, branched, velvety-haired plants.
Flowers: 1–1¼" (2.5–3.1 cm) wide; petals 5; stamens many, joined at base, forming a tube around style.
Leaves: ¾–2" (2–5 cm) wide, nearly round, divided into 3 broad or narrow lobes which may be variously divided or toothed.
Height: to 20" (50 cm), stems often leaning at base.
Flowering: April–August.
Habitat: Open ground in arid grassland and among piñon and juniper.
Range: Central Canada; south to western Montana, most of Utah, northeastern Arizona, and most of New Mexico; east to Texas and Iowa.
Comments: Globemallows are common plants on western ranges, but difficult to identify. One of the easiest species to recognize is Scaly Globemallow (*S. leptophylla*), which is covered with gray, scale-like hairs and has very narrow upper leaves,

not divided or toothed. It grows from southern Utah, southwestern Colorado, and northeastern Arizona to western Texas and northern Mexico.

### 365 Coulter's Globemallow
(*Sphaeralcea coulteri*)
Mallow Family (Malvaceae)

Description: Erect, slender stems with thin, grayish-velvety leaves have *orange or red-orange flowers in long, wand-like clusters.*
Flowers: ¾–1″ (2–2.5 cm) wide; petals 5; stamens many, joined into a tube.
Leaves: ½–1¼″ (1.3–3.1 cm) long, ovate or nearly round, not lobed, or with 3 or 5 deep or shallow lobes, edges scalloped.
Height: 8–60″ (20–150 cm).

Flowering: January–May.

Habitat: Sandy desert flats.

Range: Southeastern California, southern Arizona, and northwestern Mexico.

Comments: In years of ample winter rain this species will carpet the desert floor with red-orange.

## UNICORN PLANT FAMILY
(Martyniaceae)

Herbs covered with sticky, glandular hairs, and with large flowers in showy terminal racemes.

Flowers: bilaterally symmetrical; sepals 5, united; petals 5, united, forming a corolla with an upper and lower lip; stamens 4, fertile, and a fifth modified, sterile one. All these parts attached at base of ovary.

Leaves: alternate or opposite, often palmately veined and lobed.

Fruit: woody capsule with curved horn or hook on end.

There are about 5 genera and 20 species occurring in warm regions of the Western Hemisphere.

---

**13, 288** Devil's Claw; Unicorn Plant
(*Proboscidea altheaefolia*)
Unicorn Plant Family (Martyniaceae)

Description: A coarse plant with stems lying on the ground and a few *yellowish-green bilaterally symmetrical flowers* blooming in racemes.
Flowers: corolla 1–1½" (2.5–3.8 cm) long, commonly flecked with maroon or rust brown, the 5 lobes spreading from a broad opening.
Leaves: blades ¾–3" (2–7.5 cm) long, fleshy, roundish, edges plain, scalloped, or deeply lobed.
Fruit: pod about 2½" (6.3 cm) long, with *curved horn* nearly 5" (12.5 cm) long.
Height: creeper, with flower stalks to about 1' (30 cm) high, and stems spreading to nearly 3' (90 cm) wide.
Flowering: June–September.
Habitat: Sandy soil in deserts and arid grassland.
Range: Southern California to western Texas.
Comments: As the plump fruit matures, it divides into halves, the single "horn" forming two curved "devil's claws."

## BUCKBEAN FAMILY
(Menyanthaceae)

Perennial herbs of freshwater ponds or marshes, with flowers in showy clusters.
Flowers: radially symmetrical; sepals 5, united; petals 5, united; stamens 5. All these parts attached to base of ovary.
Leaves: undivided, or with 3 leaflets.
Fruit: 1-celled capsule, with many seeds.
There are 5 genera and 33 species occurring in temperate regions and tropical Asia. The family is often united with the Gentianaceae.

155 Buck Bean
(*Menyanthes trifoliata*)
Buckbean Family (Menyanthaceae)

Description: Large leaves with long stalks and racemes or narrow clusters of *white or purple-tinged, star-like flowers* at top of stout stalks, about as high as the leaves.
Flowers: corolla about ½" (1.3 cm) wide, with a tube ¼–⅜" (6–9 mm) long (about twice the length of calyx) and 5 or 6 pointed lobes covered with short scales.
Leaves: 4–12" (10–30 cm) long; leaflets 1½–5" (3.8–12.5 cm) long, broadly lanceolate.
Height: aquatic, with leaves and flower stalks 4–12" (10–30 cm) above water.
Flowering: May–August.
Habitat: Bogs and shallow lakes.
Range: From the southern Sierra Nevada and central Colorado north to Canada; eastern United States.
Comments: A species with similar flowers, Deer Cabbage (*Nephrophyllidium crista-galli*), has undivided kidney-shaped leaves, and grows in wet places on the Olympic Peninsula and around the northern Pacific.

## FOUR O'CLOCK FAMILY
(Nyctaginaceae)

Mostly herbs, also shrubs, vines, or small trees in the tropics, with flowers borne in leaf axils, in umbels, heads, racemes, or openly branched clusters.

Flowers: usually bisexual, radially or slightly bilaterally symmetrical; sepals 4 or 5 petal-like, usually united into a trumpet-shaped structure; petals absent; stamens 1–30; ovary tightly enclosed by the lower part of the calyx, which becomes part of the fruit, and, therefore, all parts appear to be attached to top of ovary.

Leaves: simple, opposite; those of a pair often unequal in size.

Fruit: 1-seeded, smooth, glandular, or winged, fleshy or dry.

The 30 genera and 300 species of this family are best represented in the New World. The warm deserts of North America are one area of high diversity. Beneath the flowers are often bracts, an involucre, which may be mistakenly interpreted as a calyx. In Bougainvillea the bracts are brightly colored. Other ornamentals are Four O'Clocks and Sand Verbenas.

---

151 **Snowball; Sweet Sand Verbena**
(*Abronia elliptica*)
Four O'Clock Family (Nyctaginaceae)

Description: *Many fragrant, white, trumpet-shaped flowers bloom in heads* at ends of long stalks in upper leaf axils.
Flowers: head 1–3" (2.5–7.5 cm) wide; 5 lobes on end of "trumpet."
Leaves: blades ½–2½" (1.3–6.3 cm) long, opposite, ovate to diamond-shaped, on long stalks.
Fruit: 1-seeded, usually with 5 papery wings, each with a flat, diamond-shaped pad at top.

Height: 4–20" (10–50 cm), the stems often leaning on the ground.

Flowering: April–September.

Habitat: Sandy, arid grassland and among piñon and juniper.

Range: Central Nevada to northern Arizona, northwestern New Mexico, western Colorado, and northern Wyoming.

Comments: Throughout most of its range this is the only Sand Verbena with white flowers. *A. fragrans,* also called Snowball or Sweet Sand Verbena, has sweet-smelling flowers, but lacks pads atop the wings of the fruit and is often taller, with stems up to 3' (90 cm). It grows in eastern Montana and western North and South Dakota, south to eastern Utah, northeastern Arizona, southern New Mexico, and western and central Texas. White Sand Verbena (*A. mellifera*), from eastern Washington and Oregon to southern Idaho, has nearly scentless flowers.

---

### 330 Yellow Sand Verbena
(*Abronia latifolia*)
Four O'Clock Family (Nyctaginaceae)

Description: *Many yellow, trumpet-shaped flowers in hemispherical heads* bloom atop long stalks in leaf axils of trailing stems.
Flowers: head 1–2" (2.5–5 cm) wide; 5 lobes on end of "trumpet."
Leaves: ½–2½" (1.3–6.3 cm) long, opposite, fleshy, roundish.
Fruit: with 3–5 wings.
Height: creeper, with flower stalks to 6" (15 cm) high, but stems to 3' (90 cm) long.

Flowering: May–August.

Habitat: Dunes along the Pacific Coast.

Range: Southern California to British Columbia.

Comments: This is the only yellow Sand Verbena. Two similar species, each differing primarily by flower color, grow along the Pacific Coast. Beach Pancake (*A.*

*maritima*), from southern California to
Mexico, has wine-red flowers, and
Beach Sand Verbena (*A. umbellata*),
from British Columbia to Baja
California, has flowers varying from
deep pink to white.

## 542  Desert Sand Verbena
(*Abronia villosa*)
Four O'Clock Family (Nyctaginaceae)

Description:  A soft-haired, sticky plant with *bright
pink, trumpet-shaped flowers in heads* that
bloom on stalks growing from leaf
axils.
Flowers: head 2–3″ (5–7.5 cm) wide,
with 5 lobes on end of "trumpet."
Leaves: ½–1½″ (1.3–3.8 cm) long,
opposite, ovate, with slightly wavy,
scalloped edges.
Fruit: with 3–5 wings.
Height: creeper, with flower stalks to
about 10″ (25 cm) high, but stems
trailing on the sand, up to 3′ (90 cm)
long.
Flowering:  March–October.
Habitat:  Sandy desert soil.
Range:  Southeastern California, southern
Nevada, and western Arizona; south
into northwestern Mexico.
Comments:  Following ample winter rains, Desert
Sand Verbena may carpet miles of
desert with pink.

## 83  Angel Trumpets
(*Acleisanthes longiflora*)
Four O'Clock Family (Nyctaginaceae)

Description:  The highly branched stems spread on
the ground or sprawl over shrubs; *erect,
white flowers stand like miniature trumpets*
in leaf axils.
Flowers: 3½–6½″ (8.8–16.3 cm) long,
½–¾″ (1.3–2 cm) wide.

Leaves: about 1″ (2.5 cm) long,
opposite, triangular.
Fruit: about ¼″ (6 mm) long, with 5
roundish angles.
Height: creeper, with branches to 8″
(20 cm) high, and reclining stems to 3′
(90 cm) long.

Flowering: May–September.
Habitat: Rocky slopes in deserts or on plains.
Range: Southeastern California to central New
Mexico and western Texas; south into
Mexico.

Comments: During the day, flowers that bloomed
the night before are bent like melted
candles, and those yet to bloom are
held rigidly erect as brownish-green
tubes that blend with the foliage. In
the cool of evening new flowers open,
flaring their white funnel tops, which
attract night-flying moths that drink
the nectar and, more importantly,
pollinate the flowers.

### 458 Trailing Four O'Clock; Trailing Windmills
(*Allionia incarnata*)
Four O'Clock Family (Nyctaginaceae)

Description: Brilliant *deep pink flowers* bloom near the
ground on this trailing plant, *3 crowded
together and resembling a single radially
symmetrical flower.*
Flowers: cluster ¼–1″ (6–25 mm)
wide; on a short stalk, in a leaf axil;
beneath the cluster is a calyx-like
involucre of 3 bracts, each partly
enclosing a fruit. *Individual flowers
bilaterally symmetrical.*
Leaves: ½–1½″ (1.3–3.8 cm) long,
opposite, ovate.
Fruit: less than ¼″ (6 mm) wide,
convex on one side, with 2 rows of 3 or
5 curved teeth on the other.
Height: creeper, with flower stalks to 4″
(10 cm) tall, stems to 3′ (90 cm) long.

Flowering: April–September.

Habitat:  Dry gravelly or sandy soils in sun.
Range:  Southeastern California to southern
Utah and Colorado; south to Texas,
Mexico, and beyond.
Comments:  The flowers remain open most of the
day, not just in the evening as
suggested by the name. The other
species, Smooth Trailing Four O'Clock
(*A. choisyi*), from Arizona to Texas and
southward, has a perianth ³⁄₁₆″ (5 mm)
long or less, and the curved edges of
the fruit each bear 5–8 slender, gland-
tipped teeth.

## 82 Southwestern Ringstem
(*Anulocaulis leiosolenus*)
Four O'Clock Family (Nyctaginaceae)

Description:  An ungainly, spindly plant with large,
*fleshy leaves* near the base, and *pale pink
or pink and white, trumpet-shaped flowers*
scattered about the widely branched
top.
Flowers:  1¼–1½″ (3.1–3.8 cm) long;
slightly bilateral; 3 stamens project
about 1½″ (3.8 cm) beyond perianth,
the slender style even farther.
Leaves:  to 10″ (25 cm) wide, opposite,
nearly round, rough with small, wart-
like hairs.
Fruit:  resembles a wrinkled little pot
with conical lid.
Height:  to 4′ (1.2 m).
Flowering:  June–November.
Habitat:  On rocky soil containing gypsum.
Range:  Southern Nevada, central Arizona, and
western Texas.
Comments:  In the heat of the day, the tubes of
spent flowers hang bedraggled. At
sundown, new flowers open, the long
stamens and style unraveling and
aligning in a graceful sweep from the
narrow opening. The name Ringstem
derives from the sticky glandular rings
encircling the stem.

### 555 Red Four O'Clock
(*Mirabilis coccineus*)
Four O'Clock Family (Nyctaginaceae)

Description: A spindly plant with *very narrow leaves, and trumpet-shaped, deep pink flowers in small clusters.*
Flowers: ½–¾″ (1.3–2 cm) long, without petals; calyx petal-like, with 5 lobes; beneath each little cluster of flowers is a calyx-like ring of joined bracts which becomes larger and papery as fruits mature.
Leaves: ¾–5″ (2–12.5 cm) long, opposite.
Fruit: seed-like, club-shaped, ³⁄₁₆″ (5 mm) long, with 5 broad angles.
Height: 1–3′ (30–90 cm).
Flowering: May–September.
Habitat: Dry rocky, brushy hillsides.
Range: Central Arizona to western Texas and northern Mexico.
Comments: This night-flowering plant has the deepest pink flowers of all the small-flowered species of Four O'Clocks.

### 84 Sweet Four O'Clock; Maravilla
(*Mirabilis longiflora*)
Four O'Clock Family (Nyctaginaceae)

Description: A leafy plant with stout, forking stems and *slender, white or pale pink, trumpet-shaped flowers,* rarely darker, that bloom in cups in axils of upper leaves.
Flowers: 3–7″ (7.5–17.5 cm) long; purple stamens and style extend as much as 2″ (5 cm) beyond end of flower.
Leaves: to 5″ (12.5 cm) long, opposite, broadly ovate or heart-shaped.
Fruit: hard and seed-like, roundish, dark gray or black, about ¼″ (6 mm) long.
Height: 1½–5′ (45–150 cm).
Flowering: July–September.
Habitat: Brushy canyons and banks.

Range:    Western Texas to southern Arizona;
          south into Mexico.
Comments: *Mirabilis,* in Latin, and Maravilla, in
          Spanish, mean "marvelous"—which
          these flowers certainly are. They open
          in the shade of the late afternoon. This
          lovely native species is a close relative of
          the Common Four O'Clock (*M. jalapa*),
          named for Xalapa, Mexico, which
          commonly "escapes" from gardens,
          establishing itself in the wild. It has
          purple, yellow, or sometimes white
          flowers that generally do not exceed
          2½" (6.3 cm) in length.

---

### 439  Desert Four O'Clock; Colorado Four O'Clock; Maravilla
(*Mirabilis multiflora*)
Four O'Clock Family (Nyctaginaceae)

Description: *Vibrant deep pink, broadly tubular flowers*
             *bloom in 5-lobed cups* growing in leaf
             axils of this bushy plant.
             Flowers: about 1" (2.5 cm) wide; petal-
             like calyx has 5 lobes; stamens 5.
             Leaves: 1–4" (2.5–10 cm) long,
             opposite, broadly ovate or heart-shaped,
             with short stalks.
             Fruit: seed-like, ½" (1.3 cm) long,
             roundish, nearly brown or black.
             Height: to 18" (45 cm).
Flowering:  April–September.
Habitat:    Common in open sandy areas among
            juniper and piñon, extending into
            deserts and grassland.
Range:      Southern California to southern
            Colorado; south into northern Mexico.
Comments:   Flowers open in the evening. The large
            root was chewed or powdered by
            Indians and applied as a poultice for
            various ailments. An infusion in water
            was used to appease the appetite. Two
            similar species occur in totally separate
            areas. They are Green's Four O'Clock
            (*M. greenei*), on dry slopes in northern
            California, and MacFarlane's Four
            O'Clock (*M. macfarlanei*), in canyons in

northeastern Oregon and adjacent
Idaho.

## 446 Mountain Four O'Clock
### (*Mirabilis oblongifolia*)
Four O'Clock Family (Nyctaginaceae)

Description: A leafy plant with erect or leaning
stems and *lavender-pink flowers in little
cups* on branches.
Flowers: about ½" (1.3 cm) wide,
broadly funnel-shaped; calyx petal-like,
with 5 lobes; 3 flowers in each little
cup, which expands into a 5-lobed
papery saucer as fruits mature.
Leaves: 1¼–4" (3.1–10 cm) long,
opposite, broadly lanceolate.
Fruit: seed-like, club-shaped, barely
over ⅛" (3 mm) long, with 5 ribs,
minutely hairy.
Height: to 3' (90 cm).

Flowering: June–October.

Habitat: Open woods or brush in the mountains.

Range: Southern Colorado to Arizona and
western Texas; south into Mexico.

Comments: Flowers open in the evening and remain
open through the cool part of the next
day. They are visited by many insects
and seem to be a favorite morning
flower of hummingbirds.

## WATER LILY FAMILY
### (Nymphaeaceae)

Perennial aquatic herbs, usually with floating round or heart-shaped leaf blades, and large flowers either floating or held above the water surface on long stalks.

Flowers: radially symmetrical; sepals 3 to many, often intergrading into many petals; stamens 3 to many; pistils 3 to numerous, sometimes held together in a common fleshy base.

Leaves: simple, with very long stalks.

Fruit: each pistil may open on one side, or each may form a little nut, or all may be grown together as a leathery berry.

There are about 7 genera and nearly 70 species occurring in aquatic habitats throughout temperate and tropical regions. Several are cultivated as ornamentals in garden ponds.

---

60  **Fragrant Water Lily**
(*Nymphaea odorata*)
Water Lily Family (Nymphaeaceae)

Description: Aquatic plant with *floating round leaves and large white floating flowers.*
Flowers: 3–6″ (7.5–15 cm) wide; petals 20 to 30; stamens 50–100.
Leaves: blades to 10″ (25 cm) wide, attached at the base of a deep notch to a long, submerged stalk.
Height: aquatic, the submerged leaf and flower stalks 2–4′ (60–120 cm) long; stems buried in the mud.

Flowering: July–October.

Habitat: Quiet, fresh water.

Range: A native of the eastern United States now found in ponds in many places in the West.

Comments: The fragrant flowers open in the morning and close in the afternoon. The only other species in the West, Pygmy Water Lily (*N. tetragona*), with flowers about 2½″ (6.3 cm) wide and only 7–15 petals, is found only in a few places in Washington and Idaho, but is native to the northeastern United States.

### 222 Indian Pond Lily; Yellow Water Lily; Spatterdock; Wakas
(*Nuphar polysepala*)
Water Lily Family (Nymphaeaceae)

Description: *Heart-shaped, leathery leaves* with roundish tips float on water, and *cup-shaped, bright yellow flowers* either float on the surface or are held just above it, both attached by long stalks to stout stems buried in the mud.
Flowers: 2½–4″ (6.3–10 cm) wide; sepals usually 9, outer ones greenish, inner bright yellow or tinged with red, 1¼–2½″ (3.1–6.3 cm) long, bluntly fan-shaped; petals narrow, inconspicuous, about as long as numerous stamens.
Leaves: 4–18″ (10–45 cm) long.
Height: aquatic, the flowers 1–3″ (2.5–7.5 cm) above water surface.

Flowering: April–September.

Habitat: Ponds and slow streams.

Range: Alaska to southern California; eastward to Colorado.

Comments: The seeds of this species were ground by Indians for flour and roasted as popcorn. When the mud in which the stems grow loses oxygen, a small amount of alcohol instead of carbon dioxide is produced by this and some other aquatic plants, including rice.

## OLIVE FAMILY (Oleaceae)

Small or large shrubs, trees, or woody
vines, with flowers borne in racemes or
branched clusters.
Flowers: radially symmetrical; sepals
usually 4, united; petals usually 4,
united, or occasionally the corolla
absent; stamens 2. All these parts
attached at base of ovary.
Leaves: simple or pinnately compound,
opposite.
Fruit: berry, stone-fruit, or capsule.
The 29 genera and 600 species are
especially frequent in temperate and
tropical Asia. Ornamentals are Lilac,
Privet, Jasmine, Golden Bells
(*Forsythia*), and others. Ash is used as
an ornamental and is an important
lumber tree. Olives and olive oil are
obtained from the tree *Olea europea*.

204 **Rough Menodora**
(*Menodora scabra*)
Olive Family (Oleaceae)

Description: Numerous erect, rough, leafy stems
have *pale yellow flowers* in loose
clusters.
Flowers: ½–¾" (1.3–2 cm) wide;
corolla with a short, narrow tube and
5 spreading lobes; hidden within are
2 stamens.
Leaves: ½–1½" (1.3–3.8 cm) long,
broadly lanceolate, usually erect.
Fruit: capsule of 2 translucent spheres
side by side, each nearly ¼" (6 mm)
wide.
Height: 14" (35 cm).
Flowering: March–September.
Habitat: Grassy slopes and brushy deserts.
Range: Southeastern California and southern
Utah to western Texas and northern
Mexico.
Comments: A small genus with species only in
southern North America, southern
South America, and southern Africa.

## EVENING PRIMROSE FAMILY
### (Onagraceae)

Usually herbs, rarely shrubs or trees, often with showy flowers borne singly, in racemes or spikes, or in branched clusters.

Flowers: usually radially symmetrical, sepals usually 4; petals 4; sepals and petals united into a long, short, or barely discernable tube at the base; stamens usually 4 or 8. All these parts attached at top of ovary.

Leaves: simple, alternate or opposite.

Fruit: commonly 4-chambered capsule, less commonly berry or hard nut-like structure.

The family of about 17 genera and 675 species is found worldwide, but is especially abundant in temperate regions of the New World. Evening Primroses, Fuschsia, and Lopezia are popular ornamentals. "Primrose" ultimately derives from a Latin word meaning "first" and the true Primroses (Primulaceae), unrelated to Evening Primroses, are among the first flowers to bloom in the spring. Apparently in the early 1600's when an eastern United States species of *Oenothera* was being described, its sweet scent reminded the botanist of wild Primroses of Europe. He gave the name to these plants and it stuck.

---

## 97 Enchanter's Nightshade
### (*Circaea alpina*)
Evening Primrose Family (Onagraceae)

Description: Slender stems with several pairs of heart-shaped leaves and *tiny white flowers in racemes.*

Flowers: about ⅛" (3 mm) wide; sepals 2; petals 2, each notched and having 2 lobes; stamens 2.

Leaves: to 2½" (6.3 cm) long.

Height: 4–20" (10–50 cm).

Flowering:  May–July.
  Habitat:  Cool damp woods.
    Range:  Across northern North America; south
            mostly in the mountains to southern
            California, Arizona, and New Mexico;
            in the East to Georgia.
Comments:  Circe, the Greek enchantress for whom
           the genus is named, possessed magical
           powers, a knowledge of poisonous
           herbs, and could change men to swine.
           An Old World species of Enchanter's
           Nightshade, with races in eastern
           North America, was one of her magical
           plants.

## 466  Farewell to Spring
(*Clarkia amoena*)
Evening Primrose Family (Onagraceae)

Description:  An open plant with *showy, pink, cup-*
              *shaped flowers* in a loose inflorescence.
              Flowers: sepals 4, reddish, remain
              attached by tips, twisted to one side;
              petals 4, fan-shaped, ¾–1½″ (2–3.8
              cm) wide, each often with a red-purple
              blotch in center; stamens 8.
              Leaves: ¾–3″ (2–7.5 cm) long,
              lanceolate.
              Height: 6–36″ (15–90 cm).
Flowering:  June–August.
  Habitat:  Dry grassy slopes and openings in brush
            and woods.
    Range:  Southern British Columbia to central
            California.
Comments:  As the lush grass watered by spring
           rains begins to turn gold in the dry
           heat of summer, Farewell to Spring
           begins to flower. The flowers close at
           night, and reopen in the morning. The
           genus name honors Captain William
           Clark of the Lewis and Clark expedition
           to the Northwest in 1806. There are
           about 30 species, most in California,
           some very rare.

485 **Lovely Clarkia**
(*Clarkia concinna*)
Evening Primrose Family (Onagraceae)

Description: A low plant, highly branched, with *elaborate bright pink flowers* crowded in leaf axils.
Flowers: 1½–2″ (3.8–5 cm) wide; sepals 4; petals 4, slender at base, with 3 lobes at end, the middle lobe at least as wide as 2 lateral lobes.
Leaves: ½–2″ (1.3–5 cm) long, broadly lanceolate.
Height: rarely more than 1′ (30 cm).
Flowering: May–June.
Habitat: Loose slopes where partly shaded.
Range: Coast Ranges of California.
Comments: In the very similar Beautiful Clarkia (*C. pulchella*), sometimes also called Deerhorn Clarkia or Ragged-robin Clarkia, from southern British Columbia to southeastern Oregon and east to western Montana, the middle lobe of each petal is twice as wide as the side ones. Brewer's Clarkia (*C. breweri*), of central California, has central lobe of petal about half as wide as side ones. Gunsight Clarkia (*C. xantiana*), of southern California, has a needle-like middle lobe.

531 **Elegant Clarkia**
(*Clarkia unguiculata*)
Evening Primrose Family (Onagraceae)

Description: A slender plant with a few lanceolate leaves and *buds nodding along an erect raceme of a few pink flowers.*
Flowers: 1–1½″ (2.5–3.8 cm) wide; sepals 4, reddish, joined by ends and turned to one side after flower opens; petals 4, with circular, diamond-shaped, or broadly triangular ends with a reddish blotch, and narrowly stalked bases.
Leaves: ¾–3″ (2–7.5 cm) long.
Height: 6–36″ (15–90 cm).

Flowering:  June—July.
  Habitat:  Dry slopes, often where the soil has
            been disturbed.
    Range:  Southern two thirds of California.
Comments:  The long, slender petal stalks help
            distinguish this from several similar
            species in the West, most limited to
            California.

536  **Fireweed; Blooming Sally**
     (*Epilobium angustifolium*)
     Evening Primrose Family (Onagraceae)

Description:  *Pink spires of flowers* bloom at tops of
              tall, erect, leafy stems.
              Flowers: sepals 4; petals 4, ½–¾"
              (1.3–2 cm) long, usually deep pink but
              occasionally white.
              Leaves: 4–6" (10–15 cm) long, with
              veins joined in loops near edge of
              leaf.
              Fruit: pod 2–3" (5–7.5 cm) long,
              slender, stands out rigidly from stem.
              Height: 2–7' (60–210 cm).
 Flowering:  June—September.
   Habitat:  Disturbed soil in cool areas, from the
             lowlands well into the mountains,
             frequent along highways and in burned
             areas; hence one common name.
     Range:  Throughout.
 Comments:  Often grows in spectacular dense
             patches, and though attractive, it is
             aggressive in a moist garden, spreading
             from persistent underground stems.

220  **Yellow Willow Herb**
     (*Epilobium luteum*)
     Evening Primrose Family (Onagraceae)

Description:  Erect, leafy stems grow in patches; in
              upper leaf axils bloom *yellow flowers*.
              Flowers: 1–1½" (2.5–3.8 cm) wide;
              petals 4, notched at tip; stamens 8.
              Leaves: ¾–3" (2–7.5 cm) long,
              opposite, lanceolate.

Fruit: slender pod, containing seeds with long hairs.

Height: 8–28" (20–70 cm).

Flowering: July–September.

Habitat: Moist places in the mountains.

Range: South to northern California.

Comments: Yellow Epilobiums are unusual in the West. The Shrubby Willow Herb, (*E. suffruticosum*), with smaller flowers, is found in the mountains of central Idaho, western Montana, and Wyoming. Such plants were formerly known as *Oenothera*.

---

### 460 Rock Fringe; Rose Epilobium
(*Epilobium obcordatum*)
Evening Primrose Family (Onagraceae)

Description: A *matted plant* with a short creeping stem and, in the upper leaf axils, *deep pink flowers* seemingly too large for the plant and often hiding its foliage.

Flowers: ¾–1¼" (2–3.1 cm) wide; petals 4, shaped like perfect hearts.

Leaves: ¼–½" (6–13 mm) long, opposite, crowded, ovate.

Height: creeper, with flower stalk about 2" (5 cm) high, and stems to 6" (15 cm) long.

Flowering: July–September.

Habitat: High mountain meadows, rocky slopes, and ledges.

Range: Central Idaho to Oregon, Nevada, and the Sierra Nevada of California.

Comments: Most *Epilobium* species are tall, but this, like many other alpine plants, is low and compact, and so derives protection from cold, drying mountain winds and freezing temperatures.

---

### 532 Scarlet Gaura
(*Gaura coccinea*)
Evening Primrose Family (Onagraceae)

Description: The leafy stems of this grayish plant are branched, grow in clumps, and bear at

the tips *reddish-pink, nodding racemes.*
Flowers: about ½" (1.3 cm) wide;
bilaterally symmetrical; petals 4,
narrow, all spreading upward, *white in
the evening, by midmorning deep pink;*
stamens 8.
Leaves: ½–2½" (1.3–6.3 cm) long,
crowded, narrowly lanceolate.
Fruit: pod less than ½" (1.3 cm) long,
hard, shaped somewhat like an old-
fashioned toy top.
Height: usually 6–24" (15–60 cm).

Flowering: May–September.

Habitat: Sandy soil in grassland and among
piñon and juniper.

Range: Central Canada and western Montana to
Wyoming and Colorado; southwest to
southern California; south to Mexico;
east to Minnesota, Missouri, and
Texas.

Comments: The whiteness of the newly opened
flowers attracts night-flying moths, the
primary pollinators of these plants. By
early the next day the flowers are pink,
the color intensifying throughout the
morning. The flower remains open less
than a day.

### 329 Desert Primrose
(*Oenothera brevipes*)
Evening Primrose Family (Onagraceae)

Description: From a basal rosette of leaves grows a
nearly leafless, reddish stem with a
*broad raceme of bright yellow flowers* just
below its drooping top.
Flowers: ¼–1½" (6–38 mm) wide;
petals 4, nearly round; stamens 8, with
stalks about ¼" (6 mm) long; style at
least ½" (1.3 cm) long with a large
round knob at tip.
Leaves: 1–5" (2.5–12.5 cm) long,
pinnately lobed, the end lobe largest.
Fruit: slender pod ¾–3½" (2–8.8 cm)
long.
Height: 1–30" (2.5–75 cm).

Flowering: March–May.

Habitat: Desert slopes and washes.
Range: Southeastern California to southwestern Utah and western Arizona.
Comments: This species, distinguished by the knob on the style, blooms at sunrise rather than sunset. It is also known as *Camissonia brevipes*.

---

### 195 Beach Primrose
(*Oenothera cheiranthifolia*)
Evening Primrose Family (Onagraceae)

Description: *Leafy stems lie on the sand,* radiating from a central rosette of grayish leaves, with *bright yellow flowers* facing upward near the ends.
Flowers: ½–1¼" (1.3–3.1 cm) wide; petals 4, nearly round; stamens 8.
Leaves: ½–2" (1.3–5 cm) long, ovate, covered with grayish hairs.
Fruit: slender pod, 4-sided.
Height: creeper, with branches to about 6" (15 cm) high, and stems 2–4' (60–120 cm) long.
Flowering: April–August.
Habitat: Beach sands along the Pacific Coast.
Range: Southern Oregon to Baja California.
Comments: The large knob on the end of the style, as well as several technical characteristics, shows that this is a fairly close relative of Desert Primrose (*O. brevipes*). It is also known as *Camissonia cheiranthifolia*.

---

### 61 Birdcage Evening Primrose
(*Oenothera deltoides*)
Evening Primrose Family (Onagraceae)

Description: A grayish plant with *large, white, tissue-like flowers* blooming on a short central stalk or at the leafy ends of otherwise nearly leafless reclining stems that grow from a *dense basal rosette.* Buds at the stem tips droop.
Flowers: 1½–3" (3.8–7.5 cm) wide;

petals 4, broad; tube between sepals and top of ovary ¾–1½" (2–3.8 cm) long.

Leaves: ¾–3" (2–7.5 cm) long, broadly ovate or diamond-shaped.

Height: creeper, with branches to 2–12" (5–30 cm) high, and reclining stems 4–40" (10–100 cm) long.

Flowering: March–May.

Habitat: Sandy deserts.

Range: Eastern Oregon to southern California, Arizona, and Utah.

Comments: In some years, when desert rains have been ample, these plants grow in profusion. Each evening hundreds or thousands of flowers quickly pop open. In the early morning light, before the large flowers close, the desert may appear as if strewn with tissue paper. When plants die, their stems curve upward, forming a "birdcage."

### 219 Hooker's Evening Primrose
(*Oenothera hookeri*)
Evening Primrose Family (Onagraceae)

Description: A tall, erect, usually unbranched stem with *large yellow flowers* in a raceme.

Flowers: 2–3" (5–7.5 cm) wide; sepals 4, reddish; petals 4, broad; becoming rather orange as they age the following day; stamens 8.

Leaves: 6–12" (15–30 cm) long, lanceolate, numerous, progressively smaller from base to top of stem.

Fruit: slender, rigid pod 1–2" (2.5–5 cm) long.

Height: 2–3' (60–90 cm).

Flowering: June–September.

Habitat: Open slopes, road banks, and grassy areas from the plains well into the mountains.

Range: Eastern Washington to Baja California; east to western Texas and southern Colorado.

Comments: Common Evening Primrose (*O. strigosa*), found throughout most of the United States, has similar erect stems, but its petals are less than 1" (2.5 cm) long. Both are closely related to the garden Evening Primrose (*O. erythrosepala*), scattered in the wild from western Washington to California, which is a taller plant, with redder sepals, paler petals about 1½" (3.8 cm) long, and crinkled leaves.

## 206 Tansy-leaved Evening Primrose
(*Oenothera tanacetifolia*)
Evening Primrose Family (Onagraceae)

Description: *Resembles a Dandelion,* but the *bright yellow flowers* have four broad petals.
Flowers: about 1" (2.5 cm) wide; stamens 8; tube between petals and ovary 1–3½" (2.5–8.8 cm) long.
Leaves: 2–8" (5–20 cm) long, in a rosette, lanceolate, the edges deeply cut and lobed.
Fruit: hard pod about ¾" (2 cm) long, 4-sided, the angles narrow and wing-like, sitting in the center of the rosette.
Height: 1–4" (2.5–10 cm).

Flowering: June–August.

Habitat: In soil moist in spring but drying by summer, from sagebrush plains to pine forests.

Range: Eastern Washington to the Sierra Nevada of California; east to Idaho and Montana.

Comments: This is representative of several low, yellow-flowered Evening Primroses with no stems. The rootstock of this plant branches beneath the ground, the plants forming patches on the surface. It is also known as *Camissonia tanacetifolia.*

405 **California Fuchsia; Hummingbird's Trumpet; California Firechalice**
(*Zauschneria californica*)
Evening Primrose Family (Onagraceae)

Description: A somewhat shrubby green or grayish plant, often with many branches with *brilliant red, trumpet-shaped flowers* blooming in profusion near ends, commonly all oriented in the same direction.
Flowers: 1½–2½" (3.8–6.3 cm) long; 4 red sepals and 4 red petals growing from a red tubular base; 8 red stamens that protrude.
Leaves: ½–1½" (1.3–3.8 cm) long, very narrow and gray with hair, or broader, lanceolate, and greener.
Height: 1–3' (30–90 cm).

Flowering: August–October.

Habitat: Dry slopes and ridges from sea level to high in the mountains; in the Southwest in damp canyons.

Range: Southwestern Oregon to Baja California; east to southwestern New Mexico.

Comments: Related to the popular ornamental Fuchsias, most originally from the American tropics. In California, species of *Zauschneria* bloom late in the season, after the summer heat has turned grasses brown and driven most wildflowers to seed. The bright scarlet flowers produce nectar, supplying hummingbirds with food for the start of their southward migration.

## ORCHID FAMILY (Orchidaceae)

Perennial herbs with complicated, unusual and often beautiful flowers borne singly or in spikes, racemes, or branched clusters.

Flowers: usually bisexual, bilaterally symmetrical, twisting one-half turn during development, the top of the flower originally the bottom; sepals 3, separate, often resembling petals; petals 3, separate, the lower usually different from the other two and modified into an elaborate lip, often bearing a backward projecting spur or sac; stamens 1 or 2, united with the style and stigma, forming a complex structure called the column. All these parts attached to top of ovary.

Leaves: simple, usually alternate.

Fruit: 3-chambered capsule.

This is the largest family of flowering plants in terms of number of species, but rarely, if ever, is it dominant. The 600-700 genera and 20,000 species are most abundant in the tropics, where they most frequently grow upon other vegetation. Elsewhere they are usually terrestrial. Vanilla is obtained from the fruits of the tropical genus *Vanilla,* and many species are grown as beautiful greenhouse novelties. Certain species and hybrids, once very rare and difficult to acquire, are now reproduced in great numbers by cloning. The elaborate flower is involved with highly specialized relationships with pollinators. Pollen is usually held together in masses and in many cases must be positioned correctly on the insect for pollination of another flower to occur.

### 484 Calypso; Fairy Slipper
(*Calypso bulbosa*)
Orchid Family (Orchidaceae)

Description: 1 mostly *pink bilateral flower* hangs at tip of an erect, reddish flower stalk that grows above *1 basal leaf.*
Flowers: about 1¼" (3.1 cm) long; 3 sepals and 2 upper petals similar, rose-pink, narrowly lanceolate, spreading sideways or upward and also forward. Lip divided into a white, spoon-like tip with reddish-purple spots and a 2-lobed, sack-like base with reddish-purple stripes.
Leaves: 1¼–2½" (3.1–6.3 cm) long, shallowly plaited, tapered to a purplish stalk.
Height: to 8" (20 cm).
Flowering: March–July.
Habitat: Thick duff and mossy ground in woods.
Range: Northern California, northeastern Arizona, and southern New Mexico; north through much of northern North America; Eurasia.
Comments: Named for the sea nymph Calypso of Homer's *Odyssey,* who detained the willing Odysseus on his return from Troy; like Calypso, the plant is beautiful and prefers secluded haunts.

### 387 Spotted Coral Root
(*Corallorhiza maculata*)
Orchid Family (Orchidaceae)

Description: 1 to many *yellowish-, reddish-, or purplish-brown, nearly leafless stems* with several or many bilaterally symmetrical flowers of the same color in loose racemes.
Flowers: about ¾" (2 cm) wide; 3 sepals and 2 petals lanceolate, spreading sideways and upward; lip white, usually purple-spotted, bent downward near base, about ½" (1.3 cm) long and nearly as wide having 2 small lobes near base.
Leaves: a few tubular sheaths on stem.

Height: 8–32″ (20–80 cm).
Flowering: April–September.
Habitat: Shady woods.
Range: From Guatemala north to Canada.
Comments: This is the most common Coral Root in the United States. Clumps of stems often occur in extensive colonies.

390 **Striped Coral Root**
(*Corallorhiza striata*)
Orchid Family (Orchidaceae)

Description: A nearly leafless plant, the several or many erect, reddish-purple stems with several or many *pale pinkish and brownish-striped bilaterally symmetrical flowers* in a raceme.
Flowers: about 1″ (2.5 cm) wide; sepals 3, with 3 veins; 2 upper petals similar to sepals, with 5 veins; ovate lip ⅜–½″ (9–13 mm) long, bent downward at base, spoon-like near tip, the deep purplish-brown stripes at base tending to merge at tip.
Leaves: reduced to sheaths on lower part of stem.
Height: 6–20″ (15–50 cm).
Flowering: May–August.
Habitat: Deep woods.
Range: Canada to Mexico.
Comments: *Corallorhiza* means "coral root," though the "root" is actually a hard mass of rhizomes associated with a fungus that aids in absorbing nutrients from the duff of the forest floor. After producing flower stalks, the rhizomes may remain dormant for several years.

7 **Early Coral Root; Pale Coral Root**
(*Corallorhiza trifida*)
Orchid Family (Orchidaceae)

Description: Several or many erect, *pale yellowish or greenish, nearly leafless stems* in a clump, each stem with a raceme of small

bilaterally symmetrical flowers the same
color as the stem except for the *white,
lower lip.*

Flowers: about ¼″ (6 mm) long; sepals
3, petals 2, both arched upward and
forward; lip bent downward, sometimes
with a few purple spots at base,
irregularly and minutely scalloped
around end.

Leaves: reduced to sheaths on the lower
part of the stem.

Height: 3–12″ (7.5–30 cm).

Flowering: May–August.

Habitat: Moist woods at moderate or high
elevations.

Range: Northern New Mexico to western South
Dakota and eastern Washington; north
to Canada and Alaska.

Comments: Of all the Coral Roots, this small pale
species is perhaps the least showy.

## 86 California Lady's Slipper
(*Cypripedium californicum*)
Orchid Family (Orchidaceae)

Description: 3–10 bilaterally symmetrical *yellow-
green flowers with white pouches* bloom 1
in each upper leaf axil of unbranched,
clumped stems.

Flowers: sepals seemingly 2, lanceolate,
yellow-green, ⅝–¾″ (1.5–2 cm) long,
1 directed upward, the second (actually
2 sepals fused almost their entire
length) directed downward beneath
pouch; petals 2, like upper sepal; lip a
bulbous white pouch about ¾″ (2 cm)
long, sometimes blushed with pink or
spotted with purple, with a small
opening on top near base.

Leaves: 2–6″ (5–15 cm) long, broadly
lanceolate.

Height: 1–4′ (30–120 cm).

Flowering: May–July.

Habitat: Along streams and seeps in open shade.

Range: Southwestern Oregon and northern
California.

Comments: This is one of the most charming of

Lady's Slippers, often having many flowers all turned in the same direction, seeming to peer from cool hideaways among Western Azaleas, Maidenhair Ferns, Salal, and Red Columbines. *Cypripedium* refers to Aphrodite, the goddess of love and beauty.

## 376 Clustered Lady's Slipper
(*Cypripedium fasciculatum*)
Orchid Family (Orchidaceae)

Description: Several short stems in a cluster, each stem with only *2 broad leaves, and 2–4 drooping, brownish to greenish, bilaterally symmetrical flowers.*
Flowers: about 1½″ (3.8 cm) wide; 3 sepals and 2 petals similar, the 2 lower sepals joined and appearing as one with 2 tips; lip about ½″ (1.3 cm) long, a greenish pouch streaked or mottled with purple.
Leaves: 2–6″ (5–15 cm) long, ovate.
Height: 2–8″ (5–20 cm).
Flowering: April–July.
Habitat: Forests at moderately high elevations.
Range: British Columbia southward to central California and northern Colorado.
Comments: Lady's Slippers attract insects into their pouch, from which there is only one exit, past the stigma, where pollen from a previously visited flower is brushed off. Then the insect must go under one of the anthers where new pollen is picked up. This procedure reduces chances of self-fertilization of the flower.

## 85 Mountain Lady's Slipper
(*Cypripedium montanum*)
Orchid Family (Orchidaceae)

Description: A leafy plant with few stems in a clump, and near the top 1–3 *white and dull purple bilaterally symmetrical flowers,*

1 in each upper leaf axil.
Flowers: sepals lanceolate, dull purple,
1 directed upward, 2 almost completely
joined and pointing downward, 1¼–3″
(3.1–7.5 cm) long; petals 2, like
sepals, twisted; lip a bulbous white
pouch ¾–1¼″ (2–3.1 cm) long,
blushed with pink or purple, with
opening on top near base.
Leaves: 2–6″ (5–15 cm) long, ovate.
Height: 8–28″ (20–70 cm).

Flowering: May–July.

Habitat: Dry or moist, open or lightly shaded,
brushy or wooded valleys and slopes.

Range: Alaska to northern California, northern
Idaho, and northwestern Wyoming.

Comments: Most Lady's Slippers are handsome
plants, all the more charming because
of the mystique and romance
surrounding Orchids. So many species
have been dug up that most are now
rare in the wild. Although many
enthusiasts try to cultivate these plants
as ornamentals, they will die in the
garden.

## 91 Phantom Orchid; Snow Orchid
(*Eburophyton austinae*)
Orchid Family (Orchidaceae)

Description: A *waxy, white, nearly leafless plant* with
stems in clusters and racemes of 5–20
*bilaterally symmetrical white flowers.*
Flowers: sepals 3 and upper petals 2,
similar, lanceolate, each ½–¾″ (1.3–
2 cm) long, gently curving inward and
surrounding lip; lip divided into
2 parts, constricted in middle, the tip
with a yellow fleck.
Leaves: reduced to sheaths on the lower
part of the stem.
Height: 9–20″ (22.5–50 cm).

Flowering: June–August.

Habitat: Occasional in dense, moist, usually
coniferous woods.

Range: From northern Washington to the
mountains of northern California and

the southern Sierra Nevada; east to
Idaho.

Comments: This aptly named plant appears ghostly
in the dim light of the forest floor.
Since it is not green and is therefore
incapable of photosynthesis, it absorbs
all its nutrients from the forest duff,
aided by a fungus in its roots.

---

389 **Stream Orchid; Chatterbox; Giant
Helleborine**
(*Epipactis gigantea*)
Orchid Family (Orchidaceae)

Description: Leafy stems usually growing in dense
patches and in the axils of each upper
leaf 1 *bilaterally symmetrical greenish-
brown and pinkish flower.*
Flowers: 1–1½" (2.5–3.8 cm) wide;
sepals 3, coppery-green, lanceolate;
petals 2, pinkish-rose or purplish,
lanceolate, with purple veins, pointing
forward, about as long as sepals; lip ⅝–
¾" (1.5–2 cm) long has 2 parts
separated by deep constriction in
middle; spoon-like half at base has
purple veins; waxy, triangular tip or
"tongue" is pink or salmon.
Leaves: 2–8" (5–20 cm) long, broadly
lanceolate with prominent veins.
Height: 1–3' (30–90 cm).

Flowering: March–August.

Habitat: Deserts to mountains in springs or
seeps, near ponds, along streams.

Range: British Columbia to Mexico; from the
Pacific Coast east to the Rocky
Mountains and the Black Hills.

Comments: The lower lip and "tongue" move when
the flower is touched or shaken; thus
the name Chatterbox.

## 101   Bog Rein Orchid; Bog Candles
(*Habenaria dilatata*)
Orchid Family (Orchidaceae)

Description:   Erect, leafy stems have many *fragrant,
              white bilaterally symmetrical flowers in a
              spike.*
              Flowers: upper sepal joined to 2 upper
              petals, forming a hood about ¼"
              (6 mm) long; 2 lanceolate sepals ³⁄₁₆–
              ³⁄₈" (5–9 mm) long, spread
              horizontally; lip hangs down and is
              about as long as sepals, the base almost
              3 times as wide as slender tip; slender
              or stout spur extends from back of lip
              downward and forward beneath flower.
              Leaves: middle ones largest, 2–12" (5–
              30 cm) long, narrowly or broadly
              lanceolate, clasping.
              Height: 6–52" (15–130 cm).
Flowering:   June–September.
Habitat:   Wet or boggy ground.
Range:   Northern New Mexico to southern
         California; north through most of the
         West and northern North America.
Comments:   Plants in the Rocky Mountain region
            often have stouter, shorter spurs.
            *Habena,* Latin for "reins" or "narrow
            strap," refers to the narrow lip of some
            species of *Habenaria.*

## 102   Coastal Rein Orchid
(*Habenaria greenei*)
Orchid Family (Orchidaceae)

Description:   Many *white, fragrant, bilaterally
              symmetrical flowers* in a raceme at tip of a
              stout stem with leaves near base.
              Flowers: petals 3 and sepals 3, bluntly
              lanceolate, about ¼" (6 mm) long, each
              with a pale green central stripe; 2 upper
              petals barely joined to upper sepal; base
              of lip constricted slightly, bearing a
              slender, almost straight spur about ½"
              (1.3 cm) long extending behind flower.
              Leaves: to 5" (12.5 cm) long, oblong,
              withering before flowering ends.

Height: 8–16″ (20–40 cm).
Flowering: July–September.
Habitat: Bluffs and open slopes along the coast.
Range: Central California to northern Washington.
Comments: This comparatively stout species intergrades with the slender inland Elegant Habenaria (*H. elegans*), of dry open woods from British Columbia to California, east to Montana, which has an open inflorescence and pale greenish-yellow flowers each with a spur more than ¼″ (6 mm) long. Alaska Rein Orchid (*H. unalascensis*), in dry woods, on gravelly stream banks, or on open slopes from Alaska to Baja California, east to Colorado, is similar to Coastal Rein Orchid but has smaller flowers.

## 98 Round-leaved Rein Orchid
(*Habenaria orbiculata*)
Orchid Family (Orchidaceae)

Description: Between *2 broadly elliptic or round basal leaves, lying on ground,* grows a single flower stalk with up to *25 white or greenish-white bilaterally symmetrical flowers in a raceme.*
Flowers: upper sepal and 2 upper petals arch forward; 2 sepals at side bent back; lip narrow, ½–¾″ (1.3–2 cm) long, hanging down; slender spur ⅝–1″ (1.5–2.5 cm) long extends back, and often slightly upward, from beneath base of lip.
Leaves: 2½–6″ (6.3–15 cm) long.
Height: 8–24″ (20–60 cm).
Flowering: June–August.
Habitat: Moist floor of forests.
Range: Northern Oregon and northwestern Montana northward; east across Canada to the eastern United States.
Comments: This species has the largest flowers of all western Rein Orchids. Several moths feed on nectar in the spur, and probably pollinate the flower.

### 11   **Alaska Rein Orchid**
(*Habenaria unalascensis*)
Orchid Family (Orchidaceae)

Description:   One or a few stems, leafy near base, have *pale green bilaterally symmetrical flowers* in long, slender, open racemes.
Flowers: sepals 3, broadly lanceolate and about ⅛″ (3 mm) long, each with 1 vein; two of the sepals spread to the sides and downward; petals about as long as sepals, the two upper ones joined to upper sepal, forming a hood; lip fleshy, lanceolate, projecting forward, bearing at the base a backward- or downward-projecting spur ⅛″ (3 mm) long.
Leaves: to 10″ (25 cm) long, lanceolate.
Height: 8–32″ (20–80 cm).
Flowering:   June–August.
Habitat:   Dry woods, gravelly stream banks, open slopes.
Range:   Alaska to Baja California; east to northern Nevada, Utah, Colorado, western South Dakota; also near the Great Lakes.
Comments:   The species name comes from Unalaska, an island in the Aleutians.

### 388   **Texas Purple Spike**
(*Hexalectris warnockii*)
Orchid Family (Orchidaceae)

Description:   Slender, *nearly leafless, reddish-brown stems* have up to 10 mostly *reddish-brown flowers in a loose raceme.*
Flowers: 1–1¼″ (2.5–3.1 cm) wide; sepals 3 and petals 2, similar, narrow; lip broad, curved upward, widest near base, where edges are pinkish; white or yellowish center of lip has 3 fringed ridges; tip of lip fringed, blunt, often maroon.
Leaves: represented by a few bracts.
Height: to 12″ (30 cm).
Flowering:   June–August.
Habitat:   Open brushy woods.

Range: Southeastern Arizona; central Texas and the Big Bend region.

Comments: This is the most common *Hexalectris* in Big Bend National Park. There are 4 other species in the Southwest, all also in the park, all with yellowish or reddish stems. Crested Coral Root (*H. spicata*), from southeastern Arizona to the eastern United States, has yellowish-brown sepals, petals with darker veins, and a yellowish or white lip with purple veins.

12 **Broad-leaved Twayblade**
(*Listera convallarioides*)
Orchid Family (Orchidaceae)

Description: A little plant that has at midstem *1 pair of leaves,* and above these a slender raceme of about 20 *small, green bilaterally symmetrical flowers.*
Flowers: 3 sepals and 2 upper petals much alike, narrowly lanceolate, short, sharply bent backward; lip ⅜–½" (9–13 mm) long, 2 round lobes at end, widest near tip, evenly tapered and then abruptly narrowed to a stalk-like base.
Leaves: ¾–3" (2–7.5 cm) long, elliptic.
Height: 2–14" (5–35 cm).

Flowering: June–August.

Habitat: Moist woods.

Range: Sierra Nevada and central Colorado; north to Canada; also southern Arizona.

Comments: The small green flowers attract little insects. The insect trips a "trigger," and pollen with a spot of "glue" is fired onto its body, to be carried to another flower. There are 3 other species in the West, all with the characteristic pair of leaves at midstem, but none with sepals and upper petals sharply bent backward.

**100 Hooded Ladies' Tresses**
*(Spiranthes romanzoffiana)*
Orchid Family (Orchidaceae)

Description:   1 stem, or several in a clump, with
3—6 leaves near base and *up to 60 creamy
white bilaterally symmetrical flowers*
blooming in *1—4 gently spiraled rows* in
a dense spike.
Flowers: ⅜—½″ (9—13 mm) long;
sepals 3, lanceolate, projecting forward,
the tips of the 2 at side often curled
back; 2 upper petals form a hood; lip
bent downward at middle and
projecting from beneath hood,
constricted behind its finely fringed tip.
Leaves: 2—10″ (5—25 cm) long,
lanceolate, about ½″ (1.3 cm) wide or
less.
Height: 4—24″ (10—60 cm).

Flowering:   July—October.

Habitat:   Generally moist open places, but
variable, occurring from coastal bluffs
to high in the mountains.

Range:   Southern California to New Mexico;
north through most of northern North
America.

Comments:   Western Ladies' Tresses (*S. porrifolia*),
which grows in similar habitats from
southern California to southern
Washington and also in northern Utah,
has a triangular lip barely constricted
behind the tip, the sepals only about
⅜″ (9 mm) long.

## BROOMRAPE FAMILY
(Orobanchaceae)

Herbaceous root parasites, annual or
perennial, usually somewhat fleshy,
that lack chlorophyll, and are some
shade of yellow, brown, violet, or red.
Flowers: bilaterally symmetrical, in
racemes, spikes, or borne singly at the
top of a slender stem; sepals 2–5,
united; petals 5, united, forming an
upper and lower lip; stamens 4. All
these parts attached at base of ovary.
Leaves: simple, scale-like, alternate.
Fruit: 1-chambered capsule.
There are about 13 genera and 180
species of primarily north temperate
regions.

### 386 California Ground Cone
(*Boschniakia strobilacea*)
Broomrape Family (Orobanchaceae)

Description: An unusual plant resembling a slender,
*dark reddish-brown pine cone;* stands erect
on the ground, with cupped, spoon-like
bracts, widest near blunt tip.
Flowers: about ⅝″ (1.5 cm) long,
bilaterally symmetrical, in axils of
bracts; corolla bent at middle of tube,
upper lip hood-like, lower 3-lobed.
Leaves: bracts among flowers.
Height: 4–10″ (10–25 cm).
Flowering: May–July.
Habitat: In forests or brush, associated with the
shrub manzanita (*Arctostaphylos*) or the
tree madrone (*Arbutus*).
Range: Southern California to southern
Oregon.
Comments: A perennial parasite that flowers each
season and causes large knobs to form
on the roots of manzanita and madrone.
Small Ground Cone (*B. hookerii*), which
grows near the coast from Canada to
northern California, is half the size of
California Ground Cone, with pointed
bracts widest at about the middle.

### 613  Spike Broomrape
(*Orobanche multiflora*)
Broomrape Family (Orobanchaceae)

Description:  The *thick, purple cone-like stems* of this
plant grow singly or clustered, have
*purple or yellowish bilaterally symmetrical
flowers* in axils of bracts; corolla tube
lighter than lobes.
Flowers: corolla ½–1½″ (1.3–3.8 cm)
long, upper lip bent back and erect, 2-
lobed, lower lip 3-lobed, lobes
roundish at tips or bluntly pointed;
style remains on developing capsule.
Leaves: reduced to bracts on stems.
Height: 4–20″ (10–50 cm).

Flowering:  March–September.

Habitat:  Prairies, rangeland, and deserts.

Range:  Eastern Washington to Mexico; east to
Texas, Oklahoma, and Wyoming.

Comments:  A parasite on roots of certain Asteraceae
species. The name Broomrape refers to
any species parasitic on the shrub
Broom (*Cytisus*).

### 602  Naked Broomrape
(*Orobanche uniflora*)
Broomrape Family (Orobanchaceae)

Description:  *Purple, lavender, or yellowish bilaterally
symmetrical flowers bloom singly* at tips of
slender, *yellowish-brown, leafless stalks.*
Flowers: about 1″ (2.5 cm) long; corolla
slightly bent downward in middle of
tube, with 2 yellow stripes on lower
side; lobes fringed with fine hairs.
Leaves: represented by tiny scales.
Height: stalks 1¼–4″ (3.1–10 cm);
main stem mostly underground.

Flowering:  April–August.

Habitat:  Open places from lowlands to moderate
elevations in the mountains.

Range:  Throughout, except western portion of
the Great Plains.

Comments:  This species is parasitic on several kinds
of plants, often Stonecrops (*Sedum*).

## WOOD SORREL FAMILY
## (Oxalidaceae)

Herbs with alternate or basal leaves, the plants varying to shrubs or rarely trees; sap often sour.

Flowers: radially symmetrical, usually borne singly or in an umbel; sepals 5, separate; petals 5, separate or united at base; stamens 10, joined by their stalks. All these parts attached at base of ovary; ovary with 5 styles.

Leaves: usually palmately compound and resembling 3-leaved Clovers in the United States; sometimes leaves with more leaflets, or only 1 by evolutionary reduction, or pinnately compound.

Fruit: 5-chambered capsule, rarely berry.

There are about 8 genera and 1,000 species occurring primarily in tropical and subtropical regions. Several are cultivated as ornamentals, and one tree-like tropical species produces gooseberry-like, edible fruits.

---

447 **Mountain Wood Sorrel**
*(Oxalis alpina)*
Wood Sorrel Family (Oxalidaceae)

Description: A few leaves in a cluster, with 3 *heart-shaped leaflets* attached by their points, bearing a *few yellowish or orange spots*. Flowers generally red-violet, but ranging from bluish to lavender or white.
Flowers: ½–1″ (1.3–2.5 cm) wide; petals 5, joined at base into a greenish tube; 1–13 flowers in a loose umbel, the branches ¼–2½″ (6–63 mm) long.
Leaves: leaflets ¼–1″ (6–25 mm) long.
Fruit: several-seeded capsule ³⁄₁₆–½″ (5–13 mm) long.
Height: 1–10″ (2.5–25 cm).
Flowering: July–September.
Habitat: In pockets of rich soil among rocks in coniferous or pine-oak forests.

Range: Northern New Mexico and central
Arizona; south to Guatemala.

Comments: Styles on this species are of 3 different
lengths, insuring cross-pollination.
Violet Wood Sorrel (*O. violacea*), from
central Arizona and northern New
Mexico to the eastern United States, is
similar but has spots only at the notch
of the leaves; the leaves are generally ⅕
the height of the flowers, the capsules
less than ¼″ (6 mm) long. Ten-leaved
Wood Sorrel (*O. decaphylla*), from the
Southwest and Mexico, has 4–11
leaflets.

## 443 Redwood Sorrel
(*Oxalis oregana*)
Wood Sorrel Family (Oxalidaceae)

Description: A low plant in patches, with *3 heart-
shaped leaflets on each leaf* and *1 funnel-
shaped, white or rose-pink flower* at end of
each stalk; leaf and flower stalks both
about the same length and attached to
the plant at ground level.
Flowers: ½–¾″ (1.3–2 cm) wide;
petals 5, often with purple veins.
Leaves: leaflets ½–1½″ (1.3–3.8 cm)
long, often with pale blotch in center,
attached by points to tip of erect stalk.
Height: 2–7″ (5–17.5 cm).

Flowering: April–September.

Habitat: Forest shade.

Range: Coastal central California to
Washington; east to the eastern side of
the Cascade Mountains.

Comments: This species forms lush, solid, inviting
carpets on the cool floor of coastal
redwood forests. The sour juice is
characteristic of this genus, and gives
the generic name, from the Greek *oxys*
("sour"). A similar species in the same
general region and habitat, Great
Oxalis (*O. trilliifolia*), has 2 or more
flowers on a stalk. There are also several
yellow-flowered species of *Oxalis* in the
West, some aggressively weedy.

## PEONY FAMILY (Paeoniaceae)

Somewhat succulent, occasionally rather shrubby, herbs with large flowers.
Flowers: radially symmetrical; sepals 5, separate; petals 5 or 10, separate; stamens many, maturing from inside to outside; pistils 2–5, separate. Partially surrounding ovaries is a conspicuous fleshy disk.
Leaves: alternate, divided.
Fruit: leathery pods with many seeds.
There is one genus with about 33 species occurring in northern temperate regions. Many species, hybrids, and horticultural forms are cultivated, most with "doubled" flowers.

### 375 Western Peony
(*Paeonia brownii*)
Peony Family (Paeoniaceae)

Description: A rather fleshy, bluish-green, leafy plant, usually with several clustered stems, divided leaves, and *greenish and reddish-brown globose flowers,* 1 hanging at end of each stalk.
Flowers: 1–1½" (2.5–3.8 cm) wide; sepals 5 or 6, greenish, spoon-shaped; petals 5, maroon or bronze in center, green on margins, about as long as sepals.
Leaves: blades to 2½" (6.3 cm) long, divided into 3 main segments on short stalks, segments again divided into 3 parts, these with lobes at end.
Height: 8–24" (20–60 cm).
Flowering: April–June.
Habitat: Chaparral, sagebrush, and pine forests.
Range: Eastern Washington; south through the northern two thirds of California; east to Utah, western Wyoming, and Idaho.
Comments: The genus name comes from Paeon, the physician of Greek gods; northwestern Indians made tea from the roots to treat lung ailments.

## POPPY FAMILY (Papaveraceae)

Annual or perennial herbs, occasionally shrubs, rarely trees, often with colored sap.

Flowers: radially symmetrical, most borne singly; sepals 2 or 3, separate or united, quickly drop off; petals 4–6 separate, showy, often crumpled in the bud; stamens numerous. All these parts attached at base of ovary.

Leaves: alternate, simple or deeply divided.

Fruit: usually capsule, often oddly shaped, and opening by pores.

There are about 26 genera and 200 species, most occurring in temperate and subtropical regions; they are well represented in western North America. Several species are grown as ornamentals and opium is extracted from one.

---

62 **Great Desert Poppy; Great Bear Poppy**
(*Arctomecon merriami*)
Poppy Family (Papaveraceae)

Description: *1 large, white flower* blooms atop each of several stalks that have *hairy leaves, most near base.*
Flowers: 2–3″ (5–7.5 cm) wide; sepals 3, hairy, drop when flower opens; petals 6, widest near tip; stamens many, yellow.
Leaves: 1–3″ (2.5–7.5 cm) long, pale blue-green, narrowly fan-shaped, toothed across blunt end, covered with long, straight hairs.
Height: 8–20″ (20–50 cm).
Flowering: April–May.
Habitat: Loose rocky slopes and deserts.
Range: Southeastern California and southern Nevada.
Comments: Little Desert Poppy (*A. humilis*), in southwestern Utah and northwestern Arizona, generally less than 10″

(25 cm) tall, has 4 white petals. Yellow Desert Poppy (*A. californica*), in southern Nevada and northwestern Arizona, has 6 yellow petals.

## 64 Prickly Poppy
(*Argemone polyanthemos*)
Poppy Family (Papaveraceae)

Description: A branched, pale blue-green, leafy plant, with *white flowers, yellow sap, and slender yellow prickles all over.*
Flowers: about 3″ (7.5 cm) wide; petals 4–6, broad, crumpled; stamens many, yellow; buds with 2 or 3 sepals bearing erect prickles and at tip a stout "horn" ¼–⅝″ (6–15 mm) long, but sepals drop as flower opens.
Leaves: to 8″ (20 cm) long, deeply lobed, prickly only on veins.
Fruit: capsule; largest spines without small prickles at base.
Height: to 4′ (1.2 m).
Flowering: April–July.
Habitat: Sandy or gravelly soil on plains or brushy slopes.
Range: South-central New Mexico and northern half of Texas; north to South Dakota and eastern Wyoming.
Comments: *Argema,* in Greek, means "cataract of the eye," for which species of this genus were supposedly a remedy. There are several species in the West, all similar, a few with yellow, pinkish, or lavender petals. All parts of the plants are poisonous (including the seeds), but the herbage is so prickly and distasteful that livestock avoid them.

## 346 Tree Poppy
(*Dendromecon rigida*)
Poppy Family (Papaveraceae)

Description: A stiff roundish *shrub with brilliant yellow, cup-shaped flowers* at ends of short

branches or on long stalks in leaf axils.
Flowers: 1–2½″ (2.5–6.3 cm) wide;
sepals 2, fall when flower opens;
petals 4, broad; stamens many,
short.
Leaves: 1–4″ (2.5–10 cm) long,
leathery, lanceolate, bluish green, the
stalk twisted so that flat sides of blade
face sideways.
Height: 4–20′ (1.2–6 m).

Flowering:  April–June.
Habitat:  Dry slopes in chaparral.
Range:  Northern California to Mexico.
Comments:  The Tree Poppy may be very common
several years after a fire in chaparral.
There is only one other species, Island
Tree Poppy (*D. harfordii*), on islands off
the coast of southern California.

### 361  California Poppy
(*Eschscholtzia californica*)
Poppy Family (Papaveraceae)

Description:  A *smooth, bluish-green plant* with several
stems, *fern-like leaves,* and usually *orange
flowers* borne singly on a long stalk.
Flowers: 1–2″ (2.5–5 cm) wide; petals
4, fan-shaped, deep orange or yellow-
orange, sometimes yellow at tips and
orange at base, rarely cream; sepals
joined into a cone (calyptra) which is
pushed off as flower opens; stamens
many; beneath ovary a flat,
conspicuous, pinkish rim.
Leaves: ¾–2½″ (2–6.3 cm) long,
divided into narrow segments, on long
stalks.
Fruit: capsule 1¼–4″ (3.1–10 cm)
long, slender, slightly curved.
Height: 8–24″ (20–60 cm).

Flowering:  February–September.
Habitat:  Open areas, common on grassy slopes.
Range:  Southern California to southern
Washington; often cultivated.
Comments:  On sunny days in spring, California
Poppies, the state flower, often turn
hillsides orange. Responsive to

sunlight, the flowers close at night and on cloudy days. The spicy fragrance attracts mainly beetles, which serve as pollinators. Flowers produced early in the season tend to be larger than those later on. There are other species in California, but none has the conspicuous pink rim at the base of the ovary.

### 227 Mexican Gold Poppy; Amapola del Campo
(*Eschscholtzia mexicana*)
Poppy Family (Papaveraceae)

Description: A low, *smooth, pale bluish-green* plant with *fern-like leaves*, mostly near base, and *orange-yellow cup-shaped flowers* borne singly on stalks.
Flowers: ¾–1½" (2–3.8 cm) wide; petals 4, yellow, orange, or yellow near tips and orange at base, occasionally cream; stamens many; sepals joined into a cone which is pushed off as flower opens; a conspicuous, flat, pinkish rim at ovary base.
Leaves: about 2" (5 cm) wide, about as long, divided into narrow segments, on a stalk as long or longer.
Height: to 16" (40 cm).
Flowering: March–May.
Habitat: Open gravelly desert slopes.
Range: Southeastern California to the western tip of Texas and northern Mexico.
Comments: The Spanish name means "Poppy of the countryside." When there have been ample winter rains, this Poppy sometimes grows in dense patches.

### 363 Fire Poppy; Western Poppy
(*Papaver californicum*)
Poppy Family (Papaveraceae)

Description: A single bowl-shaped flower at top of each stem has 4 *fan-shaped, reddish-*

*orange petals* with a greenish spot at base; before the flowers open, the *buds droop.*

Flowers: about 1″ (2.5 cm) wide; sepals 2, hairy, drop as flower opens; stamens many, yellow; atop nearly cylindiic ovary, a cap-shaped stigma witli lines radiating from center.

Leaves: 1¼–3½″ (3.1–8.8 cm) long, pinnately divided into a few segments with teeth or lobes.

Height: 12–24″ (30–60 cm).

Flowering: April–May.

Habitat: Open brush and woods, especially after fires.

Range: The Coast Ranges from San Francisco Bay to southern California; not common in the northern half of the range.

Comments: Opium is extracted from the sap of an Old World species, once commonly (and innocently) grown in gardens and still found scattered in the country.

### 223 Alpine Poppy
(*Papaver kluanense*)
Poppy Family (Papaveraceae)

Description: A low, tufted plant with brownish hairs, the *4 pale yellow or white petals forming bowl-shaped flowers* that bloom singly, 1 at end of each stalk.

Flowers: ¾–1½″ (2–3.8 cm) wide; sepals 2, drop as flower opens, covered with brown hairs; stamens many.

Leaves: ¾–4″ (2–10 cm) long (including stalk), pinnately lobed, lobes generally with a few teeth.

Height: 2–6″ (5–15 cm).

Flowering: June–August.

Habitat: Tundra and rocky alpine slopes.

Range: Canada; northern New Mexico.

Comments: Alpine Poppy was only recently named, after completion of a study of all Poppies from northern Canada and high in the Rocky Mountains. The smaller Pigmy Poppy (*P. pygmaeum*), only 1¼–

2½" (3.1—6.3 cm) tall, with pale salmon petals ½" (1.3 cm) long, grows at high elevations in the Waterton-Glacier International Park.

## 208 Cream Cup
(*Platystemon californicus*)
Poppy Family (Papaveraceae)

Description: A softly-haired plant with several stems, each with 1 small, bowl-shaped flower at top which *resembles a pale yellow or cream buttercup.*
Flowers: ½—1" (1.3—2.5 cm) wide; petals 6; sepals 3, drop as flower blooms; stamens many, with flat stalks; stigmas 6—25 on an ovary that separates into as many sections when fruit forms.
Leaves: ¾—3" (2—7.5 cm) long, opposite, narrowly lanceolate, mostly on lower half of plant.
Height: 4—12" (10—30 cm).
Flowering: March—May.
Habitat: Open grassy areas.
Range: Most of California; west to southwestern Utah, central Arizona, and northern Baja California.
Comments: Only one species, some races with nearly white petals, some with yellow petals, others with cream petals yellow at base.

## 63 Matilija Poppy
(*Romneya coulteri*)
Poppy Family (Papaveraceae)

Description: Tall, heavy, leaning, leafy, branched stems grow in patches and have 5—8 *large, fragrant, white flowers* blooming near ends.
Flowers: 4—7" (10—7.5 cm) wide; petals 6, fan-shaped; sepals 3, smooth; stamens many, yellow, forming ball in center; bristly-haired ovary.
Leaves: 2—8" (5—20 cm) long, gray-

green, pinnately divided into 3 or 5 main divisions that may have a few teeth or again be divided.

Fruit: capsule with bristly hairs.

Height: 3–8′ (90–240 cm).

Flowering: May–July.

Habitat: Brush in coastal mountains.

Range: Southern California.

Comments: The large white flowers are conspicuous from a distance in early summer. A second species, Bristly Matilija Poppy (*R. trichocalyx*), has bristly hairs on the sepals and on the stalk beneath the flower. Hybrids between the two are grown as ornamentals.

## PASSION FLOWER FAMILY
(Passifloraceae)

Herbaceous vines climbing by tendrils,
woody vines, shrubs, or trees, with
bizarre, elaborate flowers.
Flowers: radially symmetrical, usually
in pairs in leaf axils; sepals usually 5,
often petal-like, usually separate but
sometimes united at the base; petals 5,
separate or absent; at the base of the
corolla are numerous thread-like
structures forming a corona; stamens 3–
5, or 10; ovary bears 3–5 styles, often
on a stalk that also bears stamens.
Leaves: alternate, simple, often lobed.
Fruit: capsule or berry.
There are about 12 genera and 600
species in this mostly tropical American
family.

## 2 Green Passion Flower
(*Passiflora tenuiloba*)
Passion Flower Family (Passifloraceae)

Description: Vines with *tendrils in axils* of leaves and
*bizarre greenish flowers.*
Flowers: about ¾″ (2 cm) wide; sepals
5, but no petals; between stamens and
sepals is a fringed crown (corona) with
2 circles of many hair-like segments.
Stamens and ovary borne on stalk in
center of flower, the 5 stamens bent
down, the 3 styles arching outward.
Leaves: to 6″ (15 cm) wide, broader
than long, divided into 3 main narrow
lobes; stalk with large glands.
Height: vine, stems to 7′ (2.1 m) long.
Flowering: April–October.
Habitat: Climbing over shrubs and grasses.
Range: Southern New Mexico to southwestern
Texas.
Comments: The name Passion Flower comes from
the impressions of early explorers, to
whom the flower suggested Christ's
torture. There are several species in the
Southwest.

## PLANTAIN FAMILY
### (Plantaginaceae)

Herbs with basal leaves and small flowers borne in spikes or heads.
Flowers: radially symmetrical; calyx and corolla each have 4 united membranous or papery sepals or petals; stamens 4, protruding from flower. All these parts attached at base of ovary.
Leaves: alternate, basal, simple, with predominantly parallel veins.
Fruit: capsule, with top lifting free, or small nut.
There are 3 genera and about 270 species, most inconspicuous, a few weedy, found nearly throughout the world.

---

## 94 English Plantain
*(Plantago lanceolata)*
Plantain Family (Plantaginaceae)

Description: A *narrow, cylindrical spike* of tiny, *brownish-white flowers* tops a long, slender, leafless stalk that grows from a basal rosette of leaves.
Flowers: spike ¾–3″ (2–7.5 cm) long; each crowded flower with 4 parchment-like petals about ⅛″ (3 mm) long; stamens 4, projecting on hair-like stalks and ending in large, cream-colored anthers.
Leaves: 2–16″ (5–40 cm) long, lanceolate, dark green, veins parallel.
Height: 6–24″ (15–60 cm).
Flowering: April–August.
Habitat: Lawns, roadsides, and pastures.
Range: Throughout.
Comments: A common companion of the Dandelion. The name Plantain, from the Latin *planta* ("sole of the foot"), refers to the broad, flat, low-lying leaves of some species.

## LEADWORT FAMILY
## (Plumbaginaceae)

Herbs or shrubs with leaves often in
basal rosettes, and small flowers.
Flowers: radially symmetrical, in heads,
modified racemes, or branched clusters;
sepals 5, united, often plaited, showy,
stiff and membranous; petals 5, united,
but corolla often deeply lobed and
seeming to have separate petals;
stamens 5, each positioned opposite a
lobe of the corolla. All these parts
attached at base of ovary.
Leaves: alternate.
Fruit: 1-chambered; often leathery
and does not open, or opens very late,
1-seeded.
There are about 10 genera and 300
species predominantly found in dry
parts of the Mediterranean region and
in central Asia.

---

### 553 California Thrift
(*Armeria maritima*)
Leadwort Family (Plumbaginaceae)

Description: A low plant with a basal cluster of
many narrow leaves and, atop a slender,
leafless stalk, a *globe of pale lilac flowers,*
beneath which are several broad,
purplish, papery bracts.
Flowers: head ¾–1″ (2–2.5 cm) wide;
flower with calyx in the form of a
funnel of pinkish parchment; 5 lobes on
corolla joined at base.
Leaves: 2–4″ (5–10 cm) long.
Height: 2–16″ (5–40 cm).

Flowering: March–August.

Habitat: Beaches and coastal bluffs, or slightly
inland on prairies.

Range: Pacific Coast from British Columbia to
southern California; Arctic North
America; Eurasia.

Comments: It resembles a small onion, but the two
families are only related in that they are
flowering plants.

## PHLOX FAMILY (Polemoniaceae)

Usually leafy herbs, rarely small shrubs, commonly with showy flowers.
Flowers: radially symmetrical or slightly bilaterally symmetrical, in open or dense clusters branched in a forked manner; sepals 5, united; petals 5, united; stamens 5. All these parts attached at base of ovary; usually 3 branches at tip of style.
Leaves: alternate or opposite, simple or pinnately compound.
Fruit: 3-chambered capsule.
This chiefly North American family is especially well developed in the western United States. About 18 genera and 300 species occur, a few grown as ornamentals.

---

30, 434 **Alpine Collomia**
(*Collomia debilis*)
Phlox Family (Polemoniaceae)

Description: *Numerous sprawling stems form a loose mat,* with leaves and flowers crowded at ends. Flowers cream, white, pink, lavender, or blue.
Flowers: about ¾" (2 cm) wide; corolla trumpet-shaped, ½–1½" (1.3–3.8 cm) long, with 5 lobes.
Leaves: ½–1¼" (1.3–3.1 cm) long, from lanceolate to highly divided.
Height: creeper, with floral stalks about 2" (5 cm) high, and mats 6–18" (15–45 cm) wide.
Flowering: June–August.
Habitat: Shifting, rocky, high mountain slopes.
Range: Washington to northern California; east to central Utah, western Wyoming, and western Montana.
Comments: *Debilis* means "weak," referring to the sprawling stems, which might, however, be considered a strength, for the low, compact habit helps protect the plant from cold mountain winds.

442 **Bridge's Gilia**
(*Gilia leptalea*)
Phlox Family (Polemoniaceae)

Description: *Many slender branches* and small leaves
form a bushy, airy plant with *small,
deep pink, funnel-shaped flowers* growing
on thread-like stalks in the leaf axils.
Flowers: ⅜–¾" (9–20 mm) long, the
5 lobes about ³⁄₁₆" (5 mm) long;
stamens 5, attached at different levels
to inside of corolla.
Leaves: ½–2" (1.3–5 cm) long, very
narrow, with glandular hairs, often
pinnately divided into a few lobes.
Height: 2–14" (5–35 cm).
Flowering: June–September.
Habitat: Openings in brush and dry woods.
Range: Southern Oregon to southern
California.
Comments: The pink color of the flowers is among
the richest in the genus; the flowers of
many other species are nearly white,
pale pink, or lavender. The species of
this large western genus are difficult to
identify, but usually can be recognized
as *Gilia* by the fairly small, trumpet-
shaped or funnel-shaped flowers, the
3 branches on the style, and the
alternate, often pinnately parted,
leaves.

590 **Blue Gilia**
(*Gilia rigidula*)
Phlox Family (Polemoniaceae)

Description: A low plant, often tufted, with *dense,
rigid, prickly, divided leaves* and *deep, rich
blue flowers* borne singly or a few in a
loose cluster near the foliage, often
hiding it when the plant is in full
bloom.
Flowers: corolla nearly ¾" (2 cm) wide,
the 5 round lobes spreading from a
narrow tube; around opening to tube is
a yellow ring, the "eye."
Leaves: ½–1½" (1.3–3.8 cm) long.

Height: to 10″ (25 cm).
Flowering: April–September.
Habitat: Sandy or rocky slopes on prairies or among piñon and juniper.
Range: Eastern Arizona to western Texas; north to southeastern Colorado and western Kansas; also northern Mexico.
Comments: The deep blue flower with the bright yellow center is unique. The "eye" serves to guide insects to the nectar.

### 413 Skyrocket; Scarlet Gilia; Desert Trumpets; Skunk Flower
(*Ipomopsis aggregata*)
Phlox Family (Polemoniaceae)

Description: In upper leaf axils and at tops of sparsely-leaved stems are clusters of showy, *bright red or deep pink, trumpet-shaped flowers.*
Flowers: corollas ¾–1¼″ (2–3.1 cm) long, with 5 pointed lobes.
Leaves: mostly 1–2″ (2.5–5 cm) long, densest near base, pinnately divided into narrow segments.
Height: 6–84″ (15–210 cm).
Flowering: May–September.
Habitat: Dry slopes from sagebrush to forest.
Range: Eastern Oregon to southern California; east to western Texas; north through the Rocky Mountains and the western edge of the plains to western North Dakota; also northern Mexico.
Comments: Skyrocket, one of the most common western wildflowers, grows readily from seed; its brilliant red trumpets are handsome in the native garden. Its beauty compensates for the faint skunky smell of its glandular foliage, responsible for the less complimentary name Skunk Flower. *Ipomopsis* was once considered part of *Gilia*, explaining the name Scarlet Gilia.

## 137 Ballhead Gilia
(*Ipomopsis congesta*)
Phlox Family (Polemoniaceae)

Description: Branched and woody near base, with *roundish heads of small, trumpet-shaped, dingy white flowers* at ends of stems and branches.
Flowers: about ¼" (6 mm) long; heads about ¾–1" (2–2.5 cm) wide.
Leaves: usually less than 1" (2.5 cm) long, divided into 3–5 very narrow lobes which again may be divided.
Height: 8–12" (20–30 cm).
Flowering: June–September.
Habitat: Dry open slopes from lowlands to high mountain elevations.
Range: Eastern Oregon and eastern California to northwestern New Mexico, western Nebraska, and western North Dakota.
Comments: Some forms may at first be mistaken for Sandworts (*Arenaria*), but the latter have simple leaves and 5 separate petals.

## 580 Pale Trumpets
(*Ipomopsis longiflora*)
Phlox Family (Polemoniaceae)

Description: Slender, *pale blue-violet, pale blue, or white, trumpet-shaped flowers* bloom singly or in pairs, spreading from axils of upper bracts on this spindly, openly branched, sparsely-leaved plant.
Flowers: corolla 1–1½" (2.5–3.8 cm) long, with a very narrow tube and a flared end resembling a 5-pointed star.
Leaves: near base, to 1½" (3.8 cm) long, pinnately divided into a few narrow lobes; those above, shorter and less divided.
Height: to 2' (60 cm).
Flowering: March–October.
Habitat: Sandy deserts and arid grassland.
Range: Southern Utah to western Nebraska; south to western Texas, Arizona, and northern Mexico.

Comments:    The slender, pale flowers look almost
too delicate for the intense heat of the
desert and plains, but these rather
ungainly plants are vigorous and often
grow in profusion. At night, moths
attracted to the pale flowers feed on the
nectar.

---

488    **Desert Calico**
(*Langloisia matthewsii*)
Phlox Family (Polemoniaceae)

Description:    *Small bristly tufts or mats and colorful
white to pink or lavender, bilaterally
symmetrical flowers nestled among the
leaves.*
Flowers: corolla about ½" (1.3 cm)
wide, the 3 *upper lobes marked with red
and white,* the lower 2 generally
unmarked.
Leaves: ½–1½" (1.3–3.8 cm) long,
with bristles at tips of sharp teeth.
Height: 1–2" (2.5–5 cm); 1–12" (2.5–
30 cm) wide.
Flowering:    March–June.
Habitat:    Open gravelly or sandy desert.
Range:    Southern California to northwestern
Arizona and Sonora.
Comments:    All species are tufted and rather bristly.
Schott's Calico (*L. schottii*), also
bilaterally symmetrical, has a pale
lavender corolla with purple spots, or a
purple, arch-shaped patch.

---

594    **Spotted Langloisia; Lilac Sunbonnet**
(*Langloisia punctata*)
Phlox Family (Polemoniaceae)

Description:    *Low bristly tufts with pale violet or lilac,
purple-dotted flowers* peering from among
the leaves.
Flowers: corolla about ½" (1.3 cm)
wide, the 5 lobes with *many fine purple
spots* and, near base of each, 2 yellow
dots.

Leaves: ¾–1¼″ (2–3.1 cm) long,
broadest near the top, with 3–5 bristle-
tipped teeth, the bristles on the stalk-
like base often with 2 or 3 branches.
Height: 1½–6″ (3.8–15 cm), forming
a tuft to 10″ (25 cm) wide.

Flowering: April–June.

Habitat: In dry gravelly places in deserts, among
creosotebush, and among piñon and
juniper.

Range: Southeastern California, southern
Nevada, and western Arizona.

Comments: A relative, Bristly Langloisia
(*L. punctata*), is the most widespread
and northern of the few species, has
bluish-lavender flowers commonly with
a few dark lines. It grows from eastern
Oregon and southern Idaho to northern
Sonora.

438 **Prickly Phlox**
(*Leptodactylon californicum*)
Phlox Family (Polemoniaceae)

Description: Slightly woody stems covered with
*small, prickly leaves,* form a loose clump
with *pink flowers in small clusters* near the
top.
Flowers: about 1″ (2.5 cm) wide, with a
narrow tube, and an abruptly flared top
with 5 broad, round lobes, usually
pink, but often white, cream, or lilac,
and brownish on the back.
Leaves: about ½″ (1.3 cm) long, in
clusters along the stem, palmately cleft
into 5–9 narrow, rigid, prickly lobes.
Height: 1–3′ (30–90 cm).

Flowering: March–June.

Habitat: Dry places and rocky ridges in brush.

Range: Southern California.

Comments: The genus name refers to the finger-
like division of the leaves. A more
widespread species, Granite Gilia
(*L. pungens*), from southern British
Columbia to Baja California, eastward
to New Mexico, western Nebraska, and
Montana, is 4–16″ (10–40 cm) tall.

### 31  Nuttall's Linanthastrum
(*Linanthastrum nuttallii*)
Phlox Family (Polemoniaceae)

Description:   *White or cream flowers* are clustered at the
top of many leafy stems.
Flowers: about ½″ (1.3 cm) wide, the
tube narrow, the 5 broad lobes widely
flared.
Leaves: ¾″ (2 cm) long, opposite, each
cleft into 5–9 narrow lobes, the
appearance being that of *rings of many
narrow leaves*.
Height: about 1′ (30 cm).
Flowering:   June–September.
Habitat:   Open or sparsely wooded, often rocky
slopes in the mountains.
Range:   Eastern Washington to southern
California; east to New Mexico,
Colorado, western Wyoming, and
Idaho.
Comments:   These attractive plants are sweetly
aromatic.

### 448  False Baby Stars
(*Linanthus androsaceus*)
Phlox Family (Polemoniaceae)

Description:   A *knob-like cluster of prickly leaves and
deep pink, lilac, white, or yellow, trumpet-
shaped flowers* top this small, spindly
plant.
Flowers: corolla ½–¾″ (1.3–2 cm)
wide, tube slender, with 5 lobes; calyx
with 5 needle-pointed lobes, membrane
between them short and inconspicuous.
Leaves: ½–1¼″ (1.3–3.1 cm) long,
most in the cluster at top, but several
in pairs widely spaced apart on the
slender stem; each leaf divided into 5–9
narrow, pointed lobes, the pair of leaves
seeming to form a ring of needles.
Height: 2–12″ (5–30 cm).
Flowering:   April–June.
Habitat:   Grassy slopes and open places.
Range:   Through most of California west of the
Sierra Nevada to the edge of the

southern desert.

Comments: The many *Linanthus* species are mostly slender, perky little annuals, commonly forked, with opposite, palmately divided, prickly leaves, often clustered near the top, and colorful flowers that seem almost too big for the plant. Almost 40 species occur in California alone, few elsewhere.

## 218 Desert Gold
(*Linanthus aureus*)
Phlox Family (Polemoniaceae)

Description: A tiny, spindly plant, usually with 3 branches at a fork, and *pale to deep yellow, funnel-shaped flowers* on very slender stalks.
Flowers: corolla ¼–½" (6–13 mm) wide, with 5 lobes, often purple spots in center, and a narrow tube.
Leaves: opposite, divided into 3 narrow, pointed lobes about ¼" (6 mm) long which form a ring of needles around stem.
Height: 2–4" (5–10 cm).
Flowering: April–June.
Habitat: Desert floor and sandy slopes.
Range: Southern California to southern Nevada and southwestern New Mexico; south to northern Mexico.
Comments: Northern Linanthus (*L. septentrionalis*), from Colorado to Alberta, west to the Sierra Nevada and Cascade Mountains, has a similar manner of branching but grows up to 10" (25 cm) tall and has white, pale blue, or lavender corollas only about ⅛–¼" (3–6 mm) long.

## 437 Mustang Linanthus; Mustang Clover
(*Linanthus montanus*)
Phlox Family (Polemoniaceae)

Description: Erect stems have a *dense cluster of prickly bracts* near top and long, *pink, trumpet-*

*shaped flowers* projecting from bracts.
Flowers: about ¾″ (2 cm) wide, 1–2″
(2.5–5 cm) long, paler in center, with
purple spot at base of each of 5 lobes;
outside of tube minutely glandular-
hairy.
Leaves: ¾–1¼″ (2–3.1 cm) long,
opposite, palmately divided into 5–11
lobes, each pair resembling a ring of
needles around stem.
Height: 4–24″ (10–60 cm).

Flowering: May–August.

Habitat: Dry gravelly places in open woodland.

Range: Western slope of the Sierra Nevada in
California.

Comments: The unusually long flowers of this
species make it one of the showiest of
this California-based genus.

---

### 577 Tufted Phlox
(*Phlox caespitosa*)
Phlox Family (Polemoniaceae)

Description: Low, tufted, slightly woody plant with
*prickly, needle-like leaves and pale-purple,
pink, or white flowers.*
Flowers: narrowly tubular corolla base
¼–½″ (6–13 mm) long, the flared,
5-lobed end ½–¾″ (1.3–2 cm) wide;
calyx with 5 narrow, pointed lobes
joined by a flat translucent membrane.
Leaves: ¼–½″ (6–13 mm) long, not
divided, opposite.
Height: 2–6″ (5–15 cm).

Flowering: April–June.

Habitat: Commonly in dry, open pine woods,
sometimes among sagebrush.

Range: Southern British Columbia to central
Washington, northeastern Oregon,
northern Idaho, and northwestern
Montana.

Comments: Tufted Phlox resembles small Granite
Gilia (*Leptodactylon pungens*), which has
leaves divided into needle-like
segments. Cushion Phlox (*P. pulvinata*),
from eastern Oregon to southwestern
Montana, and throughout the Rocky

Mountains to New Mexico, has been mistakenly called *P. caespitosa.* Unlike Tufted Phlox, it forms tight mats and its stems are not at all woody.

---

**538 Long-leaved Phlox**
(*Phlox longifolia*)
Phlox Family (Polemoniaceae)

Description: Slender stems often grow in dense clumps and have *bright pink, pale lilac, or chalky white flowers* in loose clusters.
Flowers: corolla about 1″ (2.5 cm) wide, with 5 round lobes and a slender tube about ½–¾″ (1.3–2 cm) long; membranes between pointed calyx lobes folded outward; style several times as long as 3 branches at tip.
Leaves: to 3″ (7.5 cm) long, very narrow, opposite.
Height: 4–16″ (10–40 cm).
Flowering: April–July.
Habitat: Dry, open rocky places from low to moderate elevations.
Range: Southern British Columbia to southern California; east to the Rocky Mountain region from New Mexico to western Montana.
Comments: Phloxes are beautiful and popular wildflowers found in nearly all western habitats. The most spectacular have densely clumped stems which, when in bloom, are completely hidden under a hemisphere of pink, white, or pale lilac.

---

**658 Western Polemonium**
(*Polemonium occidentale*)
Phlox Family (Polemoniaceae)

Description: Many *broadly funnel-shaped, sky-blue flowers* are crowded in a branched cluster near top of this leafy plant.
Flowers: corolla ½–¾″ (1.3–2 cm) wide, with 5 round lobes.

Leaves: narrow, pinnately compound, bearing 19–27 lanceolate leaflets, each ½–1½" (1.3–3.8 cm) long.

Height: 1–3' (30–90 cm).

Flowering: June–August.

Habitat: Wet places at moderate elevations.

Range: British Columbia to southern California; east to Colorado and Alberta.

Comments: The leaves resemble long overlapping ladders, giving a common name for the genus, Jacob's Ladder. Leafy Polemonium (*P. foliosissimum*), which grows from Idaho and Wyoming south to Arizona and New Mexico, is somewhat more leafy, the upper leaves not much smaller than those at the base, as in Western Polemonium.

---

645  **Sky Pilot**
(*Polemonium viscosum*)
Phlox Family (Polemoniaceae)

Description: A leafy plant with stems in clumps; has a skunk-like scent from the *sticky, glandular hairs* that cover leaves and stems; *funnel-shaped, blue-violet flowers* bloom in *loose heads* atop stem.

Flowers: corolla ½–¾" (1.3–2 cm) wide, with 5 round lobes.

Leaves: to 6" (15 cm) long, narrow, pinnately compound, each leaflet divided to its base into 3–7 tiny lobes.

Height: to 4–16" (10–40 cm).

Flowering: June–August.

Habitat: Open, rocky ridges in high mountains.

Range: Eastern Washington, northern Oregon, and central Nevada; east to the Rocky Mountain region from New Mexico to Alberta.

Comments: The name Sky Pilot comes from its preferred high habitat. Elegant Polemonium (*P. elegans*), in the high Cascade Mountains of Washington and British Columbia, has undivided leaflets.

## MILKWORT FAMILY
(Polygalaceae)

Herbs, shrubs, or small trees with oddly shaped flowers.
Flowers: bilaterally symmetrical, borne in spikes, racemes, or branched clusters; sepals usually 5, separate, the inner 2 larger and petal-like; petals 3, often fringed; stamens usually 8, united. All these parts attached at base of ovary.
Leaves: alternate, simple.
Fruit: usually 2-chambered capsule.
There are about 13 genera and 800 species occurring nearly throughout the world. A few are grown as ornamentals. The flowers are often confused with those of the Pea Family (Fabaceae).

120 **White Milkwort**
(*Polygala alba*)
Milkwort Family (Polygalaceae)

Description: *Tiny, white, bilaterally symmetrical flowers in a narrowly cone-shaped raceme* top each of numerous, slender, erect stems.
Flowers: raceme ¾–3" (2–7.5 cm) long; sepals 5, 3 small, but inner 2 white, extending to side like wings, each ⅛" (3 mm) long; petals 3, white, often greenish at base, the lowest like a keel, often tipped with purple.
Leaves: ¼–1" (6–25 mm) long, very narrow, the lowest in 1 or 2 whorls, but many also scattered on stem.
Height: 8–14" (20–35 cm).
Flowering: March–October.
Habitat: Sandy flats or rocky hills.
Range: Eastern Montana to eastern Colorado, New Mexico, and central Arizona; east to Texas; north through much of the plains to Minnesota; also Mexico.
Comments: *Polygala* comes from Greek meaning "much milk," because some species were thought to stimulate the flow of milk in cattle.

## BUCKWHEAT or KNOTWEED FAMILY (Polygonaceae)

Mostly herbs, sometimes shrubs or vines, rarely trees, with small flowers. Stems commonly have swollen nodes. Flowers: usually bisexual, radially symmetrical, in racemes, spike-like clusters, or in heads; sepals 3–6, separate, petal-like, sometimes in two series of 3 each, the outer series differing somewhat from the inner; petals absent; stamens 3–9. All these parts attached at base of ovary. Leaves: simple, usually alternate, at the base often forming a membranous sheath around the stem above the node. Fruit: small, hard, seed-like, generally 3-sided or lens-shaped.
There are about 40 genera and 800 species chiefly occurring in north temperate regions. Rhubarb and Buckwheat are sources of food, and a few species are grown as ornamentals.

---

### 148 Northern Buckwheat
(*Eriogonum compositum*)
Buckwheat Family (Polygonaceae)

Description: Matted clumps of basal leaves have *leafless stems, with roundish clusters of tiny, whitish to deep yellow flowers.*
Flowers: clusters 1–4″ (2.5–10 cm) wide; individual flowers clustered in cups with several teeth, each flower about ⅛″ (3 mm) long, tapered to a slender base about as thick as the slender stalk joined to flower; 6 petal-like lobes not hairy on outside.
Leaves: 1–10″ (2.5–25 cm) long, the stalk about as long as the heart-shaped, triangular, or ovate blade, whitish beneath, but lightly-haired on top.
Height: 4–20″ (10–50 cm).
Flowering: May–July.
Habitat: Rocky open ground from lower elevations well into the mountains.

Range: Eastern Washington to northern
California; east to Idaho.

Comments: A highly variable species in a genus of
many species, most difficult to identify.
The seeds are an important food for
small wildlife, even ants. *Eriogonum*,
from the Greek *erion* ("wool") and *gony*
("knee" or "joint"), refers to the hairy
stems of many species.

### 275 Desert Trumpet; Bladder Stem; Indianpipe Weed
(*Eriogonum inflatum*)
Buckwheat Family (Polygonaceae)

Description: A *spindly plant* with 1 or a few leafless,
erect *stems swollen just below the branches*.
Flowers: tiny, yellow flowers, on very
slender stalks, grow from woolly cups
at ends of branches; cups with 6 teeth.
Leaves: ½–2" (1.3–5 cm) long, oval,
on long stalks in a basal rosette.
Height: 8–40" (10–100 cm).

Flowering: March–July.

Habitat: Sandy or rocky ground in deserts.

Range: Southern California to southern Utah,
much of Arizona, and Baja California.

Comments: A common desert plant, conspicuous
because of the stark swollen, gray-green
stems, which have a pleasant sour taste.
Dried stems were used by Indians as
tobacco pipes.

### 415 Cushion Buckwheat
(*Eriogonum ovalifolium*)
Buckwheat Family (Polygonaceae)

Description: Matted plants, often grayish-haired,
with basal leaves and *round heads of tiny
reddish or purplish to cream flowers* on
long, erect leafless stems.
Flowers: head about 1" (2.5 cm) wide;
individual flowers on slender stalks
growing from cylindrical, 5-toothed
cups, each flower about ⅛" (3 mm)

long, with 6 petal-like segments.
Leaves: ½–5″ (1.3–12.5 cm) long,
varying from short and spatula-shaped,
without stalks, to long-stalked with
roundish blades.
Height: 1–12″ (2.5–30 cm).

Flowering: May–August.

Habitat: In open areas from sagebrush plains to
open coniferous woodland, alpine
ridges, and rocky mountain slopes.

Range: British Columbia to northern
California; east to the Rocky Mountains
from New Mexico to Alberta.

Comments: As to be expected in a widespread
species such as this, which occurs over a
broad elevational range, there is much
variation. Alpine plants are generally
dwarf; plants among sagebrush are
usually taller. Flowers vary from cream
to yellow when young; as they age,
they may become reddish or purple.

### 336  Sulphur Flower

(*Eriogonum umbellatum*)
Buckwheat Family (Polygonaceae)

Description: Leaves at base, and on long, erect stalks
bloom *tiny, yellow or cream flowers in
balls* at ends of branches of an umbel-
like cluster.
Flowers: each individual, ball-like
cluster 2–4″ (5–10 cm) wide,
composed of numerous little cups, from
which grow several flowers on very
slender stalks; flowers about ¼″ (6 mm)
long, the 6 petal-like lobes hairy on
outside; circle of bract-like leaves
immediately beneath umbel.
Leaves: ½–1½″ (1.3–3.8 cm) long,
clustered at ends of short woody
branches, on slender stalks, ovate, 2–3
times as long as wide, very hairy on
lower side.
Height: 4–12″ (10–30 cm).

Flowering: June–August.

Habitat: Dry areas from sagebrush deserts to
foothills and alpine ridges.

Range: British Columbia to southern
California; east to the eastern flank of
the Rocky Mountains from Colorado to
Montana.

Comments: Sulphur Flower, highly variable, adds
to the difficulties of identification in a
complex group of similar western
species.

---

527 **Water Smartweed; Water Lady's
Thumb**
(*Polygonum amphibium*)
Buckwheat Family (Polygonaceae)

Description: Long, prostrate *stems grow across mud, or
in water,* and end with erect, dense,
*narrowly egg-shaped pink flower clusters.*
Flowers: clusters ½–1½″ (1.3–3.8 cm)
long; each flower with 5 petal-like
segments less than ¼″ (6 mm) long.
Leaves: to 6″ (15 cm) long, narrowly
elliptic.
Height: aquatic, with floral stalks 3–6″
(7.5–15 cm) high, and stems up to 7′
(2.1 m) long.

Flowering: June–September.

Habitat: In mud or floating on still fresh water.

Range: Throughout.

Comments: The pink flower masses are very
attractive, but since the plants grow
quickly, they can become an
unwelcome weed in decorative ponds.
Their seeds provide food for water fowl.
The similar species *P. coccineum,* also
called Water Smartweed and very
common, has narrower, longer clusters
of flowers on stalks covered with
glandular hairs. Both are often
considered as variable species of
*P. coccineum.*

## 114  **Western Bistort; Smokeweed**
(*Polygonum bistortoides*)
Buckwheat Family (Polygonaceae)

Description:  At tops of slender, erect, reddish stems
bloom *dense white or pale pink flower
clusters.*
Flowers: clusters 1–2" (2.5–5 cm)
long; individual flowers less than ¼" (6
mm) long, with 5 petal-like segments.
Leaves: 4–8" (10–20 cm) long,
lanceolate, mostly near the base of the
stem; a brownish, papery sheath where
leaf joins stem.
Height: 8–28" (20–70 cm).

Flowering:  May–August.

Habitat:  Moist mountain meadows or along
mountain streams.

Range:  Western Canada southward to southern
California, Arizona, and New Mexico.

Comments:  One of the most frequent mountain
wildflowers, sometimes covering
meadows with thousands of clusters of
white flowers. The stout roots were
once prepared by Indians for food.
Young leaves may be cooked as greens.

## 374  **Winged Dock**
(*Rumex venosus*)
Buckwheat Family (Polygonaceae)

Description:  Stout, erect, leafy, reddish stems with
conspicuous white sheaths where leaves
join, have *reddish-orange flowers in thick
clusters.*
Flowers: at first inconspicuous, with 6
sepal-like segments, the inner 3 greatly
enlarging to broadly heart-shaped
bracts, each ½–1½" (1.3–3.8 cm)
long, which surround a tiny fruit.
Leaves: up to 6" (15 cm) long,
numerous, ovate or lanceolate.
Height: 6–20" (15–50 cm).

Flowering:  April–June.

Habitat:  Open banks, ravines, grassland or
sagebrush desert, often where sandy.

Range:  Southern British Columbia to

northeastern California; east to central Canada, and throughout the Great Plains.

Comments: The reddish-orange flower clusters are conspicuous in the late spring; later the broad sepals catch the wind and tumble the seed to new places. The similar Canaigre (pronounced *can-i'-gray*) or Desert Rhubarb (*R. hymenosepalus*) grows in sandy areas from Wyoming to southern California and western Texas. Its sepals are rarely more than ¾" (2 cm) wide and its stout stems grow from a cluster of thick roots. Tannin extracted from the roots was used by early Spanish settlers to tan hides. Roots were also used medicinally. An English name for many of the more weedy *Rumex* species is Sour Dock. The sour flavor comes from oxalic acid.

## PURSLANE FAMILY
### (Portulacaceae)

Herbs, often succulent, with delicate flowers.
Flowers: radially symmetrical, borne singly or in branched clusters; sepals usually 2, united or separate; petals 4–6 or more, separate or united at the base; 1 stamen opposite each petal, or stamens many. All these parts attached at base of ovary.
Leaves: simple, alternate, opposite or in a dense basal rosette.
Fruit: usually capsule, often opening at top.
There are about 19 genera and nearly 600 species occurring throughout the world, especially in the Americas. A few are grown as ornamentals and some are eaten as potherbs.

---

### 457 Red Maids
(*Calandrinia ciliata*)
Purslane Family (Portulacaceae)

Description: Small, *brilliant, bright reddish-pink, shallowly bowl-shaped flowers* bloom on short stalks growing from axils of upper leaves on this *succulent plant* with spreading or erect stems.
Flowers: about ½" (1.3 cm) wide; petals 5, sepals 2, with coarse hairs.
Leaves: ½–3" (1.3–7.5 cm) long, narrow, upper ones much smaller.
Height: 2–16" (5–40 cm).
Flowering: April–May.
Habitat: Open places where the soil is moist, at least early in the year; often with weeds.
Range: California to Washington; east to southwestern New Mexico.
Comments: This species is a member of a large genus of the western Americas and Australia named for a Swiss botanist of the 18th century, J. L. Calandrini.

### 554 Pussy Paws
(*Calyptridium umbellatum*)
Purslane Family (Portulacaceae)

Description: *Pink clusters of densely packed flowers* at
ends of ascending or prostrate stems
*resemble upturned pads of cats' feet.*
Flowers: sepals 2, pale pink, papery and
translucent, become larger, to ½" (1.3
cm) long; petals 4, quickly withering,
pinkish, ¼" (6 mm) long; stamens 3.
Leaves: ¾–3" (2–7.5 cm) long,
narrow, in a dense rosette.
Height: creeper, with branching stalks
2–10" (5–25 cm) high.

Flowering: May–August.
Habitat: Loose soil in coniferous forests.
Range: British Columbia to Baja California;
east to Utah, Wyoming, and Montana.
Comments: Stems often lie on the ground with the
relatively heavy "pussy paws" forming a
perfect ring around the leaf rosette.

### 444 Spring Beauty
(*Claytonia lanceolata*)
Purslane Family (Portulacaceae)

Description: A small, slender, delicate plant with
*1 pair of succulent leaves at midstem* and a
*loose raceme of white, pink, or rose, bowl-
shaped flowers.*
Flowers: ¼–¾" (6–20 mm) wide;
petals 5, if pale then often with darker
veins; sepals 2; stamens 5.
Leaves: ½–3½" (1.3–8.8 cm) long,
narrow, lanceolate, commonly also 1 or
2 narrow leaves near base of stem, but
often withered by time of flowering.
Height: 2–10" (5–25 cm).

Flowering: April–July.
Habitat: Moist ground, especially near
snowbanks, from foothills to high
mountains.
Range: British Columbia to southern
California; east to the Rocky Mountains
from New Mexico to Alberta.
Comments: As the name suggests, Spring Beauty

hurries to flower, barely waiting for the
snow to melt. This perennial grows
from a deeply buried spherical corm,
that is edible and, when cooked, tastes
like a potato.

---

### 547   Siskiyou Lewisia
(*Lewisia cotyledon*)
Purslane Family (Portulacaceae)

Description: From a dense basal rosette of succulent
leaves grow leafless, branched flower
stalks with flowers that have *8–10 pink,
white-and-red-striped, or deep pink petals.*
Flowers: 1–1¼" (2.5–3.1 cm) wide;
sepals 2, with glandular teeth; stamens
5–8; bracts on flower stalk.
Leaves: to 5" (12.5 cm) long, spatula-
shaped.
Height: 4–12" (10–30 cm).
Flowering: April–May.
Habitat: Rock crevices, often on cliffs.
Range: Southwestern Oregon and northern
California.
Comments: This plant forms beautiful bouquets on
precipitous cliffs, to which it clings by
a massive root tightly wedged in a tiny
cleft. Because of its precise adaptation
to its rugged habitat, it finds the
gentle environment of the garden
inhospitable, and though it may persist
for a number of years, ultimately it
perishes.

---

### 548   Bitterroot
(*Lewisia rediviva*)
Purslane Family (Portulacaceae)

Description: A low, little plant with comparatively
big, *deep pink to nearly white flowers* that
bloom on short stalks, nearly within a
*rosette of narrow succulent leaves.*
Flowers: 1½–2½" (3.8–6.3 cm) wide;
petals 12–18; sepals 6–8; stamens 30–
50; at middle of each flower stalk is a

ring of 5–8 narrow bracts.
Leaves: ½–2″ (1.3–5 cm) long.
Height: ½–2″ (1.3–5 cm).

Flowering: May–July.
Habitat: Open places among sagebrush or pines.
Range: British Columbia to southern California; east to Colorado, and Montana.
Comments: Of the several pretty species of ground-hugging Lewisias, this one is the Montana state flower and perhaps the most showy. It was first collected by Meriwether Lewis of the Lewis and Clark expedition, who is honored by the genus name.

## 21 Broad-leaved Montia
(*Montia cordifolia*)
Purslane Family (Portulacaceae)

Description: A succulent plant with most leaves at base, but *on stem is 1 pair of broadly ovate or heart-shaped leaves,* and above these *3–10 white flowers in a very open raceme* without bracts.
Flowers: about ½″ (1.3 cm) long; petals 5; sepals 2; stamens 5.
Leaves: ¾–2½″ (2–6.3 cm) wide, opposite, those at base on long stalks.
Height: 4–16″ (10–40 cm).
Flowering: May–September.
Habitat: Wet soil near springs and streams, more common in the mountains.
Range: Southern British Columbia to northern California; east to northern Utah and western Montana.
Comments: All Montia species have edible, rather pleasant-tasting leaves. The very similar Western Spring Beauty (*M. sibirica*), growing in shaded places from Alaska to southern California, east to Montana and Utah, has smaller flowers, tinged with pink, with a bract at the base of each individual flower stalk in the raceme.

## 35  Miner's Lettuce; Indian Lettuce
(*Montia perfoliata*)
Purslane Family (Portulacaceae)

Description:   The slender stems of this *succulent plant*
seem to grow through the middle of a
*single succulent, circular leaf* above which
is a *raceme of tiny, white flowers.*
Flowers: ⅛–¼" (3–6 mm) wide;
sepals 2.
Leaves: circular leaf to 2" (5 cm) wide;
several leaves at base from half to fully
the height of the flowering stems,
almost uniformly narrow, or with a
lanceolate blade and a slender stalk.
Height: 1–14" (2.5–35 cm).

Flowering:   March–July.

Habitat:   Loose, moist soil in shady places.

Range:   British Columbia to Baja California;
east to Arizona, Utah, and North and
South Dakota.

Comments:   The circular stem leaf is actually two,
paired side by side and grown together.
Sometimes they are not grown together
at all, or grown together only on one
side. As the common names indicate,
the leaves are edible.

## 201  Common Purslane; Pusley; Verdolagas
(*Portulaca oleracea*)
Purslane Family (Portulacaceae)

Description:   A *very succulent and fleshy matted weed,*
commonly with smooth, lustrous,
prostrate, bronze-green stems with
*small, yellow flowers* borne singly or in
small clusters in leaf axils or at end.
Flowers: about ¼" (6 mm) wide; petals
5; sepals 2.
Leaves: ½–1½" (1.3–3.8 cm) long,
fleshy, spatula-shaped, commonly
broadest in upper half.
Height: usually a low creeper, the
stems to 2'. (60 cm) long, sometimes
erect and to 6" (15 cm) high.

Flowering:   June–September.

Habitat: Open places, especially where the ground has been disturbed, frequent as a garden weed.

Range: Throughout.

Comments: Noted not for its beauty but for its ubiquity, it grows rapidly and produces thousands of tiny black seeds. If pulled and left as mulch, it will live on stored water and food, and, even with roots turned upward, will continue to mature seeds. Purslane was eaten in India and Persia over 2,000 years ago, and brought to the New World as a potherb and a medicinal plant. Spanish Americans now call it Verdolagas and use it with tomatoes, onions, and various seasonings. The genus name *Portulaca* may derive from *portula*, "little gate," referring to the lid on the capsule.

## 370 Flame Flower
(*Talinum aurantiacum*)
Purslane Family (Portulacaceae)

Description: Rather stout, erect stems bear *evenly distributed, narrow, succulent leaves* and *1 orange or reddish-orange flower* in each upper leaf axil.
Flowers: about 1″ (2.5 cm) wide; petals 5, broad; sepals 2, drop as flower matures; stamens 20 or more.
Leaves: ¾–2″ (2–5 cm) long, ¹⁄₁₆–⅛″ (1.5–3 mm) wide.
Height: 6–14″ (15–35 cm).

Flowering: June–October.

Habitat: Rocky slopes of desert canyons.

Range: Southern Arizona to western Texas.

Comments: Indians once cooked the fleshy roots. A very similar species, which grows in the same region, is Narrow-leaved Flame Flower (*T. angustissimum*). Its petals are paler, generally yellow-orange, its leaves less than ¹⁄₁₆″ (1.5 mm) wide.

455 **Pigmy Talinum**
(*Talinum brevifolium*)
Purslane Family (Portulacaceae)

Description: A low plant with *crowded, narrow,*
*succulent leaves* and comparatively large,
*deep pink flowers* in upper axils.
Flowers: about ¾" (2 cm) wide; petals
5, broad; sepals 2, oval; stamens
about 20.
Leaves: ⅛–½" (3–13 mm) long, almost
cylindrical.
Height: 1–3" (2.5–7.5 cm).
Flowering: May–September.
Habitat: On rocky slopes, especially limestone.
Range: Southern Utah and northern Arizona to
western Texas.
Comments: The bright deep pink flowers seem to
sit on the ground, often obscuring the
short, erect stems. This species is
representative of several others, most
more open and spindly, but all with
white to rose flowers. In one, in central
Washington, Spiny Talinum (*T.
spinescens*), the midribs persist as spines
as the leaves wither and dry.

## PRIMROSE FAMILY (Primulaceae)

Leafy herbs, usually with showy
flowers.
Flowers: radially symmetrical, borne
singly or in clusters; sepals 5, often
united at base; petals 5, united or
separate, or no petals; stamens 5,
opposite the petals or lobes of the
corolla, or alternate with sepals in
flowers lacking petals. All these parts
usually attached at base of ovary.
Leaves: opposite, whorled, or basal;
usually simple.
Fruit: 1-chambered capsule.
There are about 28 genera and 800
species with most occurring in the
north temperate zone. In the United
States the family is most diverse in the
eastern region. Primroses, Cyclamens
and several others are grown as
ornamentals.

369 Scarlet Pimpernel; Poor Man's
Weatherglass
(*Anagallis arvensis*)
Primrose Family (Primulaceae)

Description: A matted plant with *creeping 4-sided
stems,* shiny, bright green leaves, and
*small, flat, bright pinkish-orange blossoms*
on the ends of very slender stalks.
Flowers: corolla about ¼" (6 mm) wide,
with 5 round lobes attached to each
other only at base.
Leaves: to ¾" (2 cm) long, opposite or
in whorls of 3 along stem.
Fruit: capsule.
Height: creeper, with stems 4–10"
(10–25 cm) long.
Flowering: March–July.
Habitat: Open, disturbed ground at low
elevations, usually where weedy, or as a
weed on lawns and in gardens.
Range: Nearly throughout; most frequent in
California and Oregon.
Comments: The name Scarlet Pimpernel is not

entirely apt, for the flowers are pinkish-orange, and there is even a rarer blue phase. Flowers close in cloudy or humid weather, giving the name Poor Man's Weatherglass, and open again when the sun shines, probably inspiring the genus name, derived from the Greek *ana* ("again") and *agallein* ("to delight in"). However, this charming plant is poisonous.

---

### 29 Northern Fairy Candelabra
(*Androsace septentrionalis*)
Primrose Family (Primulaceae)

Description: A small plant with a *basal rosette of leaves* and several erect stalks ending in an *open umbel of small, white flowers*.
Flowers: corolla slightly more than ⅛" (3 mm) wide, with a broad tube and 5 roundish lobes; calyx lobes shorter than tubular part, broadly pointed.
Leaves: ½–1¼" (1.3–3.1 cm) long, lanceolate, sometimes with low, irregular teeth near tip.
Height: 1–10" (2.5–25 cm).
Flowering: May–August.
Habitat: Moist mountain soil.
Range: Throughout the western mountains.
Comments: These plants are often overlooked, for they are small and very slender. Their umbels of white flowers resemble miniature star bursts.

---

### 503 Alpine Shooting Star
(*Dodecatheon alpinum*)
Primrose Family (Primulaceae)

Description: At top of a smooth stalk growing from a basal rosette is an umbel of *1–9 flowers, each resembling a small rocket*.
Flowers: ¾–1" (2–2.5 cm) long; corolla with *4 narrow lobes sharply bent back* at the yellow base; dark purple stamens form nose of "rocket;" *stigma a*

*conspicuous knob at least as thick as style.*
Leaves: 1¼–4" (3.1–10 cm) long, narrow, usually less than ½" (1.3 cm) wide.
Height: 4–12" (10–30 cm).

Flowering: June–July.
Habitat: Mountain meadows and along mountain streams.
Range: Eastern Oregon to southern California; east to Arizona and Utah.
Comments: There are about 10 western species with reddish-lavender corollas, two also with a large bead at the end of the style. Tall Mountain Shooting Star (*D. jefferyi*), from Alaskan mountains to the southern Sierra Nevada of California, east to Idaho and Montana, has 4 or 5 corolla lobes, and minute glandular hairs on the leaves and flower cluster. Sticky Shooting Star (*D. redolens*), from the mountains of southern California east to Nevada and Utah, is densely covered with glandular hairs, its corolla has 5 lobes; the tubular portion covers the base of the anthers.

## 88 Northwestern Shooting Star
(*Dodecatheon dentatum*)
Primrose Family (Primulaceae)

Description: *White flowers like small darts* point in all directions from ends of branches of an umbel that grows on a stalk above a basal rosette.
Flowers: about 1" (2.5 cm) long; corolla with 5 narrow, white lobes, yellow at base above the purple ring in center; deep reddish-purple stamens form point of "dart."
Leaves: 1¼–4" (3.1–10 cm) long, on narrow stalks toothed on edges.
Height: 6–16" (15–40 cm).

Flowering: May–July.
Habitat: Moist soil near waterfalls and streams and in shady damp places.
Range: Southern British Columbia to northern

Oregon; east to northern Utah and central Idaho.

Comments: This popular and aptly named wildflower decorates many western landscapes. Only two consistently have white corollas. The other is Southwestern White Shooting Star (*D. ellisiae*), from Arizona and New Mexico.

## 504 Few-flowered Shooting Star
(*Dodecatheon pulchellum*)
Primrose Family (Primulaceae)

Description: A few *flowers like deep pink darts* point in all directions from an umbel atop a long, erect stalk growing from a basal cluster of leaves.
Flowers: ¾–1″ (2–2.5 cm) long; corolla with 4 or 5 narrow lobes sharply bent back from a yellowish ring that usually has dark purplish lines; stamens form yellowish to purplish point of "dart," the tube beneath the anthers not wrinkled, or slightly wrinkled lengthwise; stigma barely broader than stalk.
Leaves: 2–16″ (5–40 cm) long, broadly lanceolate, gradually tapered to long stalks, the margins smooth or with small teeth.
Height: 4–24″ (10–60 cm).
Flowering: April–August.
Habitat: From coastal prairies to mountain meadows and streamsides.
Range: Throughout.
Comments: This is a common species, varying in color of the tube below the anthers, presence or absence of glandular hair on foliage, and shape of leaves.

### 433 Smooth Douglasia
(*Douglasia laevigata*)
Primrose Family (Primulaceae)

Description: Stems spread on ground and form rather *extensive mats,* with 2–10 *deep reddish-pink flowers* (aging to lavender) blooming in tight umbels on short, leafless stalks.
Flowers: about ⅜" (9 mm) wide; corolla has 5 round lobes flaring from a narrow tube.
Leaves: ½–¾" (6–20 mm) long, smooth, lanceolate, gathered in dense rosettes at ends of stems.
Height: creeper, with floral stalks ¾– 2½" (2–6.3 cm) high, stems to 1' (30 cm) long.

Flowering: March–August.

Habitat: Moist coastal bluffs to rocky alpine slopes and ledges.

Range: Western Washington and northwestern Oregon.

Comments: Douglasia, named for David Douglas, an early-19th-century plant explorer of western North America, are prized rock-garden subjects, but need not be dug up, for they grow well from cuttings or seed.

### 295 Fringed Loosestrife
(*Lysimachia ciliata*)
Primrose Family (Primulaceae)

Description: A plant with stems forming open patches and *yellow flowers* growing on slender, arched stalks in the leaf axils.
Flowers: about ¾" (2 cm) wide; corolla with 5 round lobes, each generally with a tiny point at the middle of the broad end, the base granular with minute hairs.
Leaves: 1–2½" (2.5–6.3 cm) long, opposite, ovate, evenly distributed on stem, the blade and stalk fringed with stiff hairs.
Height: 1–4' (30–120 cm).

Flowering: June–August.
  Habitat: Ponds, along streams, and in wet
           meadows.
    Range: Eastern Washington to Arizona; east
           across most of the United States.
Comments: This species is distinguished by having
           5 sterile stamens, which appear as small
           points of tissue between the bases of the
           fertile stamens. Much less frequent in
           the West is Lance-leaved Loosestrife
           (*L. lanceolata*), which also has flowers
           on slender stalks in axils, but its yellow
           corollas are only about ⅝″ (1.5 cm)
           wide.

---

### 296  Bog Loosestrife
(*Lysimachia terrestris*)
Primrose Family (Primulaceae)

Description: Erect stems with opposite leaves and
             *racemes of star-like, yellow flowers.*
             Flowers: ½–¾″ (1.3–2 cm) wide, flat,
             the 5 lobes pointed, streaked with
             purplish black.
             Leaves: 2–6″ (5–15 cm) long.
             Height: 8–32″ (20–80 cm).
Flowering: June–August.
  Habitat: Swampy or boggy areas.
    Range: Western Washington.
Comments: This handsome species was introduced
             into Cranberry bogs in the Northwest
             from the East.

---

### 294  Tufted Loosestrife
(*Lysimachia thyrsiflora*)
Primrose Family (Primulaceae)

Description: Erect stems bear evenly distributed
             leaves, and *yellow flowers in dense, slender*
             *racemes in axils of leaves near midstem;*
             entire plant is finely dotted with black
             or dark purple.
             Flowers: corolla with 5 narrow lobes
             about ¼″ (6 mm) long, with narrow
             stalks leading to the united base; sepals

and petals also dotted with dark purple.
Leaves: to 6" (15 cm) long, opposite,
lanceolate
Height: 8–32" (20–80 cm).

Flowering: May–July.

Habitat: Swamps, lakes, and ditches.

Range: Northern California to northern
Colorado; north throughout much of
North America.

Comments: The tight racemes of yellow flowers
immediately distinguish this species,
the erect stamens giving a fuzzy
appearance.

---

### 544 Parry's Primrose
(*Primula parryi*)
Primrose Family (Primulaceae)

Description: Atop a rather stout, leafless flower stalk
growing from a basal rosette of rather
fleshy, oblong leaves bloom *3–12 deep
pink flowers in a loose umbel.*
Flowers: corolla ⅝–1¼" (1.5–3.1 cm)
wide, with 5 round lobes flared from a
slender tube; calyx and individual
flower stalks covered with minute
glandular hairs.
Leaves: 2–12" (5–30 cm) long.
Height: 3–16" (7.5–40 cm).

Flowering: June–August.

Habitat: Wet ground, often along streams, at
high elevations.

Range: Idaho and Montana to Nevada,
northern Arizona, and northern New
Mexico.

Comments: In spite of the plant's carrion odor, its
brilliant color makes it a favorite with
mountain hikers.

---

### 543 Sierra Primrose
(*Primula suffrutescens*)
Primrose Family (Primulaceae)

Description: Atop leafless stalks growing above
mats of basal leaf rosettes are *2–9*

*reddish-lavender flowers in umbels.*
Flowers: corollas about ¾" (2 cm) wide,
the 5 lobes, each notched at end, flare
abruptly from a narrow tube whose
opening is circled with yellow.
Leaves: ¾–1¼" (2–3.1 cm) long,
thick, wedge-shaped, the ends with
even teeth (as if cut by pinking shears),
all clustered in rosettes at ends of
creeping, woody branches.
Height: creeper, with flower stalks
3–6" (7.5–15 cm) high.

Flowering: July–August.
Habitat: Rocky areas at high elevations.
Range: Mountains of northern California; south
through the Sierra Nevada.
Comments: Although this plant is extremely small,
and often escapes attention, it is one of
the most handsome native species.

---

449  **Western Starflower; Indian Potato**
(*Trientalis latifolia*)
Primrose Family (Primulaceae)

Description: A delicate stem has a *whorl of 3–8 ovate
leaves* at top, in the center of which
blooms 1 or several *pink, star-shaped
flowers,* each on its own thread-like
stalk.
Flowers: corolla about ½" (1.3 cm)
wide, with 5–9 pointed lobes.
Leaves: 1¼–4" (3.1–10 cm) long.
Height: 4–10" (10–25 cm).

Flowering: April–June.
Habitat: Open woods and prairies.
Range: British Columbia; south through the
northern two-thirds of California; east
to northern Idaho.
Comments: The name Indian Potato refers to the
small underground swelling at the base
of the stem; modern references do not
mention edibility, so caution is
advised. Northern Starflower
(*T. arctica*), which grows in wet places
from Alaska to Oregon, has white
flowers; leaves are widest beyond
middle.

## WINTERGREEN FAMILY
### (Pyrolaceae)

Perennial herbs with or without leaves.
Flowers: radially symmetrical, borne
singly, in racemes, or in a branched
cluster; sepals 4 or 5, separate or
slightly united; petals 4 or 5, separate;
stamens usually 10, the anthers
opening by terminal pores. All parts
attached at base of ovary.
Leaves: alternate or nearly whorled,
simple, often dish-shaped.
Fruit: 4 or 5-chambered capsule, more
or less spherical.
There are 4 genera and about 40
species, most of north temperate
regions.

---

403 **Candystick; Sugarstick**
(*Allotropa virgata*)
Wintergreen Family (Pyrolaceae)

Description: Lustrous, erect, *leafless, scaly stems
resembling peppermint sticks* have red
flowers hanging in a raceme along top.
Flowers: 5 white or reddish petal-like
segments about ¼" (6 mm) long form
an inverted bowl.
Leaves: represented by scales.
Height: 4–12" (10–30 cm).
Flowering: May–August.
Habitat: Coniferous forests.
Range: British Columbia to the southern Sierra
Nevada in California.
Comments: Lacking chlorophyll, these plants
absorb nutrients from the rich, thick
duff.

---

445 **Little Pipsissewa**
(*Chimaphila menziesii*)
Wintergreen Family (Pyrolaceae)

Description: 1–3 shallowly *bowl-shaped, pink or
pinkish-green flowers* hang at ends of

branches above leathery, dark-green leaves, atop this low plant.

Flowers: about ½″ (1.3 cm) wide; petals 5, roundish; stamens 10, the bases of the stalks swollen and hairy.

Leaves: ¾–2½″ (2–6.3 cm) long, lanceolate, commonly with small sharp teeth on edges.

Height: 2–6″ (5–15 cm).

Flowering: June–August.

Habitat: Coniferous woods.

Range: British Columbia to southern California.

Comments: The genus name, from the Greek *cheima* ("winter") and *philos* ("loving"), refers to the evergreen nature of the plant. The common name Pipsissewa is believed to be derived from the Cree Indian word *pipisisikweu,* meaning "it breaks it into small pieces;" the plant was once used in preparations for breaking up kidney stones or gallstones. The similar Prince's Pine or Common Pipsissewa (*C. umbellata*), common throughout, usually has more than 3 flowers and the swollen bases of its stamens have a few stiff hairs. Spotted Wintergreen (*C. maculata*), in Arizona, Mexico, and the eastern United States, has whitish mottling along the leaf veins.

## 20 Wood Nymph; Single Delight; Waxflower
(*Moneses uniflora*)
Wintergreen Family (Pyrolaceae)

Description: A little plant with *1 white or pale pink, saucer-shaped flower nodding* from the top.

Flowers: ¾″ (2 cm) wide; petals 5, roundish; stamens 10, with swollen bases; greenish ovary with 5 lobes.

Leaves: ½–1″ (1.3–2.5 cm) long, opposite or in whorls of 3 or 4 toward base of stem, nearly round with tiny round teeth above middle.

Height: 2–6″ (5–15 cm).

Flowering: May–August.
Habitat: Coniferous forests.
Range: Alaska to eastern Washington and Oregon; east to the Rocky Mountain region and to the Black Hills; thence south to New Mexico.
Comments: *Moneses,* from the Greek words *monos* ("single") and *hesis* ("delight"), refers to the single pretty flower.

## 92 Indian Pipe
(*Monotropa uniflora*)
Wintergreen Family (Pyrolaceae)

Description: *Waxy white plant* that blackens with age; the several clustered stems are bent like a shepherd's hook at top.
Flowers: about ¾" (2 cm) long; 1 hanging at end of each stem like a narrow bell; petals 5 (4–6), separate; stamens 10.
Leaves: scales pressed against stem.
Height: 2–10" (5–25 cm).
Flowering: June–August.
Habitat: Deep shaded woods.
Range: Northwestern California to Alaska; east across the northern part of the West.
Comments: These plants were once believed to absorb all nutrients from the duff, but it is now known that they are associated with a fungus, which obtains nutrients directly from the roots of green plants. Indian Pipe, therefore, is more of a parasite, with the fungus as a "bridge" between it and its host.

## 392 Pinedrops; Albany Beechdrops
(*Pterospora andromedea*)
Wintergreen Family (Pyrolaceae)

Description: The stiffly erect, leafless stems of this *reddish-brown plant* often grow in clusters, and are covered with glandular hairs. *Pale yellowish-brown egg-shaped flowers* hang in a long raceme.

Flowers: corolla about ¼" (6 mm) long, with 5 tiny lobes around opening.
Leaves: represented by scales.
Height: 1–3' (30–90 cm).

Flowering: June–August.
Habitat: Deep humus of coniferous forests, in the West especially common under ponderosa pine.
Range: Throughout.
Comments: Stems grow for only one year, but remain as dried stalks for several years. The genus name, from Greek words for "winged seeds," refers to the net-like wing at one end of each minute seed that carries it to a new site as it is sprinkled from the capsule.

### 528   Bog Wintergreen
(*Pyrola asarifolia*)
Wintergreen Family (Pyrolaceae)

Description: A little woodland plant with *shiny, leathery leaves* near base and *5–25 pink to reddish-pink flowers hanging in racemes* at top.
Flowers: corolla about ½" (1.3 cm) wide; petals 5, roundish, forming a bowl; style curved outward.
Leaves: to 3" (7.5 cm) long, broadly elliptic or heart-shaped, on long stalks.
Height: 6–16" (15–40 cm).
Flowering: June–September.
Habitat: Moist ground, generally in woods.
Range: Throughout.
Comments: *Pyrola* species are common woodland wildflowers. Sometimes they are leafless, in which case they are saprophytes, absorbing their nutrients from the rich soil humus. All such, regardless of their biological species, have been classified as Leafless Pyrola (*P. aphylla*). Leafless phases with pink flowers are probably Bog Wintergreen (*P. asarifolia*).

**8, 105   One-sided Wintergreen; Side-Bells**
(*Pyrola secunda*)
Wintergreen Family (Pyrolaceae)

Description: This plant forms low patches of shiny,
bright green leaves, above which grow
*racemes of 6–20 whitish-green or white*
*flowers all turned to one side.*
Flowers: corolla ¼" (6 mm) long; petals
5, white; stamens 10.
Leaves: ½–2½" (1.3–6.3 cm) long,
ovate, with minutely scalloped or
toothed edges.
Height: 2–8" (5–20 cm).
Flowering: June–August.
Habitat: Moist coniferous woods.
Range: Throughout.
Comments: *Pyrola,* from the Latin *pyrus* ("pear
tree"), refers to the leaves of some
species that resemble those of pears.
Leaves remain green throughout the
winter, giving the common name.
There are several other, very similar
species in the West.

**404   Snow Plant**
(*Sarcodes sanguinea*)
Wintergreen Family (Pyrolaceae)

Description: An unusual plant that is stout, fleshy,
*entirely bright red,* with bracts
overlapping on lower stem, and curled
among racemes of flowers above.
Flowers: corolla bell-shaped, ½–¾"
(1.3–2 cm) long, with 5 round lobes.
Leaves: represented by scales.
Height: 8–24" (20–60 cm).
Flowering: April–July.
Habitat: Coniferous woods.
Range: Southern Oregon to southern
California.
Comments: Once seen, never forgotten; the
brilliant red is startling in the filtered
sunlight against a dark background of
forest duff. Plants poke through the
forest floor as snow recedes, drawing
their nutrients from the rich humus.

## BUTTERCUP FAMILY
(Ranunculaceae)

Usually leafy herbs, sometimes woody vines or shrublike.
Flowers: usually bisexual, radially or bilaterally symmetrical, borne singly, in racemes, or in branched clusters; sepals and petals variable in number, separate, often all petal-like; stamens usually many; pistils vary in number from 1 to many.
Leaves: alternate, rarely opposite, commonly palmately lobed or divided.
Fruit: pod, seed-like, or berry.
The family has 35–70 genera and about 2,000 species that occur mostly in cool regions of the Northern Hemisphere. Several are grown as ornamentals, others provide drugs, and some are poisonous. The family is most likely to be confused with the Rose Family (Rosaceae), from which it is distinguished by the absence of a cup-like base.

---

**635 Western Monkshood; Aconite**
(*Aconitum columbianum*)
Buttercup Family (Ranunculaceae)

Description: A usually tall, leafy plant with *bilaterally symmetrical, hood-like, blue or blue-violet flowers in a showy raceme.*
Flowers: sepals 5, resembling petals, the uppermost forming a large arched hood ⅝–1¼" (1.5–3.1 cm) long, the 2 at sides broadly oval, the 2 lowermost narrow; petals 2, concealed under hood, with 3 others that generally do not develop.
Leaves: 2–8" (5–20 cm) wide, palmately lobed and jaggedly toothed.
Height: 1–7' (30–210 cm).

Flowering: June–August.
Habitat: Moist woods and subalpine meadows.
Range: Alaska to the Sierra Nevada of California; east to New Mexico,

Colorado, South Dakota, and western Montana.

Comments: Some species have been a source of drugs, and most are poisonous to humans and livestock. A European species of Monkshood (*A. napellus,*) is the celebrated "wolfbane" of werewolf lore.

108, 427 **Baneberry**
(*Actaea rubra*)
Buttercup Family (Ranunculaceae)

Description: Usually branched, with *racemes of many small, white flowers* in leaf axils or at end of stem.
Flowers: sepals 3–5, quickly drop as flower opens; petals 4 or 5, spatula-shaped, ⅛" (3 mm) long, also drop; stamens many.
Leaves: few, very large, pinnately and repeatedly divided into sharply toothed leaflets, each ¾–3½" (2–8.8 cm) long.
Fruit: glistening red (or pearly white) berry ¼–½" (6–13 mm) wide.
Height: 1–3' (30–90 cm).
Flowering: May–July.
Habitat: Moist woods and along stream banks.
Range: Throughout.
Comments: The attractive berries are poisonous, but are not reported to have caused death to humans or livestock in the United States. European species have fatally poisoned children.

58 **Western Pasque Flower; Mountain Pasque Flower**
(*Anemone occidentalis*)
Buttercup Family (Ranunculaceae)

Description: A hairy plant with finely divided leaves and several stems that have *1 white or cream flower at tip.*
Flowers: 1¼–2" (3.1–5 cm) wide;

sepals 5–8, hairy on back, resembling petals; petals absent; stamens many.

Leaves: at base and 3 in a whorl on the stems beneath flower, 1½–3″ (3.8–7.5 cm) wide, divided into narrow, crowded segments.

Fruit: seed-like base has a hairy style that becomes a silvery plume to 1½″ (3.8 cm) long.

Height: 8–24″ (20–60 cm).

Flowering: May–September.

Habitat: Mountain slopes and meadows.

Range: British Columbia to the Sierra Nevada of California; east to northeastern Oregon and western Montana.

Comments: The common name Pasque refers to the Easter or Passover blooming time of other species, and to the purity of the white sepals.

### 593  Blue Anemone
(*Anemone oregana*)
Buttercup Family (Ranunculaceae)

Description: Forms open patches and has an erect stem with *1 usually bluish-lavender flower.*

Flowers: 1–1½″ (2.5–3.8 cm) wide; sepals 5–8, long, generally bluish-lavender, but varying to reddish-lavender or pale pink (rarely white), resembling petals; no true petals; stamens 35–100.

Leaves: 1 at base and 3 in a whorl on stem, divided into 3 leaflets to 3″ (7.5 cm) long, each often deeply divided and toothed.

Height: 4–12″ (10–30 cm).

Flowering: March–June.

Habitat: Open woods and brushy hillsides.

Range: Northern Washington to central Oregon.

Comments: This plant spreads by stout underground stems. It intergrades with the white-flowered Western Wood Anemone (*A. lyallii*).

### 591 Pasque Flower; Wild Crocus; Lion's Beard
(*Anemone patens*)
Buttercup Family (Ranunculaceae)

Description: A hairy plant with 1 to many stems, each bearing at tip *1 lavender, purple, or blue, deeply cup-shaped flower.*
Flowers: about 1½–2″ (3.8–5 cm) wide; sepals 5–7, resembling petals, hairy on back; petals absent; stamens many, yellow.
Leaves: at base and 3 in a whorl on stem below flower, 1½–4″ (3.8–10 cm) wide, repeatedly divided into narrow lobes.
Fruit: seed-like base has a hairy style that in fruit becomes a silky plume ¾–1¼″ (2–3.1 cm) long.
Height: to 14″ (35 cm).

Flowering: May–August.
Habitat: Well-drained soil from prairies to mountain slopes.
Range: Alaska to central Washington and Montana; south, east of the Rocky Mountain region, to Texas; east across the northern plains to Illinois.
Comments: South Dakota's state flower. Other common names are Prairie Anemone, Blue Tulip, Wild Crocus, and American Pulsatilla, with "Crocus" and "Tulip" referring to the shape of the flower. On some plants the sepals may be white, and such plants are most easily distinguished from Western Pasque Flower (*A. occidentalis*) by their longer, less crowded leaf segments.

### 71 Desert Anemone
(*Anemone tuberosa*)
Buttercup Family (Ranunculaceae)

Description: This plant has several stems in a cluster, and *1 pinkish-purple or white flower* at end of each erect branch.
Flowers: 1–1½″ (2.5–3.8 cm) wide; sepals 5–8, generally darker and hairy

on back, resembling petals; petals
absent; stamens many.
Leaves: at base and in a whorl of 3
about midway on stem, 1¼–2″ (3.1–
5 cm) wide, repeatedly divided into
narrow short sections.
Fruit: many individual pistils, each
woolly, all maturing into a round head.
Height: 4–16″ (10–40 cm).
Flowering: March–April.
Habitat: Among rocks on desert slopes.
Range: Southeastern California to southern
Utah and southern New Mexico.
Comments: These Anemones differ from Pasque
flowers by the absence of hairs on the
style. There are several similar species
in the western mountains.

### 289 Golden Columbine
(*Aquilegia chrysantha*)
Buttercup Family (Ranunculaceae)

Description: Several stems and highly divided leaves
form a bushy plant with handsome
*bright yellow flowers that face upward* on
long stalks.
Flowers: 1½–3″ (3.8–7.5 cm) wide;
sepals 5, long, spreading, lanceolate,
petal-like; petals 5, scoop-shaped, with
backward-projecting spurs 1½–3″
(3.8–7.5 cm) long; stamens many and
styles 5, protruding from center of
flower.
Leaves: large, repeatedly divided,
leaflets to 1½″ (3.8 cm) long, about as
wide, deeply cleft and lobed on ends.
Height: 1–4′ (30–120 cm).
Flowering: July–August.
Habitat: Moist places in sheltered spots.
Range: Arizona to southern Colorado, western
Texas, and northern Mexico.
Comments: Columbine comes from *columbinus,* in
Latin "dove," referring to the flower's
resemblance to a cluster of 5 doves. The
spurs represent the birds' heads and
shoulders, the spreading sepals, the
wings, the blade of the petal each bird's

body. The genus name, from the Latin *aquila* ("eagle"), alludes to the petals, which resemble the eagle's talons. There are several yellow-flowered species in the West, some rare and now considered "endangered." Yellow Columbine (*A. flavescens*), a mountain species growing from southern British Columbia to northern Oregon, east to Colorado, western Wyoming, and Alberta, has bent tips on the spurs, which form hooks.

### 605 Blue Columbine
(*Aquilegia coerulea*)
Buttercup Family (Ranunculaceae)

Description: Several stems and many divided leaves form bushy plants with beautiful *white and blue flowers that tip upward* at ends of stems.
Flowers: 2–3" (5–7.5 cm) wide; sepals 5, spreading, lanceolate, petal-like, pale to sky blue; petals 5, shaped like sugar scoops, generally paler than sepals or even white, extending into backward-projecting spurs 1¼–2" (3.1–5 cm) long; stamens many and styles 5, protruding from center of flower.
Leaves: repeatedly divided into leaflets ½–1¼" (1.3–3.1 cm) long, about as wide, deeply cleft and lobed.
Height: to 3' (90 cm).
Flowering: June–August.
Habitat: Mountains, commonly in aspen groves.
Range: Western Montana to northern Arizona and northern New Mexico.
Comments: Colorado's state flower. Popular in cultivation, with several color phases and "doubled" flowers. Hybridization with other species has produced further cultivated variants. Phases in the wild with pale or white sepals are frequent. A species with blue sepals and white petal tips, but only 2–8" (5–20 cm) tall, is Alpine Blue Columbine

(*A. saximontana*), whose blue spurs are
hooked at the tip; it grows high in the
Colorado mountains.

---

400   **Crimson Columbine; Red**
      **Columbine; Sitka Columbine**
      (*Aquilegia formosa*)
      Buttercup Family (Ranunculaceae)

Description:   Handsome *red and yellow flowers* hang at
ends of branches above this bushy plant
with several stems and many divided
leaves.
Flowers: about 2″ (5 cm) wide; sepals 5,
petal-like, red, lanceolate, spreading;
petals 5, yellow, shaped like sugar scoops,
extending into backward-projecting
spurs; stamens many, yellow, and styles
5, protruding from center of flower.
Leaves: repeatedly divided into leaflets
¾–1½″ (2–3.8 cm) long, about as
wide, each lobed and cleft across ends.
Height: 6–36″ (15–90 cm).

Flowering:   May–August.
Habitat:   Open woods, on banks, near seeps.
Range:   Southern Alaska to Baja California; east
to western Montana and Utah.
Comments:   The species name *formosa*, Latin for
"beautiful," aptly describes this large
plant, especially when it has hundreds
of lovely flowers nodding over it. There
are other species with mostly red
flowers, which also attract
hummingbirds as pollinators.

---

604   **Limestone Columbine**
      (*Aquilegia jonesii*)
      Buttercup Family (Ranunculaceae)

Description:   *Deep blue or blue-violet flowers tip upward,*
held barely above the low, densely
tufted, divided leaves.
Flowers: 1½–2″ (3.8–5 cm) wide;
sepals 5, sometimes darker than the 5

petals, which have slender, straight
spurs ¼–⅝" (6–15 mm) long.
Leaves: leaflets crowded, leathery,
forming compact blades about ½" (1.3
cm) wide, barely longer.
Height: 2–5" (5–12.5 cm).

Flowering: June–August.
Habitat: Rocky slopes or in crevices in rock high
in the mountains, on limestone.
Range: Southern Alberta to northwestern
Wyoming.
Comments: As is characteristic of plants from
limestone, it does not transplant
successfully. It is also rare; if fortunate
enough to find it, leave it for others to
enjoy.

## 80 Coville's Columbine
(*Aquilegia pubescens*)
Buttercup Family (Ranunculaceae)

Description: A tufted plant with highly divided
leaves; *large cream flowers, tipped upward,
tinted with pastel blue, pink, or yellow.*
Flowers: about 1½" (3.8 cm) wide;
sepals 5, broadly lanceolate, spreading;
petals 5, shaped like sugar scoops,
extending into backward-projecting
spurs 1–1½" (2.5–3.8 cm) long; many
stamens and 5 styles protrude from
center of flower.
Leaves: repeatedly divided into leaflets
½–1¼" (1.3–3.1 cm) wide, about as
long, deeply cleft and scalloped.
Height: 8–14" (20–35 cm).

Flowering: June–August.
Habitat: Rocky places high in the mountains.
Range: Southern Sierra Nevada of
California.
Comments: The pale flowers and long, straight,
nectar-filled spurs attract moths as
pollinators. Where this species and
Crimson Columbine (*A. formosa*) grow
in the same region, cross-pollination
between the two species may result in
hybrid plants.

## 59 Marsh Marigold; Elk's Lip
(*Caltha leptosepala*)
Buttercup Family (Ranunculaceae)

Description:   There are several leaves at the base of
each erect, leafless flowering stem, with
usually only *1 white, bowl-shaped flower
at tip.*
Flowers: ½–1½" (1.3–3.1 cm) wide;
petal-like sepals 5–12; petals absent;
stamens many, pistils several.
Leaves: to 3" (7.5 cm) long, oblong,
with minutely scalloped edges, on
stalks either shorter than blade or much
longer.
Height: 1–8" (2.5–20 cm).

Flowering:   May–August.

Habitat:   Wet places high in the mountains.

Range:   Idaho and Montana to northern Arizona
and northern New Mexico.

Comments:   Marsh Marigolds bloom very close to
receding snowbanks. The name Elk's
Lip refers to the shape of the long leaf
of this species. Twin-flowered Marsh
Marigold (*C. biflora*), from Alaska to
California, east to Colorado, is very
similar but has leaves about as wide as
long and nearly always 2 flowers on
each stem.

## 662 Columbia Virgin's Bower; Bell Rue
(*Clematis columbiana*)
Buttercup Family (Ranunculaceae)

Description:   A vine, creeping on ground or climbing
over other vegetation, with *1 pale purple
to blue-violet, bell-shaped flower* at end of
each leafless stalk growing from leaf
axil.
Flowers: sepals 4, lanceolate, petal-like,
1¼–2½" (3.1–6.3 cm) long; no petals;
many yellow stamens inside "bell."
Leaves: opposite, each with 3 broadly
lanceolate, toothed or deeply lobed
leaflets, each 1–2½" (2.5–6.3 cm)
long.
Fruit: silvery plumes to 2½" (6.3 cm)

long, forming a feathery sphere.

Height: vine, to 10' (3 m) long.

Flowering: May–July.

Habitat: Wooded or brushy areas in the mountains, often on steep rocky slopes.

Range: British Columbia to northeastern Oregon; east to Montana and Wyoming.

Comments: As pretty in fruit as in flower. Rocky Mountain Clematis (*C. pseudoalpina*), from Montana to New Mexico and northeastern Arizona, is similar, but each of the 3 leaflets is divided into 3 smaller, jaggedly toothed leaflets. Matted Purple Virgin's Bower (*C. tenuiloba*), in Montana, Wyoming, and western South Dakota, has similar flowers, but plants form low mats rather than vines and the leaves are even more finely divided.

---

381, 508 **Vase Flower; Sugar Bowls; Leather Flower**
(*Clematis hirsutissima*)
Buttercup Family (Ranunculaceae)

Description: A hairy plant generally with several stems in a dense clump, and at the end of each stem a *purplish-brown, dull reddish-lavender, or dull violet flower hanging like a small, inverted urn.*
Flowers: about 1" (2.5 cm) long; sepals 4, leathery, lanceolate, petal-like, hairy on outside, joined at base, their tips flared outward; petals absent; stamens many inside "urn."
Leaves: up to 5" (12.5 cm) long, opposite, finely divided, carrot-like.
Fruit: styles form plumes 1–2" (2.5–5 cm) long above the seed-like base, all together forming a shaggy, silvery cluster.
Height: 8–24" (20–60 cm).

Flowering: April–July.

Habitat: Grassland, among sagebrush, and in open pine forests.

Range: British Columbia to eastern

Washington; east to Montana and
Wyoming; south to northern Arizona
and New Mexico.

Comments:   Unlike most other *Clematis* species, it is
not a vine. Another common name for
this species, Lion's Beard, refers to the
shaggy fruit head.

---

172   **White Virgin's Bower; Pipestems;**
**Traveler's Joy**
(*Clematis liguisticifolia*)
Buttercup Family (Ranunculaceae)

Description:   A *woody vine* which clambers over other
vegetation and, when in bloom, is
covered with *hundreds of cream flowers*.
Flowers: about ¾" (2 cm) wide;
generally 5 petal-like sepals; petals
absent; some plants have flowers with
stamens only; others, flowers with
ovaries only.
Leaves: opposite, pinnately compound,
with 5–7 broadly lanceolate, toothed
leaflets, each to 3" (7.5 cm) long.
Fruit: styles form silvery plumes 1–2"
(2.5–5 cm) long above the seed-like
base; the many styles on each flower
form a feathery ball.
Height: vine, to 10' (3 m) long.

Flowering:   May–September.

Habitat:   Along creek or gully bottoms from
deserts to pine forests.

Range:   Throughout.

Comments:   The stems and leaves of this plant have
an acrid, peppery taste, giving the old
common name, Pepper Vine, and were
chewed by Indians as a remedy for colds
and sore throats. It is said that the
crushed roots were placed in the nostrils
of tired horses to revive them. Caution
is advised: the genus is known to have
poisonous species.

### 634 Nuttall's Larkspur
(*Delphinium nuttallianum*)
Buttercup Family (Ranunculaceae)

Description: Generally only 1 stem with a few
leaves, mostly at base, and *blue or blue-
violet bilateral flowers* in one or several
open racemes.
Flowers: about 1" (2.5 cm) wide; sepals
5, blue, with ovate blades, the
uppermost also bearing a backward-
projecting spur ½–1" (1.3–2.5 cm)
long; petals 4, blue or white with blue
marks, about ³⁄₁₆" (5 mm) long, deeply
notched on lower edge, upper petals
white or bluish, angling upward from
center of flower.
Leaves: to 3" (7.5 cm) wide, nearly
round, palmately divided into narrow,
forked lobes.
Height: 4–16" (10–40 cm).
Flowering: March–July.
Habitat: Well-drained soil in sagebrush deserts
and open pine forests.
Range: British Columbia to northern
California; east to Colorado, Nebraska,
Wyoming, and Montana.
Comments: Representative of a host of low Larkspur
species with blue or blue-violet flowers
occurring in many habitats, from dry
California grasslands and chaparral to
southwestern deserts and high
mountaintops. They are difficult to
distinguish, and in the West are second
only to Locoweeds (*Astragalus* and
*Oxytropis*) as a livestock poison,
especially among cattle.

### 632 Parry's Larkspur; Parry's Delphinium
(*Delphinium parryi*)
Buttercup Family (Ranunculaceae)

Description: Stiffly erect, hairy stems bear *deeply
palmately divided leaves* and end in a
dense, *spike-like raceme of bright blue
bilateral flowers*.

Flowers: about 1″ (2.5 cm) wide; sepals 5, petal-like, about ½″ (1.3 cm) long, cupped forward, the upper sepal extending into a backward-projecting spur about ½″ (1.3 cm) long; petals 4, center of flower has whitish hairs.
Leaves: those at midstem 2–3″ (5–7.5 cm) wide, about as long, divided into very narrow, lobed segments; leaves at base usually withered before plant flowers.
Height: 1–3′ (30–90 cm).

Flowering: April–May.
Habitat: Grassy slopes in chaparral, pine forests, and bluffs near the coast.
Range: Southern California to Baja California.
Comments: This is a common, but variable, Larkspur frequenting grassy areas, recognized by its very narrow leaf divisions.

---

### 633  Poison Delphinium
(*Delphinium trolliifolium*)
Buttercup Family (Ranunculaceae)

Description: The stout, hollow, leafy, generally tall stems of this stately plant have *bilaterally symmetrical deep blue flowers in long, loose racemes,* the upper stem and individual flower stalks commonly covered with minute, yellowish hairs.
Flowers: 1–1½″ (2.5–3.8 cm) wide; sepals 5, broadly lanceolate, blue, the uppermost bearing a backward-projecting spur about ¾″ (2 cm) long; petals 4, the broad lower pair blue, notched on the lower edge, the 2 smaller upper ones white.
Leaves: 4–8″ (10–20 cm) wide, nearly round, divided into 3 or 5 main lobes, deeply cut and toothed.
Height: 2–6′ (60–180 cm).

Flowering: April–June.
Habitat: Moist shady woods and wet banks.
Range: Southern Washington to northern California.
Comments: A common Delphinium in the wet

parts of the Northwest and one of the most handsome native species. Gardeners generally call tall perennial species "Delphinium" and smaller annual species "Larkspur." Cattlemen, who despise them because of their toxicity, call all species "Larkspur," and botanists usually call all "Delphinium."

## 126 Plains Larkspur; White Larkspur
(*Delphinium virescens*)
Buttercup Family (Ranunculaceae)

Description: Stiffly erect, felt-covered stems have *palmately divided leaves*, and at the top a *spike-like raceme of white or very pale blue bilaterally symmetrical flowers.*
Flowers: about 1″ (2.5 cm) wide; sepals 5, petal-like, crinkled, the upper with a backward-projecting spur about ½″ (1.3 cm) long; petals 4, in center.
Leaves: about 3″ (7.5 cm) wide, about as long, the main leaf divisions again divided into very narrow segments.
Height: to about 5′ (1.5 m).

Flowering: May–July.

Habitat: Open hills, prairies, and fields.

Range: Northeastern Colorado to southeastern Arizona; east to eastern Texas, Iowa, and Minnesota.

Comments: Although most blue species occasionally have white-flowered variants, a few species are consistently white or very pale. They are: Alkali Larkspur (*D. gypsophilum*), from the San Joaquin Valley and southern Coast Ranges of California; Peacock Larkspur (*D. pavonaceum*), with brightly glandular-hairy petals, from western Oregon; and Pale Larkspur (*D. leucophaeum*), without glandular petals, from the vicinity of Portland, Oregon.

### 44  Water Buttercup; Water Crowfoot
*(Ranunculus aquatilis)*
Buttercup Family (Ranunculaceae)

Description: Stems float under and upon the surface
of water, generally forming fairly dense
beds, the *white flowers held by stalks*
*slightly above water.*
Flowers: ½–¾″ (1.3–2 cm) wide;
petals 5, white, may be yellow at base.
Leaves: underwater leaves droop when
stems are lifted from water, the blades
about 1″ (2.5 cm) long on stalks ½–¾″
(1.3–2 cm) long, and *finely divided into*
*forked, hair-like segments;* leaves that float
on surface of water are less divided.
Height: aquatic, with flowers held
about 1″ (2.5 cm) above water surface;
stems to 3′ (90 cm) long.
Flowering: May–August.
Habitat: Ponds and slow streams.
Range: Much of North America and Europe.
Comments: The genus name, from the Latin *rana*
("frog"), refers to the wet habitat of
some species.

### 200  Subalpine Buttercup
*(Ranunculus eschscholtzii)*
Buttercup Family (Ranunculaceae)

Description: *5 shiny, brilliant yellow petals* are part of
flowers that are sometimes so numerous
as nearly to hide the foliage of this low
plant.
Flowers: ¾–1½″ (2–3.8 cm) wide;
sepals drop as flower opens.
Leaves: ¼–1¼″ (6–31 mm) long,
roundish to ovate, varying from having
3 shallow lobes to being highly divided
into narrow segments.
Height: 2–10″ (5–25 cm).
Flowering: June–August.
Habitat: High in mountain meadows and on
rocky slopes.
Range: Alaska to southern California; east to
Alberta; throughout the Rocky
Mountains to northern New Mexico.

Comments: Subalpine Buttercup has the largest
flowers of North American species.
There are many Buttercups, most with
shiny yellow petals, and most difficult
to identify. Yellow Marsh Marigold
(*Caltha asarifolia*), from coastal bogs in
Oregon to Alaska, resembles a
Buttercup but lacks green sepals.

## 199 Sagebrush Buttercup
(*Ranunculus glaberrimus*)
Buttercup Family (Ranunculaceae)

Description: A *small fleshy plant* with most of the
leaves at the base and *shiny yellow
flowers.*
Flowers: ¾–1¼" (2–3.1 cm) wide;
sepals 5, purplish-tinged; petals 5–8,
yellow; stamens and pistils many.
Leaves: ½–2" (1.3–5 cm) long, rather
fleshy, blades varying from elliptic to
nearly round, often with 3 lobes at end.
Fruit: seed-like, about half as thick as
broad, in oval heads.
Height: 2–8" (5–20 cm).
Flowering: March–June.
Habitat: Mostly among sagebrush and in open
pine woods.
Range: British Columbia to northern
California; east to New Mexico,
Nebraska, and North Dakota.
Comments: Among the first wildflowers to bloom
in the spring. The very smooth, rather
fleshy leaves are characteristic. Most
Buttercups are to some degree
poisonous, but the toxin is unstable and
is rendered harmless by drying or
boiling the leaves.

## 384 Meadow Rue
(*Thalictrum occidentale*)
Buttercup Family (Ranunculaceae)

Description: The branched stems bear *highly divided,
soft, thin leaves;* flowers in open,

branched clusters with stamens and pistils on separate plants.

Flowers: about ⅜″ (9 mm) wide; sepals 4–5, greenish-brown, eventually dropping off; petals absent; stamens, on plants that have them, hang from purplish, thread-like stalks.

Leaves: leaflets, each ½–1½″ (1.3–3.8 cm) long, about as wide, usually with 3 lobes, shallowly notched and cleft.

Fruit: pistils develop into small, spreading or reflexed, pointed, narrow fruits.

Height: 1–3′ (30–90 cm).

Flowering: May–July.

Habitat: Moist ground, often in shady woods.

Range: British Columbia to northern California; east to Colorado, Wyoming, and Montana.

Comments: The common name comes from its resemblance to Common Rue (*Ruta*), grown for its aromatic and medicinal properties.

---

**57 Globeflower**
(*Trollius laxus*)
Buttercup Family (Ranunculaceae)

Description: At the top of each of the 1 or several leafy stems blooms 1 *greenish-white or white, bowl-shaped flower.*
Flowers: 1–1½″ (2.5–3.8 cm) wide; sepals 5–9, broad, petal-like, ½–¾″ (1.3–2 cm) long; petals absent; stamens many, yellow, the outer 5–15 modified into flat structures without anthers.
Leaves: about 2″ (5 cm) long, about as wide, deeply cleft into 5 lobes, each jaggedly cut and toothed.
Fruit: pod-like, nearly ½″ (1.3 cm) long, many from each flower, each with several seeds and at tip a short beak.
Height: 4–20″ (10–50 cm).

Flowering: May–August.

Habitat: Wet places in the mountains.

Range: British Columbia to Washington; in

the Rocky Mountains south to
Colorado.

Comments: The name Globeflower refers to the
shape of the flower in cultivated species
(the native western species is much
flatter).

## BUCKTHORN FAMILY
### (Rhamnaceae)

Shrubs, trees, or vines, usually with small flowers in clusters.
Flowers: radially symmetrical; sepals 5 or rarely 4, separate; petals often 5, sometimes 4 or none, separate; 1 stamen, opposite each petal or, if petals are absent, between the sepals, attached to the flower near the edge of a disk that surrounds the ovary.
Leaves: simple, alternate or opposite.
Fruit: 2- or 3-chambered berry.
There are nearly 60 genera and 900 species occurring throughout the world. Edible fruits are obtained from the tropical Jujube, and Cascara bark was once collected for its purgative properties.

---

### 175, 665 Deer Brush
(*Ceanothus integerrimus*)
Buckthorn Family (Rhamnaceae)

Description: An openly branched shrub with thin leaves, gray bark, and *tiny white or pale blue flowers in conical clusters* at ends of flexible twigs.
Flowers: cluster 3–6″ (7.5–15 cm) long; sepals 5, petal-like, triangular, curved toward center; petals 5, spoon-shaped.
Leaves: to 2½″ (6.3 cm) long, elliptic, with 3 main veins.
Fruit: small, 3-lobed capsule.
Height: 3–13′ (90–390 cm).
Flowering: May–June.
Habitat: Dry slopes in chaparral and open forests.
Range: Eastern Washington to southwestern Oregon and Baja California; east to western New Mexico.
Comments: In the spring, Deer Brush covers hillsides with a mixture of white and pale blue, and fills the air with its sweet, spicy, honey scent.

## ROSE FAMILY (Rosaceae)

Herbs, shrubs, or trees with mostly prickly stems.

Flowers: usually bisexual, radially symmetrical; sepals 5; petals 5, separate or sometimes none; stamens usually numerous; sepals, petals, and stamens attached at edge of cup (which is attached at bottom of ovary), or attached at top of ovary.

Leaves: alternate, simple or compound, usually with small, leaf-like structures at the base of the leaf stalk.

Fruit: dry or fleshy, opening at maturity or remaining closed.

There are about 100 genera and 3,000 species in this worldwide family. Apples, pears, quinces, cherries, plums, peaches, apricots, loquats, blackberries, raspberries, and strawberries are important fruits. Roses, Cotoneaster, Firethorn, Mountain Ash, Spirea, and Hawthorne are common ornamentals.

---

171 **Western Serviceberry**
(*Amelanchier alnifolia*)
Rose Family (Rosaceae)

Description: *A shrub with many white flowers.*
Flowers: 1–2″ (2.5–5 cm) wide; petals 5, growing from the rim of a little cup; stamens 20; styles 5.
Leaves: ¾–1½″ (2–3.8 cm) long, oval, usually with teeth on edges, hairless or sparsely-haired when old.
Fruit: berry about ½″ (1.3 cm) long, purplish, juicy, round.
Height: 4–30′ (1.2–9 m).
Flowering: April–July.
Habitat: Slopes, canyons, and open coniferous woods from low to high elevations.
Range: Alaska and Alberta; south to southern California, Arizona, New Mexico, Nebraska, and Minnesota.
Comments: Serviceberries are variable and species

not easily identified. The berries produced by this species were once used to make jelly or wine.

---

117  **Goatsbeard**
     (*Aruncus sylvester*)
     Rose Family (Rosaceae)

Description:   *Large filmy sprays of tiny white flowers* nod or arch at the top of stems of this rather tall, leafy plant.
              Flowers: less than ⅛" (3 mm) wide; petals 5, white, which drop off; on some plants flowers have only stamens 15–20, on others only pistils 3–5.
              Leaves: large, divided into ovate leaflets to 6" (15 cm) long, the edges with many sharp teeth.
              Height: 3–7' (90–210 cm).
Flowering:    May–July.
Habitat:      Moist places in woods.
Range:        Alaska to northwestern California.
Comments:     *Aruncus,* from the Greek *aryngos* ("goat's beard"), refers to the long cluster of white flowers.

---

46  **White Mountain Avens**
    (*Dryas octopetala*)
    Rose Family (Rosaceae)

Description:   A small, *prostrate plant often in large patches,* the woody stems rooting, with 1 *cream or white flower* at the end of each erect, leafless flower stalk.
              Flowers: about 1" (2.5 cm) wide; 8–10 narrow, pointed calyx lobes, hairy, darkened by stalked glands; petals 8–10, broad; stamens many.
              Leaves: to 1¼" (3.1 cm) long, lanceolate, often very hairy on lower surface, edges scalloped and rolled downward.
              Fruit: many, seed-like, with long plumes, all packed together in a round, feathery head.

Height: creeper, flower stalks 2—10"
(5—25 cm) high.
Flowering: June—August.
Habitat: Open, often rocky places from middle
elevations to above the timberline.
Range: Across northern North America; south
to northern Washington, northeastern
Oregon, central Idaho, and Colorado.
Comments: This species often grows with dwarf
willows, the prostrate habits of each
providing protection against cold,
drying winds.

## 41 Apache Plume
(*Fallugia paradoxa*)
Rose Family (Rosaceae)

Description: A shrub with *white flowers* and *silvery
puffs of fruit heads* borne at the tips of
very dense, intertangled, twiggy,
slender branches.
Flowers: 1—1½" (2.5—3.8 cm) wide;
petals 5, round, growing from rim of a
small cup; stamens many.
Leaves: ½—1" (1.3—2.5 cm) long,
thick, divided into 5 or 7 narrow lobes,
edges strongly curled downward.
Fruit: styles form a feathery plume ¾—
2" (2—5 cm) long, above a seed-like
base; many in a head.
Height: to 7' (2.1 m).
Flowering: May—October.
Habitat: Gravelly or rocky slopes, and in washes,
from deserts to open pine forests.
Range: Southeastern California and southern
Nevada to southern Colorado, western
Texas, and northern Mexico.
Comments: These rather thick shrubs appear
unkempt, but in full flower their white
petals are attractive against the dark
foliage.

45 **Beach Strawberry**
(*Fragaria chiloensis*)
Rose Family (Rosaceae)

Description:   A low plant connected to others by
"runners," at least when young, often
growing in patches, with *white flowers*
on stalks slightly shorter than the
leaves.
Flowers: about ¾" (2 cm) wide; sepals
5, green, pointed, with little bracts
between; petals 5, broadly ovate, each
with a short stalk at base; stamens
many.
Leaves: compound; 3 broad, leathery
leaflets, each ¾–2" (2–5 cm) long,
toothed at end, shiny, dark green on
top, hairy and grayish on lower side, on
stalk 2–8" (5–20 cm) long.
Fruit: berry, ⅝–¾" (1.5–2 cm) wide,
enlarges from a cone-shaped flower
center that has many pistils.
Height: creeper, with floral stalks 2–8"
(5–20 cm) high.

Flowering:   March–August.

Habitat:   Coastal dunes and bluffs.

Range:   Alaska; south through the northern two
thirds of California.

Comments:   The word "strawberry" comes from the
Anglo-Saxon *streawberige,* and refers to
the berries "strewing" their runners out
over the ground. Chilean plants of this
species were used as parents in the
production of hybrid, domestic
Strawberries. Several species of wild
Strawberries in the West strongly
resemble the Beach Strawberry but have
thin leaflets.

198 **Large-leaved Geum**
(*Geum macrophyllum*)
Rose Family (Rosaceae)

Description:   A leafy plant with 1 or several stems,
and a few *yellow flowers* on branches at
the top.

Flowers: about ½" (1.3 cm) wide; sepals 5, pointed, bent downward; petals 5, broad, ¼" (6 mm) long; stamens and pistils many, each with a slender style consisting of a persistent basal part hooked at tip and a terminal part that drops off.

Leaves: to 1' (30 cm) long, pinnately compound, the segments becoming progressively larger from base of leaf to tip, the end segment by far the largest.

Fruit: seed-like, hooked at tip, many in a head.

Height: to 3' (90 cm).

Flowering: April–August.

Habitat: Moist woods or meadowland from low to high elevations.

Range: Alaska; south to Baja California; east to South Dakota and the Rocky Mountain region as far south as northern New Mexico.

Comments: Geums with yellow flowers are difficult to distinguish from Cinquefoils (*Potentilla*), but Geum's style is divided into an upper and lower part, and in most western species its leaves are also narrow at the base and broad at the tip.

---

### 501 Prairie Smoke; Purple Avens; Old Man's Whiskers
(*Geum triflorum*)
Rose Family (Rosaceae)

Description: Several *pink or reddish-pink, bell-shaped flowers, sometimes yellowish, hang* from long, reddish, branched stalks above thick clumps of mostly basal leaves.

Flowers: about ½" (1.3 cm) long; calyx with 5 very narrow bracts between the 5 pointed main lobes; 5 tiny petals.

Leaves: 1¼–6" (3.1–15 cm) long, pinnately compound, jaggedly toothed blades.

Fruit: seed-like, bearing reddish plumes to 2" (5 cm) long, many in a head.

Height: to 16" (40 cm).

Flowering: April–August.
Habitat: Sagebrush plains to mountain ridges and meadows.
Range: Across northern North America; south in the West to the Sierra Nevada of California, in the Rocky Mountain region to Utah, and New Mexico.
Comments: After fertilization, the bell-like flowers turn upward and plumes begin to grow from the pistils, ready to be caught by the wind or a passing animal and the seed so dispersed.

## 334 Gordon's Ivesia
(*Ivesia gordonii*)
Rose Family (Rosaceae)

Description: *Yellow flowers* bloom in a *crowded, head-like cluster* on each of several nearly leafless stalks that grow from *basal leaves*.
Flowers: cluster ½–¾" (1.3–2 cm) wide; petals 5, narrow, on small stalks, shorter than lobes of sepals; stamens 5.
Leaves: ¾–4" (2–10 cm) long, pinnately compound, usually with more than 20 leaflets, each with 3–5 rounded segments.
Height: to 8" (20 cm).
Flowering: June–August.
Habitat: Open gravelly or rocky places, at lower elevations along riverbanks, at higher elevations on open ridges.
Range: Central Washington to the Sierra Nevada of California; east to Utah, northern Colorado, and western Montana.
Comments: Ivesia is a western genus with mostly yellow flowers, a few species with white or pink ones, and is closely related to *Horkelia,* which has broad stalks on the stamens. Cinquefoil (*Potentilla*) species are similar but usually do not have stalks at the base of the petals, and the 3 uppermost leaflets do not grow together as in many Ivesia species.

### 111 Partridge Foot
(*Luetkea pectinata*)
Rose Family (Rosaceae)

Description: From *dense patches or mats of dark green divided leaves* grow erect stalks with *white flowers in dense clusters* at the top.
Flowers: cluster 1–2″ (2.5–5 cm) long; petals 5, white, about ⅛″ (3 mm) long; stamens about 20.
Leaves: ¼–½″ (6–13 mm) long, mostly crowded at base, *fan-shaped, dissected into very narrow lobes*, on a stalk about as long.
Height: 2–6″ (5–15 cm).

Flowering: June–August.

Habitat: Usually well-drained soil high in the mountains where snow persists until late in the season.

Range: Alaska to northern California, eastern Idaho, and western Montana.

Comments: The name Partridge Foot refers to the divided leaves, shaped like birds' feet.

### 161 Rocky Mountain Rockmat
(*Petrophytum caespitosum*)
Rose Family (Rosaceae)

Description: This plant resembles stone with *thick, impenetrable, gray cushions* above which *white flowers bloom in dense racemes*.
Flowers: cluster ¾–1¼″ (2–3.1 cm) wide; petals 5, about ⅛″ (3 mm) long; stamens 20.
Leaves: to ½″ (1.3 cm) long, narrow, crowded, hairy, gray.
Height: mat to about 3″ (7.5 cm) thick and 3′ (90 cm) wide; flower stalks 1–3″ (2.5–7.5 cm) high.

Flowering: June–August.

Habitat: Barren rock, growing from crevices.

Range: Northeastern Oregon to southern California; east to Montana, South Dakota, Colorado, and western Texas.

Comments: This strange plant is found almost exclusively in the inhospitable habitat of barren rock, clinging by stout roots jammed in crevices. There are only two other species. Chelan Rockmat (*P. cinerascens*), in central Washington, and Olympic Mountain Rockmat (*P. hendersonii*), in the Olympic Mountains of western Washington.

---

### 197  Common Silverweed
(*Potentilla anserina*)
Rose Family (Rosaceae)

Description:  A low plant with *silky leaves in tufts,* connected by runners to other tufts, forming patches; 1 *yellow flower* at tip of each leafless stalk in axil of leaf on runner.
Flowers: about ¾" (2 cm) wide; petals 5, broad; stamens 20–25.
Leaves: 4–12" (10–30 cm) long, pinnately compound, usually bearing 15–29 rounded, sharply toothed leaflets.
Height: creeper, with flowers on stalks 2–12" (5–30 cm) high, the runners 3–6' (90–180 cm) long.
Flowering:  May–August.
Habitat:  Moist ground, meadows, and stream banks.
Range:  Alaska to southern California; east across the continent; also Eurasia.
Comments:  In ancient times this plant was grown for food and medicine. The root, when cooked, is said to have the flavor of parsnips or sweet potatoes, and an extract from the root has been used to tan leather. Its supposed medicinal properties inspired the genus name, from the Latin *potens* ("powerful") and meaning "powerful little one." To treat scrofula Pliny recommended an ointment compounded of Cinquefoil (*Potentilla* spp.), honey, and axle grease. The very similar Pacific Silverweed (*P. pacifica*), grows along the coast from Alaska to southern California; the runners and stalks of its leaves lack hairs or have a few hairs that lie flat.

## 351 Shrubby Cinquefoil
(*Potentilla fruticosa*)
Rose Family (Rosaceae)

Description: A *small shrub with reddish-brown, shredding bark* on the young twigs, and *yellow flowers,* 1 in each upper leaf axil, or a few in clusters at ends of branches.
Flowers: about 1″ (2.5 cm) wide; petals 5, broad, stamens 25–30.
Leaves: pinnately divided, generally with 5 crowded leaflets, each ½–¾″ (1.3–2 cm) long, hairy and grayish, especially on lower side.
Height: 6–36″ (15–90 cm).

Flowering: June–August.

Habitat: Ridges, open forests, and plains from low to high elevations.

Range: Throughout.

Comments: This handsome shrub, common in the West, adapts well to cultivation and among the many horticultural variants are dwarf, low-growing, and unusually large-flowered forms, some with white flowers, others with yellowish-orange ones.

## 215 Sticky Cinquefoil
(*Potentilla glandulosa*)
Rose Family (Rosaceae)

Description: A leafy plant with several stems, often reddish and *sticky with minute, glandular hairs; yellow flowers bloom in loose, branched clusters* at the top.
Flowers: ½–¾″ (1.3–2 cm) wide; 5 pointed calyx lobes, with smaller bracts between, at edge of a nearly flat saucer; petals 5, broad; stamens 25–40; numerous pistils, the style attached to lower side of ovary and thickest in middle.
Leaves: pinnately compound, with 5–9 ovate leaflets ½–2″ (1.3–5 cm) long, each with sharp teeth on edges.
Height: to 20″ (50 cm).

Flowering: May–July.

Habitat:   In dry or moist soil, generally in open
           situations.
Range:     British Columbia to northern
           California; east to Arizona, Colorado,
           and Montana.
Comments:  Attractive wildflowers common in the
           West and generally recognizable as
           "Cinquefoil," a word ultimately
           deriving from Latin through French,
           meaning "5 leaves." Some species have
           leaves with 5 leaflets. The genus differs
           from very similar-appearing species of
           Buttercups (*Ranunculus*) in having a
           hypanthium (a cup or saucer at the edge
           of which are attached stamens, petals,
           and sepal lobes). Some species
           hybridize, others reproduce asexually,
           or hybrids may produce asexually, and
           populations of intermediate plants are
           frequent. Thus, identification of
           Cinquefoil species is difficult.

### 396 Red Cinquefoil
(*Potentilla thurberi*)
Rose Family (Rosaceae)

Description:  *Rich, deep crimson flowers* bloom in loose
              clusters on long stalks on 1 or several
              leafy, branched stems.
              Flowers: about 1" (2.5 cm) wide; petals
              5, broad; stamens many.
              Leaves: pinnately divided into 5–7
              closely adjacent, toothed leaflets, each
              1–2" (2.5–5 cm) long.
              Height: 1–2½' (30–75 cm).
Flowering:    July–October.
Habitat:      Rich soil in coniferous forests, damp
              meadows, and along streams.
Range:        Central Arizona to central New Mexico
              and northern Mexico.
Comments:     The rich red, darkest in the flower's
              center, seems to have a velvety glow,
              the surface dull but the color intense. A
              second *Potentilla* species with reddish
              flowers, Purple Cinquefoil (*P. palustris*),
              is relatively humble with tiny dark red
              petals placed between dull red, larger

sepals; it grows in bogs across North America, extending south in the West to northern California and Wyoming.

571 **Nootka Rose**
(*Rosa nutkana*)
Rose Family (Rosaceae)

Description: A *thorny shrub* with *pale pink flowers,* the largest (often only) thorns in pairs near leaf stalks.
Flowers: 2–3″ (5–7.5 cm) wide; petals 5, broad; sepals 5, slender, usually tapered from base to narrow middle, then expanded slightly near tip; stamens many.
Leaves: pinnately compound, with 5–9 ovate leaflets ½–3″ (1.3–7.5 cm) long, sharply toothed on edges.
Fruit: berry-like, ½–¾″ (1.3–2 cm) long, round, smooth, reddish-purple.
Height: 2–13′ (60–400 cm).
Flowering: May–July.
Habitat: Woods and open places in the mountains.
Range: Alaska to northern California, northeastern Oregon, northern Utah, and Colorado.
Comments: The hips, or fruit, of any wild roses may be eaten and are often used to make jams and jellies. Sweetbrier (*R. eglanteria*), the "Eglantine" of Shakespeare and Chaucer, has many down-curved prickles on the stem, and minute glands on the leaves and sepals, giving a pleasant rose aroma.
Introduced to North America, it is fairly common west of the Cascade Mountains and the Sierra Nevada.

## 42 Dwarf Bramble
(*Rubus lasiococcus*)
Rose Family (Rosaceae)

Description: *Trailing, thornless, freely rooting, leafy
stems* have short, erect flowering stems
bearing 1 leaf and *1 or 2 white flowers.*
Flowers: about ½" (1.3 cm) wide;
petals 5, broad; stamens many.
Leaves: 1–2½" (2.5–6.3 cm) wide,
about as long, cleft into 3 lobes, the
edges toothed.
Fruit: small red raspberry.
Height: creeper, with stems to 7'
(2.1 m) long, and floral stalks 4"
(10 cm) high.

Flowering: June–August.

Habitat: Thickets and woods.

Range: British Columbia to northern
California.

Comments: Species of the large and complicated
genus *Rubus,* the Roman name for
"bramble," are more often shrubs or
formidable patches of thorny brambles
than low creepers and produce
blackberries, raspberries, and many
horticultural varieties that have been
improved through hybridization and
selection. However, berries of the wild
progenitors are equally sweet, juicy,
and flavorful.

## MADDER FAMILY (Rubiaceae)

Herbs, shrubs, or trees, with flowers borne in a branched cluster.

Flowers: usually radially symmetrical; sepals 4 or 5; petals 4 or 5, united; stamens 4 or 5. All these parts attached at top of ovary.

Leaves: opposite or whorled, the bases often connected by fused scales that extend across the node, or the scales large and leaflike.

Fruit: usually 2-chambered capsule or berry.

There are about 500 genera and 6,000 species that occur primarily in tropical regions, where woody representatives are most frequent. Madder (a dye), coffee, and quinine are obtained from the family. Gardenias are popular ornamentals in mild climates.

---

### 424 Scarlet Bouvardia; Trompetilla
(*Bouvardia ternifolia*)
Madder Family (Rubiaceae)

Description: A *shrub with brilliant scarlet, tubular flowers* in loose clusters at ends of *numerous erect branches.*
Flowers: corolla ⅝–1¼" (1.5–3.1 cm) long, with 4 short lobes at end.
Leaves: to 3" (7.5 cm) long, ovate, 3 or 4 in a whorl on branches.
Height: to 3' (90 cm).

Flowering: May–November.

Habitat: Dry rocky slopes and among boulders.

Range: Southern Arizona and western Texas; south to Mexico.

Comments: The spectacular red corolla attracts and provides nectar for hummingbirds. The Spanish name, which means "little trumpet," refers to the corolla's shape.

142  **Bedstraw**
(*Galium boreale*)
Madder Family (Rubiaceae)

Description:  A leafy plant with 4 *leaves in each whorl*
on the 4-sided stems, short branches
often in axils, and at ends of branches
*many round-topped clusters of tiny, white
flowers.*
Flowers: petals 4, less than ⅛" (3 mm)
long, spreading from top of ovary; no
sepals.
Leaves: to 2" (5 cm) long, narrow, with
3 veins.
Height: 8–32" (20–80 cm).

Flowering:  June–August.

Habitat:  Open, moist areas from sea level to
high in the mountains.

Range:  Extending south in the West to
northern California, Arizona, New
Mexico, and Texas; also the northern
plains and the eastern United States.

Comments:  Most *Galium* species have inconspicuous
flowers borne singly or in small
clusters, but the 4 spreading corolla
lobes, the attachment of flower plants
above the ovary, and whorled leaves are
consistent features. Sweet-scented
European species were once used as
mattress stuffing, giving the name
Bedstraw to all species in the genus.
Those bearing tiny hooks all over the
surface of the round fruits are called
Cleavers, for the fruits "cleave" to
fabric or fur. The genus name, from the
Greek *gala* ("milk"), comes from the
use of one species to curdle milk.

## PITCHER PLANT FAMILY
### (Sarraceniaceae)

Carnivorous herbs with tubular leaves and large, nodding flowers.

Flowers: radially symmetrical, borne singly or in racemes; sepals 4 or 5, often petal-like; petals 5; stamens 12 or more. All these parts attached at base of ovary; ovary topped by an umbrella-like style.

Leaves: basal, long, commonly with a decorative opening to the tubular base.

Fruit: 3- to 6-chambered capsule.

There are 3 genera and 17 species in North America and northern South America; in the United States all but one are in the East. A few species are grown as curiosities, and collecting for this purpose threatens the rarest.

---

10 **California Pitcher Plant; Cobra Plant; Cobra Lily**
*(Darlingtonia californica)*
Pitcher Plant Family (Sarraceniaceae)

Description: Several *tubular leaves with hood-like tops* grow in a cluster; *1 yellow-green and maroon flower hangs at the tip* of a leafless stalk.
Flowers: sepals 5, yellow-green petal-like, 1½–3½" (3.8–8.8 cm) long; petals 5, maroon, shorter than sepals; green, bell-shaped ovary.
Leaves: 4–20" (10–50 cm) long; 2 long, flat appendages beneath hood.
Height: to 3' (90 cm).
Flowering: April–August.
Habitat: Coastal bogs and mountain streams and seeps.
Range: Most of western Oregon to northwestern California and the central Sierra Nevada.
Comments: Insects, or other small organisms, attracted to the nectar secreted by the hood and appendages, enter the hole beneath the hood. Once inside,

numerous down-pointing hairs
discourage escape, and they are
decomposed by microorganisms in the
fluid in the tubular base. Nutrients
thus released are absorbed by the
Pitcher Plant.

## LIZARD TAIL FAMILY
### (Saururaceae)

Herbs, mostly of moist places, with small flowers often associated with colored bracts.

Flowers: radially symmetrical, in dense spikes or racemes, or in clusters often resembling single flowers; calyx and corolla absent; stamens 3, 6, or 8; pistils 3 or 4, sometimes partly joined at the base.

Leaves: alternate, simple.

Fruit: succulent capsule.

There are 5 genera and 7 species that are restricted to the Northern Hemisphere.

---

72 **Yerba Mansa**
(*Anemopsis californica*)
Lizard Tail Family (Saururaceae)

Description: A grayish-green plant that grows in patches, with conical spikes resembling *1 white flower.*
Flowers: spike 1–2″ (2.5–5 cm) long, at its base several broad, white, petal-like bracts ½–1″ (1.3–2.5 cm) long; beneath each tiny flower in the spike is a small, white bract.
Leaves: to 6″ (15 cm) long, mostly oblong, erect.
Height: to 1′ (30 cm).
Flowering: May–August.
Habitat: Low, moist, saline or alkaline places.
Range: Oregon, Utah, Colorado, and Texas; south into Mexico.
Comments: "Mansa" in Spanish means "mild" or "tame," the whole name supposedly meaning "herb of the tamed Indian." The aromatic rootstock has been put to many medicinal uses: treatment of abrasions, cuts, and burns; a cure for a variety of gastrointestinal upsets; a poultice for rheumatism; a tonic for blood purification.

## SAXIFRAGE FAMILY
## (Saxifragaceae)

Usually herbs with small flowers.
Flowers: radially symmetrical, in
raceme-like or branched clusters; sepals
5, petals 5 or 10, separate; stamens 5 or
10; all these parts attached to edge of
cup-like flower base, with ovary in
center.
Leaves: alternate usually, and basal.
Fruit: capsule, small pod, or berry.
There are about 30 genera and 580
species, with most occurring in cooler
regions of the Northern Hemisphere.
Species of *Saxifraga, Bergenia,* and
*Astilbe* are commonly grown as
ornamentals.

---

## 26 Coast Boykinia
(*Boykinia elata*)
Saxifrage Family (Saxifragaceae)

Description: A plant with leaves mostly at base and
*openly branched clusters of small, white
flowers* that tend to turn upward at the
tops of several reddish stems covered
with minute glandular hairs.
Flowers: about ¼″ (6 mm) wide;
5 short, pointed calyx lobes on rim
of a cup; petals 5, narrow, with
narrow, stalk-like bases; stamens 5.
Leaves: broadly heart-shaped or kidney-
shaped, cleft into 5–7 lobes, the edges
bearing sharp, irregular teeth tipped
with bristles, those near base on long
stalks.
Height: 6–24″ (15–60 cm).
Flowering: June–August.
Habitat: Moist woods at springs and seeps, and
along streams.
Range: British Columbia to western
Washington, Oregon, and the northern
half of California.
Comments: There are several species of *Boykinia* in
North America, most occurring in the
West. The genus name honors an early-

19th-century Georgia naturalist, Dr. Samuel Boykin.

---

112 **Poker Heuchera; Poker Alumroot**
(*Heuchera cylindrica*)
Saxifrage Family (Saxifragaceae)

Description: *Leathery leaf blades* varying from ovate to broadly heart-shaped on *long stalks clustered at base* of flower stalks; upper part of plant densely covered with glandular hairs, especially in the *narrow, greenish-white flower cluster.* Flowers: a cream or greenish-yellow cup ¼–½" (6–13 mm) deep, with 5 round calyx lobes forming the rim, the lobes on the lower side slightly longer; petals 5 (or fewer, or none), white, shorter than calyx lobes; stamens 5. Leaves: 1–3" (2.5–7.5 cm) wide. Height: 6–36" (15–90 cm).
Flowering: April–August.
Habitat: Rocky flats, slopes, and cliffs.
Range: British Columbia to northeastern California; east to northern Nevada, Wyoming, and Montana.
Comments: The dense, narrow flower cluster helps distinguish this species from several others. Alumroot species hybridize, making identification of many plants difficult.

---

420 **Coral Bells**
(*Heuchera sanguinea*)
Saxifrage Family (Saxifragaceae)

Description: *Bright coral-red bells hang in a narrow cluster* from upper part of a nearly leafless stalk; leaves mostly basal. Flowers: ¼–½" (6–13 mm) long; sepals 5, on rim of colorful bell-shaped cup; petals 5, as long as sepals; stamens 5. Leaves: 1–3" (2.5–7.5 cm) wide, nearly round, leathery, most on long stalks.

Height: 10–20″ (25–50 cm).
Flowering: March–October.
Habitat: Moist, shaded, rocky places.
Range: Southern Arizona to northern Mexico.
Comments: The dainty bells and dark green leaves
make this a highly popular ornamental.
Several other western species have
smaller pink or purplish flowers in
more open clusters.

### 140  Leatherleaf Saxifrage
(*Leptarrhena pyrolifolia*)
Saxifrage Family (Saxifragaceae)

Description: *A dense, roundish cluster of tiny, white
flowers* blooms atop an erect, nearly
leafless flower stalk that grows from a
basal rosette.
Flowers: cluster ¾–1″ (2–2.5 cm)
wide; calyx with 5 erect lobes attached
near rim of saucer-like base; petals 5,
narrow, white; stamens 10, slender, as
long as or longer than petals; pistil has
2 segments attached to saucer-like base
only at bottom and not by sides.
Leaves: 1–6″ (2.5–15 cm) long,
elliptic, smooth, leathery, widest above
middle, scalloped on edges.
Fruit: tiny rusty-red pods.
Height: 2–10″ (5–25 cm).
Flowering: June–August.
Habitat: Wet places along streams, in meadows,
or on mountain slopes.
Range: Alaska to central Oregon, northern
Idaho, and western Montana.
Comments: The only species. The plants are
attractive for the dark green, persistent
foliage and the rusty-red fruits that
mature from the flowers. *Leptarrhena*
differs from similar species of *Saxifraga*
in the attachment of the pistils.

## 28 Prairie Star; Starflower
(*Lithophragma parviflorum*)
Saxifrage Family (Saxifragaceae)

Description: Flowers in open, slender racemes have
*white or pale pink petals cleft into 3 or 5
finger-like lobes*; the leaves of plant
mostly at base and lower part of stem.
Flowers: ½–1″ (1.3–2.5 cm) wide;
sepals 5, short, triangular, attached
near rim of bell-shaped base; petals 5;
stamens 5.
Leaves: ½–1¼″ (1.3–3.1 cm) wide,
roundish, deeply cleft into 3 or 5
sections, these less deeply divided into
narrow lobes.
Height: to 20″ (50 cm).
Flowering: March–June.
Habitat: Prairies, among sagebrush, and in open
forest at lower elevations.
Range: British Columbia to northern
California; east to western Nebraska,
western South Dakota, Montana, and
Alberta.
Comments: The white or pinkish petals on star-like
flowers in racemes are characteristic of
the genus. Those species that grow in
woods are called Woodland Star. Some
species have tiny maroon beads
(bulblets) in leaf axils and in place of
some flowers; these can grow into new
plants.

## 9 Five-point Bishop's Cap
(*Mitella pentandra*)
Saxifrage Family (Saxifragaceae)

Description: A small plant with *tiny, greenish flowers,
in slender racemes,* and leaves in a basal
cluster.
Flowers: about ¼″ (6 mm) wide; petals
5, each with a slender central rib from
which project at right angles even finer
strands, each tiny petal like a fine
double comb with sparse, slender teeth.
Leaves: 1–3″ (2.5–7.5 cm) wide,
roundish, on long stalks.

Height: 4–16″ (10–40 cm).
Flowering: June–August.
Habitat: Damp woods, stream banks, and wet meadows.
Range: Alaska to the Sierra Nevada of California; east to Colorado and Alberta.
Comments: There are several species of this dainty little plant, all in damp, shady places in the West. One species, Bare-stem Mitella (*M. nuda*), has 10 stamens, the others 5.

24 **Fringed Grass of Parnassus**
(*Parnassia fimbriata*)
Saxifrage Family (Saxifragaceae)

Description: *A white or cream, saucer-shaped flower* blooms atop each of several stems, with most leaves at base.
Flowers: about 1″ (2.5 cm) wide; petals 5, fringed on lower edges; a yellowish, fan-shaped structure with gland-tipped "fingers" between each of the 5 stamens.
Leaves: to 2″ (5 cm) wide, all except the one at midstem with long stalks, broadly heart-shaped or kidney-shaped, with several major veins arching from notched base to tip.
Height: 6–20″ (15–50 cm).
Flowering: July–September.
Habitat: Wet places in the mountains.
Range: Alaska to central California; east to the Rocky Mountains from New Mexico to Alberta.
Comments: Grass of Parnassus is the translation of the Latin name of a European species, *Gramen parnassi.* The word *gramen* was used for many herbs, not only grasses. Parnassus, in both common and scientific names, probably dedicates the plant to the Muses, for snowcapped Mount Parnassus was celebrated as their home. The 5 fan-shaped, finger-tipped staminodia of *Parnassia* are distinctive.

### 552 Umbrella Plant
(*Peltiphyllum peltatum*)
Saxifrage Family (Saxifragaceae)

Description: This plant forms large masses of *nearly round, jaggedly toothed leaf blades* on *rough, hairy stalks; small, pink flowers in large, round, branched clusters* grow on stalks slightly taller than leaves.
Flowers: petals 5, pink or white, about ¼" (6 mm) long; stamens 10; pistil with 2 reddish-purple sections.
Leaves: to 16" (40 cm) wide.
Height: 2–6' (60–180 cm).
Flowering: April–June.
Habitat: In and along edges of cold streams.
Range: Central Oregon to central California.
Comments: This plant, usually anchored firmly among water-washed rocks, sometimes gives a verdant, almost tropical aspect to mountain streams owing to its luxuriant foliage.

### 17 Spotted Saxifrage
(*Saxifraga bronchialis*)
Saxifrage Family (Saxifragaceae)

Description: This *matted plant,* resembling a small evergreen or large moss, has *small, white flowers* in an open, branched, reddish cluster.
Flowers: about ⅜" (9 mm) wide; petals 5, white, spotted with maroon or orange; stamens 10; purplish ovary.
Leaves: ¼–¾" (6–20 mm) long, narrow, rigid, mostly near base, with tiny, stiff hairs on edges.
Height: 2–6" (5–15 cm).
Flowering: June–August.
Habitat: Open slopes, usually among rocks, generally high in the mountains.
Range: Throughout the Northern Hemisphere; in the West, south to northern Oregon, Idaho, and New Mexico.
Comments: A common plant along mountain trails. The genus name, from the Latin *saxum* ("rock") and *frangere* ("to break"),

alludes to the species' rocky habitat; the plants grow in rock crevices, looking as if they had split the rock. Also, herbalists once used some species in a treatment for "stones" in the urinary tract.

---

104 **Merten's Saxifrage**
(*Saxifraga mertensiana*)
Saxifrage Family (Saxifragaceae)

Description: *Nearly circular leaf blades with hairy stalks* grow in a basal cluster around a taller, branched flower stalk with *tiny, white flowers*.
Flowers: nearly ¼" (6 mm) wide; petals 5, oblong; stamens 10, with club-like stalks and pink anthers; some flowers replaced by pink bulbs.
Leaves: blades 1–4" (2.5–10 cm) wide, lobed on the edge, the larger lobes with roundish, shallow teeth; stalks up to 4 times the length of blade; at base of stalk is a membranous sheath around stem.
Height: 4–16" (10–40 cm).
Flowering: April–August.
Habitat: Wet banks or along streams in coniferous woods.
Range: Alaska to central California, northeastern Oregon, central Idaho, and western Montana.
Comments: The tiny bulbs that replace some flowers can grow into new plants when they drop to the ground.

---

139 **Western Saxifrage**
(*Saxifraga occidentalis*)
Saxifrage Family (Saxifragaceae)

Description: A small clump of basal leaves surrounds an erect, *reddish-glandular stem with tiny, white flowers in a branched cluster*.
Flowers: cluster ¾–2" (2–5 cm); petals 5, ovate or oblong, about ⅛" (3 mm)

long, sometimes with 2 yellow spots at base; stamens 10, with slender or club-shaped stalks; 2 chambers of ovary nearly separate from each other.
Leaves: blades to 2½" (6.3 cm) long, ovate, coarsely toothed, tapered to a short or long stalk.
Fruit: capsule nearly divided into 2 separate pod-like sections less than ¼" (6 mm) long, greenish or reddish.
Height: 2–12" (5–30 cm).

Flowering: April–August.

Habitat: Moist slopes, meadows, and rocks.

Range: British Columbia to northwestern Oregon, eastern Nevada, Idaho, and northwestern Wyoming.

Comments: This complex and highly variable species intergrades with several other species distinguished by technical features only.

## 432 Purple Saxifrage
(*Saxifraga oppositifolia*)
Saxifrage Family (Saxifragaceae)

Description: A *dense, little cushion plant with oval leaves*, often tinged with maroon, and *bright reddish-lavender flowers*.
Flowers: about ¼" (6 mm) wide; petals 5, erect, spatula-shaped; stamens 10; pistil with 2 projections at top, each tipped with a tiny knob.
Leaves: about ⅛" (3 mm) long, opposite, in 4 rows on stem, strongly overlapping, the edges with stiff, short hairs.
Height: about 2" (5 cm); tuft to 8" (20 cm) wide.

Flowering: June–August.

Habitat: Rocky areas and crevices in mountains.

Range: Northern Hemisphere; south in the West to Washington, northeastern Oregon, central Idaho, and northern Wyoming.

Comments: The richly colored flowers are unusual in this genus, which commonly has white ones. The plant resembles Moss

Pink (*Silene acaulis*), which is
distinguished from it by 3 styles and
generally a notch in the end of the
slender petals.

---

141 **Diamond-leaf Saxifrage**
    (*Saxifraga rhomboidea*)
    Saxifrage Family (Saxifragaceae)

Description: 1 erect, glandular-hairy stem with a
*tight cluster of tiny, white flowers,* grows
from a basal cluster of leaves.
Flowers: petals 5, ovate, about ⅛″
(3 mm) long; stamens 10, with stalks
thickest near the middle; ovary has 2–4
nearly separate chambers; flower cluster
may resemble a round head about ¾″
(2 cm) wide, or the cluster may be
more openly branched, the flowers
grouped near ends of branches.
Leaves: blades ½–2″ (1.3–5 cm) long,
thick, with blunt teeth, diamond-
shaped or nearly triangular, on broad,
flat stalks.
Height: 2–12″ (5–30 cm).

Flowering: May–August.

Habitat: Moist places from sagebrush hills to
high in the mountains.

Range: Alberta to Utah and Colorado.

Comments: This species belongs to a complex of
closely similar species found in most
parts of the West.

---

138 **Alpine Saxifrage**
    (*Saxifraga tolmiei*)
    Saxifrage Family (Saxifragaceae)

Description: Low, *mat-forming plants with tiny white
flowers in clusters* at the top of mostly
leafless stems.
Flowers: petals 5, white, up to ¼″
(6 mm) long; stamens 10, the stalks
thickest near the tip, like small bats.
Leaves: ⅛–½″ (3–13 mm) long,
narrow, crowded at the base, becoming

stiff and dry and remaining on the stem when dead.

Fruit: capsule with usually only 2 beak-like projections at tip.

Height: 1–3″ (2.5–7.5 cm).

Flowering: July–August.

Habitat: Meadows or moist rocky areas in the mountains.

Range: Alaska south to central California; east to western Montana.

Comments: This attractive alpine plant has two varieties. The common one in California has no hairs on leaves, whereas those of other areas usually have a few long hairs on leaf bases.

---

## 440 Violet Suksdorfia
(*Suksdorfia violaceae*)
Saxifrage Family (Saxifragaceae)

Description: A *slender, delicate plant* with a few branches at top bearing several *deep pink or violet, funnel-shaped flowers.*

Flowers: petals 5, slender, ⅜″ (9 mm) long; stamens 5.

Leaves: to 1″ (2.5 cm) wide, roundish, edges deeply lobed; those at base with long stalks; those on stem on shorter stalks with very broad bases, or with leaf-like flaps at base.

Height: 4–8″ (10–20 cm).

Flowering: March–June.

Habitat: Moist, sandy, shaded areas, mossy banks, cliffs, and rock crevices.

Range: British Columbia to northern Oregon; east to northern Idaho and northwestern Montana.

Comments: W. N. Suksdorf, whom the genus name honors, was, around the turn of the 20th century, one of the foremost plant collectors of the Pacific Northwest. The only other species, Buttercup-leaved Suksdorfia (*S. ranunculifolia*), has white petals, but its 5 stamens and broad leaf-stalk bases distinguish it from similar species of *Saxifraga*.

## 520 Telesonix
(*Telesonix jamesii*)
Saxifrage Family (Saxifragaceae)

Description: 1 or several short stems, frequently purplish in the upper parts, with *largest leaves at base,* and *pinkish-lavender flowers* in little clusters on short branches in axils of very small upper leaves.
Flowers: base narrowly bell-shaped, showy; petals 5, less than ⅛" (3 mm) long, attached near rim of bell-like base; pistil in center with 2 styles.
Leaves: ½–2½" (1.3–6.3 cm) wide, kidney-shaped, the edges bluntly toothed and lobed, those at base with long stalks.
Height: 2–8" (5–20 cm).
Flowering: July–August.
Habitat: Moist rock crevices and rocky slopes high in the mountains.
Range: Alberta to Idaho, Colorado, eastern Utah, and southern Nevada.
Comments: The only species in the genus. Though beautiful, it does not transplant well; attempts at cultivation should be done from seed.

## 106 Fringe Cups
(*Tellima grandiflora*)
Saxifrage Family (Saxifragaceae)

Description: Grows in clumps with most leaves near base, and *cream or pale pink, fringed flowers blooming in several long racemes.*
Flowers: about ½" (1.3 cm) wide; sepals 5, short; petals 5, white or pink, fringed across end; both are attached to the edge of cup-like base; stamens 10.
Leaves: 1–4" (2.5–10 cm) wide, roundish, hairy, shallowly lobed and scalloped, those at base on long stalks.
Height: to 32" (80 cm).
Flowering: April–July.
Habitat: Moist places in woods.
Range: Alaska to coastal central California; east to northern Idaho.

Comments: A beautiful plant of shaded woods, the slender wands of flowers arching upward or standing erect above the rich green foliage. The curious petals are at first white or cream but often become deep pink with age.

## 99 False Mitrewort
(*Tiarella unifoliata*)
Saxifrage Family (Saxifragaceae)

Description: *Tiny, white flowers hang in loose clusters in narrow, branched racemes* at tops of leafy stems.
Flowers: about ¼″ (6 mm) wide, with a pale green cup-like base about ¹⁄₁₆″ (1.5 mm) long, the upper calyx lobe largest; petals 5, white, hair-like, about ⅛″ (3 mm) long; stamens 10, white, protruding.
Leaves: blades to 3½″ (8.8 cm) wide, the lower ones, on long stalks, rather triangular, indented and toothed or divided into 3 leaflets which may be deeply cut.
Fruit: capsule that opens by a split between 2 unequal halves.
Height: 8–16″ (20–40 cm).

Flowering: May–August.

Habitat: Moist woods, along stream banks.

Range: Alaska to central California; east to Idaho and western Montana.

Comments: The form with the most highly cut leaf blades grows in western Washington. The genus name is from the Greek *tiara*, an ancient Persian headdress, which the fruit resembles.

## FIGWORT OR SNAPDRAGON FAMILY
### (Scrophulariaceae)

Mostly herbs, sometimes shrubs, rarely trees, often with showy flowers.
Flowers: bilaterally symmetrical; sepals 4 or 5, united; petals 4 or 5, united, usually forming a corolla with upper and lower lips; stamens usually 4, sometimes 2 or 5, when 5 the fifth often sterile and different from the rest. All these parts attached at base of ovary.
Leaves: alternate, opposite, or whorled, simple or pinnately divided.
Fruit: 2-chambered capsule or berry.
There are about 220 genera and 3,000 species occurring nearly throughout the world. Several are grown as ornamentals.

---

### 123 White Snapdragon
(*Antirrhinum coulterianum*)
Figwort Family (Scrophulariaceae)

Description: Slender, wand-like racemes with *white bilaterally symmetrical flowers* grow on sparsely-leafed stems.
Flowers: corolla about ½" (1.3 cm) long; the 2 upper lobes bent upward, the 3 lower bent downward, hairy, lightly lined and spotted with violet on the hump that closes opening to the tube; stamens 4.
Leaves: few, the lower 1–2½" (2.5–6.3 cm) long, opposite, lanceolate; slender tendrils in the flower cluster cling to other vegetation.
Height: to 4½' (1.4 m).
Flowering: April–June.
Habitat: Flats and slopes in loose soil in brush.
Range: Southern California and northern Baja California.
Comments: This Snapdragon's tall, slender spires are sparsely distributed, and so never provide dense color displays. The genus

name, from the Greek *anti* ("against")
and *rhinos* ("nose"), refers to the snout-
like corolla's lower lip pressed against
the upper.

---

342 **Yellow Twining Snapdragon**
(*Antirrhinum filipes*)
Figwort Family (Scrophulariaceae)

Description: *Many slender stems twist and twine*
through other vegetation, and *yellow*
*bilaterally symmetrical flowers* bloom on
thread-like stalks growing from leaf
axils.
Flowers: corolla about ½" (1.3 cm)
long; the 2 upper lobes bent upward,
the 3 lower bent downward and dotted
with black on the hump that closes
opening to the tube; stamens 4.
Leaves: to 2" (5 cm) long, lanceolate.
Height: vine, with stems to about 3'
(90 cm) long.
Flowering: February–May.
Habitat: Sandy deserts.
Range: Southeastern Oregon to southern
California and southwestern Utah.
Comments: The flowers are brilliant yellow, but the
plant, hidden and tangled in low
bushes, is hard to find, its twining
stems ordinarily obscured by leaves and
twigs.

---

639 **Alpine Besseya**
(*Besseya alpina*)
Figwort Family (Scrophulariaceae)

Description: A *small, pale plant, woolly* in younger
parts, the *pale bluish-violet flowers in dense*
*spikes* with conspicuous bracts.
Flowers: woolly calyx; bilaterally
symmetrical corolla about ¼" (6 mm)
long, the upper lip cupped forward, the
lower lip with 3 lobes, bent down,
middle lobe shortest; stamens 2.
Leaves: ¾–2" (2–5 cm) long, mostly at

base, the blades broadly ovate, edges
scalloped; those on stem beneath spike
much smaller and bract-like.
Height: barely 6″ (15 cm).

Flowering: July—September.

Habitat: High cold meadows and tundra.

Range: Wyoming and Utah to New Mexico.

Comments: The several *Besseya* species have corollas
varying from violet to yellow or white,
or lacking entirely. The genus name
honors the great American botanist
Charles E. Bessey (1845—1915).

### 417 Desert Paintbrush
(*Castilleja chromosa*)
Figwort Family (Scrophulariaceae)

Description: Several erect *stems with bright orange to
red, flower-like tips,* the bracts brightly
colored.
Flowers: corolla bilaterally symmetrical,
beak-like, very slender, ¾–1¼″ (2–
3.1 cm) long, lower lip a green bump
at about midlength, upper lip
projecting as a beak, lightly hairy on
top, usually pale with orange to red
edges; calyx bright reddish-orange, as
deeply cleft on upper side as lower,
shallowly cleft on sides, the resulting
4 lobes bluntly pointed.
Leaves: about 1–2″ (2.5–5 cm) long,
lower ones very narrow, undivided,
upper ones divided into 3 or 5 very
narrow lobes; bracts in flower cluster
similarly divided, but bright reddish-
orange.
Height: 4–16″ (10–40 cm).

Flowering: April—August.

Habitat: Dry open soil, often with sagebrush.

Range: Southern Idaho to eastern Oregon and
eastern California; east to northern
Arizona, northwestern New Mexico,
western Colorado, and central
Wyoming.

Comments: This is one of the West's most common
dry-land Paintbrushes. The genus is
easily recognized but many species are

notoriously difficult to identify. The
genus name, which honors the Spanish
botanist Domingo Castillejo, is usually
pronounced *cas-til-lay'-yah*.

### 418 Giant Red Paintbrush
(*Castilleja miniata*)
Figwort Family (Scrophulariaceae)

Description: The flower cluster of this leafy plant
resembles a *ragged, crimson or scarlet
paintbrush,* calyx and bracts beneath
each flower brightly colored.
Flowers: conspicuous, tubular calyx has
4 pointed lobes, cleft between upper
lobes as deep as cleft between lower;
bilaterally symmetrical corolla,
relatively inconspicuous, ¾–1½" (2–
3.8 cm) long, lower lip merely a green
bump, upper lip a "beak," at least as
long as the pale, tubular lower portion,
its edges thin and red.
Leaves: on stem, to about 4" (10 cm)
long, lanceolate, usually without lobes,
some of the upper leaves and the
colorful bracts with 3 pointed
lobes.
Height: 1–3' (30–90 cm).
Flowering: May–September.
Habitat: Mountain meadows, thickets, and
forest openings.
Range: Throughout.
Comments: Most Indian Paintbrushes are partial
parasites on other plants, their roots
establishing connections with roots of
other species. For this reason, they
usually cannot be transplanted, and are
difficult to grow from seed.

### 525 Great Plains Paintbrush
(*Castilleja sessiliflora*)
Figwort Family (Scrophulariaceae)

Description: Hairy plants with clustered stems,
often the *bracts and flowers pinkish,* the

corollas protruding like long, pale,
curved beaks.

Flowers: bilaterally symmetrical corolla
1¼–2½" (3.1–6.3 cm) long, pale
yellow to pale pink, upper lip beak-
like, about ½" (1.3 cm) long, lower
with 2 flared lobes about ¼" (6 mm)
long; calyx same color as bracts, its 4
lobes long and narrow.

Leaves: about 1–2" (2.5–5 cm) long,
lower ones very narrow, upper usually
with pair of narrow lobes.

Height: 4–12" (10–30 cm).

Flowering: March–September.

Habitat: Dry, open, rocky or sandy knolls and
slopes on plains, and among piñon and
juniper.

Range: Throughout the Great Plains to western
Texas and southeastern Arizona; also
northern Mexico.

Comments: In very dry, infertile areas the species
forms diminutive tufts; where soil and
moisture are better, plants are taller
and more open.

---

310 **Sulfur Paintbrush**
(*Castilleja sulphurea*)
Figwort Family (Scrophulariaceae)

Description: The flower cluster of this leafy plant
resembles *a ragged, pale yellow
paintbrush,* each calyx, and the bracts
beneath the flowers, brightly colored.

Flowers: tubular calyx with 4 short,
pointed lobes; bilaterally symmetrical
corolla ¾–1¼" (2–3.1 cm) long,
relatively inconspicuous, the lower lip a
green bump on the lower side well
above the middle, the upper lip pale,
barely extending beyond the calyx as a
short "beak."

Leaves: 1–3" (2.5–7.5 cm) long,
lanceolate, usually not cleft or lobed;
bracts of flower cluster similar, but
yellowish.

Height: 6–20" (15–50 cm).

Flowering: June–September.

Habitat: Moist meadows and slopes from
moderate to high elevations.

Range: Southern Alberta and western Montana
to Utah, New Mexico, and western
South Dakota.

Comments: Most Indian Paintbrushes are bright
red; this is one of the few yellow ones.
The large genus is found primarily in
western North America.

---

521 **Purple Chinese Houses; Innocence**
(*Collinsia heterophylla*)
Figwort Family (Scrophulariaceae)

Description: Bilaterally symmetrical flowers in *several
widely spaced whorls at top* of a sparsely
leafy stem.
Flowers: about ¾" (2 cm) long; upper
lip of corolla has *2 lavender, pale blue-
violet, or whiie lobes bent upward,* with
many maroon dots at base; lower lip has
*2 violet lobes projecting forward, the third
lobe folded between them,* hiding the style
and 4 stamens.
Leaves: to 2½" (6.3 cm) long, few,
paired, lanceolate, scalloped on edges.
Height: 1–2' (30–60 cm).

Flowering: March–June.

Habitat: Sandy soil on shaded flats or slopes.

Range: Southern two thirds of California and
northern Baja California.

Comments: Few of California's spectacular
wildflowers are as charming as this one.
The flowers grow in perfect rings of
widely spaced bands around the stem,
forming a fairytale pagoda, the
"Chinese houses." There are about 20
*Collinsia* species, most in California,
distinguished from other genera by the
corolla's folded middle lower lobe. In
this respect it resembles members of the
Pea Family, which, however, have 5
petals not joined into a tubular base,
and usually 10 stamens rather than 4.

### 599   Maiden Blue-eyed Mary
(*Collinsia parviflora*)
Figwort Family (Scrophulariaceae)

Description:   *Tiny, blue and white bilaterally
symmetrical flowers* bloom on slender
stalks in an open cluster on this small,
widely branched plant.
Flowers: about ¼" (6 mm) wide; upper
lip of corolla has 2 white lobes, bent
upward, often tinged with violet near
tips; lower lip has 2 blue-violet lobes
projecting forward and a middle lobe
folded between them, hiding the style
and 4 stamens.
Leaves: to 2" (5 cm) long but usually
much shorter, narrowly lanceolate,
opposite near base, in whorls of 4 in the
flower cluster.
Height: 2–16" (5–40 cm).

Flowering:   April–July.

Habitat:   Open gravelly flats and banks, often in
sparse grass.

Range:   British Columbia to southern
California; east to Colorado, Michigan,
and Ontario.

Comments:   This Collinsia has among the smallest
flowers in the genus. The similar Little
Tonella (*Tonella tenella*), from western
Washington to northern California, has
a bilateral white corolla barely ⅛"
(3 mm) long, the 5 lobes tipped with
violet, none folded.

### 486   Salt-marsh Club-flower
(*Cordylanthus maritimus*)
Figwort Family (Scrophulariaceae)

Description:   A softly hairy, loosely branched, low
plant with *pinkish and white bilaterally
symmetrical corollas nearly hidden* within
the tubular calyx and leafy racemes.
Flowers: corolla ¾" (2 cm) long, lower
end a slender tube, the upper end
swollen, blushed with pink or dull red-
violet, opening almost closed by the
very short, pale yellow, beak-like upper

lip and the equally short, 4-toothed lower lip; stamens 4.

Leaves: ¼–1" (6–25 mm) long, broadly lanceolate.

Height: 8–16" (20–40 cm).

Flowering: May–September.

Habitat: Salt marshes along the Pacific Coast.

Range: Southern Oregon to northern Baja California.

Comments: Although hardly pretty, this curious flower attracts attention. The genus name, from the Greek *kordyle* ("club") and *anthos* ("flower"), describes the corolla's shape.

## 291 Wright's Birdbeak
(*Cordylanthus wrightii*)
Figwort Family (Scrophulariaceae)

Description: This openly branched, spindly plant has *yellow or dull purplish bilaterally symmetrical flowers resembling a bird's beak* in clusters at ends of branches.

Flowers: ¾–1¼" (2–3.1 cm) long; corolla with upper and lower pointed lips nearly equal in length, with edges of upper lip flared to the side near base; calyx with a tubular base and 1 lobe, and opposite this lobe there is a bract, giving the effect of a 2-lobed calyx; outer bracts around flowers have up to 7 very slender lobes.

Leaves: about 1–2" (2.5–5 cm) long, divided into 3 or 5 very narrow segments.

Height: 2' (60 cm).

Flowering: July–October.

Habitat: Open sandy areas on plains and in pine forests.

Range: Central Arizona to western Texas.

Comments: Most of the nearly 40 species of Birdbeaks are found in western North America. The plants tend to grow in dry places, blooming late in the season when most other flowers have passed. The color of the corolla varies from white to dull violet, mauve, or yellow.

511  **Foxglove**
     (*Digitalis purpurea*)
     Figwort Family (Scrophulariaceae)

Description:   Spectacular *spires of hanging flowers all
               turned to one side* in long, dense racemes
               top this tall, leafy plant.
               Flowers: bilaterally symmetrical corolla
               with a flared white to pinkish-lavender
               tube 1½–2½″ (3.8–6.3 cm) long and
               ¾″ (2 cm) wide, conspicuously speckled
               with many red or maroon dots on lower
               side of interior, the rim with 5 short
               lobes.
               Leaves: largest at base, to 1′ (30 cm)
               long, ovate, edges scalloped or toothed.
               Height: 2–7′ (60–210 cm).
Flowering:     June–July.
Habitat:       Along road banks and other disturbed
               open sites.
Range:         British Columbia to central California
               mostly west of the Cascade Mountains
               and the Sierra Nevada.
Comments:      Unlike most plants introduced from
               foreign lands and now unwelcome
               weeds, Foxglove lends spectacular
               columns of color to the green brushy
               and wooded slopes of the Pacific region.
               The heart stimulant digitalis, toxic
               when not properly administered, is
               derived from the species. Plants are
               poisonous to livestock but are rarely
               eaten; however, in hay they are deadly
               toxic.

576  **Texas Silverleaf; Purple Sage; Cenizo**
     (*Leucophyllum frutescens*)
     Figwort Family (Scrophulariaceae)

Description:   A *gray shrub* with leaves covered with
               silvery hairs, and *bright pink-lavender
               bilaterally symmetrical flowers* blooming
               singly in crowded leaf axils.
               Flowers: corolla ¾–1″ (2–2.5 cm)
               long, about as wide, funnel-shaped
               with 5 round lobes, the lower lobes
               hairy inside; stamens 4.

Leaves: generally about 1″ (2.5 cm) long, nearly oval, the base long and tapered.

Height: to 8′ (2.5 m).

Flowering: June—November.

Habitat: Rocky limestone plains, brushland, and deserts.

Range: Southern Texas and northern Mexico.

Comments: As one travels from west to east in the Southwest, near the Mexican border, the olive-green creosotebush gives way to the gray of Texas Silverleaf, with its display of bright lavender flowers. These burst into bloom for only a few days at a time, in the summer and fall, depending on the rainfall.

---

**621 Blue Toadflax; Old-field Toadflax**
(*Linaria canadensis*)
Figwort Family (Scrophulariaceae)

Description: The slender, erect stem of this plant has short, prostrate branches at base, and *blue-violet bilaterally symmetrical flowers* blooming in a raceme.

Flowers: corolla about ½″ (1.3 cm) long, with a slender spur about ¼″ (6 mm) long projecting backward and curving downward; the 2 lobes of upper lip bent upward, the lower lip extending forward, its 2 broad lobes hanging to the sides of a central hump, 1 narrower lobe hanging at end.

Leaves: to 1¼″ (3.1 cm) long, narrow.

Height: to 28″ (70 cm).

Flowering: March—June.

Habitat: Moist, open, sandy areas.

Range: Throughout.

Comments: The eastern *L. texana,* also called Blue Toadflax, and rarely found in the West, has slightly larger flowers.

### 301  Butter and Eggs; Common Toadflax
*(Linaria vulgaris)*
Figwort Family (Scrophulariaceae)

Description:    Erect stems that grow in dense patches
and numerous, mostly *pale yellow,
bilaterally symmetrical flowers all tipped
upward in a dense spike.*
Flowers: 1–1½" (2.5–3.8 cm) long;
2 lobes of upper lip pointing forward,
the 3 lobes of lower lip bending
downward, with an orange patch of
hairs on hump at base which closes
opening to the tube; beneath, a straight
spur projects backward.
Leaves: to 4" (10 cm) long, many,
narrow, grayish green.
Height: 1–3' (30–90 cm).

Flowering:    June–September.
Habitat:    Open, often disturbed places.
Range:    Throughout.
Comments:    The common name Toadflax refers to
the corolla's "mouth," resembling that
of a toad, and the leaves, which look
like those of Flax (*Linum*). The name
Butter and Eggs refers to the corolla's
color combination. A similar species,
Dalmatian Toadflax (*L. dalmatica*), also
introduced from Eurasia and spreading,
has ovate leaves that clasp the
stem.

### 660  Little Snapdragon Vine; Violet
Twining
*(Maurandya antirrhiniflora)*
Figwort Family (Scrophulariaceae)

Description:    *Stems twine* through other vegetation;
*flowers pale blue-violet or reddish-lavender,*
their stalks and those of leaves curved
and twisted.
Flowers: corolla bilaterally symmetrical,
¾–1" (2–2.5 cm) long, with a hairy
cream patch at base of lower lip near
opening, 2 lobes of upper lip bent
upward, the 3 lobes of lower lip bent
downward.

Leaves: about 1″ (2.5 cm) long, shaped
like arrowheads.

Height: vine, with stems to 7′ (2.1 m)
long.

Flowering: June–September.

Habitat: Sandy or gravelly soil, in deserts,
sometimes on rock walls, and among
piñon and juniper.

Range: Southeastern California to western
Texas; south into Mexico.

Comments: These little Snapdragons, attractive and
well worth cultivating, can be grown
from seed. They will produce small,
scrambling vines that die back to the
ground each winter.

### 659 Net-cup Snapdragon Vine
(*Maurandya wislizenii*)
Figwort Family (Scrophulariaceae)

Description: *Vine* with rather *arrow-shaped leaves and
pale blue-violet snapdragon flowers* in axils
of bract-like leaves.

Flowers: bilaterally symmetrical corolla
1″ (2.5 cm) long; sepals enlarging as
fruit matures, with a rigid, net-like
pattern throughout, the base of each
becoming swollen and pouch-like.

Leaves: to 2″ (5 cm) long, on stalks
about as long.

Fruit: capsule.

Height: vine, to 10′ (3 m) long.

Flowering: April–July.

Habitat: Among shrubs and on dunes.

Range: Southeastern Arizona to western Texas
and northern Mexico.

Comments: This species is much coarser-looking
than its close relative, Little
Snapdragon Vine (*M. antirrhiniflora*).

### 357   Orange Bush Monkeyflower
(*Mimulus aurantiacus*)
Figwort Family (Scrophulariaceae)

Description: A plant with woody, branched stems,
covered with a sticky, varnish-like
secretion and *pale to deep orange
bilaterally symmetrical flowers.*
Flowers: 1¼–2″ (3.1–5 cm) long;
upper lip of corolla has 2 lobes bent
upward, lower lip has 3 lobes bent
downward; calyx smooth.
Leaves: to 3″ (7.5 cm) long, lanceolate,
dark green on top, pale and sparsely
hairy on underside, edges with fine
teeth.
Height: 2–4′ (60–120 cm).
Flowering: March–August.
Habitat: Slopes and banks in chaparral and open
woods.
Range: Southwestern Oregon to southern
California; inland to the base of the
Sierra Nevada.
Comments: Its long blooming season makes Orange
Bush Monkeyflower a reliable source of
nectar for hummingbirds. At the end of
the style, two flaps (the stigmas) will
slowly but visibly move and close
together when touched by a blade of
grass, a pollen-laden insect, or a
hummingbird, providing a protective
chamber for the pollen to begin its
growth.

### 545   Fremont's Monkeyflower
(*Mimulus fremontii*)
Figwort Family (Scrophulariaceae)

Description: A small, branched, glandular-hairy,
reddish plant with *slightly bilaterally
symmetrical rose-lavender flowers.*
Flowers: ¾–1″ (2–2.5 cm) wide;
corolla with 5 nearly equal round lobes
and a broadly tubular base; calyx with 5
prominent angles and 5 nearly equal
triangular lobes; stamens 4, hidden
within.

Leaves: ½–1¼" (1.3–3.1 cm) long,
oblong, opposite.
Height: 1–8" (2.5–20 cm).

Flowering: April–June.
Habitat: Dry open places such as recent burns,
road banks, and dry gullies.
Range: Southern California to Baja California,
west of the desert.
Comments: This species will be very frequent for a
few years after a fire sweeps through the
chaparral, decreasing as the vegetation
closes in.

## 286 Seep-spring Monkeyflower; Common Monkeyflower
(*Mimulus guttatus*)
Figwort Family (Scrophulariaceae)

Description: An extremely variable, leafy plant
ranging from spindly and tiny to large
and bushy, with *yellow bilaterally
symmetrical flowers* on slender stalks in
upper leaf axils.
Flowers: corolla ½–1½" (1.3–3.8 cm)
long, often with reddish spots near
opening, 2 lobes of upper lip bent
upward, the 3 lobes of lower lip bent
downward; at base of lower lip is a
hairy hump that almost closes the
opening.
Leaves: ½–4" (1.3–10 cm) long, ovate,
opposite, edges with sharp teeth.
Height: to 3' (90 cm).
Flowering: March–September.
Habitat: Wet places from sea level to mountains.
Range: Throughout.
Comments: In this large genus of several look-alikes
with yellow corollas, Seep-spring
Monkeyflower is distinguished by the
longer upper tooth on the angular
calyx.

### 564  Lewis' Monkeyflower
(*Mimulus lewisii*)
Figwort Family (Scrophulariaceae)

Description:  Showy, *deep pink to red bilaterally symmetrical flowers* bloom in profusion near the top of this leafy, several-stemmed plant.
Flowers: 1¼–2″ (3.1–5 cm) long; corolla with 3 lobes bent down, 2 bent upward, marked with yellow patches of hairs and darker red-violet lines near opening.
Leaves: 1–4″ (2.5–10 cm) long, with toothed or plain edges, opposite.
Height: 1–3′ (30–90 cm).
Flowering:  June–August.
Habitat:  Wet open places in the mountains.
Range:  Western Canada; south to the southern Sierra Nevada in California and to the higher mountains of Utah, Wyoming, and Montana.
Comments:  This is among the most handsome of mountain wildflowers, its deep pink to red flowers probably attracting hummingbirds during their summer stay in the mountains.

### 435  Dwarf Purple Monkeyflower
(*Mimulus nanus*)
Figwort Family (Scrophulariaceae)

Description:  A little plant, covered with glandular hairs, with single or highly branched stems, and *rich reddish-lavender bilaterally symmetrical flowers* on short stalks in upper leaf axils.
Flowers: corolla ½–1″ (1.3–2.5 cm) long, marked inside near opening with yellow and deep red lines.
Leaves: to 1½″ (3.8 cm) long, lanceolate, opposite.
Height: to 4″ (10 cm).
Flowering:  May–August.
Habitat:  Dry open areas on sagebrush plains and in open pine forests.
Range:  Central Washington to northern

California; east to northeastern Nevada, northwestern Wyoming, and southwestern Montana.

Comments: Like other desert annuals, in a year of poor rainfall Dwarf Purple Monkeyflower puts all its efforts into producing a new crop of seeds to insure future generations. After growing only about ¼" (6 mm) tall, it flamboyantly produces one, comparatively huge, flower that seems to sit right on the ground.

228 **Ghost Flower; Mojave Flower**
(*Mohavea confertiflora*)
Figwort Family (Scrophulariaceae)

Description: In the upper leaf axils of this erect plant are *large, bilaterally symmetrical, translucent, yellow flowers, tipped upward* or even vertical.
Flowers: corolla about 1¼" (3.1 cm) long, with 5 ragged-edged lobes, lower ones with maroon speckles inside and a maroon blotch at base; opening to base closed by a hairy bump on lower side; only 2 stamens.
Leaves: 2–4" (5–10 cm) long, hairy, narrowly lanceolate.
Height: 4–20" (10–50 cm).
Flowering: March–April.
Habitat: Desert washes and rocky slopes.
Range: Southeastern California to southern Nevada, western Arizona, and northwestern Sonora.
Comments: The translucent, pale corolla gives the name Ghost Flower. There is only 1 other species, Lesser Mohavea or Golden Desert Snapdragon (*M. breviflora*), which grows in the same region and has bilaterally symmetrical yellow corollas only about ½" (1.3 cm) long.

## 306  Yellow Owl's Clover
*(Orthocarpus luteus)*
Figwort Family (Scrophulariaceae)

Description:  *Many golden-yellow flowers, angled upward, protruding from glandular-hairy bracts* near top of this erect plant. Flowers: corolla bilaterally symmetrical, about ½" (1.3 cm) long, with a pouch on lower side near tip; at end of pouch are 3 tiny teeth; above pouch, upper lip forms a short beak; stamens 4, inside. Leaves: ½–1½" (1.3–3.8 cm) long, very narrow, sometimes divided into 3 narrow lobes. Height: 4–16" (10–40 cm).

Flowering:  July–September.

Habitat:  Plains and open woods.

Range:  British Columbia to southeastern California, mostly east of the Cascade Mountains and the Sierra Nevada; east to New Mexico, Nebraska, Minnesota, and Manitoba.

Comments:  There are about 25 species of Owl's Clover, all but one in western North America, several with yellow corollas, and some with a 3-lobed pouch. The name Owl's Clover may refer to the eye-like spots on the petals of some species or, picturesquely, to the swollen head-like ends of the erect corollas that seem to peer from the bracts as owls peer from the leaves of a tree.

## 526  Common Owl's Clover; Escobita
*(Orthocarpus purpuracens)*
Figwort Family (Scrophulariaceae)

Description:  The flower cluster of this erect, little plant is *rose and yellow, or rose and white,* for the floral *bracts are velvety and rose-purple* on their divided tips. Flowers: bilaterally symmetrical corollas 1–1¼" (1.3–3.1 cm) long, each exposing a white or yellow 3-lobed pouch as they "peer" from bracts, strongly angled upward; at end of

pouch are 3 tiny teeth; above pouch's upper lip is a short, hooked, velvety, rose-purple beak.
Leaves: ½–2" (1.3–5 cm) long, divided into a few very narrow segments.
Fruit: capsule about ½" (1.3 cm) long.
Height: 4–16" (10–40 cm).

Flowering: March–May.

Habitat: Fields and open wooded areas.

Range: Southern California to western Arizona and northern Mexico.

Comments: Following a wet spring, acre upon acre is carpeted with this beautiful wildflower, whose Spanish name means "little broom," descriptive of the broom-like flower cluster. *Orthocarpus* comes from Greek words meaning "straight fruit," but by the time most fruits form, the late-spring sun has "burned off" the colorful display and the plants are overlooked.

### 304 Yellow Parentucellia
(*Parentucellia viscosa*)
Figwort Family (Scrophulariaceae)

Description: An erect, leafy, *glandular-hairy plant with small, bilaterally symmetrical, yellow flowers* tucked among the upper leaf-like bracts.
Flowers: corolla about ¾" (2 cm) long, upper lip like a hood, lower 3-lobed and slightly bent downward.
Leaves: ½–1½" (1.3–3.8 cm) long, ovate, the edges toothed, at least the lower ones opposite.
Height: 4–28" (10–70 cm).

Flowering: June–August.

Habitat: Moist open areas.

Range: Western Washington to northwestern California.

Comments: Introduced from Europe, this species grows in such profusion that grassy hillsides and flats often acquire a yellow hue.

### 305  Towering Lousewort
(*Pedicularis bracteosa*)
Figwort Family (Scrophulariaceae)

Description:  An erect plant with *divided, rather fern-like leaves* and *bilaterally symmetrical, beak-like flowers in a dense raceme.*
Flowers: corolla ½–¾" (1.3–2 cm) long; varies from yellow to purple, maroon, or reddish, its upper lip narrow, arched outward like the prow of an overturned canoe, the lower lip shorter, the 3 lobes projecting forward, the central the narrowest.
Leaves: 3–10" (7.5–25 cm) long, fern-like, divided into narrow leaflets with jagged teeth; upper leaves about as large as lower.
Height: to 3' (90 cm).

Flowering:  June–August.
Habitat:  Moist woods and meadows in the mountains.
Range:  British Columbia to northern California; east to Colorado, Utah, Montana, and Alberta.
Comments:  Western Louseworts vary from plants 3' (2.1 m) tall, to miniature ones only 1" (2.5 cm) high. The genus name, from the Latin *pediculus* ("little louse"), alludes to a superstition that livestock that ate these plants would suffer from an infestation of lice.

### 534  Elephant Heads; Little Red Elephants
(*Pedicularis groenlandica*)
Figwort Family (Scrophulariaceae)

Description:  Dense racemes of *flowers that are perfect little pink elephant heads* (ears, trunk, and all) bloom on leafy stems.
Flowers: strongly bilaterally symmetrical corolla; exclusive of the "trunk" about ½" (1.3 cm) long; "trunk" the upper lip, curving forward well beyond the lower lip, of which 3 lobes form the ears and lower part of

the "elephant's head."

Leaves: 2–10" (5–25 cm) long, narrow, pinnately divided into sharp-toothed lobes.

Height: to 28" (70 cm).

Flowering: June–August.

Habitat: Wet meadows and small cold streams.

Range: Throughout the western mountains.

Comments: The flower's charming structure facilitates pollination while at the same time reducing the chances of hybridization with other species. Little Elephant Heads (*P. attollens*), only to 16" (40 cm) tall, has a corolla marked with white and rose, and head proportions are not so perfectly elephantine—the "trunk," raised as if trumpeting, is only as long as the lower lip. It grows from the Cascade Mountains of Oregon to the Sierra Nevada in California.

---

121 **Sickletop Lousewort**
(*Pedicularis racemosa*)
Figwort Family (Scrophulariaceae)

Description: A bushy, leafy plant with several stems, and *twisted white or pink flowers* in short branches in upper leaf axils.

Flowers: irregular corolla about ½" (1.3 cm) long, white, pale pink, or pink; the narrow upper lip an arched, beak-like hook twisting to one side, touching the lower lip, which is broad, with 2 big lateral lobes and a small central one.

Leaves: 2–4" (5–10 cm) long, lanceolate, with many tiny blunt teeth on edges.

Height: 6–20" (15–50 cm).

Flowering: June–September.

Habitat: Coniferous woods and dry meadows in the mountains.

Range: British Columbia and Alberta; south to eastern Arizona and western New Mexico.

Comments:  A common trailside plant in the mountains. The corolla's contorted beak is distinctive, and the undivided leaves are unusual among western Lousewort species.

---

### 287  Dwarf Lousewort
(*Pedicularis semibarbata*)
Figwort Family (Scrophulariaceae)

Description:  A little plant with *fern-like leaves in a tuft,* among which is a short raceme of flowers with *pale yellow, bilaterally symmetrical corollas.*
Flowers: corolla about ¾" (2 cm) long; upper and lower lips tinged with purple, upper lip resembling the prow of an overturned canoe, lower lip about as long, with 3 lobes.
Leaves: to 6" (15 cm) long, pinnately divided into many leaflets, with jagged lobes and teeth.
Height: less than 4" (10 cm).
Flowering:  May–July.
Habitat:  Dry coniferous woods in the mountains.
Range:  Southern Oregon to southern California and western Nevada.
Comments:  Among the shortest of the many Lousewort species. The flowers often sit almost upon the ground.

---

### 414  Golden-beard Penstemon
(*Penstemon barbatus*)
Figwort Family (Scrophulariaceae)

Description:  *Slender, bilaterally symmetrical, scarlet corollas hang slightly* in a long, open cluster above sparsely leafy stems.
Flowers: corolla 1–1½" (2.5–3.8 cm) long, upper lip projecting forward, like a visor, with 2 small teeth at tip; lower lip with 3 lobes, bent downward and backward, with usually a few yellow hairs near opening; 4 stamens have anthers, the fifth has none.

Leaves: 2–5″ (5–12.5 cm) long, smooth, gray-green, opposite, narrow. Height: to 3′ (90 cm).

Flowering: June–September.

Habitat: Dry rocky slopes in open forests.

Range: Southern Colorado to Arizona and western Texas; south into Mexico.

Comments: This species is one of several Penstemons with scarlet corollas. The genus name, from the Greek *pente* ("five") and *stemon* ("thread"), refers to the slender fifth stamen.

409 **Scarlet Bugler**
(*Penstemon centranthifolius*)
Figwort Family (Scrophulariaceae)

Description: Few, erect, sparsely leafy stems have *bright red, nearly radially symmetrical, tubular flowers* in a long, narrow, but open cluster near the top.
Flowers: corolla 1–1¼″ (2.5–3.1 cm) long, the 5 lobes very short, barely spreading, round at tips; stamens 5, the fifth without an anther.
Leaves: 1¼–3″ (3.1–7.5 cm) long, spatula-shaped or lanceolate, opposite. Height: 1–4′ (30–120 cm).

Flowering: April–July.

Habitat: Dry open places in brush, commonly where the soil has been disturbed.

Range: Coast Ranges from central California to Baja California.

Comments: In certain situations this species will produce extensive, nearly solid patches of brilliant red. The nearly radially symmetrical corollas are unusual.

406 **Red Shrubby Penstemon**
(*Penstemon corymbosus*)
Figwort Family (Scrophulariaceae)

Description: A *low, dark green shrub with bright, brick-red, bilaterally symmetrical flowers* in bunches at ends of branches.

Flowers: 1–1½″ (2.5–3.8 cm) long,
the 2 lobes of upper lip project forward,
the 3 lobes of lower lip bend
downward; stamens 5, with stalks hairy
at base, the fifth stamen lacking an
anther but tipped with golden hairs.
Leaves: ¾–1½″ (2–3.8 cm) long,
*opposite,* leathery, ovate, often with
small teeth.
Height: 12–20″ (30–50 cm).

Flowering: June–October.

Habitat: Open rocky slopes and cliffs.

Range: Coast Ranges and Sierran foothills of
northern California.

Comments: After the summer heat dries the low
mountains, driving most wildflowers to
seed and browning the grasses, Red
Shrubby Penstemon begins to flower,
providing a final source of nectar before
the hummingbirds must seek food
higher in the cooler mountains or, if
late in the season, migrate south. This
and several other shrubby species have
been suggested to belong to the genus
*Keckiella,* honoring David Keck, a
student of *Penstemon* and California
plants.

---

625  **Platte River Penstemon**
(*Penstemon cyananthus*)
Figwort Family (Scrophulariaceae)

Description: An erect plant with several leafy stems,
and *blue-violet bilaterally symmetrical
flowers in rings* near the top.
Flowers: corolla ¾–1¼″ (2–3.1 cm)
long, smooth, the 5 lobes blue, the
tube violet and swollen; stamens 4,
with anthers, the fifth sterile, densely
bearded at tip with golden hairs;
anthers hairy on the sides, not opening
across the region where the 2 pollen
sacs are joined to the stalk.
Leaves: ¾–4″ (2–10 cm) long,
narrowly lanceolate or ovate, without
stalks, opposite.
Height: 8–40″ (20–100 cm).

Flowering: May–July.
Habitat: Sagebrush hills and openings in mountain forests.
Range: Southeastern Idaho to northern Utah and western Wyoming.
Comments: This is a common spring wildflower in its area, often filling disturbed ground with handsome patches of blue. An alternate common name for the genus is Beardtongue, referring to the bearded sterile stamen, as in this species.

### 494 Davidson's Penstemon
(*Penstemon davidsonii*)
Figwort Family (Scrophulariaceae)

Description: A *matted plant* with woody stems and base, opposite, crowded leaves, and *blue-lavender bilaterally symmetrical flowers* clustered on short, erect stems.
Flowers: corolla ¾–1¼" (2–3.1 cm) long, upper lip with 2 lobes projecting forward, lower lip with 3 lobes bent downward, hairy inside at base of lower lip; 4 stamens have long wool on anthers, the fifth stamen without an anther, hairy at tip.
Leaves: ¼–¾" (6–20 mm) long, thick, firm, oval but tapered to the stalk, with or without small teeth; leaves nearer flowers represented by small bracts.
Height: 2–6" (5–15 cm).
Flowering: June–August.
Habitat: On rock ledges and slopes from middle to high elevations.
Range: British Columbia to northern California.
Comments: In full flower this plant forms spectacular lavender mats. Plants in the southern part of the range have toothless leaves; to the north teeth are frequent.

## 122 Hot Rock Penstemon
(*Penstemon deustus*)
Figwort Family (Scrophulariaceae)

Description: The stems grow in clusters from a woody base and have *dingy white or cream bilaterally symmetrical flowers* in several whorls in axils of leafy bracts. Flowers: corolla ½–¾" (1.3–2 cm) long, generally with fine purplish lines inside, upper lip with 2 round lobes bent upward, lower lip with 3 lobes bent downward; stamens 5, the fifth lacking an anther, the tip hairy or not. Leaves: to 3" (7.5 cm) long, opposite, bright green, ovate, with sharp teeth. Height: 8–24" (20–60 cm).

Flowering: May–July.

Habitat: Dry open rocky places from the lowlands to the mountains.

Range: Central Washington to central California; east to Nevada, Utah, northern Wyoming, and western Montana.

Comments: In a huge western genus of more than 200 species, this will serve to represent the few with white flowers. Few species of these lovely wildflowers are fragrant, most having a mildly unpleasant odor, especially noticeable in Hot Rock Penstemon.

## 622 Jones' Penstemon
(*Penstemon dolius*)
Figwort Family (Scrophulariaceae)

Description: A low plant with stems prostrate to erect, and with *light blue and violet bilaterally symmetrical flowers in short clusters* near the tips. Flowers: corolla ½–¾" (1.3–2 cm) long, the 2 lobes of upper lip arched forward, the lower 3 spreading downward, light blue, the tubular base violet and glandular-hairy on the outside; 4 stamens with anthers, fifth without an anther, bearded at tip.

Leaves: ½–2″ (1.3–5 cm) long, narrowly lanceolate, opposite.
Height: 2–8″ (5–20 cm).
Flowering: May–June.
Habitat: Dry gravelly or clay slopes in sagebrush or among piñon and juniper.
Range: Eastern Nevada to northeastern Utah.
Comments: This little Penstemon with its short flower clusters and bright, short flowers is a common sight among the arid bushy lands of the Great Basin region.

## 562 Lowbush Penstemon
(*Penstemon fruticosus*)
Figwort Family (Scrophulariaceae)

Description: A bushy plant usually much broader than tall, with large, showy, *pale lavender or pale blue-violet bilaterally symmetrical flowers* in crowded, narrow clusters at ends of stems.
Flowers: corolla 1–2″ (2.5–5 cm) long, plump, with long white hairs inside near base of lower lip, the 2 lobes of upper lip arched forward, the 3 lobes of lower lip bent downward; 4 stamens have hairy pollen sacs, the fifth stamen has a bearded tip but no pollen sac.
Leaves: to 2½″ (6.3 cm) long, opposite, lanceolate or ovate, the edges with or without teeth.
Height: 6–16″ (15–40 cm).
Flowering: May–August.
Habitat: Rocky open or wooded sites from the foothills well into the mountains.
Range: Southern British Columbia to central Oregon; east to western Montana and Wyoming.
Comments: In a genus with many beautiful species, this one may be the most spectacular. Bright green leafy patches cascade down banks and between rocks, topped with a dense display of subtly shaded flowers that butterflies seem to find especially attractive.

### 623  Narrowleaf Penstemon
(*Penstemon linarioides*)
Figwort Family (Scrophulariaceae)

Description:   *Bilaterally symmetrical blue-violet corollas turned to one side* in a narrow, long, open flower cluster above a leafy base.
Flowers: corolla about ¾″ (2 cm) long, the very narrow tubular base expanding abruptly into a broad throat without 2 ridges on bottom, the 2 lobes of upper lip bent upward, the 3 lobes of lower lip bent downward; stamens 5, the fifth bearded at tip but bearing no anther.
Leaves: ½–1″ (1.3–2.5 cm) long, *very narrow, grayish-green, usually downy,* crowded near base.
Height: 6–16″ (15–40 cm).

Flowering:   June–August.
Habitat:   Open, often rocky soil at moderate elevations.
Range:   Southern Utah and Colorado, to much of New Mexico and Arizona.
Comments:   This is a common Penstemon in dry open woodland in the Southwest. Of several species in this huge, beautiful genus that have blue-violet flowers and narrow leaves, some have 2 ridges inside the corolla.

### 492  Mountain Pride
(*Penstemon newberryi*)
Figwort Family (Scrophulariaceae)

Description:   From a matted base grow short, erect, leafy stems with *deep pink bilaterally symmetrical flowers* usually all turned to one side in a short raceme.
Flowers: corolla ¾–1¼″ (2–3.1 cm) wide, the 2 lobes of upper lip arched forward, the 3 lobes of lower lip bent downward, 2 densely hairy ridges on the lower inside of tube; stamens 4, with densely hairy anthers, the fifth stamen without an anther, densely golden-bearded at tip.
Leaves: ½–1½″ (1.3–3.1 cm) long,

toothed, ovate, thick, opposite.
Height: 6–12″ (15–30 cm).
Flowering: June–August.
Habitat: Rocky places at moderate to high elevations.
Range: Southwestern Oregon to the southern Sierra Nevada of California.
Comments: This handsome species commonly adds bright swatches of color to highway road cuts through the rocky California mountains.

### 523 Balloon Flower
(*Penstemon palmeri*)
Figwort Family (Scrophulariaceae)

Description: A few sparsely-leaved, erect, stout stems have *swollen white to reddish-pink bilaterally symmetrical flowers mostly turned to one side* in a long, narrow cluster.
Flowers: corolla 1–1½″ (2.5–3.8 cm) long, the short tube at base abruptly expanded into a large swollen chamber with reddish lines on the lower inside, the opening with the 2 upper lobes bent sharply upward, the 3 lower bent downward; 4 stamens with anthers, the fifth without an anther, densely golden-bearded at tip.
Leaves: largest to 10″ (25 cm) long, lanceolate, opposite, the bases of the paired upper leaves often joined, the stem appearing to go through them.
Height: 2–7′ (60–210 cm).
Flowering: May–July.
Habitat: Open rocky areas among sagebrush, piñon and juniper, or pine woods.
Range: Southeastern Arizona to central Arizona, southern Utah, and central New Mexico.
Comments: This is one of the most delightful species of Penstemon, its cheery puffed-up flowers exquisitely fragrant.

**524 Parry's Penstemon**
*(Penstemon parryi)*
Figwort Family (Scrophulariaceae)

Description: Several erect, sparsely leafy stems have *pinkish-lavender bilaterally symmetrical flowers* in a long, open, interrupted cluster.
Flowers: corolla about ¾" (2 cm) long, glandular-hairy on outside, broadly funnel-shaped, the lobes short and round, 2 bent upward, 3 bent downward; stamens 4, with anthers, the fifth without an anther, bearded at tip.
Leaves: 2–5" (5–12.5 cm) long, lanceolate, those at midstem broadest at base, without stalks, smooth.
Height: to 4' (1.2 m).
Flowering: March–May.
Habitat: Grassy or bushy slopes or flats.
Range: Southern Arizona and northern Sonora.
Comments: This handsome species commonly grows on road shoulders and freeway medians, providing spectacular splashes of color against the still brown grasses.

**493 Cliff Penstemon; Rock Penstemon**
*(Penstemon rupicola)*
Figwort Family (Scrophulariaceae)

Description: A few large, *brilliant pink or rose bilaterally symmetrical flowers in many racemes* often form a dense display above thick mats of stems and leaves.
Flowers: corolla 1–1½" (2.5–3.8 cm) long, with 5 lobes, 2 bent upward, 3 bent downward; 4 stamens with long wool on anthers, the fifth stamen has no anther, but may have a few hairs at tip.
Leaves: ½–¾" (1.3–2 cm) long, opposite, ovate, thick, with small, irregular teeth on edges.
Height: creeper, flower stalks to 4" (10 cm) high.
Flowering: May–August.
Habitat: Rock slopes, ledges, and cliffs.

Range: Central Washington to northern California.

Comments: Although there are only a few flowers in any one raceme, there are many racemes, and in full bloom the plant is a swatch of bright, glowing pink, among the West's most beautiful wildflowers.

## 624 Rydberg's Penstemon
*(Penstemon rydbergii)*
Figwort Family (Scrophulariaceae)

Description: *Small, dark blue-violet bilaterally symmetrical flowers form 1 or several dense whorls* at, or along, the upper part of the erect stems.
Flowers: corolla ½–¾" (1.3–2 cm) long, narrowly funnel-shaped, the 2 upper lobes projecting forward, the 3 lower spreading downward, hairy near opening on the lower inside; stamens 4, with anthers, the fifth without an anther, densely bearded at tip.
Leaves: 1½–3" (3.8–7.5 cm) long, lanceolate, opposite, those at midstem without stalks.
Height: 8–24" (20–60 cm).

Flowering: June–July.

Habitat: Open mountain slopes.

Range: Eastern Washington to eastern California; east to northern Arizona, Colorado, Wyoming, and southwestern Montana.

Comments: The dark blue-violet whorls of small flowers help distinguish this common Penstemon from most other species.

## 626 Cascade Penstemon
*(Penstemon serrulatus)*
Figwort Family (Scrophulariaceae)

Description: Several erect, leafy stems with 1 or several whorls of *deep blue to dark purple bilaterally symmetrical flowers* at the top.

Flowers: corolla ¾–1″ (2–2.5 cm) long, without hairs, 2 upper lobes bent slightly upward, 3 lower spreading downward; stamens 4, with anthers, the fifth without an anther, golden-hairy at tip.

Leaves: 1¼–3″ (3.1–7.5 cm) long, opposite, broadly lanceolate or ovate, not hairy, sharply toothed on edges, usually without stalks.

Height: 8–28″ (20–70 cm).

Flowering: June–August.

Habitat: Moist places from low to moderate elevations.

Range: British Columbia to southern Oregon.

Comments: One of the few Penstemons to occur west of the Cascade Mountains. *Serrulatus* in the technical name refers to the little teeth (*serrate*) on the leaves.

---

### 522  Whipple's Penstemon
(*Penstemon whippleanus*)
Figwort Family (Scrophulariaceae)

Description: *Deep wine-lavender to black-purple bilaterally symmetrical flowers* bloom in several clusters in the upper half of leafy stems.

Flowers: ¾–1¼″ (2–3.1 cm) long, finely glandular-hairy outside, usually with sparse, long hairs inside at base of lower lip, with the tubular base expanding abruptly to the much broader middle portion; upper lip arched forward, lower lip projecting forward farther than upper lip; 4 stamens with anthers, fifth stamen without an anther but usually with a tuft of hair at tip.

Leaves: ½–6″ (1.3–15 cm) long, ovate, opposite, the edges smooth or with small teeth.

Height: 4–28″ (10–70 cm).

Flowering: July–September.

Habitat: In meadows or on wooded slopes, often where moist.

Range: Southern Montana southward through

the Rocky Mountain regions to northern Arizona and southern New Mexico.

Comments: This common mountain Penstemon can ordinarily be recognized by its plump, dark purple, glandular-hairy corollas. However, phases with dingy yellow or white corollas blushed with brown, purple, or blue are frequent.

### 303 Yellow Rattle
(*Rhinanthus crista-galli*)
Figwort Family (Scrophulariaceae)

Description: An erect plant with *widely spaced opposite leaves* on the stem and *bilaterally symmetrical flowers in spikes* at the top, *all turned to one side,* each *yellow corolla protruding from a flat calyx* (as if pressed from the sides).
Flowers: calyx oval, becoming larger as fruit develops, bearing 4 teeth at tip, corolla about ½" (1.3 cm) long, with a hoodlike upper lip with 2 small round teeth, the smaller lower lip with 3 round teeth projecting forward.
Leaves: up to 2½" (6.3 cm) long, lanceolate, with teeth on edges.
Height: 6–32" (15–80 cm).
Flowering: June–August.
Habitat: Meadows and moist slopes.
Range: Northern Hemisphere extending south to northwestern Oregon, Colorado, and New York.
Comments: The scientific name means " snout-flower cock's-comb," probably referring to the comb-like row of calyces (plural for calyx) and the snout-shaped corolla.

## 641 Mountain Kittentails
*(Synthyris missurica)*
Figwort Family (Scrophulariaceae)

Description: *Dense racemes of bilaterally symmetrical*
*flowers with deep blue-violet corollas* bloom
above basal leaves on generally low,
erect plants.
Flowers: corolla about ¼" (6 mm) long,
the 4 lobes somewhat spreading;
stamens 2.
Leaves: 1–3" (2.5–7.5 cm) wide,
round, coarsely toothed, on long stalks.
Height: 4–24" (10–60 cm).

Flowering: April–July.

Habitat: Moist open or shaded slopes from
foothills to moderate elevations.

Range: Northern Idaho to southeastern
Washington, northeastern Oregon, and
northeastern California.

Comments: The intense blue-violet of the corolla
seems to deepen in the shade where
these plants are often found. Although
pretty, they are surpassed by a close
relative, Fringed Synthyris,
(*S. schizantha*), in which the edges of
the corolla lobes are cut into many
strips, forming a beautiful fringe; it
grows only on a few moist, shaded cliffs
in northern Oregon and western
Washington.

## 647 Snow Queen; Round-leaf Synthyris
*(Synthyris reniformis)*
Figwort Family (Scrophulariaceae)

Description: *Several weak, leafless flowering stems* curve
upward from a cluster of leaves on
long stalks, and in short racemes bloom
*deep blue-violet, slightly bilaterally*
*symmetrical flowers.*
Flowers: corolla about ¼" (6 mm) long,
1 of the 4 slight spreading lobes
broader than the rest; stamens 2.
Leaves: to 3" (7.5 cm) wide, heart-
shaped, but the tip round, the edges
irregularly scalloped.

Height: to 6″ (15 cm).
Flowering: March–May.
Habitat: Coniferous woods.
Range: Southwestern Washington to central California.
Comments: One of the humbler, early-flowering *Synthyris* species; in the dim light of the early-spring woods its low, dark flowers are easily overlooked.

---

### 297 Moth Mullein
(*Verbascum blattaria*)
Figwort Family (Scrophulariaceae)

Description: Slender spires of flowers with *pale yellow corollas* bloom atop erect, leafy stems.
Flowers: corolla about 1″ (2.5 cm) wide, almost radially symmetrical, the 5 round lobes nearly the same size; stamens 5, with stalks covered with red-purple hairs.
Leaves: largest in a rosette at base, 2–6″ (5–15 cm) long, the edges variously lobed or toothed, those on stem becoming progressively smaller toward the flower cluster.
Height: 1–5′ (30–150 cm).
Flowering: May–September.
Habitat: Roadsides, fields, and vacant lots.
Range: Throughout.
Comments: Corollas are sometimes white. The common name alludes to the resemblance of the flowers to moths resting on the stem.

---

### 298 Woolly Mullein; Common Mullein; Flannel Mullein
(*Verbascum✸thapsus*)
Figwort Family (Scrophulariaceae)

Description: A spike resembling *stout poles,* with the *yellow flowers densely packed,* above the leafy stems.
Flowers: corolla ¾–1″ (2–2.5 cm) wide, almost radially symmetrical, the

5 round lobes spreading out flat;
stamens 5, the upper 3 with yellow
hairs on stalks.
Leaves: 4–16″ (10–40 cm) long, ovate,
covered with felt-like gray hair.
Height: 2–7′ (60–210 cm).
Flowering: June–August.
Habitat: Open places.
Range: Throughout.
Comments: No one wishes to claim a weed. A
wildflower book written near the turn
of the 20th century cites that Europeans
call *V. thapsus* "American Velvet
Plant." Although only a few of the
many Eurasian *Verbascum* species have
crossed the seas to North America, this
species makes up for the lack of variety
in the genus by sheer numbers. Ancient
Greeks and Romans dipped the stalks
in tallow for funeral torches. In
medieval Europe it was called "Hag-
taper" because witches used it. Today
children hurl the dried stalks as
javelins, the light weight and pointed
root sailing them far and straight.

## 627 American Brookline
(*Veronica americana*)
Figwort Family (Scrophulariaceae)

Description: Erect or leaning, leafy stems have *small,
blue flowers in several open racemes,* 1 in
each upper leaf axil.
Flowers: ¼–½″ (6–13 mm) wide, with
4 lobes joined at base, lower lobe
narrowest; stamens 2.
Leaves: ½–3″ (1.3–7.5 cm) long,
opposite, broadly lanceolate, the edges
toothed or nearly smooth, all leaves
with short stalks.
Height: 4–40″ (10–100 cm).
Flowering: May–July.
Habitat: Wet places.
Range: Common in much of the West.
Comments: Plants spread from rhizomes shallowly
buried in the mud, and can quickly
form dense patches in slow-moving or

still water. The genus name may
commemorate St. Veronica.

## 628 Cusick's Speedwell
(*Veronica cusickii*)
Figwort Family (Scrophulariaceae)

Description: Erect stems grow in little patches and
*deep blue-violet, flat flowers* bloom on
hair-like stalks in racemes.
Flowers: corolla about ½" (1.3 cm)
wide, 4 lobes, the lowest the narrowest;
stamens 2, spread apart; style more
than ¼" (6 mm) long.
Leaves: ½–1" (1.3–2.5 cm) long,
opposite, shiny, ovate.
Height: 2–8" (5–20 cm).
Flowering: July–August.
Habitat: Open, moist areas in the mountains.
Range: Western Washington to northeastern
Oregon and the Sierra Nevada of
California; east to northern Idaho and
western Montana.
Comments: This perky little wildflower is common
along mountain trails. In other
species—some weeds in lawns or
ditches—the corolla varies from nearly
white to clear blue. The structure of
flowers and leafy stems is distinctive.

## NIGHTSHADE FAMILY
(Solanaceae)

Herbs, shrubs, vines, or trees with often showy flowers, generally in branched clusters.
Flowers: usually radially symmetrical; sepals 5, united; petals 5, united; stamens usually 5, sometimes fewer. All these parts attached at base of ovary.
Leaves: simple, alternate.
Fruit: berry or 2-chambered capsule.
There are about 85 genera and 2,300 species occurring in tropical and warm temperate regions, especially in Central and South America. Several are poisonous, but others supply foods such as chili, bell pepper, tomato, potato, eggplant, and groundcherry. Tobacco comes from the family. Petunia, Painted-Tongue, and Butterfly Flower are grown as ornamentals.

1 **Dingy Chamaesaracha**
(*Chamaesaracha sordida*)
Nightshade Family (Solanaceae)

Description: A low, dull green plant covered with fine glandular hairs, with a *flat, round, dingy whitish-green flower* blooming in each upper axil.
Flowers: corolla about ½" (1.3 cm) wide, with 5 pale bands radiating from center to the tips of the 5 low lobes; near center hairy, greenish-yellow pads between bases of 5 slender stamens.
Leaves: to 1½" (3.8 cm) long, pointed at tip, tapering to base, edges usually wavy and sometimes with low lobes.
Fruit: berry tightly enveloped by calyx.
Height: creeper, stems to 1' (30 cm) long, mostly hugging ground.
Flowering: May–September.
Habitat: Plains and deserts.
Range: Southern Arizona to western Texas and northern Mexico.

Comments: This and other *Chamaesaracha* species
are frequent but rarely very
conspicuous. The corollas are dull and
the foliage often has an earthen hue.

---

52 **Southwestern Thorn Apple**
(*Datura wrightii*)
Nightshade Family (Solanaceae)

Description: Large, *trumpet-shaped, white corollas,*
generally withered by early morning,
protrude from the *coarse foliage* of this
stout, branched, rank-smelling plant.
Flowers: corolla 6″ (15 cm) long, flared
portion with 5 slender teeth on rim.
Leaves: to 6″ (15 cm) long, ovate,
covered with minute, low hairs.
Fruit: 1½″ (3.8 cm) in diameter,
spherical, hangs down, its surface
prickly with many slender spines less
than ½″ (1.3 cm) long.
Height: to 5′ (1.5 m).

Flowering: May–November.

Habitat: Loose sand, in arroyos, on plains.

Range: Central California to northern Mexico;
east across the Southwest to Texas.

Comments: Extracts from this plant and its relatives
are narcotic and, when improperly
prepared, lethal. The narcotic
properties of species have been known
since before recorded history. They once
figured importantly in religious
ceremonies of southwestern Indians.
Among several species, all with round,
thorny fruits, is Jimsonweed
(*D. stramonium*); the fruit has many
small spines and does not hang; the
corolla is only about 3″ (7.5 cm) long.
The common name is a corruption of
Jamestown Weed, so named because of
the poisoning of many soldiers sent
there to stop Bacon's Rebellion in
1676. In early days the plant may have
been imported for medicinal use. In all
species corollas may be tinged to
varying degrees with violet.

### 341  Tree Tobacco
(*Nicotiana glauca*)
Nightshade Family (Solanaceae)

Description: An open *shrub or small tree* with few branches, the *yellow, trumpet-shaped flowers* tending to spread or hang on slender branches.
Flowers: corolla 1¼–2″ (3.1–5 cm) long; stamens 5.
Leaves: 2–7″ (5–17.5 cm) long, smooth, ovate, gray-green.
Height: to 26′ (8 m).
Flowering: April–November.
Habitat: Roadsides, slopes, and washes.
Range: Central California, southern Arizona, and western Texas; south into Mexico.
Comments: A common and conspicuous plant along roadsides in southern California. All species of *Nicotiana* contain the highly toxic alkaloid nicotine. An effective insecticide against aphids can be prepared by steeping tobacco in water and spraying the solution on affected parts of the plant. Tree Tobacco contains a more potent poison for aphids, anabasine.

### 95  Desert Tobacco; Tabaquillo
(*Nicotiana trigonophylla*)
Nightshade Family (Solanaceae)

Description: *Sticky-glandular stems and leaves,* with *trumpet-shaped, white flowers* in a loosely branched cluster at the top.
Flowers: corolla ½–¾″ (1.3–2 cm) long, the flared ends with 5 low, bluntly pointed lobes; stamens 5.
Leaves: 2–6″ (5–15 cm) long, broadly lanceolate, lower ones on broad, flat stalks, upper ones without stalks, the bases with ear-like lobes on either side of stem.
Height: 1–3′ (30–90 cm).
Flowering: November–June in the western part of the range, March–November in the eastern part.

Habitat: Sandy areas and washes.

Range: Southeastern California and southern Nevada to western Texas and northwestern New Mexico.

Comments: The Spanish name, pronounced *tah-bah-kee'-oh,* means "little tobacco." Also once called Punche ("a punch") by Spanish Americans, who carefully tended it for tobacco and medicinal use, it is still smoked by Indians in traditional ceremonies. Coyote Tobacco (*N. attenuata*), from British Columbia to Baja California, east to New Mexico, Colorado, and northern Idaho, has fewer glands, short triangular calyx lobes, and dingy white, trumpet-shaped corollas 1–1½" (2.5–3.8 cm) long. All wild Tobaccos are poisonous, but strong-smelling and distasteful, and usually are not eaten by livestock.

### 581 Purple Groundcherry
(*Physalis lobata*)
Nightshade Family (Solanaceae)

Description: *Blue-violet or violet, nearly round, saucer-shaped flowers* bloom on slender stalks in leaf axils of short, erect stems that grow from a rosette of leaves, or on longer, leafy stems that lie on ground, their ends turning upward.
Flowers: corolla about ¾" (2 cm) wide; hairy pads alternate with bases of 5 slender stamens near center of flower, the anthers like small yellow knobs; calyx enlarges as fruit matures and forms a 5-sided bladder ¾" (2 cm) long.
Leaves: to 4" (10 cm) long, lanceolate, pinnately lobed or divided.
Fruit: berry about ¼" (6 mm) in diameter enclosed in the calyx.
Height: creeper, with some branches to about 6" (15 cm).

Flowering: March–September.

Habitat: Open areas in desert plains, frequent in agricultural areas.

Range: Arizona to Kansas, south to Mexico.
Comments: The berry is edible, but caution is advised, for the flower resembles some of those of *Solanum,* a genus with both edible and deadly berries, and unripe berries of some species of *Physalis* are also poisonous. The large tomatillo, meaning "little tomato," common in Mexican and Southwestern markets, adds a pleasant tang to salads. Purple Groundcherry is sometimes put in the genus *Quincula.*

## 661 Bittersweet; Climbing Nightshade
(*Solanum dulcamara*)
Nightshade Family (Solanaceae)

Description: The long stems of this plant climb or scramble over other vegetation, and *blue or deep violet, star-like flowers* with 5 points of the corolla often bent backward, bloom in roundish, open clusters.
Flowers: ½–¾" (1.3–2 cm) wide; 5 long yellow anthers usually form a narrow, blunt cone in center of flower.
Leaves: to 3" (7.5 cm) long, heart-shaped or ovate with 2 lobes at base.
Fruit: berry about ½" (1.3 cm) wide, red, shiny.
Height: vine, with stems to 10' (3 m) long.
Flowering: May–September.
Habitat: Thickets, cleared areas, open woods, and along fencerows.
Range: Throughout, but infrequent or absent in arid regions.
Comments: Since herbage and fruits of this species are mildly poisonous, *Solanum* species are expensive pests in agricultural regions. Truckloads of dried beans have been discarded because agricultural inspectors found a few *Solanum* berries harvested along with the crop, a necessary precaution even though all Nightshades are not poisonous.

## 584 White Horsenettle; Silver Horsenettle; Silverleaf Nightshade; Bullnettle
(*Solanum elaeagnifolium*)
Nightshade Family (Solanaceae)

Description: Stems grow in patches and bear *fine prickles, bluish-gray lanceolate leaves,* and *bluish-violet, violet, or lavender, star-like flowers.*
Flowers: ¾–1¼" (2–3.1 cm) wide, with 5 points on corolla; long anthers form a slender yellow cone in center of flower, especially when young.
Leaves: 1–4" (2.5–10 cm) long, usually with wavy edges.
Fruit: berry ½" (1.3 cm) wide, shiny, yellow.
Height: to 3' (90 cm).

Flowering: May–September.

Habitat: Dry open areas, now common along roads, in old lots, and in agricultural regions.

Range: Across the Southwest to central California; south into Mexico.

Comments: The lavender stars with yellow centers are beautifully set off by the silvery foliage, and large patches of the plant in full bloom are striking. However, the plants are aggressive, poisonous weeds, spreading steadily from deep rootstocks. The genus name, from the Latin *solamen* ("quieting"), alludes to the narcotic properties of many species. Southwestern Indians used the crushed berries to curdle milk in making cheese, and they have also been used in various preparations for sore throat and toothache. Many economically important plants also are in this family, including potato, tomato, chili, tobacco, eggplant, and petunia.

**14, 210  Buffalo Bur**
(*Solanum rostratum*)
Nightshade Family (Solanaceae)

Description:  Dense, *golden-yellow prickles* cover the
stems and calyx of each *yellow, star-like
flower* on this leafy weed.
Flowers: corolla ¾–1″ (2–2.5 cm)
wide, with 5 points; unequal anthers
form a slender, irregular, blunt cone at
center of flower.
Leaves: 2–6″ (5–15 cm) long,
including the stalks, the blades deeply
parted into irregularly pinnate lobes,
the stalks and backs of veins covered
with prickles.
Fruit: berry enclosed by spiny, tight-
fitting calyx, including spines about 1″
(2.5 cm) wide.
Height: 16–32″ (40–80 cm).
Flowering:  May–September.
Habitat:  Roadsides, edges of fields, and old lots.
Range:  Throughout most of the West,
probably more common in the southern
part.
Comments:  The prickles on this plant help to
discourage grazing by livestock; it is
also highly toxic. An equally prickly
species of about the same habit,
Melonleaf Nightshade (*S. citrullifolium*),
has blue-violet corollas.

## CACAO FAMILY (Sterculiaceae)

Trees, shrubs, or herbs, often covered with star-like hairs, sometimes with large showy flowers.

Flowers: usually bisexual, radially symmetrical; sepals 3 or 5, joined at the base, often petal-like; corolla is absent or has 5 small petals; stamens separate and in one whorl, or in two whorls and then united by the stalks. All these parts attached at base of ovary.

Leaves: alternate, simple or palmately compound.

Fruit: leathery or fleshy, 4, 5, or more chambers.

There are about 50 genera and 750 species that occur mostly in warm regions of the world. Chocolate comes from fermented seeds of one species.

---

### 358 Flannel Bush; Fremontia
(*Fremontia californica*)
Cacao Family (Sterculiaceae)

Description: A spreading shrub with many *large, saucer-shaped, yellow-orange flowers.*
Flowers: 1½–2½" (3.8–6.3 cm) wide; sepals petal-like, ovate, with long hairs in pits at base; petals absent; stamens 5, united at base into tube.
Leaves: ½–3" (1.3–7.5 cm) long, dark green, 3 shallow lobes, 1–3 veins.
Height: 5–30' (1.5–9 m).
Flowering: May–June.
Habitat: Dry slopes brush or pine forests.
Range: Much of California to central Arizona.
Comments: The flowers bloom in showy masses, making this a popular ornamental. Mexican Fremontia (*F. mexicana*), found along the southern California border, has flowers hidden among the leaves and 5–7 veins at the base of the leaves and long hairs in pits at the base of the sepals.

## VALERIAN FAMILY
### (Valerianaceae)

Leafy herbs with small flowers in
branched or head-like clusters.
Flowers: bisexual or unisexual,
bilaterally symmetrical; calyx barely
developed, when present often feathery;
petals 5, united, often bearing a
backward-projecting spur; stamens 1–
4. All these parts attached at top of
ovary.
Leaves: opposite or basal, often
pinnately divided.
Fruit: seed-like.
There are about 13 genera and 400
species occurring in north temperate
regions and the Andes. Red Valerian is
grown as an ornamental.

---

160 **Downy-fruited Vervain**
(*Valeriana acutiloba*)
Valerian Family (Valerianaceae)

Description: *Small, slightly bilaterally symmetrical,*
*white flowers* in branched clusters bloom
atop a stem *with largest leaves at*
*base.*
Flowers: about ¼" (6 mm) long, the
tubular portion slightly swollen in the
lower side, the 5 roundish lobes sharply
bent outward; stamens 3, protruding.
Leaves: blades to 3" (7.5 cm) long,
ovate, those at base usually not divided,
tapered to a long stalk, those on stem
pinnately divided into 1 or 2 pairs of
lobes, without stalks.
Fruit: seed-like, shortly hairy, with a
number of plume-like bristles that
unroll at the top when the fruit is
mature.
Height: 4–24" (10–60 cm).
Flowering: June–July.
Habitat: Open rocky slopes in the mountains,
often near water or snowbanks.
Range: From southwestern Montana to
southern Oregon, the southern Sierra

Nevada of California, northern Arizona, and New Mexico.

Comments: The mostly undivided basal leaves help to distinguish this from other, similar species, which have divided leaves. *Valeriana* comes from the Latin *valere* ("to be strong"), and refers to the medicinal qualities of the plants; extracts were used as a nerve tonic and are said, under certain circumstances, to relax better than opium. Valerian was one of 72 ingredients Mithridates, King of Pontus, compounded as an antidote to poison, using poisoned slaves as test subjects.

## VERBENA FAMILY (Verbenaceae)

Herbs, shrubs, or trees usually with flowers in spike-like or branched clusters or in heads.

Flowers: bilaterally symmetrical; sepals 5, united; petals 5, united, forming a corolla with a slender tube and an abruptly flared top; stamens usually 4. All these parts attached at base of ovary.

Leaves: opposite or whorled, simple.

Fruit: often separates into 4 hard nutlets, each 1-seeded.

There are about 75 genera and 3,000 species mostly of tropical and warm temperate regions. Teak is a highly prized furniture wood. Vervain, Lantana, Lippia or Frog Fruit, and Chaste Tree or Vitex are grown as ornamentals.

---

539 **Western Pink Vervain; Moradilla**
(*Verbena ambrosifolia*)
Verbena Family (Verbenaceae)

Description: *Gently rounded clusters of bilaterally symmetrical pink, lavender, or purple flowers* bloom atop stems with highly divided leaves.
Flowers: corolla ¼–½" (6–13 mm) wide, the tubular base 1–1½ times the length of the calyx; calyx glandular-hairy, the teeth at the tip of the 5 narrow lobes about ⅛" (3 mm) long.
Leaves: ¾–2½" (2–6.3 cm) long, pinnately divided, the main divisions again pinnately divided, the final divisions lanceolate.
Height: 8–16" (20–40 cm).
Flowering: February–October.
Habitat: Open fields and weedy areas.
Range: Oklahoma, Arizona, New Mexico, and Texas to northern Mexico.
Comments: This plant often forms brilliant displays covering acres of ground. The Spanish name comes from "morado" meaning

purple, and in this species means "little
purple flower."

---

495  **New Mexico Vervain**
     (*Verbena macdougalii*)
     Verbena Family (Verbenaceae)

Description: Harshly hairy plant with 4-sided stems,
            and thick, dense, long, erect spikes
            each with a *ring of small, lavender to blue-*
            *violet bilaterally symmetrical flowers* at one
            level.
            Flowers: corolla ¼" (6 mm) across,
            5 lobes, 3 bent down, the middle
            largest, and 2 bent upward.
            Leaves: blades up to 4" (10 cm) long,
            opposite, ovate, edges with coarse and
            irregular teeth.
            Fruit: separates into 4 long, seed-like
            sections.
            Height: to 3' (90 cm).
Flowering: June–October.
  Habitat: Valleys and open flats at moderate or
            high elevations.
    Range: Southern Wyoming to Arizona, New
            Mexico, and western Texas.
Comments: This species resembles members of the
            Mint Family, but lacks the aromatic
            odor. There are several species of tall
            Vervains with thick or slender spikes of
            flowers. They are usually not easy to
            identify. New Mexico Vervain is one
            with relatively thick spikes, common in
            the southern Rocky Mountain region.

## VIOLET FAMILY (Violaceae)

Rather dainty herbs with perky, colorful flowers in the United States, but often shrubby and less showy elsewhere.

Flowers: bilaterally symmetrical or radially symmetrical; sepals 5, separate; petals 5, separate, the lowermost often largest and bearing a backward-projecting spur; stamens 5, loosely united with one another around the ovary.

Leaves: alternate, simple but sometimes deeply lobed.

Fruit: berry or explosively opening capsule.

There are about 22 genera and 900 species occurring nearly throughout the world. Many species of Violets, including Pansies, are cultivated for their pretty flowers.

---

588 **Blue Violet**
(*Viola adunca*)
Violet Family (Violaceae)

Description: A small plant with Pansy-like *bluish-violet flowers* that hang at tips of slender stalks.
Flowers: ½–¾" (1.3–2 cm) wide; petals 5, upper 2 bent upward, the lower 3 white at base, outer ones with white hairs. *A slender spur extends backward.*
Leaves: blades, ½–1¼" (1.3–3.1 cm) long, on stalks, dark green, rather thick, ovate or heart-shaped, finely scalloped on edges; in tufts at base.
Height: up to 4" (10 cm).
Flowering: April–August.
Habitat: Meadows, open woods, and open slopes from sea level to timberline.
Range: Canada; south to southern California, Arizona, New Mexico, the northern Great Plains.
Comments: Violets are very popular wildflowers and

garden plants, romantically described as "shrinking" because of the way the petals fold in. Species are often difficult to identify as they may hybridize, producing intermediate forms. These hybrids, in turn, may reproduce by means of inconspicuous flowers at the base of the plant, often even underground, producing seeds without opening.

---

## 586 Western Pansy Violet; Beckwith Violet
*(Viola beckwithii)*
Violet Family (Violaceae)

Description: *Bilaterally symmetrical 2-tone flowers hang and face outward* on leafless stalks that grow from a low tuft of leaves.
Flowers: corolla ½–¾" (1.3–2 cm) across; 5 petals, 2 upper reddish-purple, 3 lower mauve and with yellowish patches and reddish-purple lines near base, of 3 lower, the lateral ones with yellow hairs, the middle one with a pouch behind it.
Leaves: blades about 1" (2.5 cm) long, grayish green, divided into 3 main sections, these into narrow segments, all attached to a long stalk.
Height: 2–5" (5–12.5 cm).

Flowering: March–May.

Habitat: Among sagebrush and in open pine woods.

Range: Northeastern Oregon to southeastern California; east to Idaho and Utah.

Comments: This species is as pretty as the garden Pansy (*V. arvensis*) a Violet native to Europe. Sagebrush Violet or Desert Pansy (*Viola trinervata*), from eastern Washington and northeastern Oregon, is very similar, but has 3-veined, leathery leaf segments.

**37  Canada Violet**
(*Viola canadensis*)
Violet Family (Violaceae)

Description: *White bilaterally symmetrical flowers hang and face outward* at tips of short stalks that grow from axils of heart-shaped leaves.
Flowers: nearly 1″ (2.5 cm) wide, the petals almost all white, yellow at the base, 2 bent upward, purplish on backs, 3 lower ones with purple lines near base; of these, the 2 at side hairy at base and the middle one with a short spur that projects beneath the flower.
Leaves: blades 1–3″ (2.5–7.5 cm) long, on slender stalks to 1′ (30 cm) long.
Height: 4–16″ (10–40 cm).
Flowering: May–July.
Habitat: Moist woodland.
Range: From Alaska to Oregon and Arizona, eastward in the Rocky Mountains.
Comments: The flowers growing from axils of upper leaves, and the yellow petal bases, help distinguish this lovely Violet from other white-flowered species.

**191  Douglas' Violet**
(*Viola douglasii*)
Violet Family (Violaceae)

Description: *Bilaterally symmetrical orangish-yellow flowers hang and face outward* atop leafless stalks growing from a low tuft of leaves.
Flowers: ½–¾″ (1.3–2 cm) wide; petals 5, the 2 upper ones maroon on back, 3 lower ones with purple lines near the base, the middle lower one with a short pouch behind it.
Leaves: blades ¾–2″ (2–5 cm) long, pinnately divided into several main divisions, these again divided into narrow segments, all attached to a comparatively long stalk.
Height: 2–6″ (5–15 cm).

Flowering: March—May.
Habitat: Dry open gravelly slopes at low
elevations.
Range: Southern Oregon and the northern two-
thirds of California.
Comments: This Violet grows on very sparsely
vegetated banks, often in rather sterile
soil, the perky little flowers peering
from the bank like golden faces among
the grayish foliage. As summer
progresses the soil becomes hard and
crusty and the plants wither, their stout
root preserving life until the next
flowering season.

## 190 Stream Violet; Pioneer Violet; Smooth Yellow Violet
(*Viola glabella*)
Violet Family (Violaceae)

Description: Slender leaning or erect stems with
leaves only in upper one-third, and
*bilaterally symmetrical, yellow flowers
facing outward,* hanging from slender
stalks.
Flowers: ½–¾" (1.3–2 cm) wide;
petals 5, the 3 lower ones with fine
maroon lines at base, of these three the
lateral ones bearded, the middle one
with a short pouch that projects
backward under flower; 2 upper petals
yellow on backside.
Leaves: blades 1¼–3½" (3.1–8.8 cm)
long, heart-shaped, with finely toothed
edges, on long stalks.
Height: 2–12" (5–30 cm).
Flowering: March—July.
Habitat: In moist woods or along streams.
Range: Alaska to the southern Sierra Nevada of
California, eastward to western
Montana.
Comments: A very common species in moist,
shaded places in woods. Most western
Violets have yellow rather than purple
corollas, but all have the perky little
flower with a spur or pouch behind the
lower petal. The lower petal forms a

landing platform for insects seeking nectar within the spur.

---

### 192   Yellow Wood Violet; Pine Violet
(*Viola lobata*)
Violet Family (Violaceae)

Description:   Leaves and *bright yellow bilaterally symmetrical flowers* are crowded near the top of the stem.
Flowers: ¾–1″ (2–2.5 cm) wide; petals 5, yellow, the upper 2 brown on back, the lower 3 with fine brown lines at base; middle lower petal with a pouch barely extending back beneath the flower.
Leaves: 1–4″ (2.5–10 cm) wide, palmately cleft into 3–9 narrow lobes, or the leaves broadly heart-shaped and irregularly scalloped.
Height: 4–14″ (10–35 cm).
Flowering:   April–July.
Habitat:   Dry slopes in open woods.
Range:   Southwestern Oregon to southern California.
Comments:   Phases of this species with unlobed leaves occur in the same region as those with deeply lobed leaves. However, in northwestern California and southwestern Oregon, the phase with lobed leaves is nearly absent.

---

### 587   Larkspur Violet
(*Viola pedatifida*)
Violet Family (Violaceae)

Description:   *Bilaterally symmetrical blue-violet flowers face outward,* hanging atop leafless stalks barely taller than the tufted leaves.
Flowers: ½–¾″ (1.3–2 cm) wide; petals 5, of the 3 lower ones the 2 toward sides have hairs at base, the one in middle has a prominent spur.
Leaves: ¾–2½″ (2–6.8 cm) long, on long stalks, blades divided into one or

two main sections, these divided into narrow lobes.

Height: 3–8″ (7.5–20 cm).

Flowering: May–June.

Habitat: Forest openings, valleys, plains.

Range: Central Arizona to western Colorado and northern New Mexico; east to Ohio and northward east of the Rocky Mountain region to central Canada.

Comments: The deep blue-violet flowers and divided leaves resemble those of Larkspur (*Delphinium*), giving the common name.

### 193 Goosefoot Violet
(*Viola purpurea*)
Violet Family (Violaceae)

Description: *Bilaterally symmetrical yellow flowers face outward, hanging at tips of slender stalks* growing from axils of *purplish-green leaves.*

Flowers: ½–¾″ (1.3–2 cm) wide, often with a purplish or brownish tinge, and with five brownish lines on the lower 3 petals near the base, lowest petal with a very short spur that extends beneath the flower.

Leaves: blades ½–2″ (1.3–5 cm) long, lanceolate to nearly round, thick and fleshy, the veins deeply impressed on the upper surface, raised on the lower, edges with shallow or deep rounded teeth.

Height: 2–6″ (5–15 cm)

Flowering: May–August.

Habitat: In open or partly shaded places from the lowlands to high mountains.

Range: Eastern Washington to southern California, east to Arizona, Colorado, Wyoming, and Montana.

Comments: This variable Violet often has a purplish hue to the foliage and the prominently veiny leaves. Some forms of the leaves are reminiscent of a goose's foot, giving the common name.

189  **Redwood Violet; Evergreen Violet**
(*Viola sempervirens*)
Violet Family (Violaceae)

Description:  Stems creep across ground, producing
*mats of thick, leathery, broadly heart-
shaped leaves,* and *bilaterally symmetrical
clear yellow flowers* that face outward,
hanging on short stalks barely as tall as
the leaves.
Flowers: about ½″ (1.3 cm) wide;
petals 5, the 3 lower with maroon veins
near base, the middle one with a short
spur behind it; 2 upper petals bent
upward.
Leaves: ½–1¼″ (1.3–3.1 cm) wide,
each with finely scalloped toothed
edges, on long stalks.
Height: creeper, flower stalks to 1–5″
(2.5–12.5 cm) high, stems to 1′ (30
cm) long.

Flowering:  March–June.

Habitat:  Moist woods.

Range:  West of the Cascade Mountains from
British Columbia to southern Oregon,
and in the Coast Ranges to central
California.

Comments:  One of the most common wildflowers
within the dim redwood forest, lining
many of the trails in the parks of the
region. The mats of leaves persist
throughout the winter, giving one
common name and making this a
choice plant for the woodland garden.

## CALTROP FAMILY
### (Zygophyllaceae)

Herbs or shrubs, rarely trees, with flowers borne singly or in branched clusters.

Flowers: usually bisexual, radially symmetrical; sepals usually 5, separate; petals 5, separate; stamens 5, 10, or 15, often with scale-like appendages on stalks. All these parts attached at base of ovary.

Leaves: opposite, pinnately compound.

Fruit: usually 5-chambered capsule.

There are about 30 genera and 250 species with most occuring in warm temperate or tropical regions.

Creosotebush is the common shrub on Southwestern deserts. The densest of woods, lignum vitae, is obtained from a tropical tree.

---

### 453 Fagonia
(*Fagonia californica*)
Caltrop Family (Zygophyllaceae)

Description: These are low, round, open plants with green, *forking, angular stems,* and *flowers like pale lavender stars* scattered all over plant on ends of branches.
Flowers: about ½″ (1.3 cm) wide; petals 5, narrow; ovary has 5 lobes.
Leaves: opposite, each leaf divided into 3 lanceolate leaflets, each ⅛–½″ (3–13 mm) long.
Height: 8–24″ (20–60 cm).

Flowering: March–May, and depending upon rains, again in November–January.

Habitat: Rocky slopes and washes in desert.

Range: Southeastern California and southern Utah to northwestern Mexico.

Comments: Fagonias are so open that they cast little shadow. The stems and small leaves present little surface area to the sun and hot dry air, an adaptation to desert conditions that conserves precious water.

360 Desert Poppy; Mexican Poppy;
Arizona Poppy
(*Kallstroemia grandiflora*)
Caltrop Family (Zygophyllaceae)

Description: *Brilliant orange, bowl-shaped corollas,*
*crimson in center,* face upward on stalks
above sprawling, forked, hairy stems.
Flowers: 2" (5 cm) across; 5 broad
petals; 10 stamens, ovary with 5 lobes.
Leaves: ¾–2½" (2–6.3 cm) long,
opposite, pinnately compound.
Height: creeper, flowering branches to
1' (30 cm) high, stems to 3' (1 m)
long.

Flowering: May–November.

Habitat: Open sandy areas in desert.

Range: Southern Arizona to western Texas,
southward through much of Mexico.

Comments: These are not Poppies, and they are not
closely related, but the resemblance is
there and large patches provide a
display as brilliant and spectacular as
those of California Poppies (*Eschscholtzia*
*californica*). This is one of the most
handsome wildflowers in the
Southwest, frequent along roadsides.
There are several other *Kallstroemica*
species that can be recognized by the
opposite, pinnately compound leaves on
trailing stems. They have corollas only
about ½" (1.3 cm) wide. All species are
Southwestern. One, Small-flowered
Carpetweed (*K. parviflora*), has orange
flowers, and a beak on the fruit that is
longer than the round body. Two have
yellow flowers and short beaks, On
Hairy Carpetweed (*K. hirsutissima*)
sepals do not drop off, and the base of
the fruit's beak is bristly-hairy.
California Carpetweed (*K. californica*)
has sepals that usually drop off after the
flower opens, and has no hairs, or only
small ones at the base of the beak.

### 205 Goat's Head; Puncture Vine
(*Tribulus terrestris*)
Caltrop Family (Zygophyllaceae)

Description: This plant has sprawling stems and *small yellow flowers* on short stalks in the leaf axils.
Flowers: ¼–½" (6–13 mm) wide; 5 broad petals; 10 stamens.
Leaves: 1–2" (2.5–5 cm) long, opposite, pinnately compound, with 4–8 pairs of leaflets, each ¼–½" (6–13 mm) long.
Fruit: a hard star-shaped capsule that divides into 5 sharply 2-horned segments.
Height: creeper, flowers and leaves rarely more than 2" (5 cm) high, but forming mats to 3' (90 cm) wide.
Flowering: April–November.
Habitat: Weedy open areas.
Range: Much of the arid West.
Comments: A native of the Mediterranean region, this is one of the West's most unloved weeds. The sharp spines on the fruit segments (the "goat's head") cause painful injury to bare feet and to livestock. The spines easily pierce bicycle tires, hence the common name Puncture Vine.

# Part III
Appendices

# GLOSSARY

**Achene** A small, dry, hard fruit that does not open and contains one seed.

**Alternate leaves** Arising singly along the stem, not in pairs or whorls.

**Annual** Having a life cycle completed in one year or season.

**Anther** The sac-like part of a stamen, containing pollen.

**Appressed** Pressed closely against.

**Aquatic** A plant growing in water.

**Awn** A bristle-like appendage.

**Axil** The angle formed by the upper side of a leaf and the stem from which it grows.

**Banner** Uppermost petal in a Pea flower; also called the standard.

**Basal leaves** Leaves at the base of the stem.

**Bearded** Bearing long or stiff hairs.

**Berry** A fleshy fruit with one to many seeds, developed from a single ovary.

**Bilateral symmetry** In flowers, one that can be divided into two equal halves by only one line through the middle; often called irregular, or bilateral.

**Bisexual** A flower having both female (pistil) and male (stamen) parts.

**Blade** The flat portion of a leaf, petal, or sepal.

**Bloom** A whitish, powdery or waxy covering.

**Bracts** Modified leaves, usually smaller than the foliage leaves, often situated at the base of a flower or inflorescence.

**Bulb** A short underground stem, the swollen portion consisting mostly of fleshy, food-storing scale leaves.

**Calyx** Collective term for the sepals of a flower, usually green.

**Capsule** A dry fruit with one or more compartments, usually having thin walls that split open along several lines.

**Carnivorous** Subsisting on nutrients obtained from the breakdown of animal tissue.

**Catkin** A scaly-bracted spike or spike-like inflorescence bearing unisexual flowers without petals, as in the willows.

**Clasping** A leaf whose base wholly or partly surrounds the stem.

**Claw** Narrow, stalk-like base of a petal.

**Column** In Orchids, a structure formed by the union of stamens, style, and stigma.

**Compound leaf** A leaf divided into smaller leaflets.

**Corolla** Collective term for the petals of a flower.

**Corona** A crown-like structure on some corollas, as in the Milkweed Family.

**Creeper** Technically, a trailing shoot that takes root at the nodes; but used here to denote any trailing, prostrate plant.

**Cross-pollination** The transfer of pollen from one plant to another.

**Deciduous** Shedding leaves seasonally, as do many trees, or the shedding of certain parts after a period of growth.

**Dioecious** Bearing staminate and pistillate flowers on different plants of the same species, as in the willows.

**Disk flower** The small tubular flowers in the central part of a floral head, as in most members of the Sunflower Family.

**Dissected leaf** A deeply cut leaf, the cleft not reaching to the midrib; same as a divided leaf.

**Drupe** A stone fruit; a fleshy fruit with the single seed enveloped by a hard covering (stone).

**Embryo** The small plant formed after fertilization, contained within the seed and ready to grow with the proper environmental stimulation.

**Emergent** An aquatic plant with its lower part submerged and its upper part extending above water.

**Epiphyte** A plant growing on another plant but deriving no nutrition from it; an air plant.

**Filament** A thread; the slender stalk of a stamen.

**Follicle** A dry fruit developed from a single ovary, usually opening along one line.

**Fruit** The ripened ovary or pistil, often with attached parts.

**Gland** A small structure usually secreting oil or nectar.

**Glandular** Bearing glands.

**Head** A crowded cluster of flowers on very short stalks, or without stalks as in the Sunflower Family.

**Herb** Usually a soft and succulent plant; not woody.

**Hypanthium** A cup-like base to a flower; composed of the united and modified bases of calyx, corolla, and stamens. Sepals, petals, and stamens grow from the rim of the hypanthium.

**Inferior Ovary** Ovary positioned below sepals, petals, and stamens, which seem to grow from the top of ovary.

**Inflorescence** A flower cluster on a plant or, especially, the arrangement of flowers on a plant.

**Involucre** A whorl or circle of bracts beneath a flower or flower cluster.

**Irregular flower** A flower with petals that are not uniform in shape but are usually grouped to form upper and lower "lips;" generally bilaterally symmetrical.

**Keel** A sharp ridge or rib; in a Pea flower, the two lowest petals united and resembling the prow of a boat.

**Lanceolate leaf** Lance-shaped; i.e., much longer than wide and pointed at the end; technically, the widest portion below the middle (but in this book may also refer to a leaf that is widest at middle or above).

**Leaflet** One of the leaf-like parts of a compound leaf.

**Legume** A dry fruit developed from a single ovary, usually opening along two lines, as in the Pea Family.

**Ligule** A projection at the base of the leaf blade in grasses.

**Linear** Long, narrow, with parallel sides, as in the leaf blades of grasses.

**Lip petal** The lower petal of some irregular flowers, often elaborately showy, as in Orchids.

**Lobed** Indented on the margins, with the indentations not reaching to the center or base.

**Monoecious** Having both staminate (male) and pistillate (female) flowers on the same plant.

**Node** The place on the stem where leaves or branches are attached.

**Ocrea** Stem-sheathing leaf bases of members of the Buckwheat Family.

**Opposite leaves** Occurring in pairs at a node, with one leaf on either side of the stem.

**Ovary** The swollen base of a pistil, within which seeds develop.

**Ovate leaf** Egg-shaped, pointed at the top, technically broader near the base (but in this book the term is also used for leaves broadest at the middle).

**Ovule** The immature seed in the ovary that contains the egg.

**Palate** A rounded projection of the lower lip in two-lipped flowers, closing or nearly closing the throat.

**Palmate** Having 3 or more divisions or lobes, looking like the outspread fingers of a hand.

**Pappus** A bristle, scale, or crown on seed-like fruits of the Sunflower Family, as on the fruits of Dandelions, and Thistles.

**Parasite**   A plant deriving its nutrition from another organism.

**Pedicel**   The stalk of an individual flower.

**Peduncle**   The main flowerstalk or stem holding an inflorescence.

**Perianth**   The calyx and corolla or, in flowers without 2 distinct series of outer parts (sepals and petals), simply the outer whorl (as in the Buckwheat Family and others).

**Petal**   Basic unit of the corolla, flat, usually broad, and brightly colored.

**Petaloid**   Petal-like, usually describing a colored sepal.

**Petiole**   The stalk-like part of a leaf, attaching it to the stem.

**Pinnate leaf**   A compound leaf with leaflets along the sides of a common central stalk, much like a feather.

**Pistil**   The female organ of a flower, consisting of an ovary, style, and stigma.

**Pistillate flower**   A female flower, having one or more pistils but no functional stamens.

**Pod**   A dry fruit that opens at maturity.

**Pollen**   Spores formed in the anthers that produce the male cells.

**Pollen sac**   The upper portion of the stamen, containing pollen grains; the anther.

**Pollination**   The transfer of pollen from an anther to a stigma.

**Pubescent**   Covered with hairs.

**Raceme**   A long flower cluster on which individual flowers each bloom on a small stalk all along a common, larger, central stalk.

Radial symmetry  In flowers, one with the symmetry of a wheel; often called regular.

Ray flower  The bilaterally symmetrical flowers around the edge of the head in many members of the Sunflower Family; each ray flower resembles a single petal.

Receptacle  The base of the flower where all flower parts are attached.

Regular flower  With petals and/or sepals arranged around the center, like the spokes of a wheel; always radially symmetrical.

Rhizome  A horizontal underground stem, distinguished from roots by the presence of nodes, often enlarged by food storage.

Rose hip  A smooth, rounded, fruit-like structure consisting of the cup-like calyx enclosing seed-like fruits.

Rosette  A crowded cluster of leaves; usually basal, circular, and appearing to grow directly out of the ground.

Runner  A stem that grows on the surface of the soil, often developing leaves, roots, and new plants at the nodes or tip.

Saprophyte  A plant lacking chlorophyll and living on dead organic matter.

Sepal  A basic unit of the calyx, usually green, but sometimes colored and resembling a petal.

Sessile  Without a stalk.

Sessile leaf  A leaf that lacks a petiole, the blade being attached directly to the stem.

Sheath  A more or less tubular structure

surrounding a part, as the lower portion of a leaf surrounding the stem.

**Shrub**   A woody, relatively low plant with several branches from the base.

**Simple leaf**   A leaf with an undivided blade.

**Spadix**   A dense spike of tiny flowers, usually enclosed in a spathe, as in members of the Arum Family.

**Spathe**   A bract or pair of bracts, often large, enclosing the flowers.

**Species**   A fundamental category of taxonomic classification, ranking below a genus.

**Spike**   An elongated flower cluster, each flower of which is without a stalk.

**Spur**   A slender, usually hollow projection from a part of a flower.

**Stamen**   The male organ of a flower, composed of a filament topped by an anther; usually several in each flower.

**Staminate flower**   A male flower, that is, with anthers and without pistils.

**Standard**   An Iris petal; also the upper petal or banner of a Pea flower.

**Stigma**   The tip of the pistil where the pollen lands and develops into the style.

**Stipules**   Small appendages, often leaf-like, on either side of some petioles at the base.

**Stolon**   A stem growing along or under the ground; a runner.

**Style**   The narrow part of the pistil, connecting ovary and stigma.

**Superior ovary**   An ovary in the center of a flower, with all parts attaching to receptacle near the base of the ovary.

**Succulent** Fleshy and thick, storing water; a plant with fleshy, water-storing stems or leaves.

**Tendril** A slender, coiling structure that helps support climbing plants.

**Toothed** Having a sawtooth edge.

**Tuber** A fleshy, enlarged part of an underground stem, serving as a storage organ (e.g., a potato).

**Umbel** A flower cluster in which the individual flower stalks grow from the same point, like the ribs of an umbrella.

**Undulate** Having a wavy edge.

**Unisexual** A flower of one sex only, either pistillate (female) or staminate (male).

**Whorled** A circle of three or more leaves, branches, or pedicels at a node.

**Wing** In plants, a thin, flat extension found at the margins of a seed or leafstalk or along the stem; the lateral petal of a Pea flower.

## PICTURE CREDITS

The numbers in parentheses are plate numbers. Some photographers have pictures under agency names as well as their own. Agency names appear in boldface.

Ed Alverson (143)
Dennis Anderson (25, 119, 146, 195, 203, 316, 330, 341, 347, 358, 386, 389, 505, 536 left, 552, 581, 597)
Ron Austing (444, 615)
Les Blacklock (507, 510, 609)
Donna Lee Botsford (571)
Jim Brandenburg (265)
Bullaty/Lomeo (35)
Franz J. Camenzind (483)
Norden H. Cheatham (176, 502)
Herbert Clarke (635)
Anna-Jean Cole (226, 323, 441, 553)

**Bruce Coleman, Inc.**
Gene Ahrens (605) Jen and Des Bartlett (183 left, 272, 362, 642) S. C. Bisserot (286) Bill Brooks (351 right) Jane Burton (158 right) Clara Calhoun (430) Lois and George Cox (488) John Ebeling (648) Kenneth Fink (234) Kit Flannery (649) M. P. L. Fogden (185, 233, 424, 645) Lee Foster (332, 556) David Overcash (167, 450) Hans Reinhard (618) R. Schonberg (378) Joy Spurr (10 right, 107, 428, 482, 626) Larry West (12 right) Gary R. Zahm (227)

Stephen Collins (297 left)
Ed Cooper (10 left, 36, 40, 45, 68, 99 right, 116, 148, 160, 170, 186, 187, 200, 212, 276, 278, 280, 333, 354, 417, 426 left, 434, 473 right, 477,

480, 494, 534, 536 right, 577, 611)
Thase Daniel (60, 61, 225, 381)
Kent and Donna Dannen (29, 50, 53,
70, 124, 133, 198, 268, 560, 591,
639)
E. R. Degginger (337, 584)
Harry Engels (74, 199, 222, 250)
P. R. Ferguson (87, 90, 134, 137,
147, 150, 193, 201, 246 right, 307,
329, 348, 392 left, 487, 529, 538,
644)
Ken Ferrell (473 left)
Douglas Henderson (30, 112, 113 left,
122, 216, 237, 298 left, 305, 334,
384, 472 left, 554, 592, 656)
Elizabeth Henze (95, 595)
N. Holmgren (523, 622, 623, 624,
625)
Charles Johnson (2, 3, 31, 34, 38, 42,
43, 46, 62, 65, 66, 80, 85, 88, 91,
93, 94, 102, 114 right, 120, 127,
128, 132, 135, 136, 162, 164, 166,
168, 178, 182, 190, 191, 196, 207,
217, 219, 220, 221, 240, 259,
262, 264, 281, 292, 293, 297 right,
306, 311, 313, 315, 321, 339,
344, 346, 357, 365, 367, 380, 383,
393, 396, 400, 409, 410, 414,
418, 448, 451, 453, 454, 460, 466,
479, 481, 496, 497, 509, 517,
518, 521, 522, 530, 547, 550, 562,
573, 583, 587, 621, 627, 633,
634, 637, 638, 640, 647, 650, 654,
658, 661)
L. and D. Klein (108, 328, 457)
Stephen J. Krasemann (96, 289, 350
left, 411, 526)
Carl Kurtz (598)
Bonnie Kutschenreuter (475)
Frank A. Lang (15, 202, 342, 395)
John MacGregor (387)
Steve McCutcheon (431)
Brian Milne (423, 484)
Robert W. Mitchell (469)
C. A. Morgan (24, 64, 183 right, 301,
470, 578)
T. F. Niehaus (254, 385, 543, 586,
590, 612, 636)
Dr. & Mrs. Robert T. Orr (101, 103,

110, 152, 189, 267, 320, 336,
375, 579)
H. A. Pengelly (179)
C. W. Perkins (92)
M. Peterson (664)
Willis Peterson (260, 606)

**Photo Researchers, Inc.**
A–Z Collection (197, 462) Charles
Allen (652) A.W. Ambler (500) Bob
Behme (263) John Bova (322) Gary
Braasch (372) Tom Branch (81, 144,
501, 506) Ken Brate (20, 379, 394,
519) Richard W. Brooks (245 right)
Patricia Caulfield (303) Alford W.
Cooper (141) Helen Cruickshank (504,
528) Kent & Donna Dannen (326)
Barbara K. Deans (27 left) Murl
Densing (353) R. Dimond (6 left, 361)
Robert Donne (356) Robert J. Erwin
(570) Kenneth W. Fink (563 left)
H. F. Flanders (555) Glenn Foss (158
left) Lola Graham (246 left) Sandra
Grant (524 left) Farrell Grehan (392
right, 363, 438, 515, 531) Harold W.
Hoffman (413) Inez & George Hollis
(4 right) Jane Kinne (296) Russ Kinne
(564) Stephen J. Krasemann (126)
Barry Lopez (630) Alexander Lowry
(56, 492, 513) C. G. Maxwell (16, 41,
208, 257, 319, 398, 632) Rod Moon
(123) John V. A. F. Neal (111, 117)
Raymond L. Nelson (503) Dorothy
Orians (13) Charlie Ott (298 right, 351
left) Hiram L. Parent (352 left, 436)
Richard Parker (14, 165, 244 right,
245 left, 256, 261, 266, 269, 317,
404, 474, 495, 524 right, 629, 643)
Constance Porter (558) Noble Proctor
(139, 154, 283, 452, 620) Louis Quitt
(449) Susan Rayfield (437) James R.
Simon (28 right, 544) Alvin E. Staffan
(230) Myron Wood (59) Colin Wyatt
(432)

Donald J. Pinkava (582)
Robert Potts (19, 57, 67, 172, 241,
279, 364, 371, 433, 516, 537, 588,
617)

Betty Randall (75, 78, 270, 382, 401, 422 left, 435, 465, 542, 589, 628)
Bill Ratcliffe (39, 129, 130, 209, 238, 275, 439, 662)
Susan Rayfield (184, 192, 215, 295, 335, 402, 499, 535)
Tim Reeves (6 right, 7, 12 left, 97 right, 388, 447)
Edward S. Ross (77, 79, 115, 173, 211, 299, 327, 360, 377, 407, 443, 445, 485, 548, 568, 569, 574, 575, 608)
Werner Schulz (508, 600)
Richard Spellenberg (1, 23, 32, 82, 83, 84, 104, 106, 194, 204, 205, 206, 229, 235, 236, 243, 244 left, 247, 253, 271, 277, 288, 290, 302, 304, 314, 324, 350 right, 406, 421, 429, 442, 463, 468, 486, 489, 491, 493, 514, 563 right, 565, 566, 572, 619, 663)
Bob & Ira Spring (8, 180, 282, 300, 308, 310, 464)
Joy Spurr (4 left, 9, 11, 18, 21, 22, 26, 28 left, 44, 47, 48, 49, 55, 98, 100, 105, 109, 114 left, 131, 140, 142, 145, 155, 171, 175, 231, 232, 239, 249, 252, 255, 325, 331, 352 right, 374, 376, 390 left, 403, 415, 416, 427, 440, 459, 461, 472 right, 498, 511, 512, 527, 532, 541, 546, 551, 559, 561, 585, 593, 602, 604, 607, 614, 641, 651, 665)

**Tom Stack & Associates**
Ron Hormann (359)

David M. Stone (177, 369)
Lynn M. Stone (27 right)
Edo Streekmann (33, 89, 97 left, 169)
T. K. Todsen (37, 69, 72, 73, 149, 181, 213, 214, 224, 242, 248, 345, 349, 355, 368, 370, 397, 399, 405, 408, 419, 420, 425, 446, 455, 476, 525, 533, 539, 540, 545, 549, 576, 580, 599, 601, 631, 646, 653, 659, 660, 666)
University of California at Berkeley/

# INDEX

Numbers in boldface type refer to plate numbers. Numbers in italics refer to page numbers. Circles preceding English names of wildflowers make it easy for you to keep a record of the wildflowers you have seen.

# NOTES

NOTES

NOTES

# NOTES

# NOTES

# NOTES

**NOTES**

NOTES

## STAFF

Prepared and produced by
Chanticleer Press, Inc.
Founding Publisher: Paul Steiner
Publisher: Andrew Stewart
Managing Editor: Edie Locke
Senior Editor: Amy K. Hughes
Editorial Assistant: Kristina Lucenko
Art Director: Drew Stevens
Production Manager: Susan Schoenfeld
Photo Editor: Giema Tsakuginow
Photo Assistant: Consuelo Tiffany Lee
Publishing Assistant: Alicia Mills

Staff for this book:

Editor-in-Chief: Gudrun Buettner
Executive Editor: Susan Costello
Managing Editor: Jane Opper
Project Editor: Susan Rayfield
Associate Editor: Richard Christopher
Production: Helga Lose
Art Director: Carol Nehring
Picture Library: Edward Douglas
Symbols and Silhouettes: Paul Singer
Drawings: Bobbi Angell
Series design: Massimo Vignelli

All editorial inquiries should be
addressed to:
Chanticleer Press
568 Broadway, Suite #1005A
New York, NY 10012
(212) 941-1522

To purchase this book, or other
National Audubon Society illustrated
nature books, please contact:
Alfred A. Knopf
201 East 50th Street
New York, NY 10022
(800) 733-3000